THE EUROPEAN WAY

THE EUROPEAN WAY

European Societies during the Nineteenth
and Twentieth Centuries

edited by

Hartmut Kaelble

Berghahn Books
New York • Oxford

First published in 2004 by

Berghahn Books

www.berghahnbooks.com

© 2004 Hartmut Kaelble

Library of Congress Cataloging-in-Publication Data

The European way : european societies during the nineteenth and twentieth centuries /
edited by Hartmut Kaelble.
    p. cm.
Includes bibliographical references and index.
ISBN 1-57181-860-X (cloth : alk. paper) -- ISBN 1-57181-512-0 (pbk. : alk. paper)
    1. Europe--Social conditions--19th century. 2. Europe--Social conditions--20th
century. I. Kaelble, Hartmut.

HN373 .E885 2003
306'.094--dc21

                  2002034451

British Library Cataloguing in Publication Data
A catalogue record for this book is available from the British Library.

Printed in the United States on acid-free paper

ISBN 1–57181–860–X hardback
ISBN 1–57181–512–0 paperback

CONTENTS

1   Introduction   1
    Hartmut Kaelble

Part 1. Social hierarchies

2.   The Middle Classes in Europe   15
    Jürgen Kocka (Berlin)
3.   The Landed Aristocracy during the Nineteenth and Early
    Twentieth Centuries   44
    Maria Malatesta (Bologna)
4.   The Professions in Nineteenth-Century Europe   68
    Hannes Siegrist (Leipzig)
5.   The Petite Bourgeoisie and Comparative History   89
    Geoffrey Crossick (Essex)
6.   The European Working Classes in the Late Nineteenth and Early
    Twentieth Centuries   115
    Dick Geary (Nottingham)

Part 2. Social patterns and dynamics

7.   A 'European Family' in the Nineteenth and Twentieth Centuries?   140
    Michael Mitterauer (Vienna)
8.   The History of Consumption in Western Europe in the Nineteenth
    and twentieth Centuries   161
    Heinz-Gerhard Haupt (Bielefeld)
9.   Intellectuals in Europe in the Second Half of the Nineteenth Century   186
    Christophe Charle (Paris I)
10.   Nationalism and Feminism in Europe   205
    Ida Blom (Bergen)
11.   The Jewish Project of Modernity: Diverse or Unitary?   226
    Shulamit Volkov (Tel Aviv)
12.   Religion Between State and Society in Nineteenth-Century Europe   253
    Henk van Dijk (Rotterdam)

Part 3. A general view

13   Social Particularities of Nineteenth- and Twentieth-Century Europe   276
    Hartmut Kaelble

Notes on the Contributers   318
Index   321

1

INTRODUCTION

Hartmut Kaelble

This book gives an overview of nineteenth- and twentieth-century European social history. This is not an easy task. The study of the social history of Europe has intensified in the last thirty years and become an active and accepted field of history. Social history has also changed and broadened distinctly during these years. It started mainly as a history of social classes, of the family and of state intervention in society. It was complemented later by the history of ethnicity, of gender and of identities. It was enlarged more recently by the history of values and individualisation, of religion, by the history of the body and time, by the history of debates, and also by global history. In terms of methods, the study of social history started, to a large degree, as quantitative and structural history. Later, it came to include oral history, the study of ego-documents, and narrative history. More recently, the study of comparisons and transfers, and of discourses and culture, were also integrated into social history. Social history initially joined with sociology, political science and economics. It also later learned very much from ethnology. More recently it has built up further relationships with the history of literature and art history. Social history has continued to be strongly inspired by those topics of political history which can not be treated well enough by a narrow political analysis. At the same time social history was inspired by cultural sciences, and often extended the coverage into fields of cultural history. The challenges and diversification behind these varying changes strongly enriched social history. All these alerations and enlargements are mirrored in the contributions in this volume.

The choice

Looking back over thirty to forty years of modern social history, three types of surveys can be found.

The first way of summarising the activities of social history is the *encyclopaedia*. The largest and most impressive project is the *Encyclopaedia of European Social History*, edited by Peter N. Stearns, with a large staff. It consists of six large volumes and about 200 articles, mainly by American social historians, specialists on various European countries and topics.[1] A large number of smaller encyclopaedias have been published in Britain, France and Germany, dealing wholly, or at least partly, with social history. This can be the most ambitious form of social history survey.

A second, more frequent survey of the study of social history is the *manual*. A variety of manuals on social history have been published, especially since the 1980s. Not all these surveys treat social history as such; some of them are in fact larger surveys on European economic and social history.[2] Other surveys are manuals on the comprehensive political history of Europe with aspects of social history included.[3] But, especially since the 1990s, various manuals on social history written by historians have been published in English and French.[4] They usually cover only Western Europe. Also they generally cover only a selected variety of social history topics. And they normally treat only parts of the nineteenth and twentieth centuries. Thus a manual on the social history of all of Europe between 1800 and 2000 remains to be written.

A third type of summary is the *collection of articles on the main topics* of social history, written by specialists and eminent scholars. This is the type of survey chosen in this volume. It has various advantages. It is based on more specific and profound expertise than the manual, which normally is written by only one author. For this volume leading specialists in social history from France, Britain, Italy, Norway, the Netherlands, Israel, Austria, Switzerland and Germany wrote contributions. In fact, the expertise, rather than the nationality, was the major reason why an author was chosen. It is a more modest and more easily handled project than the ambitious encyclopaedia. In a more limited period this was done in various volumes by French scholars, encouraged by the topic of a major French exam, the *aggregation*, on economy and society in Western Europe 1880–1970.[5] To be sure, this type of survey also has its limits: it is less homogeneous than a manual, since each author has his own idea of social history; it is less comprehensive since it is impossible to find adequate authors for every possible theme. But it has clear advantages.

Why European social history rather than Lyonnais or British or global social history? Would regional or national or world history not be more important than European history? There are various reasons for choosing Europe. A leading American specialist in European social history, who in fact also did work on national and global social history, gave a first reason in a simple sentence: 'Social history as a field developed in Europe.'[6] Hence, a survey of the social history of Europe is easier to write than a social history of India or the USA, Brazil or China. The number of historians dealing with various topics is larger in Europe. A second, seemingly contrasting reason, is that the social history of all of Europe is rarely written. Social history in Europe was always primarily national, regional or local history. Only very recently, and still very rarely, have social historians covered the whole of Europe. In this respect this volume is an adventure, since social history has developed unequally in Europe. It is very difficult to follow it up entirely because of the enormous linguistic diversity. Hence, the survey of social history of the whole of Europe presents almost insurmountable difficulties. A third reason is that the social history of Europe is a contested field. If this history is not written by historians, it will be treated by sociologist and ethnologists – three major, good books on the social history of Europe and Western Europe, have been published by sociologists: Göran Therborn, Henri Mendras and Colin Crouch.[7] A final reason for choosing Europe for study is that Europe is becoming more of an entity in its own right: partly due to the economic and political integration and the geographical expansion of the European Union, and partly because it is seen as an actor from the outside. For an understanding of the European Union and its historical context, but also in order to present and explain Europe to non-Europeans, the history of all of Europe is needed. For many non-Europeans it is more interesting to read about Europe in its enirety than about individual European countries. This is obvious in the case of diplomatic history or the history of ideas. But there is also a need for a social history of Europe, a field in which the writing of the history of all of Europe is much more difficult.

The goals

As a survey of European social history of the nineteenth and twentieth centuries, this volume has four basic intentions.

Firstly, the volume will explore the peculiarities of European societies in both meanings of the word. On the one hand, it treats European commonalties which may turn out to be the peculiarities of Europe in comparison with other non-European countries and civilisations. On the other hand, it treats the peculiarities within Europe, among individual countries and regions, as a major characteristic of European civilisation. Peculiarities in the second sense of the term have attracted considerable attention from historians: for example, the peculiar and often pioneering British way, the 'exception française' in the scission of French politics and the lack of intermediary structures, the German 'Sonderweg' leading to the seizure of power by Hitler, the peaceful and unerratic Scandinavian way of modernisation, the specifically Italian role of the state and the family, Spanish self-isolation, the Dutch special relation to tolerance and to the coexistence of religious minorities; all of these are important explicit or implicit themes of historical research. In clear contrast to lively debates about these specific national paths, historians have taken far less interest in European particularities in the first sense of the term. Given this context, this book will give a somewhat stronger priority to European particularities in the first sense of the term, to commonalties and common trends. There is no doubt, however, that the two meanings are strongly intertwined in European historical reality, and European civilisation feeds off its internal divergences. Hence, European commonalties can not be artificially separated from internal differences. This will also be strictly avoided in this volume.

These two types of European particularities are treated in different ways by the individual contributors. Some contributions treat differences and commonalties as two distinctly different sides of a story; others present their object primarily as a European topic, continuously mentioning national and regional variations. Still other contributions look only at variations, and some international trends and transfers. The strength of this volume is that it shows the varying ways in which the topic of European history can be treated, without completely leaving aside the differences in Europe, and without forgetting that Europe is more than just a geographic term.

Secondly, the volume deals with the nineteenth and twentieth centuries. Up to now the debate on European peculiarities has largely concentrated upon medieval and early modern Europe and has almost completely neglected the last two centuries. There are good reasons, of course, for going back further in European history and dealing with its political as well as social and cultural origins. The European way emerged in the Middle Ages and the early modern period. Any discussion of the origins and causes of European particularities has to be done from a very long-term perspective. In addition, exploring European specificities during medieval and early modern times is more easy and obvious than during the nineteenth and twentieth century predominance of the nation states. However, the reluctance to explore European particularities of the nineteenth and twentieth centuries has left important questions unanswered. Not treating the last two centuries means not knowing whether European particularities are part of a world we have lost, or part of our recent past, with a strong impact on the world we live in. Not treating the last two centuries means not finding out how European specificities possibly changed, or new European particularities emerged under the influence of industrialisation, the rise of mass democracies, and the shift of the centre of the world away from Europe. Omitting the last two centuries also means discussing the historical identity of Europe only in terms of a remote, often romanticised and foreign past, rather than in terms of recent history, which leads much more decisively to the present role and particularities of Europe. Hence the need for the exploration of European particularities during the last two centuries.

Thirdly, the volume treats social and cultural history. The recent debate on particularities of Europe has often centred upon the political particularities: on the multiplicity of power centres and the rise of the modern state. Social and cultural specificities were not left untouched, but politics largely prevailed. Treating the last two centuries, any concentration on political history could easily lead into a dead end and result in an erroneous idea of European particularities. It was in political history rather than in economic, social or cultural history that nineteenth- and twentieth-century Europe disintegrated into national or regional unities. In political history, European commonalties almost faded away. The European economy, the European social specificities and the European culture persisted, or even reemerged, in a fundamentally changing Europe. Hence, social particularities of Europe are not only a promising theme for social history in the narrow sense, but also for European history in general.

The fourth goal of the volume is the encouragement of comparative social history by Europeans. Comparative social history has a high prestige, but has only very gradually become a strength of European research in social and cultural history. There are good reasons for this. Firstly, European social historians usually concentrate on one country (usually their own), one region or even one community. When they have ventured into comparative history, they have preferred to compare two, or at most three countries, regions or communities. Treating Europe as a whole often is regarded as an impossible or at least difficult task for the historian, beyond the reach of strict historical methods. This reduces the number of cases of comparison.[8] This volume tries to reinforce comparative European social history as a potential research field among European historians.

The contributions

The book has three sections: The first section covers social hierarchies, and treats the major classical approaches to social history, the social classes and social milieux. However, this is done in a modern form and with a modern selection. Five social milieux are covered: the middle class, the landed aristocracy, the professions, the lower middle class and the working class. Unfortunately, none of the specialists on nineteenth- and twentieth-century peasants and farmers was able to write an article on the European dimension.

The first section starts with a chapter by Jürgen Kocka on the European middle class: an area in which he has worked for about fifteen years. The middle class, in his view, is based on common experiences and interests, and on common – though changing – opponents, and, above all, on a common culture. The article deals with the particularities of nations and groups of nations, as well as with European commonalties. On the one hand, he deals extensively with the important differences between Western European, Central European and Eastern European middle classes; especially, the relation of the middle class to the nobility and the relation between the business element – the *Wirtschaftsbürgertum* – and the non-business part of the middle class – the *Bildungsbürgertum*. These are differences that are also partly reflected in the differences in the scientific language of the historians. On the other hand, he not only tries to find a common notion of the European middle class, but also writes a new European history of the middle class from the era of the eighteenth century up to the era of the First World War.

Maria Malatesta discusses the Western European landed aristocracy, as another of the European elites. This was a mixed group of aristocratic and bourgeois origin, which was based upon scarce resources of land, and had various strategies of defending its identity against social change. Maria Malatesta treats the landed aristocracy of the nineteenth and early twentieth centuries as a European topic. She frequently mentions the numerous variations within Europe, pointing to the rare European societies without a landed aristocracy. She deals primarily with Western Europe, but also includes Eastern Europe. She covers the economic and political power of the landed aristocracy, the mobility of bourgeois persons into this milieu, the strategies to adapt to the rising market economy, industrialisation and even urbanisation, the defence of the aristocratic identity by inheritance, lifestyle, sociability and organisation.

The following chapter, by Hannes Siegrist, covers another elite, the professions: that is, physicians, lawyers, ministers, engineers, professors, pharmacists, architects and managers (i.e. self-employed as well as civil servants). As professions they defended professional autonomy, exercised power, claimed to be experts in the field of public interest, and tried to control the market. Hannes Siegrist treats the professions as a European topic, but continuously notes the differences within Europe and among European countries, as well as among Western Europe, Central Europe (in which he includes Germany) and Eastern Europe. He differentiates between pioneers of, and latecomers to, professionalisation. He discusses the establishment of professions, the commitment to middle-class values, the creation of markets for professionals, and the relation to the state and nation, and to the clients of the professions.

The petite bourgeoisie – shopkeepers and master artisans – is covered by Geoffrey Crossick. He also treats the nineteenth- and early twentieth-century petite bourgeoisie as a European topic, at the same time discussing the limited variations in social structure and culture, and the larger differences in politics. Geoffrey Crossick covers five elements: independence as the fundamental petit bourgeois element of self-identity and the threatened economic position; the surprisingly high mobility in and out the petite bourgeoisie; the central role of the family; the particular role of the petite bourgeoisie in working-class neighbourhoods; and the petit bourgeois culture and the relation of the petite bourgeoisie to politics. The contribution also contains many reflections on comparative history.

Dick Geary discusses the nineteenth- and early twentieth-century European working class, one of the classic themes of social history. He also presents the working class as a European topic, including many national and local variations between Barcelona and St Petersburg. He criticises any simplified notion of a homogeneous working class created by the advent of the factory in Europe. He discusses the complicated relationship between the working class and modern factory production, and the uneven rise and heterogeneity of the European working class. He argues against a simplified idea of one European working class and demonstrates the unevenness of industrialisation, and the political, religious and ethnic division of the working class in Europe. He also discussses the national divisions of the European working class.

The second section of the volume, on social patterns and dynamics, covers topics which are for the most part more recent than the classical topics of social history. These topics include the family, consumption, intellectuals, gender, ethnic groups and religion. These are topics which are crucial today and form major elements of social history research. One would have liked to include some other themes, such as European work and enterprise, the European city, the European public bureaucracy, the European perception of time, changing perceptions of European space and borders, or migration and transfers in Europe, but we were constrained by the size of the volume.

Michael Mitterauer covers the European characteristics of the family in the nineteenth and twentieth centuries, treating a large variety of themes, such as the relation of the family to the young, marriage patterns, different types of nuclear or enlarged families, family norms and values, and family cycles. Drawing on literature covering all parts of Europe, Michael Mitterauer argues that the process of accelerated change in the nineteenth and early first half of the twentieth century led to a much stronger diversity of families in Europe than in any other period of history, although brought about by similar factors. Only in the second half of the twentieth century did clear tendencies of convergence emerge, especially in the formal structure of the family. For example, in the modern family cycle there was a transition from a diverse but rigid family to a more homogenous, but more flexible European family.

The history of nineteenth and twentieth-century European consumption is treated by Heinz-Gerhard Haupt as a new topic, long neglected by historians. He mainly covers differences in Europe, not only because differences in Europe prevailed, in his view, but also because he wants to demonstrate the importance of the microstudy of consumption, which covers aspects of consumption inaccessible to macrostudies on all of Europe, and from which general conclusions are difficult to draw. He presents major results of the rich research on consumption in Europe on the local and regional level, as well as on the role of the nation states and international European transfers, fashions and trends.

The history of intellectuals in nineteenth- and early twentieth-century Europe is presented by Christophe Charle. It is a common European ascendancy and a success story of the intellectuals' claim to autonomy. It is, however, a story which is different in individual countries because of different contexts. For this reason, Charle treats the European change of the professions of the intellectuals, the new audiences and readerships, the economic market of books and journals, the state employment, the new intellectual professions (i.e. writers, journalists and state intellectuals), the public fear of this change, and the division of Europe into intellectual centres and peripheries during the nineteenth and early twentieth centuries. In addition, he presents a typology of European intellectuals, focusing particularly on the French model and the British and the German particularities. However, he also points out the convergence at the end of the long nineteenth century.

Ida Blom covers the history of gender: in particular, the idea of equal citizenship for women and men in late nineteenth- and twentieth-centuries Europe. She treats common European characteristics and compares them with two Asian countries: India and Japan. She also deals with internal European differences. To summarise a complicated thesis, she argues that equal citizenship for women and men did not only depend on the concept of gender, which could be based upon antagonistic ideas or on natural rights, but also on the concept of the nation, which could be aggressive towards the outside world and hierarchical inside, or peaceful towards neighbours and egalitarian inside. She claims that these contrasts in the concepts of the elites explain differences between European countries in the equality of citizenship for men and women: for example, the early right to vote for women in Norway and later in Sweden or Germany; also the relatively early right in most of Europe as opposed to Asia.

A particular minority of nineteenth- and twentieth-century Europe is treated in the contribution on the Jewish project of modernity by Shulamit Volkov. This project is treated as a common European project, however, with much diversity, especially between Western European and Eastern European Jews. Volkov first of all covers the mainstream history of divergences and contests between Orthodox and Reform trends in European Jewry throughout the nineteenth century, after the relative uniformity of the eighteenth century. This was also a split between Western and Eastern European Jewry. She also covers the cohesive trends: the Haskala, the Jewish enlightenment, which, in her view, was much more influential in Western and Eastern Europe than is usually thought; the Reform movement of the late nineteenth century, which also spread in the West as well as in Eastern Europe; the common memory of the Spanish–Jewish Golden Age; the rise of a European Jewish public sphere; European Jewish journals and associations; the awareness and research into Jewish history and culture, and Jewish literary production.

Religion and secularisation in nineteenth-century Europe is treated by Henk van Dijk. On the one hand, van Dijk shows that, in contrast to mainstream historiography, secularisation was not a distinct process in nineteenth-century Europe since the early nineteenth century was a period of religious revival, and in the late nineteenth century, in spite of weakening church attendance and rising agnosticism brought on by urbanisation and migration, religion remained attractive for the middle class and social movements related to church membership emerged in politics. On the other hand, Henk van Dijk treats the diversity of religion in Europe. He distinguishes between hierarchical and nonhierarchical types of Christian churches, and between four religious regions: a Catholic region, a Protestant, a mixed (Switzerland, the Netherlands, Germany and Central Europe) and an Orthodox region. Though these institutions and regions underwent similar basic changes, rapprochement did not occur during the long nineteenth century.

Finally, in the third section, Hartmut Kaelble presents a more general view of nineteenth- and twentieth-century European social history. He proposes a European social history along five lines: first, European social particularities – common characteristics of most European societies that differ from most societies outside Europe. As examples of a larger, but less well-researched process, he discusses six European social particularities: three social particularities which emerged in the nineteenth and early twentieth centuries and weakened in the second half of the twentieth century – the European family, industry – orientated European activity and European social milieux mostly treated before; and three other social peculiarities that only became more distinct in the second half of the twentieth century: the European welfare state, the European city and European consumption. European social history should also include the study of the changes in the diversity between European national and regional societies; the exchanges among European societies, bilateral as well as multilateral ones; the changing experience of the European space by Europeans as compared with other international spaces; and finally the history of the debate on Europe as a whole, on European society and culture as well as European politics.

This book brings together well-known European specialists. All authors have done research on comparative social history. Each author was asked to present the European particularities in his special field in the double sense mentioned above.[9] I am very grateful to the Maison des Sciences de l'Homme in Paris, which hosted the group originally behind this volume.ix I am also grateful to the Humboldt University Berlin and to the Research Group on the Comparison of Societies (*Forschergruppe 'Gesellschaftsvergleich'*) which was helpful in the production of this volume. For financial reasons, having to do with the translations into English, the preparation of this book took much longer than was originally expected. In the work as editor I was helped by Geoffrey Crossick,

Ruth Federspiel, Priska Jones and Jan-Henrik Meyer. Furthermore, I am grateful to Deborah Louise Cohen, Robert Kimber, Thomas Lampert and Pamela Selwyn for having translated the articles into English and to Jan-Henrik Meyer for having checked the English versions of the authors who are not native English speakers.

Notes

1. *Encyclopedia of European Social History from 1350 to 2000*, 6 vols, ed. P.N. Stearns, New York, 2000.

2. P. Bairoch, *Victoires et déboires. Histoire économique et sociale du monde du XVIe siècle à nos jours*, 3 Bde., Paris, 1997(abbrev. English version: *Economics and World History: Myths and Paradoxes*, Chicago, 1995); *Handbuch der europäischen Wirtschafts- und Sozialgeschichte*, ed. W. Fischer: vol. 5, *Von der Mitte des 19. Jahrhunderts bis zum Ersten Weltkrieg*, Stuttgart 1985; vol. 6, *Vom Ersten Weltkrieg bis zur Gegenwart*, Stuttgart, 1985/1987; G. Ambrosius and W.H. Hubbard, *Sozial- und Wirtschaftsgeschichte Europas*, München, 1986 (English version: *A Social and Economic History of Twentieth-Century Europe*, Cambridge, 1989).

3. Some examples: *Oxford History of Europe since 1945*, ed. M. Fulbrook, Oxford, 2001; M. Mazower, *Dark Continent: Europe's Twentieth Century*, New York, 1999; J.-M. Gaillard and A. Rowley, *Histoire du continent européen: de 1850 à la fin du Xxe siècle*, Paris, 1998; S. Berstein and P. Milza, *Histoire de l'Europe contemporaine*, Paris, 1992; P. Duignan and L.H. Gann, *The Rebirth of the West: The Americanization of the Democratic World*, 1945–1958, Cambridge, 1992; J.M. Roberts, *Europe, 1880–1945*, Addison-Wesley, 1989.

4. E. Bussière, P. Griset, C. Bouneau and J.-P. Williot, *Industrialisation et sociétés en Europe occidentale*, 1880–1970, Paris, 1998; P. Saly, M. Margairaz, M. Pigenet and J.-L. Robert, *Industrialisation et sociétés: Europe occidentale (1880–1970)*, Paris, 1998; A. Sutcliffe, *An Economic and Social History of Western Europe since 1945*, London, 1996; C. Crouch, *Social Change in Western Europe*, Oxford, 1999; G. Therborn, *European Modernity and Beyond: The Trajectory of European Societies*, 1945–2000, London, 1995.

5. Cf. *Western Europe: Economic and Social Change since 1945*, ed. M.-S. Schulze, London, 1999 (mainly economic history); *Histoire sociale de l'Europe: Industrialisation et société en Europe occidentale (1880–1970)*, ed. F. Guedj and S. Sirot, Paris, 1998; *Industrialisation de l'Europe occidentale, 1880–1970*, ed. J. Marseille, Paris, 1998; *Die westeuropäischen Gesellschaften im Vergleich*, ed. S. Hradil and S. Immerfall, Opladen 1997.

6. Stearns, 'Introduction', *Encyclopaedia of European Social History*, p. xix.

7. Crouch, *Social Change in Western Europe*; Mendras, *L'Europe des européens: Sociologie de l'Europe occidentale*, Paris, 1997; Therborn, *European Modernity and Beyond*.

8. Cf. *Geschichte und Vergleich: Ansätze und Ergebnisse international vergleichender Geschichtsschreibung*, ed. H.-G. Haupt and J. Kocka, Frankfurt, 1996; H. Kaelble, *Der historische Vergleich: Eine Einführung zum 19. und 20. Jahrhundert*, Frankfurt 1999.

9. The core of the authors participated in the Standing Group on Social Particularities of Modern Europe, which was established in 1988 at the Maison des Sciences de l'Homme in Paris and which was active for some years. The members of the group were: Geoffrey Crossick (Essex), Henk van Dijk (Rotterdam), Patrick Fridenson (EHESS, Paris), Hartmut Kaelble (Berlin), Jürgen Kocka (Berlin), Maria Malatesta (Bologna), Hannes Siegrist (Leipzig), Rolf Torstendahl (Uppsala).

PART 1

SOCIAL HIERARCHIES

2

THE MIDDLE CLASSES IN EUROPE*

Jürgen Kocka

The attractiveness of a concept rarely correlates with its precision. 'Middle class' would seem to be a case in point. The concept has played a central role in – and been shaped by – political discourses ever since the late eighteenth century. It has been a pivotal concept in many historical interpretations of the modern period. In recent years, the history of the middle class (the *bourgeoisie*, the *Bürgertum*, the *borghesia*) has again become a prominent topic, particularly in Central Europe.[1]

On the other hand, 'generations of unsuspecting undergraduates have found the phrase "middle class" a morass, a minefield, even a veritable Pandora's box. It is certainly a chameleon among definitions'.[2] The English *middle class* is not identical with its French, German or Italian equivalents *bourgeoisie*, *Bürgertum* and *borghesia*. *Mieszczánstwo* (Polish) and *mescane* (Russian) are even more remote. In some languages (for example, in German) the concept contains very different layers of meaning, extending from 'burgher' (in the sense of a legally privileged inhabitant of a medieval or early modern town) to 'middle class' or 'bourgeoisie' to 'citizen'. These meanings have changed over time. The descriptive, analytical and normative functions of the concept overlap; again and again it has served not only as a 'neutral' category for observers and historians, but also as a polemical or affirmative code word in public debates, social criticism and utopian visions.[3]

Still, a tendency towards conceptual convergence is apparent in the recent literature on the subject, at least in that which deals with the 'long nineteenth century' that began in the eighteenth and ended with the First

* This essay was written at the Institute for Advanced Study in the Social and Behavioral Sciences, Stanford, Cal., in 1994-5. I am grateful to Marion Berghahn and Hartmut Kaelble for permitting its prepublication in *The Journal of Modern History* 67 (1995), pp. 783-806.

World War. The concept 'middle class' comprises merchants, manufacturers, bankers, capitalists, entrepreneurs and managers, as well as *rentiers* (lumped together in German as the *Wirtschaftsbürgertum* or economic middle class). It also comprises doctors, lawyers, scientists and other professionals, professors at universities and teachers at secondary schools, intellectuals, men and women of letters and academics, including those serving as administrators or officials in public and private bureaucracies (all of whom are lumped together in German as the *Bildungsbürgertum* or educated middle class).

'Middle class' does *not* include nobles, peasants, manual workers or the mass of lower-class people in general, although it is debatable where the exact boundaries should be drawn. There are groups 'in between' that may or may not be seen as belonging to the middle classes, such as military officers or artists. In addition, there is the large, growing and heterogeneous category of groups whose status has changed. Master artisans, retail merchants, innkeepers and the like certainly were among the burghers of early modern towns. They must also be seen as part of the middle class in the eighteenth and early nineteenth centuries. In the course of time, however, they became marginal members of what was understood to be the 'middle class'. In the latter nineteenth and twentieth centuries, such professionals – together with an ever-growing number of low- and middle-ranking salaried employees and white-collar workers in both the private and public sectors – have been seen as belonging to the 'lower middle classes', the *Kleinbürgertum*, the *petite bourgeoisie* – not to the middle class in the full sense of the word.[4]

Wherever possible, this article focuses on the middle class proper, leaving the subject of the lower middle classes to another essay in this volume.[5] In other words, we shall be concentrating on a small minority. In nineteenth-century Germany, middle-class families (*Bürgertum*) made up roughly 5 percent of the population. In Europe as a whole, this percentage varied from country to country, contingent on the ratio between the urban and rural populations. It was slightly larger in England and in the West in general and smaller in the East and on the peripheries of Europe. It gradually increased over the course of time.[6]

The basic pattern

What were the defining attributes of the middle class in the late eighteenth, nineteenth and twentieth centuries? What characteristics were shared by businessmen, *rentiers*, doctors, lawyers, clergy and others that distinguished them from other social groups not belonging to the middle class? What were their common denominator and *differentia specifica*, and how did they change over time?

If the concept of 'class' is taken seriously, then the middle class, in spite of its name, has never been a class in either a Marxist or a Weberian sense, since it includes both self-employed and salaried persons and, more generally, people occupying very different market positions. Nor, in contrast to the burghers of the late medieval and early modern periods, can the nineteenth-century middle class be seen as a corporate group (*Stand*), since it had no specific legal privileges.[7] Two plausible theories have attempted to define the common and essential characteristics of the middle class. One is relational in approach, the other cultural. As we will see, the two explanations are compatible, and both are necessary to understand the evolution and devolution of the European middle class.

In general, individuals are more likely to form social groups with some cohesion, common understanding and potential for collective action if some tension or conflict exists between them and other social groups. It is well known from the history of classes, religions and ethnicities that an identity is acquired by setting oneself apart from others. The same holds true for the European middle class as it emerged as a postcorporate, supralocal social formation in the second half of the eighteenth and early nineteenth centuries.

Merchants, entrepreneurs and capitalists, professors, judges, journalists, ministers and high-ranking civil servants differed from one another in many respects, but they shared a sense of social distance from the privileged aristocracy and, on the Continent, from the absolutist monarchy. By stressing the principles of achievement and education, work and self-reliance, many members of the middle class supported the emerging vision of a modern, secularised, postcorporate, self-regulating, enlightened 'civil society' which opposed the privileges and autocracy of the *ancien régime*.

This self-differentiation was a complicated and multifaceted process with many exceptions. Still, the various subgroups of the emerging middle class were to some degree united by their common opponents: the nobility, unrestricted absolutism and religious orthodoxy. They acquired common interests and experiences, a certain degree of shared self-understanding and common ideologies. In this way, the middle class constituted itself as a social formation that encompassed various occupational groups, sectors and class positions.

In the course of the nineteenth century, this line of distinction and tension lost much of its power but did not altogether fade away. The blurring was due to the gradual abolition of the nobility's legal privileges in most parts of Europe and the increasing *rapprochement* between the upper grades of the middle classes and parts of the nobility. Simultaneously, another line of demarcation came into play, which, although it had not been completely absent around 1800, became more prominent during the second third of the nineteenth century. A sharper boundary set the middle class apart from the lower strata, the emerging working class and 'small people' in general, including the 'petty-bourgeois' lower middle class. In spite of their differences, late nineteenth-century industrialists, merchants and *rentiers*, lawyers and higher civil servants, professors, high school teachers and scientists maintained a defensive and a critical distance from 'the people', the 'working class' and the labour movement, which had a significant influence on their self-understanding, social alliances and political commitments.[8]

While developing cohesion in opposition to people above and below, the middle class defined itself by its culture. Families from various middle-class categories shared a respect for individual achievement on which they based their claims for rewards, recognition and influence. They shared a positive attitude towards regular work, a propensity for rationality and emotional control and a fundamental striving for independence, either individually or through their associations and initiatives. They emphasised education. General (usually classical) education (*Bildung*) served as a basis on which members of the middle class communicated with one another, as it distinguished them from those who did not share it. Scholarly pursuits were respected, as were music, literature and the arts.

In bourgeois culture, a specific ideal of family life was essential: that of the family as an end in itself, a community held together by emotional ties and fundamental loyalties. Strictly differentiated by sex and dominated by the paterfamilias, it was meant to be a haven protected from the world of competition and materialism, from politics and the public. It was a sphere of privacy (although not without servants, whose work made it possible for the middle-class mother to devote sufficient time to family life, transmitting 'cultural capital' to the next generation).

Bourgeois culture could flourish only in towns and cities. There had to be peers with whom one could meet in clubs and associations, at feasts and at cultural events, in numbers that a rural environment could hardly provide. In order to participate in the practices of bourgeois culture adequately, one needed a secure economic status, well beyond the subsistence minimum: means, space and time. This has excluded large, though slightly decreasing, majorities of most populations from becoming truly middle class. If one sees the cohesion and the specificity of the *Bürgertum* as defined by its culture and its *sociabilité*, one appreciates the importance of symbolic forms in middle-class daily life, of bourgeois table manners and conventions, of quotations from classical literature, titles, customs and dress.[9]

These two major arguments point to what the various middle-class groups had (and partly still have) in common: experiences and interests based on common opponents and a common culture. They also elucidate that the defining particularity of the middle class is rather thin. To have common opponents and to share a culture defines those concerned only to a limited degree. In everything else, they differ: interests and experiences based on occupations and economic status, gender and region, religion and ethnicity. At any particular time, the middle class has been heterogeneous; within it 'many separate worlds could co-exist side by side'.[10]

Comparisons

Some historians prefer the plural form and speak of the middle classes in order to stress the heterogeneity of this social formation. The plural term seems to be particularly appropriate if one considers regional and national differences. Traditionally, middle-class cultures were rooted in towns. They had strongly local components. It is true that merchants, administrators and intellectuals soon formed supralocal and supra-regional networks, and in the course of the nineteenth century something like the nationalisation of the European middle classes took place. Still, they continued to be strongly differentiated and even fragmented by locality, region and nation. It is beyond the scope of this essay to reconstruct the rich diversity of the changing European middle-class world. The following paragraphs sketch some major differences between the middle classes in Western, Central and Eastern Europe, including a few glances to the South and the North. They pertain to the 'long' nineteenth century only.

The middle classes' relation to the nobility is a crucial factor that varied substantially from country to country. It was closely related to certain characteristics of the old feudal-corporate order and the varying forms of its demise.[11] In England the feudal order of the countryside and the corporate structure of the urban economy had been eroding for centuries. Agriculture had been commercialised and feudal bonds had been replaced by contractual relations, guilds had long ceased to exist; the advance of capitalism had perforated the divide between countryside and town, between rural and urban elites. Urban wealth could give access to land. In contrast to most Continental nobles, an English aristocrat could not hand down his title to all of his offspring, but only to his eldest son (female inheritance was possible in the absence of a male heir).

Although recent scholarship has warned against exaggerating the openness of the British elite, it must still be said that in a comparative perspective the English aristocracy and gentry were well known for their openness to middle-class marriages, ideas and fortunes. In the course of the nineteenth century, their accessibility increased. The permeability of the upper class, however, did not weaken its standing, power and consistency. On the contrary, in political, social and economic respects, the English aristocracy succeeded in maintaining much of its extraordinary status right into the twentieth century. Nevertheless, the line of separation between the nobility and gentry on the one hand and upper middle-class groups, on the other, was less sharply drawn in England than in most parts of the Continent.[12] Some of this holds true for Sweden, as well, where the feudal distinction between lords and peasants, countryside and town, was also less clearly marked – for other reasons, however.

In France during the *ancien régime*, the urban rich had also not been barred from acquiring land. In some French regions and towns, close alliances had been formed between parts of the aristocracy and upper middle-class groups as early as the eighteenth century. Once the Revolution had stripped the nobility of all its legal privileges, they were never restored again. The legal distinction between town and countryside was also erased. Historians of France currently stress the limited impact of the Revolution of 1789 on the country's distribution of wealth, recruitment of elites and distribution of power. Even after the Revolution, aristocrats continued to play a strong role in governing the country, both locally and nationwide. Previously exaggerated notions of the alleged triumph of the bourgeoisie during the Revolution of 1789 have long begged for correction. However, if we compare it with those parts of Europe east of the Rhine, it becomes clear that the divide between the nobility and the upper middle classes in France, Italy, the Netherlands, Belgium and Switzerland (where the nobility had been very weak anyway) was blurred early on, both by certain flexibilities of the old order and by its revolutionary end.

The era of the *notables*, who governed France between Napoleon's demise and the early years of the Third Republic, has been interpreted as a transitory stage between the old corporate order and a modern class society. Seen from further east, its most striking aspect is neither the strong aristocratic component of this milieu, nor the undeniably important role land ownership played in the acquisition of influence and status, nor the traditional mechanisms through which it worked, that is, family connections and local elite cultures. Nor were its more modern, plutocratic characteristics – voting rights based on and steeply graded according to taxable wealth and income – exceptional either. What is most startling in the comparison of France with Central and Eastern Europe is the close proximity and interconnection between aristocratic and bourgeois elements in this elite of *notables*. Certainly, the distinction between aristocratic and middle-class cultures had not yet fully disappeared. Yet in France, as in Italy and Britain – although these cases differed in other respects – a tendency existed towards the blending of aristocratic and middle-class elements. This *mélange* permitted a gradual, relatively smooth decline of the aristocratic component and a similarly gradual ascent of the middle class, which, at least in France, had become the dominant partner in this alliance by 1914.[13]

Some regions in Germany followed the West European pattern – for example, the Rhineland, *Hessen-Kassel*, parts of Saxony, independent cities like Hamburg and the Southwest, which saw an early decline of noble influence. Yet by and large, east of the Rhine and particularly east of the Elbe, the old order remained more rigid and less commercialised (or commercialised in a different form), with clearly marked legal, political and cultural differences between lords and peasants, towns and the countryside, burghers and other city-dwellers, the middle class and other social groups. Here, the *ancien régime* had largely barred rich urbanites from acquiring land. In Central and Eastern Europe, the legal foundations of the old feudal-corporate order were not removed by one revolutionary act, but in a protracted process that began in the late eighteenth century and lasted throughout most of the nineteenth century.

Of course, the differences between Central and Eastern Europe were deep and manifold. In Prussia and Bavaria, Austria and Bohemia, Galicia and Russia, land reform, individualisation of property rights and the introduction of modern political institutions took place at different times and with very different results. But in Prussia, Austria and Russia, the nobility (or part of it) retained elements of a special legal status and other privileges until the end of the First World War, in stark contrast to Western Europe. There was, it is true, some *rapprochement*, some cooperation, even some limited fusion between parts of the aristocracy and parts of the upper middle class in Central and Eastern Europe. This mingling is demonstrated by middle-class purchases of formerly aristocratic landed estates, bourgeois–aristocratic cooperation at the upper levels of the growing state bureaucracies, the bourgeois inflow into the previously aristocratic officer corps and the imitation of aristocratic lifestyles by rich upper-middle-class families towards the end of the century. Small numbers of middle-class persons were ennobled. Some aristocratic–bourgeois intermarriage took place. By and large, however, the dividing line between nobility and middle classes remained, to the latters' disadvantage, more clearly marked in Central and Eastern Europe than in the West, right into the twentieth century. In Germany and Austria, the middle classes acquired a smaller share of political power and achieved less social and cultural dominance than did their counterparts in the West. In Russia, they remained even weaker.[14]

Another way of understanding international differences in the history of the European middle classes is to probe their composition, particularly into the relationship between *Wirtschaftsbürgertum* and *Bildungsbürgertum*.

In the economically advanced countries of the West, merchants, bankers and *rentiers* and later manufacturing entrepreneurs and industrial managers, as well, constituted the bulk and core of the middle class from the mid-eighteenth to the mid-twentieth century. A high degree of intergenerational continuity was typical of these propertied groups; they were well rooted in their regions and influential in their communities.

There were, of course, lawyers and clergy, doctors and officials, university professors and teachers at public schools and *lycées*, as well. Their numbers and importance grew, particularly in the latter part of the nineteenth century. Yet relative to the scope, wealth, status and influence of the economic middle class, they clearly remained in second place, particularly in the earlier part of the century.

In England, observers like John Stuart Mill in the 1830s and later Karl Marx virtually ignored them or saw them as a mere adjunct to the capitalist entrepreneurial class. Historians have frequently followed their lead, particularly those in the Marxist tradition. The British historian Harold Perkin wrote about the 'forgotten middle class' when he rediscovered the professional milieux and distinguished them from the entrepreneurs and businessmen as part of the emerging middle class of the 1820s.

In France, the *Bildungsbürgertum* was less marginal, but the professional element among the *notables* was relatively weak. For the *notaire* and other officeholders, real estate and local connections were more important than whatever legal training they might have had.

In both Great Britain and France, it was only in the second half of the nineteenth century that the balance started to change. By this time, the secondary school system had expanded, and formal education became more important for middle-class sons (and eventually for daughters), both as a common experience and as a marker separating them from the masses. Universities and professional schools also expanded, though more slowly. Professional careers became more common and more respected. Besides wealth and family background, talent and qualification played an increasing (though still secondary) role in granting access to the middle class. Additional opportunities opened up for sons and daughters of some lower-middle-class families, but by and large the expensive and not very numerous schools served young men and women of already solidly middle-class background.[15]

This West European model was not altogether absent in Central Europe. Those towns and regions that could look back on an old tradition of industrial or mercantile wealth and active self-government followed a similar pattern of development, as, for example, in Mannheim, Karlsruhe and Hamburg. But in most of Germany, the trend was different. Commercial and entrepreneurial activities emerged on a more moderate scale; the factory system arrived later than in England, Belgium and France. The Germans were less wealthy than their neighbours in the West, a difference manifested not only in the smaller fortunes and less impressive mansions of German aristocrats, but also in the more moderate lifestyle of the middle class.

At the same time, a strong tradition of 'reform from above' existed in Prussia, Bavaria, Austria and other Central European states. Absolutist rulers and their emerging bureaucracies had taken the lead in modernising their societies for the sake of enhancing their power. In this context one has to understand the early emphasis on modernising and expanding the state-run school systems in Prussia and other German states. Secondary schools based on Latin and classical studies (*Gymnasien*) and universities expanded remarkably, the latter primarily intended to train young men for state service. The number of students grew in the first decades and again in the last quarter of the nineteenth century, in Germany much more so than in France. The stress on education and qualification – instead of or in addition to property and family background – helped to make access to the middle class a bit easier for lower-middle-class people, but it had excluding effects as well, vis-à-vis the working classes and other parts of the lower strata. Upward mobility from the working class into the middle class usually extended over two or three generations, with the elementary school teacher being an important intermediate position. Sliding down could be faster. General education (*Bildung*) and professional qualification were matters of high prestige and public esteem in Germany, and by preparing young men for higher positions in the civil service, they were closely connected to the notion of power as well, particularly since parliamentary institutions remained weak and the bureaucratic apparatus strong throughout the nineteenth century.

With university-trained civil servants at its core, the early-nineteenth-century German *Bildungsbürgertum* was small in numbers; however, it was influential and, with regard to social recognition, power and self-esteem, ahead of most merchants, manufacturers and businessmen, although the latter usually enjoyed more income and wealth. Only in the second half of the century did the balance start to shift, when industrialisation dramatically increased the wealth, power and public reputation of part of the business community. By and large, a similar pattern was followed in the western parts of the Habsburg monarchy. In Italy the *borghesia umanistica* was relatively numerous and influential. But here, civil servants played a much less important role, members of the liberal professions, particularly lawyers, a much more important one.[16]

In both Western and Central Europe, the *Wirtschaftsbürgertum* and the *Bildungsbürgertum* were loosely connected, sharing elements of a common culture and joined by numerous contacts of different sorts, but divided by different experiences as well. Over the course of the century, they grew even closer together, as indicated by increasingly similar educational backgrounds, more frequent intermarriages (at least in the German case) and a common commitment to powerful ideologies like liberalism and nationalism.

By contrast, in most of East Central and Eastern Europe the lines of division between the various middle-class subgroups remained sharply drawn. The relative economic backwardness of most of these regions corresponded to the weakness of an indigenous entrepreneurial middle class. When opportunities arose, foreign capital moved in to fill the gap, as did foreign – or ethnically different – entrepreneurs, particularly Germans, Jews, Greeks and Armenians. The Poles, Czechs, Slovaks and peoples of the Balkans were ruled by supranational empires and governed by foreign elites. A *Bildungsbürgertum* of the Central European type could not easily develop. Rather, there was something like an indigenous *Bildungs-Kleinbürgertum* (as Jiři Kořalka has called it), an educated lower middle class, comprising elementary school teachers, Catholic clergy, perhaps some minor officials and some intellectuals. They had little contact with the merchants and entrepreneurs or the elites (except, perhaps, some indigenous aristocrats), but were close to the native population and played an important role in the rise of East European nationalism. (This was true of intellectuals in Finland, Norway and the Baltic countries, as well.) In ethnically heterogeneous East Central Europe, with increasing tensions between the different nationalities and a common culture virtually lacking, the emergence of an integrated middle class was blocked.[17]

This was even more true for Russia. It is true, there were prosperous, privileged and well-organised merchants, particularly in the large cities like Moscow and St Petersburg. Their numbers grew, and their status as well as their educational background improved in the decades before the Bolshevik Revolution. There was some mobility in and out of this group. But they were set clearly apart, not only from the artisans, tradesmen and other petit bourgeois categories below them, but also from the intelligentsia (minor officials, clergy, teachers, professionals, writers, journalists). In contrast to the Central European *Bildungsbürgertum*, the Russian intelligentsia rarely included high-ranking, academically trained government employees, who were mostly noble or eventually to be ennobled, frequently foreign-born and sometimes despised by intellectuals. It may have been different with the emerging regional and local administrative elites, who were again mostly noble but less distanced from the intelligentsia. In general, members of the intelligentsia had closer contacts with intellectuals from the nobility than with members of the lower-status commercial and industrial groups, who were the objects of intellectual hostility. Even before 1917 the Russian situation differed from the Central and Western European pattern so dramatically that the author of a survey concludes: 'The Russian middle class did not exist because its constituent elements were determined to avoid fusion and identification.' Still, ongoing research may modify this view.[18]

European middle classes differed in many ways. Seen from a bird's eye view, one can perhaps distinguish three constellations. In the West, business groups dominated within the middle class. As the borderline between aristocratic and bourgeois elites was not sharply drawn and became increasingly blurred, middle-class wealth, privilege and influence were strong and grew. In Central Europe, the educated middle class played a stronger role. The line of distinction between the aristocracy and the middle class remained more clearly marked and the profile of the middle class itself, more coherent. Yet middle-class weight and impact were limited. Further East, the middle class was even weaker. The dividing line between aristocracy and middle class was clearly drawn. In addition, the middle class remained highly fragmented. At the eastern and southeastern margins of Europe, a coherent middle class hardly existed.

Phases

What were the major tendencies in the development of the European middle classes? In a process so complex and heterogeneous, one cannot expect exact turning points. Developments differed from country to country and from region to region, not only in structure but also in timing. Any proposal for periodisation implies some arbitrariness. We distinguish among four main periods in the history of the European middle classes: the second half of the eighteenth century, the years from 1790/1800 to 1848/49, from the mid-nineteenth century to the First World War and the period since then.

Eighteenth century

It is impossible to specify the precise date of birth of the middle class. There are three overlapping social milieu to consider if one looks for its origins. First, there were the burghers of eighteenth-century towns. In most of Europe (but not in the East) the towns were islands in a sea of feudalism, enjoying legal privileges with respect to commerce and trade, self-government and the civil liberties of their inhabitants. In the towns, usually only a minority enjoyed full civic rights (*Bürgerrecht*), including the rights to own property, to trade, to marry and set up a household and to participate in corporations, guilds and associations as well as in governing the town. Most merchants, tradesmen and master artisans belonged to this legally privileged group, as did urban landowners, *rentiers*, officials and people with specific skills and professions; most of them were heads of families, usually male. The mass of the other town dwellers – servants, journeymen, labourers and members of dishonourable occupations, as well as dependent household and family members, including most women – did not enjoy full civic rights and did not qualify as burghers in the full sense. It was among the burghers of the European towns that an early bourgeois culture developed. Norms and ways of life centred around work, property, respectability, thrift and order, religion and participation in the handling of common affairs. Where a tradition of strong, self-governed burgher towns had been absent in the late medieval and early modern periods, an important condition was lacking for the rise of a middle class later on.

Second, there were the agents of capitalism, the wholesale merchants with interregional and international ties, the capitalists and the bankers, and the owners and managers of putting-out systems, manufactories and mines. They usually were part of the burgher communities. At the same time their supralocal scope of action, their postcorporate type of business, their competitiveness and wealth set them apart from the traditional corporate economy of the towns, regulated by guilds, customs and morals. Indeed, particularly in Central and even more so in Eastern Europe, they frequently enjoyed special privileges granted by the government, which exempted them from the rules of their home town and set them apart from the community of traditional burghers.

Third, there were those who served the rulers and governments, the princes, bishops, lords and numerous other authorities of the time: qualified servants and educated officials, administrators and legal experts and – with some degree of autonomy – professors and clerics. Many of them had attended universities. It was among these groups that the ideas of the Enlightenment found most support, ideas which, in turn, strongly influenced the emerging middle-class culture. These early Bildungs-bürger usually lived in towns, above all in residential towns and administrative centres. They had close contacts with burghers, but their status was different. It was based on their relation to the ruler and, increasingly, on education, academic training and expertise. Many of them came into close contact with the traditional elites, the landowners and the nobility. Many of them acquired land where this was permitted; a minority was ennobled.[19]

The European tradition of self-governed towns, the rise of capitalism and the impact of state formation were the decisive factors. The urban burgher communities, the expanding business groups and the growing educated circles inside and outside of public bureaucracies certainly differed a lot, but they were usually neither noble nor lower class. They were closely related, partly overlapped and developed elements of a common culture. Where and when this happened to more than a minimal extent, the modern middle class emerged, mostly during the second half of the eighteenth century.

1800–50

In England and Switzerland, feudal structures had broken down long before the eighteenth century. In the very North of Europe they had hardly ever existed. In Russia and other parts of the East, feudal dissolution would happen much later, after the Crimean War. In most of Europe, however, the old order was largely brought to an end between the late eighteenth and mid-nineteenth centuries, either by revolution, as in France, or by gradual, protracted reforms – and revolution – as in most parts of Germany. The legal distinctions between town and countryside, and between privileged burghers and other city dwellers were gradually removed. Land became a marketable good. Guild regulations were weakened or abandoned. Deregulation took place, the legal foundations for an unrestricted market economy were laid. Capitalism was on the rise, in commerce, industry and agriculture. Later on, industrialisation began and the factory system started to break through in England and in parts of the Continent. What had remained of the old corporate order was now dissolved or at least seriously weakened. Institutional developments differed, but nearly everywhere there was a trend towards more centralisation and intensification of government power, some control of autocratic rule by bureaucracies or parliamentary institutions, constitutional government and due process of law. State building had started much earlier; it now advanced quickly. These fundamental changes were largely brought about by middle-class actors, and they had far-reaching consequences for the middle-class world.

There had been close alliances between nobles and members of the upper middle class in the eighteenth century; the French *notables* and the London mixture of aristocratic landowners, officeholders, wealthy merchants and members of the professions being two examples. But everywhere the noble element had been dominant. Now the balance had shifted. The middle-class element gained in status because wealth became more important than title, and a move towards more meritocratic criteria took place. This redistribution of power within bourgeois–aristocratic alliances was not free of tensions and conflicts, as the revolutions of 1789, 1830 and 1848 demonstrated, but it led to only gradual change.

The eighteenth-century *Wirtschaftsbürgertum* had been relatively small, dominated by merchants, bankers and *rentiers*. When it was not acting as junior partner to dominant landed elites, it remained politically weak and socially marginal. Now this group grew in numbers, wealth and importance. In the West, the rise of the manufacturers began to change the composition of the economic middle class and to contribute to its increasing demands and claims. It was in the rising manufacturing towns (e.g., of northern England, northern France and the Rhineland) that a new type of self-confident and radical middle-class culture emerged, emphasising work and thrift, independence and self-help and directed against the capital cities and their elites, against the old order with its aristocratic leadership and its autocratic traits, and sometimes in the name of minority religions against the established church and its orthodoxy.[20]

Particularly, though not exclusively in Central Europe, public bureaucracies gained in strength, cohesion and *esprit de corps*. Schools were reformed and expanded. Universities became major avenues of access into the middle class. Civil servants and professionals put forward new claims and demands on the basis of their education and training. A rising modernising elite emphasised meritocratic standards of success and the idea of professional independence.[21]

In other words, both the economic and the educated middle classes were gaining new strength and were developing a new profile. However, in the early nineteenth century, both remained for the most part embedded in urban burgher communities, which in Central and East Central Europe still retained some legal identity and much social and cultural cohesion in distinguishing themselves from the urban lower strata and the neighbouring countryside. The middle class proper had not yet severed its ties to the large community of artisans, tradesmen, retailers and minor officials.

Membership in voluntary associations – based on an emerging common culture and centred on family and work – ideas of progress and a strict moral code, education and sometimes religion held these middle-class groups together. This culture implied a postaristocratic, modern vision of life, frequently advocated with outright criticism of the old order and the aristocracy. Out of this culture the programmes of liberalism grew and were translated into different demands and campaigns in local, regional and national politics. There were, certainly, nonliberal middle-class people and nonbourgeois liberals; but there was beyond doubt a basic affinity between middle-class culture and liberalism in the first half of the nineteenth century. This middle class was on the rise, and its main challenge was against what had survived of the old order of privilege and autocracy.[22]

1850 to the First World War

Between the mid-nineteenth century and the First World War some of those trends continued. Industrialisation reached full speed in large parts of Europe. Urbanisation accelerated. Nation states were formed in Germany and Italy, as demanded by liberals. The expansion of public bureaucracies continued, the education system grew, and after the 1880s government interventions in the economy and social relations increased again.

The *Wirtschaftsbürgertum* continued to grow in numbers, wealth and importance, with the industrialists at its core. The ascent of the manager began. More and more businessmen had attended secondary schools and universities. The *Bildungsbürgertum* also expanded and differentiated internally. Self-recruitment declined and professionalisation quickly advanced. Even in Germany self-employed professionals and those employed by private organisations began to outnumber those in public employment. Doctors and lawyers made up the largest subgroups, which grew quickly as a consequence of advancing medicalisation, growing juridification and the beginning of the welfare state.

In wealth, cultural influence and political power, the middle class had clearly outstripped the nobility in large parts of Europe by 1914. Although this claim must be qualified with respect to the distribution of political power in Germany, Central Europe and the East, it is safe to say that the last two decades before the First World War saw the middle class at its peak. Even if it remained a small minority everywhere, its members, institutions, spirit and culture prevailed in many social spheres: in the economy and in education, in the sciences and the arts, in the cities and at work and in family life. It would clearly be wrong to speak of a decline of the middle class before 1914.[23]

At the same time, the middle class became more defensive and more beleaguered. It lost some of its previous energy and much of its internal cohesion.

Long before 1848/49, there had been challenges to the middle class from below. The radicalisation of the French Revolution in the 1790s, the elements of class warfare in Britain in the aftermath of the Napoleonic Wars, the uprisings and strikes of French craftsmen and workers in Paris and Lyon in the 1830s and 1840s, the revolt of the Silesian weavers in 1844, the demand for radical reform and even some socialist stirrings in the decade that has been labelled the 'hungry forties' or the *Vormärz* (i.e., the period preceding the revolution of March 1848) did not go unnoticed in middle-class circles. The unrest helped to remind those in the middle class that there was a whole world below them to which it was difficult to reach out, that was potentially dangerous and against which it was prudent to protect oneself, even if one had to give up some progressive ideas and form closer alliances with segments of the old elites.

Although the social border between the middle class and those below them was not new, it became relevant, prominent and powerful only in the second part of the century. The experience of the revolution of 1848/49 was decisive, with the masses emancipating themselves from middle-class leadership and challenging the middle-class world.

The stepwise democratisation of voting rights for males in France as a consequence of 1848/49, in the emerging German nation state in 1867–71, in Italy in the 1880s, and in Britain and other parts of Europe more gradually brought the 'ordinary people' into the political arena more than ever before. The structure of politics changed from a system of *notables* to mass and class politics.

The strength of independent labour movements, indicating the rise of the working class as a dynamic factor, increased widespread middle-class anxieties. The Paris Commune of 1871 was a signal registered all over Europe. In different forms and to different degrees, partly disguised class tensions and conflicts permeated social relations, domestic politics and culture in most of Europe in the late nineteenth and early twentieth centuries, to a far greater extent than they had a hundred years earlier. Large parts of the middle classes turned to face a new adversary. The offensive challenge to the old elites had been central to middle-class culture and politics, but now a defensive self-distancing from those below became paramount.

Middle-class circles had to make explicit what earlier had gone without saying: that they did not belong to the ordinary people. The split between the circles of property and education and 'the people' grew. The rest of the corporate basis of the burgher communities was breaking down while the differentiation between the upper and the lower strata of the middle classes advanced. A gap widened between merchants, industrialists, professors and higher civil servants on the one hand, and artisans, retailers, innkeepers, minor officials and employees, on the other. Only in the second part of the century did the *petite bourgeoisie* establish itself as a separate entity, as the concept of 'middle class' (*Bürgertum*) was narrowing down to include only the better-off circles of property and education.[24]

At the upper margin of the middle class the constellation was changing as well. Recent research has effectively relativised the notion of the 'feudalisation' of the late nineteenth-century upper middle class, and for very good reason. To acquire land and live for part of the year in a mansion outside the city, to consume conspicuously and enjoy hunting and cricket, to mix socially with aristocrats not only during the London or Berlin 'season', to think about marrying one's daughter into an aristocratic family – all this did not really make a nobleman out of a wealthy bourgeois.

It was possible to adopt elements of an aristocratic lifestyle without leaving or neglecting one's business, and many did so. Liberalism was never a strictly defining characteristic of middle-class culture, and consequently the move to the conservative right by many well-to-do businessmen, high civil servants and professionals since the late nineteenth century cannot be seen as a betrayal of their middle-class origins. Formal ennoblement remained rare. Most of the sons of well-established businessmen seem to have stayed in the business world, and aristocratic families continued to favour endogenous marriages and to disdain industrial and commercial pursuits.

Having said all this, it must still be acknowledged that there is some kernel of truth to the 'feudalisation' thesis. In contrast to the situation in 1800, large middle-class fortunes in 1900 matched and even exceeded aristocratic wealth. An upper stratum of the middle class came very close to the aristocracy in lifestyle and culture. Intermarriage and other forms of intermingling between bourgeois and aristocratic circles reached an unprecedented high in Edwardian England and Wilhelmine Germany, as well as in prerevolutionary St Petersburg. In politics the showdowns between landed and business interests, that is, between mostly conservative noblemen and the largely liberal middle classes, were definitely over. Large parts of the nobility had accepted the modern world and adopted central elements of middle-class culture, and a large segment of the middle classes moved to the right. Confronted with challenges from below, those at the top had more concern for their common interests and common experiences than for what continued to separate them. Something like a composite elite emerged, which tended to bridge the old aristocratic middle-class divide, particularly in Western Europe.[25]

For the middle class, this meant further internal differentiation. Its upper stratum was withdrawing. One of the two traditional cornerstones of middle-class identity – the historical affinity between middle-class culture and liberalism – eroded. Middle-class progressivism became a minority phenomenon. Nationalism continued to be strong, but came to have increasingly illiberal, imperialist and sometimes racist connotations. Intellectual insecurity grew. Against this background, harsh criticism and outright rejection of the middle-class world could spread widely, directed against its philistine and hypocritical aspects, its conventionalism and rigidities, its all too 'rational' vision of life. Anti-bourgeois criticisms were usually propagated by members of the middle class themselves, by intellectuals, artists and avant-garde writers, but also by the largely middle-class youth movements of the turn of the century. There were numerous clubs and associations in which anti-bourgeois *Kulturkritik* ran high; their members were usually middle class. At the *fin de siècle* and before the First World War, the middle-class world was not only attacked from below, but also challenged from within.[26]

Since the First World War

The history of the middle classes since the First World War has been a tale of stress, victory and diffusion. In a way, the middle class has eroded, together with its two main opponents, while its culture has changed and spread.

The divide between the aristocracy and the rest of society has faded away. In the twentieth century, Europe's nobility lost all its legal privileges and most of its social particularities. In Eastern Europe, the aristocracy was destroyed and expelled by communist dictatorships. In Central Europe, it did not escape the damaging effects of fascism and war. On most of the Continent the victories of capitalism and democracy eroded what had been left of aristocratic entitlements and distinctions. Some of them may still exist, particularly in England, but, by and large, it is no longer very meaningful to distinguish between the aristocracy and the middle class at the top of the social pyramid. Consequently, historians of the second half of the twentieth century and students of contemporary societies prefer to speak of composite elites, of the *Oberschicht* or of *classes supérieures*.[27]

The second social boundary that helped to define the middle class in the nineteenth century has survived much longer. Throughout most of the twentieth century, the divide, marked by tensions and conflicts, between middle and working classes has strongly influenced social relations and domestic politics. Even now, this class line has not disappeared in any West European society, and it is reappearing in the East, where it had been eroded, suppressed and supplanted by other forms of inequality. Still, the composition of the working population has fundamentally changed as a result of the stagnation and decline of the blue-collar sector, the dramatic expansion of the white-collar workforce and other profound changes in the economic sphere. Workers' lives have changed fundamentally as a result of democratisation, the rise of the welfare state, and the unprecedented growth of mass purchasing power since the 1950s. Labour movements have become more integrated. The dictatorships and wars of the twentieth century, and the massive destruction and compulsory population transfers that accompanied them, have contributed to the erosion of traditional working-class cultures in most of Europe. However, the dramatic improvement of postwar living standards and the rise of a consumer society have been even more influential in accelerating working-class devolution.

The patterns of social and cultural inequality have become fuzzier and more elusive in recent years. Certainly, labour movements have not disappeared. In fact, their threat to the middle-class world increased after the First World War, as communism first became a domestic and later – moving beyond its original working-class base – a fundamental international challenge. But in Western societies of the post-Second World War era, labour movements have lost part of their power and nearly all of their radical thrust. Finally, the communist threat has ended in the international arena as well.

All these are complicated stories and cannot be told here. Suffice it to say that the fundamental challenge from below, which had been so closely tied to the rise of the working classes and socialist labour movements and had helped to constitute and define the middle classes in nineteenth- and early twentieth-century Europe, has not survived. In most Western countries, there are new cleavages, such as between the majority and a new underclass consisting of immigrants, the unemployed and marginal minorities. Social inequality as a whole has not decreased at all. New crises and conflicts have arisen, such as those over ecological issues. Yet all this does not compel the middle class to affirm its boundaries and stick together to the same extent as did the proletarian-socialist challenge in the nineteenth and early twentieth centuries.[28]

The middle class has proven to be stronger than its opponents. In a way, it has won. Its culture and its principles have changed and been watered down. Still, they have spread not only to all parts of the *classes supérieures*, but also, to varying extents, to the shrinking rural population, to what used to be called 'lower middle class' and even to parts of the working class. There continue to be limits to the spread of middle-class culture, and differences persist everywhere; even Western societies have not become thoroughly 'bourgeois'. But middle-class culture, which has a built-in tendency towards universalisation, has moved far beyond the social segment where it originated and which it once helped to define. Through this victory, the middle class lost much of its identity.

But there have been many internal changes as well. The salaried segment of the middle class now outnumbers its self-employed part. Consequently, the definition of middle-class 'independence' has had to change. Bureaucratisation has left its imprint. The number of *rentiers* – those living on incomes from property holdings – has dropped dramatically (except for those in old age).

Other elements of nineteenth-century middle-class culture have been lost through twentieth-century catastrophes and modernisation. Ever since the First World War, the number of servants in middle-class households has steadily declined, although they were of utmost importance in nineteenth-century middle-class families. Classical education gave way to more specialised forms of training, a change that dissolved an important bracket that had kept the middle class together. The culture of work and thrift, of progress and order, of religion and self-righteousness that defined large parts of the rising middle classes in the earlier parts of the nineteenth century is largely gone. The most central institution of middle-class culture, the family, to which a clear separation of gender roles had been essential, has changed tremendously as a result of women's emancipation. Other influences have had an effect as well, such as the changing status of youth, the rise of the media and the multiplication of choices available in modern society. As a result, the family has lost many of its nineteenth-century functions and part of its internal cohesion, with disintegrating effects on middle-class culture.[29]

However, it is worthwhile remembering that most of these changes originated in the middle-class world. This is certainly true with respect to the movements for women's emancipation. These got off the ground by taking certain middle-class promises – individual rights, education, work and achievement, active participation in public life – seriously enough to demand their extension to women, to whom they had been largely denied during the first hundred years of modern middle-class history. In order to incorporate 'the other half' into middle-class culture on a more equal basis, this culture itself had to change. The same holds true for attempts to incorporate other classes, strata and parts of the world into middle-class culture. These processes have not yet resolved themselves.

This essay has dealt with the middle class in the sense of a small but coherent and highly influential social formation defined by common opponents and a shared culture. The degree to which it has existed has varied over time and space. It emerged in the eighteenth century and devolved in the twentieth. It was more clearly established in the West and Centre of the European continent than in the East. Its existence depended on certain historical constellations, among them a clear separation between countryside and town and the tradition of Enlightenment. It seems that these were constellations characteristic of Europe, and not to be found everywhere in the world. Whether similar middle classes have existed or will emerge in other parts of the world deserves further careful study.

Notes

1. See *The German Bourgeoisie: Essays on the Social History of the German Middle Class from the Late Eighteenth to the Early Twentieth Century*, ed. D. Blackbourn and

R.J. Evans, London, 1991; *Bürgertum und bürgerliche Entwicklung in Mittel- und Osteuropa*, ed. V. Bácskai, 2 vols, Budapest, 1986; *Bürgertum in der Habsburger-monarchie*, ed. E. Bruckmüller, Vienna, 1990; R. Romanelli, 'Political Debate, Social History, and the Italian "Borghesia": Changing Perspectives in Historical Research', *Journal of Modern History* 63 (1991), pp. 717–39; *Russia's Missing Middle Class: The Professions in Russian History*, ed. H.D. Balzer, Armonk, London, 1996.

2.   P.M. Pilbeam, *The Middle Classes in Europe 1789–1914: France, Germany, Italy and Russia*, London, 1990, p. 1.

3.   See P. Gay, *The Bourgeois Experience: Victoria to Freud, vol. 1: Education of the Senses*, Oxford, 1984, pp. 18–24; J. Kocka, 'The European Pattern and the German Case', in *Bourgeois Society in Nineteenth-Century Europe*, ed. J. Kocka and A. Mitchell, Oxford, 1993, pp. 3–4, 8–15.

4.   See *Shopkeepers and Master-Artisans in Nineteenth-Century Europe*, ed. G. Crossick and H.-G. Haupt, London, 1984.

5.   See G. Crossick, 'The Petite Bourgeoisie and Comparative History' (in this volume). Having decided in favour of a relatively narrow definition of 'middle class', I shall use the adjective interchangeably with 'bourgeois'. That means neglecting, for the purpose of this article, some undeniable differences in the use and the connotations of these two words. 'Middle class' is usually broader than 'bourgeoisie', in that it reaches further down into the 'petite bourgeoisie', and more narrow in that it may exclude parts of the elites. 'Bourgeoisie' and 'bourgeois' lend themselves more to critical, political and polemical usage than the more neutral 'middle class'. See the article by R. Koselleck, U. Spree and W. Steinmetz, 'Drei bürgerliche Welten? Zur vergleichenden Semantik der bürgerlichen Gesellschaft in Deutschland, England und Frankreich', in *Bürger in der Gesellschaft der Neuzeit*, ed. H.J. Puhle, Göttingen, 1991, pp. 14–58; W. Steinmetz, 'Gemeineuropäische Tradition und nationale Besonderheiten im Begriff der "Mittelk-lasse". Ein Vergleich zwischen Deutschland, Frankreich und England', in *Bürgerschaft. Rezeption und Innovation der Begrifflichkeit vom hohen Mittelalter bis ins 19. Jahrhundert*, ed. R. Koselleck and K. Schreiner, Stuttgart, 1994, pp. 161–236; U. Spree, 'Die verhinderte "Bürgerin"? Ein begriffsgeschichtlicher Vergleich zwischen Deutschland, Frankreich und Großbritannien', in ibid., pp. 274–306.

6.   See Kocka, 'European Pattern', p. 4; R. Price, *A Social History of Nineteenth-Century France*, London, 1987, p. 122; Gay, *Bourgeois Experience*, p. 23.

7.   As to concepts see J. Kocka, *Weder Stand noch Klasse. Unterschichten um 1800*, Bonn, 1990, pp. 33–5.

8.   Tracing the changing meaning, usage and counter-concepts of 'middle class' is one way of documenting these structural changes. See J. Kocka, 'Das europäische Muster und der deutsche Fall', in *Bürgertum im 19. Jahrhundert*, ed. J. Kocka, 3 vols, Göttingen, 1995, vol. 1, pp. 9–84, esp. pp. 14–17.

9.   L. Davidoff and C. Hall, *Family Fortunes: Men and Woman of the English Middle Classes, 1780–1850*, Chicago, 1987, pp. 18–28; on Austria: U. Döcker, *Die Ordnung der bürgerlichen Welt: Verhaltensideale und soziale Praktiken im 19.Jahrhundert*, Frankfurt am Main, 1994; on Sweden: J. Frykman and O. Löfgren, *Culture Builders: A Historical Anthropology of Middle-Class Life*, New Brunswick, 1987.

10. According to our definition 'middle class' is not just a category, but a social formation whose members share situational characteristics, a sense of belonging together, common attitudes and values, as well as a disposition for common behaviour and actions.

11. See J. Blum, *The End of the Old Order in Rural Europe*, Princeton, 1978. A similar book on the end of the old corporate order in the towns has still to be written. W. Mosse 'Nobility and Middle Classes in 19th-Century Europe: A Comparative Study', in *Bourgeois Society*, ed. Kocka and Mitchell, pp. 70–102; A. Goodwin, ed., *The European Nobility in the 18th Century*, London, 1953; H. Reif, *Adel im 19. und 20. Jahrhundert*, Munich, 1999.

12. E. Hobsbawm, 'The Example of the English Middle Class', in Godwin, *European Nobility*, pp. 127–50.

13. See A. Daumard, *Les bourgeois et la bourgeoisie en France depuis 1815*, Paris, 1987; G. Chaussinand-Nogaret et al., *Histoire des élites en France du XVIe au XXe siècle: L'honneur, le mérite, l'argent*, Paris, 1991; A.M. Banti, *Terra e denaro: Una bourghesia padana dell'Ottocento*, Venice, 1989; A. Tanner, 'Bürgertum und Bürgerlichkeit in der Schweiz. Die "Mittelklassen" an der Macht', in *Bürgertum*, ed. Kocka, vol. 1, pp. 199–229.

14. See the summary article on Austria by E. Bruckmüller and H. Stekl in *Bürgertum*, ed. Kocka, pp. 166–98. On Poland W. Dlugoborski's summary 'Das polnische Bürgertum vor 1918 in vergleichender Perspektive', in *Bürgertum im 19. Jahrhundert: Deutschland im europäischen Vergleich*, ed. J. Kocka and U. Frevert, 3 vols, Munich, 1988, vol. 1, pp. 266–99. On Russia: B.R. Brower, *The Russian City between Tradition and Modernity, 1850–1900*, Berkeley, 1990; A.J. Rieber, *Merchants and Entrepreneurs in Imperial Russia*, Chapel Hill, 1982.

15. See H. Perkin, *The Origins of Modern English Society, 1780–1880*, London, 1969, pp. 252ff.; H. Berghoff and R. Möller, 'Tired Pioneers and Dynamic Newcomers? A Comparative essay on English and German Entrepreneurial History 1870–1914', *Economic History Review* 47 (1994), pp. 262–87; *The Formation of Profession: Knowledge, State and Strategy*, ed. R. Torstendahl and M. Burrage, London, 1990.

16. See H.-U. Wehler, 'Deutsches Bildungsbürgertum in vergleichender Perspektive. Elemente eines "Sonderwegs"?', in *Bildungsbürgertum im 19. Jahrhundert IV: Politischer Einfluß und gesellschaftliche Formation*, ed. J. Kocka, Stuttgart, 1989, pp. 215–37. The Southwest German middle class was less influenced by civil servants and professionals. See L. Gall, *Bürgertum in Deutschland*, Berlin, 1989; H. Kaelble, *Social Mobility in the 19th and 20th Centuries: Europe and America in Comparative Perspective*, Leamington Spa, 1985; K. Tenfelde, 'Unternehmer in Deutschland und Österreich während des 19. Jahrhunderts', in *Innere Staatsbildung und gesellschaftliche Modernisierung in Österreich und Deutschland 1867/71–1914*, ed. H. Rumpler, Munich, 1991, pp. 125–38; H. Siegrist, *Advokat, Bürger und Staat: Eine vergleichende Geschichte der Rechtsanwälte in Deutschland, Italien und der Schweiz (18.–20. Jahrhundert)*, Frankfurt am Main, 1995.

17. See Dlugoborski, 'Das polnische Bürgertum', pp. 266–99; M. Hroch 'Das Bürgertum in den nationalen Bewegungen des 19. Jahrhunderts' and E. Kaczynska, 'Bürgertum und städtische Eliten. Kongreßpolen, Rußland und Deutschland im Vergleich', in ibid., vol. 3, pp. 337–59, 466–88; G. Ránki, 'The Development of the Hungarian Middle Classes: Some East-West Comparisons', in *Bourgeois Society*, ed. Kocka and Mitchell, pp. 439–55.

18. Pilbeam, *Middle Classes*, p. 22; M. Hildermeier, *Bürgertum und Stadt in Rußland 1760–1870: Rechtliche Lage und soziale Struktur*, Köln, 1986; J. Ruckman, *The Moscow Business Elite: A Social and Cultural Portrait of Two Generations 1840–1905*, De Kalb, 1984; L. Häfner, 'Stadtdumawahlen und soziale Eliten in Kazan 1870–1913', *Jahrbücher für Geschichte Osteuropas* 44 (1996), pp. 217–54; W. Bayer, *Die Moskauer Medici: Der russische Bürger als Mäzen*, Vienna, 1996.

19. The literature abounds. A classical study is: M. Walker, *German Hometowns: Community, State and General Estate 1648–1871*, Ithaca, 1971 (on traditional burgher communities in Central Europe); Pilbeam, *Middle Classes*, pp. 212f. (referring to literature by R. Forster, L. Bergeron, Tulard etc.) on eighteenth-century *notables*; W.D. Rubinstein, 'The end of "Old Corruption" in Britain, 1780–1860', *Past and Present* 101 (1983), pp. 55–86.

20. See Perkin, *Origins*, pp. 196ff.; C. Charle, *Histoire sociale de la France au XIXe siècle*, Paris, 1991, pp. 42–55, 181–228, 239ff.; A case study on a small German region: St. Brakensiek, 'Adlige und bürgerliche Amtsträger in Staat und Gesellschaft. Das Beispiel Hessen-Kassel 1750–1866', in *Wege zur Geschichte des Bürgertums*, ed. K. Tenfelde and H.-U. Wehler, Göttingen, 1994, pp. 15–35. In general, English middle-class culture maintained closer relations to religion than middle-class cultures in Germany and France, where the stress was much more on secularised *Bildung* and laicist self-distancing from the church (with many exceptions, e.g., the pious Protestant businessmen of Barmen and the Catholics of Roubaix). The 'Old Believers' formed a nonconformist religious minority and were strong in the Moscow middle class. See A. Gerschenkron, *Europe in the Russian Mirror: Four Lectures in Economic History*, Cambridge, 1970, pp. 17ff. On Jewish entrepreneurs see W.E. Mosse, *The German-Jewish Economic Elite, 1820–1935. A Socio-Cultural Profile*, Oxford, 1989; on the Catholic middle class in the western part of Germany: Th. Mergel, *Zwischen Klasse und Konfession: Katholisches Bürgertum im Rheinland 1794–1914*, Göttingen, 1994.

21. See Pilbeam, *Middle Classes*, chap. 5.

22. See R.J. Morris, *Class, Sect and Party: The Making of the British Middle Class, Leeds 1820–1850*, Manchester, 1990; E. François, ed., *Geselligkeit, Vereinswesen und bürgerliche Gesellschaft in Frankreich, Deutschland und der Schweiz, 1750–1850*, Paris, 1986; J.J. Sheehan, *German History 1770–1866*, Oxford, 1989, chap. 9; D. Langewiesche, 'Liberalism and the Middleclasses in Europe', in *Bourgeois Society*, ed. Kocka and Mitchell, pp. 40–69; D. Langewiesche, ed., *Liberalismus im 19. Jahrhundert: Deutschland im europäischen Vergleich*, Göttingen, 1988.

23. See H.G. Haupt, *Sozialgeschichte Frankreichs seit 1789*, Frankfurt am Main, 1989, pp. 232–60; H.-U. Wehler, *Deutsche Gesellschaftsgeschichte*, 3 vols, Munich, 1995, vol. 3, pp. 727–89; idem,'Wie bürgerlich war das Deutsche Kaiserreich?', in *Bürger und Bürgerlichkeit im 19. Jahrhundert*, ed. J. Kocka, Göttingen, 1987, pp. 243–80; F.M.L. Thompson, *The Rise of Respectable Society: A Social History of Victorian Britain 1830–1900*, Cambridge, MA, 1988; D. Lieven, *The Aristocracy in Europe, 1815–1914*, London, 1992; Y. Cassis, 'Businessmen and the Bourgeoisie in Western Europe', in *Bourgeois Society*, ed. Kocka and Mitchell, pp. 103–24; H. Kaelble, 'French Bourgeoisie and German Bürgertum, 1870–1914', in ibid., pp. 273–301; M. Hildermeier, 'Sozialer Wandel im städtischen Rußland in der zweiten Hälfte des 19. Jahrhunderts', *Jahrbücher für Geschichte Osteuropas* 25 (1977), pp. 525–66.

24. See E.J. Hobsbawm, *The Age of Empire 1875–1914*, New York, 1987, chaps. 5 and 7; H.-U. Wehler, 'Die Geburtsstunde des deutschen Kleinbürgertums', in *Bürger in der Gesellschaft*, ed. H.J. Puhle, Göttingen, pp. 199–209; G. Crossick, ed., *The Lower Middle Class in Britain 1870–1914*, New York, 1977; J. Kocka, ed., *Arbeiter und Bürger im 19. Jahrhundert. Varianten ihres Verhältnisses im europäischen Vergleich*, Munich, 1986.

25. See D.L. Augustine, *Patricians and Parvenus: Wealth and High Society in Wilhelmine Germany*, Oxford, 1994; H. Kaelble and H. Spode, 'Sozialstruktur und Lebensweisen deutscher Unternehmer 1907–1927', *Scripta Mercaturae* 24 (1990), pp. 132–78; H. Berghoff, 'Aristokratisierung des Bürgertums? Zur Sozialgeschichte der Nobilitierung von Unternehmern in Preußen und Großbritannien 1870 bis 1918', *Vierteljahrschrift für Sozial- und Wirtschaftsgeschichte* 81 (1994), pp. 178–204; the articles by F.M.L. Thompson, 'Aristocracy, Gentry and the Middle Classes in Britain, 1750–1850' and P. Thane, 'Aristocracy and Middle Class in Victorian England: The Problem of "Gentrification"' on aristocracy and middle class in England in *Bürgertum, Adel und Monarchie: Wandel der Lebensformen im Zeitalter des bürgerlichen Nationalismus*, ed. A.M. Birke et al., Munich, 1989, pp. 15–35, 93–108; T. Durandin, 'Entre tradition et aventure', in *Histoire des élites*, eds. Chaussinand-Nogaret et al., pp. 319–451; A.J. Mayer, *The Persistence of the Old Regime: Europe to the Great War*, New York, 1981.

26. See H. Mommsen, 'Die Auflösung des Bürgertums seit dem späten 19. Jahrhundert', in *Bürger und Bürgerlichkeit im 19. Jahrhundert*, ed. Kocka, pp. 288–315.

27. Y. Cassis, 'Financial Elites in Three European Centres: London, Paris, Berlin, 1880s–1930s', *Business History* 33 (1991), pp. 53–71; H. Kaelble, 'Die oberen Schichten in Frankreich und der Bundesrepublik seit 1945', in *Frankreich Jahrbuch 1991*, Opladen, 1991, pp. 63–78; H. Morsel, 'La classe dominante de l' entre-deux-guerres à nos jours', in *Histoire des francais XIXe–XXe siècle*, ed. Y. Lequin, Paris, 1983, vol. 2, pp. 536ff.

28. J. Mooser, *Arbeiterleben in Deutschland 1900–1970: Klassenlagen, Kultur und Politik*, Frankfurt am Main, 1984; A.A. Jackson, *The Middle Classes 1900–1950*, Nairn, 1991; A. Marwick, *Class: Image and Realitiy in Britain, France and the USA since 1930*, New York, 1980; K. Tenfelde, 'Stadt und Bürgertum im 20. Jahrhundert', in *Wege*, ed. Tenfelde and Wehler, pp. 317–53; H. Siegrist, 'Ende der Bürgerlichkeit?' *Geschichte und Gesellschaft*, 20 (1994), pp. 549–93. On the Soviet Union: D. Beyrau, 'Die russische Intelligenz in der sowjetischen Gesellschaft', in *Die Umwertung der sowjetischen Gesellschaft*, ed. D. Geyer, Göttingen, 1991, pp. 559–86.

29. Compare L. Davidoff, 'The Family in Britain', in *The Cambridge Social History of Britain*, ed. F.M.L. Thompson, Cambridge, 1990, vol. 2, pp. 98–129 with G.-F. Budde, *Auf dem Weg ins Bürgerleben: Kindheit und Erziehung in deutschen und englischen Bürgerfamilien, 1840–1914*, Göttingen, 1994; and see K.H. Jarausch, *The Unfree Professions: German Lawyers, Teachers and Engineers 1900–1950*, New York, 1990 in contrast to R. Koselleck, ed., *Bildungsbürgertum im 19. Jahrhundert II: Bildungsgüter und Bildungswissen*, Stuttgart, 1990; C. Hall, *White, Male and Middle Class: Explorations in Feminism and History*, Cambridge, 1992; U. Frevert, ed., *Bürgerinnen und Bürger. Geschlechterverhältnisse im 19. Jahrhundert*, Göttingen, 1988.

Bibliography

Augustine, D.L. *Patricians and Parvenus: Wealth and High Society in Wilhelmine Germany.* Oxford, 1994.

Bácskai, V. (ed.). *Bürgertum und bürgerliche Entwicklung in Mittel- und Osteuropa,* 2 vols. Budapest, 1986.

Balzer, H.D. (ed). *Russia's Missing Middle Class: The Professions in Russian History.* Armonk, N.Y. and London, 1996.

Banti, A.M. *Terra e denaro: Una bourghesia padana dell'Ottocento.* Venice, 1989.

Bayer, W. *Die Moskauer Medici: Der russische Bürger als Mäzen.* Vienna, 1996.

Berghoff, H. and Möller, R. 'Tired Pioneers and Dynamic Newcomers? A Comparative Essay on English and German Entrepreneurial History 1870–1914', *Economic History Review* 47 (1994), pp. 262–87.

Berghoff, H. 'Aristokratisierung des Bürgertums? Zur Sozialgeschichte der Nobilitierung von Unternehmern in Preußen und Großbritannien 1870 bis 1918', *Vierteljahrschrift für Sozial- und Wirtschaftsgeschichte* 81 (1994), pp. 178–204.

Beyrau, D. 'Die russische Intelligenz in der sowjetischen Gesellschaft', in *Die Umwertung der sowjetischen Gesellschaft,* ed. D. Geyer. Göttingen, 1991, pp. 559–86.

Blackbourn, D. and Evans, R.J. (eds.) *The German Bourgeoisie: Essays on the Social History of the German Middle Class from the late Eighteenth to the early Twentieth Century.* London, 1991.

Blum, J. (ed.). *The End of the Old Order in Rural Europe,* Princeton, N.J., 1978.

Brakensiek, St. 'Adlige und bürgerliche Amtsträger in Staat und Gesellschaft. Das Beispiel Hessen-Kassel 1750–1866', in *Wege zur Geschichte des Bürgertums,* ed. K. Tenfelde and H.-U. Wehler. Göttingen, 1994, pp. 15–35.

Brower, B.R. *The Russian City between Tradition and Modernity, 1850–1900.* Berkeley, CA, 1990.

Bruckmüller, E. (ed.). *Bürgertum in der Habsburgermonarchie.* Vienna, 1990.

Bruckmüller, E. and H. Stekl, H. 'Zur Geschichte des Bürgertums in Österreich', in *Bürgertum im 19. Jahrhundert,* ed. J. Kocka, 3 vols. Göttingen, 1995, vol. 1, pp. 166–98.

Budde, G.-F. *Auf dem Weg ins Bürgerleben: Kindheit und Erziehung in deutschen und englischen Bürgerfamilien, 1840–1914.* Göttingen, 1994.

Cassis, Y. 'Financial Elites in Three European Centres: London, Paris, Berlin, 1880s–1930s', *Business History* 33 (1991), pp. 53–71.

—— 'Businessmen and the Bourgeoisie in Western Europe', in *Bourgeois Society in Nineteenth-Century Europe,* ed. J. Kocka and A. Mitchell. Oxford, 1993, pp. 103–24.

Charle, C. *Histoire sociale de la France au XIXe siècle.* Paris, 1991.

Chaussinand-Nogaret, G. et al. *Histoire des élites en France du XVIe au XXe siècle: L'honneur, le mérite, l'argent.* Paris, 1991.

Crossick, G. (ed.). *The Lower Middle Class in Britain 1870–1914.* New York, NY, 1977.

Crossick, G. and Haupt, H.-G. (eds.) *Shopkeepers and Master-Artisans in Nineteenth-Century Europe.* London, 1984.

Daumard, A. *Les bourgeois et la bourgeoisie en France depuis 1815.* Paris, 1987.

Davidoff, L. 'The Family in Britain', in *The Cambridge Social History of Britain,* ed. F.M.L. Thompson. Cambridge: Cambridge University Press, 1990, vol. 2, pp. 98–129.

Davidoff, L. and Hall, C. *Family Fortunes: Men and Woman of the English Middle Classes, 1780–1850.* Chicago, IL, 1987.

Dlugoborski, W. 'Das polnische Bürgertum vor 1918 in vergleichender Perspektive', in *Bürgertum, im 19. Jahrhundert. Deutschland im europäischen Vergleich,* ed. J. Kocka and U. Frevert, 3 vols. Munich, 1988, vol. 1, pp. 266–99.

Döcker, U. *Die Ordnung der bürgerlichen Welt: Verhaltensideale und soziale Praktiken im 19. Jahrhundert.* Frankfurt am Main, 1994.

Durandin, T. 'Entre tradition et aventure', in G. Chaussinand-Nogaret et al., *Histoire des élites en France du XVIe au XXe siècle: L'honneur, le mérite, l'argent.* Paris, 1991, pp. 319–451.

François, E. (ed.). *Geselligkeit, Vereinswesen und bürgerliche Gesellschaft in Frankreich, Deutschland und der Schweiz, 1750–1850.* Paris, 1986.

Frevert, U. (ed.). *Bürgerinnen und Bürger: Geschlechterverhältnisse im 19. Jahrhundert,* Göttingen, 1988.

Frykman, J. and Löfgren, O. *Culture Builders: A Historical Anthropology of Middle-Class Life.* New Brunswick, NJ, 1987.

Gall, L. *Bürgertum in Deutschland.* Berlin, 1989.

Gay, P. *The Bourgeois Experience. Victoria to Freud, vol. 1: Education of the Senses.* Oxford, 1984.

Gerschenkron, A. *Europe in the Russian Mirror: Four Lectures in Economic History.* Cambridge: Cambridge University Press, 1970.

Goodwin, A. (ed.). *The European Nobility in the 18th Century.* London, 1953.

Häfner, L. 'Stadtdumawahlen und soziale Eliten in Kazan 1870–1913', *Jahrbücher für Geschichte Osteuropas* 44 (1996), pp. 217–54.

Hall, C. *White, Male and Middle Class: Explorations in Feminism and History.* Cambridge: Cambridge University Press, 1992.

Haupt, H.G. *Sozialgeschichte Frankreichs seit 1789.* Frankfurt am Main, 1989.

Hildermeier, M. *Bürgertum und Stadt in Rußland 1760–1870: Rechtliche Lage und soziale Struktur.* Köln, 1986.

—— 'Sozialer Wandel im städtischen Rußland in der zweiten Hälfte des 19. Jahrhunderts', *Jahrbücher für Geschichte Osteuropas* 25 (1977), pp. 525–66.

Hobsbawm, E. 'The Example of the English Middle Class', in *The European Nobility in the 18th Century*, ed. A. Goodwin. London, 1953, pp. 127–50.

—— *The Age of Empire 1875–1914.* New York, NY, 1987.

Hroch, M. 'Das Bürgertum in den nationalen Bewegungen des 19. Jahrhunderts', in *Bürgertum im 19. Jahrhundert: Deutschland im europäischen Vergleich,* ed. J. Kocka and U. Frevert, 3 vols. Munich, 1988, vol. 3, pp. 337–59.

Jackson, A.A. *The Middle Classes 1900–1950.* Nairn, 1991.

Jarausch, K.H. *The Unfree Professions: German Lawyers, Teachers and Engineers 1900–1950.* New York, NY, 1990.

Kaczynska, E. 'Bürgertum und städtische Eliten. Kongreßpolen, Rußland und Deutschland im Vergleich', in *Bürgertum im 19. Jahrhundert: Deutschland im europäischen Vergleich,* ed. J. Kocka and U. Frevert, 3 vols. Munich, 1988, vol. 3, pp. 466–88.

Kaelble, H. *Social Mobility in the 19th and 20th Centuries: Europe and America in Comparative Perspective.* Leamington Spa, 1985.

—— 'Die oberen Schichten in Frankreich und der Bundesrepublik seit 1945', in *Frankreich Jahrbuch 1991.* Opladen, 1991, pp. 63–78.

—— 'French *Bourgeoisie* and German *Bürgertum,* 1870–1914', in *Bourgeois Society in Nineteenth-Century Europe,* ed. J. Kocka and A. Mitchell. Oxford, 1993, pp. 273–301.

Kaelble, H. and Spode, H. 'Sozialstruktur und Lebensweisen deutscher Unternehmer 1907–1927', *Scripta Mercaturae* 24 (1990), pp. 132–78.

Kocka, J. (ed.). *Arbeiter und Bürger im 19. Jahrhundert: Varianten ihres Verhältnisses im europäischen Vergleich.* Munich, 1986.

Kocka, J. *Weder Stand noch Klasse. Unterschichten um 1800.* Bonn, 1990.

—— 'The European Pattern and the German Case', in *Bourgeois Society in Nineteenth-Century Europe,* ed. J. Kocka and A. Mitchell. Oxford, 1993, pp. 3–39.

—— 'Das europäische Muster und der deutsche Fall', in *Bürgertum im 19. Jahrhundert,* ed. J. Kocka, 3 vols. Göttingen, 1995, vol. 2, pp. 9–84.

Koselleck, R. (ed.) *Bildungsbürgertum im 19. Jahrhundert II: Bildungsgüter und Bildungswissen.* Stuttgart, 1990.

Koselleck, R., Spree, U. and Steinmetz, W. 'Drei bürgerliche Welten? Zur vergleichenden Semantik der bürgerlichen Gesellschaft in Deutschland, England und Frankreich' in *Bürger in der Gesellschaft der Neuzeit*, ed. H.J. Puhle. Göttingen, 1991, pp. 14–58.

Langewiesche, D. (ed.) *Liberalismus im 19. Jahrhundert: Deutschland im europäischen Vergleich*. Göttingen, 1988.

—— 'Liberalism and the Middleclasses in Europe', in *Bourgeois Society in Nineteenth-Century Europe*, ed. J. Kocka and A. Mitchell. Oxford, 1993, pp. 40–69.

Lieven, D. *The Aristocracy in Europe, 1815–1914*. London, 1992.

Marwick, A. *Class: Image and Realitiy in Britain, France and the USA since 1930*. New York, NY, 1980.

Mayer, A.J. *The Persistence of the Old Regime: Europe to the Great War*. New York, 1981.

Mergel, Th. *Zwischen Klasse und Konfession: Katholisches Bürgertum im Rheinland 1794–1914*. Göttingen, 1994.

Mommsen, H. 'Die Auflösung des Bürgertums seit dem späten 19. Jahrhundert', in *Bürger und Bürgerlichkeit im 19. Jahrhundert*, ed. J. Kocka. Göttingen, 1987, pp. 288–315.

Mooser, J. *Arbeiterleben in Deutschland 1900–1970: Klassenlagen, Kultur und Politik*. Frankfurt am Main, 1984.

Morris, R.J. *Class, Sect and Party: The Making of the British Middle Class, Leeds 1820–1850*. Manchester, 1990.

Morsel, H. 'La classe dominante de l' entre-deux-guerres à nos jours', in *Histoire des français XIXe–XXe siècle*, ed. Y. Lequin. Paris, 1983, vol. 2, pp. 536ff.

—— 'Nobility and Middle Classes in 19th-Century Europe: A Comparative Study', in *Bourgeois Society in Nineteenth-Century Europe*, ed. J. Kocka and A. Mitchell. Oxford, 1993, pp. 70–102.

Mosse, W.E. *The German-Jewish Economic Elite, 1820–1935: A Socio-Cultural Profile*. Oxford, 1989.

Perkin, H. *The Origins of Modern English Society 1780–1880*. London 1969.

Pilbeam, P.M. *The Middle Classes in Europe 1789–1914: France, Germany, Italy and Russia*. London, 1990.

Ránki, G. 'The Development of the Hungarian Middle Classes: Some East–West Comparisons', in *Bourgeois Society in Nineteenth-Century Europe*, ed. J. Kocka and A. Mitchell. Oxford, 1993, pp. 439–55.

Rieber, A.J. *Merchants and Entrepreneurs in Imperial Russia*. Chapel Hill, 1982.

Romanelli, R. 'Political Debate, Social History, and the Italian "Borghesia": Changing Perspectives in Historical Research', *Journal of Modern History* 63 (1991), pp. 717–39.

Rubinstein, W.D. 'The end of "Old Corruption" in Britain, 1780–1860', *Past and Present* 101 (1983), pp. 55–86.

Ruckman, J. *The Moscow Business Elite: A Social and Cultural Portrait of Two Generations 1840–1905*. De Kalb, IL,1984.

Sheehan, J.J. *German History 1770–1866*. Oxford, 1989.

Siegrist, H. 'Ende der Bürgerlichkeit?' *Geschichte und Gesellschaft*, 20 (1994), pp. 549–93.

—— *Advokat, Bürger und Staat: Eine vergleichende Geschichte der Rechtsanwälte in Deutschland, Italien und der Schweiz (18.–20. Jahrhundert)*. Frankfurt am Main, 1995.

Spree, U. 'Die verhinderte "Bürgerin"? Ein begriffsgeschichtlicher Vergleich zwischen Deutschland, Frankreich und Großbritannien', in *Bürgerschaft. Rezeption und Innovation der Begrifflichkeit vom hohen Mittelalter bis ins 19. Jahrhundert*, ed. R. Koselleck und K. Schreiner. Stuttgart, 1994, pp. 274–306.

Steinmetz, W. 'Gemeineuropäische Tradition und nationale Besonderheiten im Begriff der "Mittelklasse". Ein Vergleich zwischen Deutschland, Frankreich und England', in *Bürgerschaft. Rezeption und Innovation der Begrifflichkeit vom hohen Mittelalter bis ins 19. Jahrhundert*, ed. R. Koselleck und K. Schreiner. Stuttgart, 1994, pp. 161–236.

Tanner, A. 'Bürgertum und Bürgerlichkeit in der Schweiz. Die "Mittelklassen" an der Macht', in *Bürgertum im 19. Jahrhundert*, ed. J. Kocka, 3 vols. Göttingen, 1995, vol. 1, pp. 199–229.

Tenfelde, K. 'Unternehmer in Deutschland und Österreich während des 19. Jahrhunderts', in *Innere Staatsbildung und gesellschaftliche Modernisierung in Österreich und Deutschland 1867/71–1914*, ed. H. Rumpler. Munich, 1991, pp. 125–38.

—— 'Stadt und Bürgertum im 20. Jahrhundert', in *Wege zur Geschichte des Bürgertums*, ed. K. Tenfelde and H.-U. Wehler. Göttingen, 1994, pp. 317–53.

Thane, P. 'Aristocracy and Middle Class in Victorian England: The Problem of "Gentrification"' in *Bürgertum, Adel und Monarchie. Wandel der Lebensformen im Zeitalter des bürgerlichen Nationalismus*, ed. A. M. Birke et al. Munich, 1989, pp. 93–108.

Thompson, F.M.L. *The Rise of Respectable Society: A Social History of Victorian Britain 1830–1900*. Cambridge, MA, 1988.

—— 'Aristocracy, Gentry and the Middle Classes in Britain, 1750–1850' in *Bürgertum, Adel und Monarchie. Wandel der Lebensformen im Zeitalter des bürgerlichen Nationalismus*, ed. A.M. Birke et al. Munich, 1989, pp. 15–35.

Torstendahl, R. and Burrage, M. (eds.) *The Formation of Professions: Knowledge, State and Strategy*. London, 1990.

Walker, M. *German Hometowns: Community, State and General Estate 1648–1871*. Ithaca NY, 1971.

Wehler, H.-U. 'Wie bürgerlich war das Deutsche Kaiserreich?', in *Bürger und Bürgerlichkeit im 19. Jahrhundert*, ed. J. Kocka. Göttingen, 1987, pp. 243–80.

—— 'Deutsches Bildungsbürgertum in vergleichender Perspektive. Elemente eines "Sonderwegs"?', in *Bildungsbürgertum im 19. Jahrhundert IV: Politischer Einfluß und gesellschaftliche Formation,* ed. J. Kocka. Stuttgart, 1989, pp. 215–37.

—— 'Die Geburtsstunde des deutschen Kleinbürgertums', in *Bürger in der Gesellschaft der Neuzeit*, ed. H.J. Puhle. Göttingen, 1991, pp. 199–209.

—— *Deutsche Gesellschaftsgeschichte*, 3 vols. Munich, 1995, vol. 3.

3

THE LANDED ARISTOCRACY DURING THE NINETEENTH AND EARLY TWENTIETH CENTURIES

Maria Malatesta

The twentieth century has inherited from nineteenth-century observers in the United States and Europe – from their independent but intersecting vantage points – a view of the difference between the New World and the Old World, based on the contrast between the aristocracy of wealth and an aristocracy of birth, between multiple patterns of social distinction and a monolithic system modelled on the aristocracy. Recent European historical enquiry has shown that processes of elite formation in nineteenth-century Europe were more complex and manifold than the theory of the refeudalisation of nineteenth-century Europe, developed by American and European scholars, would have us believe. From the European perspective, the landed aristocracy was one of the nineteenth-century elites which shared resources and power with other emerging social groups. The model of social sharing, rather than of domination, distinguishes the European approach to the study of the landowning elites from its American counterpart, which, like Henry James at the end of the nineteenth century, is still enamoured of the image of a nobility which encapsulated the whole of nineteenth-century European civilisation.[1]

An elite among elites, the landed aristocracy produced a kind of symbolic capital within which the concept of nobility interwove with the notion of a natural order deeply embedded in the land and in agriculture. This symbolic capital was the material product of an economy still dependent on agriculture and of a process of defeudalisation which maintained socially, but no longer juridically, entailed landed property. Erected on this material basis was a nonmaterial structure which enabled old and new social groups to exploit the legacy of the past to create a system of social distinction still centred on landownership.

A comparative study of the material processes whereby the Western European landowning elites produced social capital must take two crucial factors into account. The first of these is the restrictedness of social mobility via landownership, which remained the prerogative of the upper classes. In addition to the social constraints on landed property was the fact that the colonisation of land in Europe had been completed by the early modern period. The shortage of land aggravated social closure by impeding that upward mobility – from farmer to freeholder – which distinguished rural American society in the nineteenth century, not only in the West but also in the plantation system of the antebellum South.[2] The fact that land in America was less freely available than Fredereck Jackson Turner – the historian of the Frontier – maintained, as it was subject to speculation and monopoly, was a result of the logic of the market as opposed to that of social privilege. The other factor consists of the characteristics and dimensions of this mobility. Unlike in Eastern Europe, mobility took place on a vast scale in Western Europe during the nineteenth century and led to a massive influx of the urban and rural bourgeoisie into the ranks of the landowning class, thereby completing the fusion between nobility and bourgeoisie that had begun during the Old Regime.

The concept of landed aristocracy describes this characteristic social pattern in Western Europe more precisely than that of nobility, since it comprises both the notion of restricted mobility and that of the noble–bourgeois composition of the landed elites. On the basis of Michael Confino's analysis of the European nobility,[3] which provides an interpretative hypothesis for the comparative study of the landed aristocracies of Western Europe, I propose and discuss an approach which comprises the following variables:

1. that these aristocracies were an economic and power elite;

2. that they were a mixed group of aristocratic and bourgeois origin, and their restricted mobility into the higher strata favoured the fusion between the two social components;

3. that they reacted to economic and social change; and

4. that they developed reproductive (hereditary, matrimonial and cultural) and organisational strategies in order to defend their identity.

1. The landed aristocracy as an economic and power elite

The basis of the power of the landed aristocracy in the nineteenth century was the persistence of land systems dominated by large estates in most European countries. However, large landownership was not the only feature of European agriculture. It coexisted in Spain, Italy, France, Germany and Austria with small-scale farmholdings; furthermore, it was insignificant in Sweden and Denmark, countries (like in Norway and Finland) in which the eighteenth-century anti-nobiliary policies pursued by the Crown favoured the consolidation in the early nineteenth century of a stratum of independent peasant freeholders, who became the basis of the agricultural system in the Nordic countries. Elsewhere in Europe, at the centre and the periphery, disentailing – which was completed in the West by the mid-1800s but continued in the East until almost the end of the century – did not dismantle the system of large landownership, which in many cases was reinforced or created ex novo by the formation of individual landownership with free access to the market.[4] Nor was France, despite the creation of a broad stratum of self-sufficient peasant owners in the country, exempt from the process. At the end of the nineteenth century, one-quarter of French agricultural land was in the hands of large-scale landowners. In England and Ireland, countries unaffected by the market turmoil provoked by the fall of the old continental regimes, the concentration and extent of eighteenth-century agricultural holdings remained intact until the 1870s.[5]

Large landownership did not in all cases signify the concentration of landed possessions, nor necessarily large-scale farming. It could, as it was in the South and East of Europe, be part of a system which also comprised peasant smallholdings. It had dimensions which ranged from the huge estates in England and Eastern Europe to the relatively smaller size of the great French and Italian landed patrimonies. It took the capitalist form of English, Prussian, French or Northern Italian high farming or the quasi-feudal form of absentee ownership based on the tenant system (which equally involved capitalist exploitation). Moreover land could be farmed by the owner or share-cropped with the peasants. These various types of farming coexisted, as happened in France and Italy, within the same regions, and they helped to enrich the European agrarian panorama.

Diversified in the extent and forms of its exploitation, large landownership coexisted with the process of industrialisation, from which it derived undoubted economic benefits. Once the agrarian depression of the 1820s and 1830s had passed, European agriculture witnessed the astonishing rise of agricultural prices and rent provoked by the increased productivity of the land and by the boom in demand for foodstuffs generated by the growth of the urban population. The high productivity of Western capitalist agriculture developed within economic systems which, although they had set off on the road towards industrialisation, were still closely dependent on the primary sector. In 1900, only England and Belgium, followed by Switzerland and Holland, were entirely emancipated from agriculture, while in France and Germany respectively 43 percent and 40 percent of the population was employed in the sector. However, these percentages, which reached 72 percent in the South of Europe and 65 percent in Spain and Portugal, were still substantially lower than those of countries in Eastern Europe, where close dependence on the agricultural sector was combined with the persistence of a quasi-feudal tenure system.

The industrialisation of Western Europe in certain respects exacerbated the gap between economic and social development. The more rapid decline of the old order and the precocious onset of industrialisation were not enough to dismantle the socioeconomic power of the great landowners, as was demonstrated in exemplary fashion by England, Belgium and Germany. Although the landed elites of the West shared their power with the new urban elites, their social influence was still guaranteed in the first half of the nineteenth century by various factors: the wealth-based electoral systems, which privileged the political representation of landowners; the notability system, which ensured that the landed nobility and bourgeoisie in France, Spain and Italy conserved their local power; and the maintenance of their jurisdictional and policing powers by the English and Prussian aristocracies.

The Western landed aristocracies were also able to preserve their power thanks to their new, but unchallenged, role as national elites. The joining of the liberal regimes of Italy and Spain by the landed aristocracies of those countries exemplifies their ability to adapt to political changes and to exploit them in order to secure positions of power within society. The counter-example is provided by the Portuguese nobility, which was economically ruined by its refusal to join the liberal regime.[6] However, in Germany, England and Belgium the alliance of land and nation was one of the mainstays of the political and constitutional systems of the nineteenth century. The hostility of the French nobility to the Third Republic and competition between the landed aristocracy and the Republicans for control of the countryside was the concluding phase of a long period in which the landed aristocracies had adhered to the previous monarchical regimes.

The integration of the Western landowning aristocracies into the new regimes was also facilitated by the absence of the ethnic distinctiveness typical of Eastern Europe.[7] Although in countries like Poland and Hungary – as well as Italy – the nobility provided the movement for national independence with its political leadership, ethnic distinctiveness meant that the peasants' struggle for land reform came to coincide with the struggle for national revolution, while it simultaneously reinforced a social system based on a twofold elite. The landed nobility and gentry of Eastern Europe embodied a culture which was entirely distinct from that of the urban bourgeoisie composed of foreigners and Jews, and the breach between the two cultures was not healed by processes of complementarity and inclusion between the two elites.[8]

The absence of ethnic distinctiveness in the West encouraged the fusion of the various segments of the landed aristocracy and increased its social integration. It also enhanced the aristocratic landowners' role as brokers between city and countryside, two worlds brought into increasingly closer contact by urbanisation, the integration of markets and the development of communications. The importance of identification with the nation for the reproduction of the landed elites of Western Europe was manifest in the case of Ireland, which was the only country in which the land question and the national question coincided. The land war which exploded during the great depression of the last years of the century developed into a socio–political conflict that replicated patterns in Eastern Europe. In Ireland, however, the urban–rural bourgeoisie was able to assume leadership of the agrarian and national revolutionary movement and to achieve the complete changeover of its elites by overthrowing the landed aristocracy and replacing it with a new elite composed of farmers and tradesmen.[9]

2. Social mobility into the landed elites

The dismantling of the Old Regimes did not substantially change the hierarchical structure of European landed property. Noble possessions were not destroyed, while the bourgeoisie was offered a great opportunity for social mobility. Defeudalisation in continental Western Europe accelerated the process of fusion between the nobility and the bourgeoisie which had begun in the seventeenth and eighteenth centuries and had by now been accomplished in England. In Eastern Europe the land instead remained the perquisite of the nobility and the gentry. The rise of the rural bourgeoisie in the Russian countryside after 1861 did not bring major changes to the agrarian structure or to the collective mentality. The case of Bulgaria, where the agrarian reform of the 1870s created a stable class of independent peasant freeholders, may be considered the exception that proves the rule.[10]

The entry of nonaristocratic elements into the landed elites was the result of the strong mobility that affected landed property in Western Europe. Mobility in Western landownership began during the Old Regime, but was accelerated in the nineteenth century by the effects of defeudalisation and the broadening of the land market. Although more stable than its Continental equivalent because it was unaffected by the turmoil of defeudalisation, English landownership was also affected by massive transfers of landed possessions in the nineteenth century. In 1889 more than nine million hectares of English land changed hands over one or two generations. The agrarian crisis of the first half of the century accentuated the mobility of Continental landownership at the expense of the freed peasants and to the benefit of the bourgeoisie. In England too, it was the erosion of yeoman estates, exacerbated in the 1820s, that offered opportunities for upward social mobility to the mercantile classes, which were also able to join the ranks of the aristocracy by means of the purchase of small properties.[11] The expulsion of the peasants from land acquired by redemption and the erosion of yeoman possessions strengthened the hierarchical structure of landed property in Western Europe. Furthermore, its emergence from the Old Regime did not differ greatly in structural terms from defeudalisation in Japan, where the Land Tax Revision of 1873 established the percentage of peasants deprived of their land and, by 1930, pushed the proportion of tenant-managed land up to 50 percent. As in Europe, the peasants' loss of their land in Japan benefited the old seigneurs and the new urban landowners.[12]

In Western Europe, rural mobility passed mostly through the agricultural middle class of the large-scale tenant farmers. Although of negligible importance in the East European countryside, where tenancy was far surpassed by direct farming – or where the tenant was, as in Romania, a middleman similar to the Sicilian *gabellotto* – in the West these tenant farmers made a vital contribution to the development of capitalist agriculture. As holders of capital, they were the first members of the rural communities to achieve upward social mobility. In Prussia, France, Italy, Spain and England, they acquired landed property while still farming their leaseholds. In the Latin countries tenant farmers founded large family fortunes, joined the landed aristocracy and in some cases were awarded noble titles. When the agrarian depression of the last decades of the century forced part of the landed aristocracy to liquidate their rural assets, the tenant farmers remained the principal vector of rural social mobility. The phenomenon was most striking in early twentieth-century England, where the tenant farmers were forced to acquire the dismantled estates of the landed aristocracy, but it was also manifest in France. After the First World War, tenant farmers in Italy and Spain gained possession of large tracts of farmland.[13] Everywhere, indeed, they were among the protagonists of the 'ruralisation' of the countryside; that is, the process whereby, between the end of the nineteenth century and the First World War, the land abandoned by the notability was restored to the rural classes.

However, the mobility of Western landed property mainly concerned the bourgeoisie, which also acquired with the land the social power that sprang from entry into the landed aristocracy. Members of the bourgeoisie bought up the land made available by defeudalisation and in most of Europe became the largest-scale landowners. Two patterns can be distinguished here. The first, the inclusion pattern, was characteristic of Central Europe, where the diffusion of bourgeois propertyowning took place internally to aristocratic proprietorship and preserved the structure of privilege connected with it. In the first half of the nineteenth century, the Prussian bourgeoisie acquired 66 percent of the land, and by the end of the century had gained possession of the majority of estates measuring over 100 hectares. The contiguity pattern, on the other hand, was characteristic of the landed aristocracy in the Latin countries, where the sale of the *biens nationaux* and church estates led to the formation of a property-owning bourgeoisie alongside the landed aristocracy.[14] This contiguity gave rise in Spain and Italy to a cohesive noble–bourgeois social bloc. In France the two components, although both belonged to the sociopolitical sphere of the notability, were more socially distant because of the French aristocracy's traditional exclusiveness.[15]

The bourgeoisie's investment in landed property continued throughout the nineteenth century and had evident social repercussions. Emulation of the noble lifestyle was responsible for the spread of an aristocratic model which induced industrialists, financiers and professionals to purchase rural estates and country houses. While the symbolic significance of this behaviour was particularly evident, especially in the more industrialised countries, one should not underestimate the economic value of landed investments, according to context and period. Comparisons among the rates of such investment by the French, Italian and Spanish bourgeoisies clearly show the effect of the constant and indeed growing presence of the urban bourgeoisie in the rural real-estate market.

In France the tendency of the bourgeoisie to give priority to investments in real estate predominated during the Restoration but went into a marked decline thereafter. Landed investments were largely replaced by stock and state bonds, although they did not entirely disappear from the portfolios of the upper classes, and, indeed, they proportionately increased among the popular classes. In Spain and Italy, by contrast, professionals, businessmen and industrialists continued to purchase land until the First World War. Delayed industrialisation, and therefore fewer opportunities for alternative investments in stock, combined with the high value of agricultural rent, strengthened the bourgeois component of the landed aristocracy in the South of Europe.[16]

3. Economic adaptation and entrepreneurial initiative

The nobility's survival of defeudalisation and industrialisation is a prime example of the ability of the landed aristocracy to adapt to social change. Whether provided with legal protection, as in Germany, or benefiting from de facto advantages as in other countries, the survival of the Continental nobility depended on its ability to secure a steady income. The economic strategies of the landowning nobility were thus designed to transform former feudal estates into a source of income within a market economy. Still surviving – indeed, in some cases flourishing – in the first half of the nineteenth century were those noble groups who had been able to cope with the financial crisis of the last decades of the eighteenth century, absorb the loss of their feudal privileges and overcome the agrarian depression of the early decades of the century. Only the fittest of the species had survived. Hardest hit was the landed nobility, like those of Portugal and Valencia, which possessed only seigneurial estates, while those seigneurial patrimonies which were disentailed over a long period of time managed to survive.[17] The Venetian nobility succumbed to the new regime by losing 61 percent of its lands. Under the effects of indebtedness and the agrarian depression, the Prussian nobility lost one-third of its landholdings in the course of the century. The Milanese nobility entered economic decline in the 1830s. Everywhere, the dissolution of the nobility's rural estates increased the percentage of land possessed by the bourgeoisie.

The conjunctures of the first half of the century widened the gap between the rich and poor nobilities, as the French case very clearly shows. However, this patrimonial distinction did not necessarily correspond to a difference in status. Whereas in Prussia it was the minor nobility that suffered the greatest losses, in Valencia it was precisely this group that proved most adept in converting its seigneurial estates. In Italy, a number of families of recent ennoblement – the Torlonia of Rome, for example – amassed enormous landholdings. The majority of the Continental nobility – in contrast to the economic stability enjoyed by their English counterparts until the 1880s – sustained losses, but they were nevertheless able to exploit the economic situation to redeem their fortunes. In Belgium, Spain and France, as well as in England, numerous noble landowners continued to be their country's great landed magnates.

Some French noble families had restored their landed patrimonies even before the law on emigrant possessions. In the region of Paris and its adjoining regions, as well as in the northwest, southwest and Alpine regions, the landed properties of the nobility resisted the economic conjuncture and speculative assaults. Other nobilities exploited the various forms and pace of disentailing. In the south and west of Germany in the 1830s, they paid off their debts at the expense of the peasants, without selling their estates.[18] In Italy and Spain they invested the compensation paid for the loss of their feudal rights and profited from the sale of biens nationaux to restore their fortunes. The great families of the ancient Spanish nobility testify to the ability of the landed elites to adapt to the new conjuncture and to the shrewdness with which they replenished their assets.

In adapting to the new order, the European aristocracy deployed a range of economic strategies. Drawing an antithesis between an entrepreneurial strategy (i.e., adjustment to economic change by introducing capitalist methods into agriculture) and a *rentier* strategy (i.e., resistance to economic change by perpetuating a semifeudal economic logic corresponding to the extensive exploitation of the land) appears reductive, especially if it is made to coincide with the division between North and South.

It is undeniable that Northern Europe was characterised by capitalist agricultural development based on high-farming. Alongside the early entrepreneurial activities of the English aristocracy and those of the Prussian nobility during the early nineteenth century, the French, Northern Italian and even Spanish landed aristocracies also displayed a general willingness to embrace the principles of a capitalist market economy.[19] Taken as a whole, the landed aristocracy of Western Europe, both noble and bourgeois, exhibited a marked tendency towards capitalist methods of land management, and this was also the case in many areas of Southern Europe.

On the other hand, we should not forget the persistence of a latifundist mentality which sought – for example in the south of Spain and in the centre-south of Italy – to preserve estates by increasing the amount of land rather than its productivity and by insulating agricultural output against market fluctuations for as long as possible. In these cases, but also in that of aristocratic land management in Franche-Comté, capitalist rationality was subordinated to a moral economy which sought to preserve communitarian social organisation, on the one hand, and to perpetuate the nobility's status and lifestyle, on the other.[20]

The entrepreneurial mentality of the landed aristocracies of Western Europe was indicative of their adaptation to the capitalist transformation of agriculture. Nobility and bourgeoisie worked side by side in modernising the countryside. In Italy and France they formed the group of captains of rural industry which introduced new agronomic techniques and mechanisation into agriculture. This pattern of economic behaviour profoundly differentiated the landed aristocracy of Western Europe from its counterparts elsewhere. In Eastern Europe the agronomanie of the landed elites did not take the form of the capitalist transformation of agrarian systems, nor – in Russia before the emancipation of the serfs – was it able to replace the traditional farming methods of the peasant communities with new economic rationality. The modernisation of agriculture in Western Europe was mainly the achievement of the landed elites. This pattern of private enterprise in the agrarian economy brought Western Europe closer to the American model, whereas it differentiated it from that of late nineteenth-century Japan and Eastern Europe. In these two areas, in fact, it was intervention by the state which created, through reform from above, the conditions for the capitalist development of agriculture and – as instead happened in the case of Japan – tightly organised agricultural production within the rural communities.[21]

The landed aristocracies continued to be tied to the agricultural economy. Their contribution to industrialisation was mainly, but not only, indirect; that is to say, it was based on financing via share capital and on the exploitation of resources. In both cases, although their economic behaviour was shaped by the imperatives of a capitalist economy, it preserved features typical of landed property holding. The direct participation of the landed aristocracy in industrialisation largely reflected the spread of industrial development. In the south of Italy and in Spain it was nonexistent, while it was pronounced in regions like Normandy, Silesia, Bohemia and Saxony. Also in Lombardy, which was the first Italian region to industrialise, a number of aristocratic families became entrepreneurs. However, this association between early industrialisation and direct economic participation by the landed elites was not the general rule. In Belgium only a handful of nobles became businessmen, and in England the involvement of the landed elites in the metallurgical industry, which was sizeable in the first half of the nineteenth century, diminished in the following period. In Europe as a whole, including Eastern Europe, the nobility withdrew from the manufacturing sector, which it had controlled during the Old Regime, and opted for less risky and demanding forms of investment. Not only investment in state securities and banks but also shareholding in industrial firms followed the economic logic of 'safety first'. Investments in industry by the landed elites began when industrial take-off was already well advanced and when the industrial sectors had consolidated, as investment in the railways amply demonstrates.

Their adaptation to the industrial cycle did not radically change the *rentier* mentality which typified the landed aristocracies. Even the English aristocrats, who were the first in Europe to invest capital in agriculture, were not immune to this tendency and preferred to lease their iron and coal mines rather than exploit them directly. The same applied to the Silesian landowners, who appointed managers to run their enterprises, thereby replicating in industry the separation between ownership and management that typified the agricultural leasehold system. Participation in the agro-food industry – by the Junkers in the Prussian distilleries or by the Italian nobility of Emilia in sugar, cheese and tomato processing plants – does not contradict the pattern. Involvement in the agro-food sector was an extension of the agricultural economy, as the industrial transformation of an activity which remained under the control of the owner.

A further example of the economic logic followed by the nineteenth-century landed aristocracies – a logic designed to exploit the benefits deriving from industrialisation while avoiding high costs and without exposure to risk – is provided by their investment in urban real estate. In the nineteenth century, the urban aristocracies no longer sought to shape the cities in their own image. They endeavoured instead to exploit processes of urbanisation for their own economic advantage. For the landed aristocracies of northern and western France, Prussia and Piedmont – a region in northern Italy – who accentuated their rural physiognomy in the course of the century, urban rents were not a major component of their incomes. For the Spanish, English and the Italian landed aristocracies, by contrast, who preserved an urban–rural or distinctly urban physiognomy, urban rents were crucial for their economic survival.

The explosive growth of the cities provided the richer English landed aristocracy, with many of its members also being the proprietors of urban buildings and ground, with a source of income greater than that to be obtained from agriculture. And it was this factor that enabled them to cope with the agrarian crisis of the end of the century, unlike those other aristocrats who relied solely on agricultural land for their incomes. The conversion of agricultural rent into urban rent, following the agrarian crisis, was a strategy also pursued by the Italian landed aristocracies who lived in Milan. In England, where the percentage of rich aristocrats who also owned urban real estate increased until 1914, as well as in Milan, the capital of the most highly industrialised of the Italian regions, one finds once again that the economic behaviour of the landed elites displayed close awareness of the economic trend and its intelligent exploitation. In fact, at the end of the Great Depression, investments in urban real estate by the English and Lombard landed elites expanded as the building cycle revived.[23]

Assessment of the economic behaviour of the landed aristocracies in the period of industrialisation must take account of a further variable: namely the economic value – according to period and area – of extra-agricultural investment. In the phase of industrial take-off, such investment – in England, Belgium, Germany and, albeit to a lesser extent, France – took the form of the reallocation of surplus agricultural capital to the industrial and financial sectors. It was a phenomenon analogous to that which accompanied the onset of Japanese industrialisation, when the landlords invested all the revenues received as compensation for the loss of their feudal rights in banks, thereby transforming themselves into financial magnates.

At the end of the Great Depression, when the upswing in the economic cycle led to the definitive establishment of the industrial economy in Europe, the process operated in reverse. The twenty-year collapse of agricultural prices drastically reduced rents. This decline, combined with the exodus of rural labour from the countryside and the consequent increase in agricultural wages, provoked (mainly in England but also in France) massive sales of landed property. Assets were 'deruralised' out of economic necessity, due to fears for the future and the loss of confidence in the land as a shelter-good, and because the 'aura' that surrounded landed property had been dispelled. This deruralisation of rural assets shifted economic resources towards movable wealth or urban rents.

Extra-agricultural investments in this case signalled the withdrawal of the landed elites from the countryside.[24]

However, the deruralisation of assets was not a phenomenon that affected the more industrialised countries alone. It was also evident in nonindustrialised, central-southern Italy, which witnessed the large-scale transfer of agricultural rents to the financial sector and to urban real estate. In nineteenth-century Spain, by contrast, the nobility (most notably the aristocratic families of Madrid) managed instead to restore their fortunes by ruralising them. Urban properties were sold in order to recuperate rural patrimonies, and the withdrawal of the Madrid nobility from the city therefore created a space which was promptly occupied by the propertied bourgeoisie.[25]

One should not overestimate the dependence of the landed aristocracies on the economic cycle, but nor should one ignore the extent to which the survival of the landed elites of Europe depended on the level of industrialisation achieved by their various countries. The end of the nineteenth century and the beginning of the twentieth saw a 'peaceful retreat' of the landed elites from the countryside in France and England, due mainly to the downturn in the economic cycle. In Italy and Spain, countries still economically dependent on agriculture at the end of the nineteenth century, there was no mass retreat of the landed elites from the countryside. The land continued to be an extremely attractive form of investment for the urban classes because, unlike in the more industrialised countries, land value remained high and rents from land had again begun to rise. Intensified capitalist exploitation of the northern Italian countryside at the end of the century, which also benefited from the 'new colonisation' made possible by land reclamation in the Po Valley, accentuated the entrepreneurial mentality of the landed elites of Northern Italy and thus helped to sustain the process of industrialisation.

4. The defence of aristocratic identity and interest organisation

Although they may have adapted to social and economic changes, the landed aristocracies stoutly defended their identity throughout the nineteenth century. Through inheritance, culture and sociability they sought to preserve their landholdings against the onslaught of industrialism, urbanisation and mass society. Keeping landed estates within the lineage continued to be one of the most important reproductive strategies of the landed elites, but it also performed a highly significant symbolic, as well as economic and social, function. Most favoured in this respect were the landowning aristocracies of Northern Europe who exploited the laws of inheritance to prevent the dismantling of their estates.

Strict settlement was one of the factors that served most to strengthen the English aristocracy. This was a legal device which enabled aristocratic families to keep their landed estates intact by planning their inheritance strategy over several generations. It also helped to develop that farsightedness which, in the nineteenth century, was required of the landed aristocracy as they undertook large-scale improvements involving huge investments of capital. The high German nobility had maintained the privilege of strong family autonomy and the right to transmit property through the male line. Nevertheless, throughout the nineteenth century it campaigned for the reintroduction of the *fideicommissum* in order to restore a noble mien to the land by removing it from the market and from possible purchase by the bourgeoisie. Significantly, the *fideicommissum* system – which was reintroduced in Germany in 1852 – was most widespread in the 1880s, the years in which the economic losses of the nobility due to the agricultural depression were most severe.[26] In England in the same period, under the joint effect of the agricultural depression and of radical public opinion which demanded the liberalisation of the land market so that the land system could be dismantled, and the growth of smallholdings, the Settled Land Act was passed into law in 1882. The result of a compromise between radical and conservative opinions, the Settled Land Act did not eliminate strict settlement and indeed buttressed the powers of the tenant-for-life. However, it did enable disentailed land to arrive on the market, thereby accelerating the deruralisation of the aristocratic landed patrimonies.

In the European countries where Napoleonic legislation had introduced the principle of equal succession, landowners resorted to family strategies in order to impede the fragmentation of their landed possessions, which had been the ruin of so many of the Continental noble families. The transmission of undivided property was ensured by three strategies. The first of these was a marked revival in endogamy characterised – as in the south of Italy – by the flouting of the prohibition of consanguinity to the fourth degree of remove. The logic of the surname thus interwove with the economic necessities of the landed patrimonies. In southern Italy, the phenomenon involved both nobles and the bourgeoisie, but it was the agricultural bourgeoisie, loath to lose the lands that it had worked so hard to acquire, which was most concerned with restricting kinship relations. The second strategy consisted in the formation, by means of intermarriage among family groups, of extended families, which secured – as in the south of Spain – control over broad swathes of territory. Finally, the maintenance of landed possessions could be ensured by an economic strategy based on the accumulation of land, on the one hand, and the planning of the heirs' administration of the patrimony in order to prevent its fragmentation, on the other.[27]

This reliance on lineage in order to counteract the effects of the expanding land market emphasised the exclusiveness of the landed aristocracies, an observation confirmed by the matrimonial choices of many European nobilities. It was especially the old nobility that exhibited this close correlation between lineage and endogamy. Social exclusiveness, however, was contradicted in many cases by the economic imperative of injecting new capital into the family. The fusion between the nobility and the wealthy bourgeoisie continued, although it was often the outcome of marriages between male heirs and bourgeois women. In other cases, it stemmed from the linking function that the lesser nobility performed between the bourgeoisie and the high nobility, or resulted from marriages with the families of recently ennobled industrialists.[28]

The other distinctive feature of the landed aristocracies was cultural in nature. In the face of the new urban and industrial culture, the landed elites reaffirmed their identity by continuing the eighteenth-century agronomic tradition and bringing it up to date with nineteenth-century scientific and technical advances. The *agronomanie* that spread through the whole of Europe provided the landed aristocracy with further and substantial opportunities to unite and entrench themselves. The passion for science gave rise to a European agrarian 'International' comprising the cream of the landed elites. This group of agrarian reformers placed its faith in progress and firmly believed that agriculture had a leading role to play even in industrialised societies.

The elite of the landed aristocracies was rich, cultivated and fluent in the principal European languages. It attended agricultural conferences, visited the Great Exhibitions and undertook study journeys. It broadcast information on crop- and soil-management techniques and on the agrarian systems of various countries, thereby helping to ensure that the landed elites kept abreast of developments in agronomy. These exchanges were further boosted by the growth of agrarian associations throughout Europe.

Agrarian sociability inherited from the Old Regime or the fruit of the Napoleonic age did not restrict itself to reinforcing the conservative demeanour of the landed aristocracies. It provided the model which, via a process of direct branching or transformation and diversification, engendered the agrarian associationism of the last decades of the nineteenth century. The cultural capital of the landed aristocracies was invested in the new terrain of the organisation of interests. The newly-founded agrarian associations were the evolutionary outcome of the long-standing sociability of academies, clubs and small local agrarian associations. But they were also entirely new institutions pursuing more complex goals than in the past: defending agricultural production against market fluctuations and obtaining economic, fiscal and social policies favourable to landownership. These associations were created in the aftermath of the Great Depression at the end of the century and for a variety of purposes: in Germany and Italy to defend agricultural production against foreign competition; in France in 1868, or England in 1907, to counteract the laissez-faire economic policy or the new pro-popular tax policy introduced by the respective governments of those countries; in the case of the agrarian associations of Northern Italy, to contend with the agricultural strikes of the early years of the twentieth century.[29]

The landed aristocracies used these associations to pursue a strategy of reproduction and conversion which achieved two results. By means of collective action and participation they created the new figure of the landed proprietor/agricultural professional. They redrew the social boundaries of the landed elites by completing the integration of the great tenant farmers and by marking them off from the smallholder and the agricultural labourer. The professionalisation of agriculture and the defence of agricultural interests gave rise to a collective and defensive identity. This, however, was less the outcome of the opposition raised by the old notability and aristocracy against social change than – once again – the result of their signal capacity to adapt. The landed aristocracies, especially in France and Germany, pursued their projects of social engineering by exploiting old techniques (paternalism, for example, or forging alliances with the Catholic church) and new ones (such as nationalism and the organisation of mass consensus) in order to maintain their control over the countryside threatened by industrialisation and socialism.

The depopulation of the countryside in the industrialised countries was not only economically threatening in so far as it pushed up agricultural wages; it was also socially hazardous because it undermined the system of deference on which the landed aristocracies' identity crucially depended. The downswing in the economic cycle of the 1880s and 1890s coincided with the land's loss of social value. Significantly, landownership ceased to be the indispensable prerequisite for ennoblement, as the cases of Belgium and England aptly demonstrate. The new nobility of state, industry and the professions was by now entrenched and wrested symbolic capital away from the landed aristocracies. In this epoch-making change, the landed aristocracies defended their identity by means of collective pressure organisations and groups. Via their associations, they developed strategies to regain the countryside using techniques which varied according to the social environment: paternalism or violence; the development of agrarian education; the organisation of production and distribution.

The modernising action of the agrarian organisations was deployed principally in the economic sphere. The spread of the agricultural co-operative movement – the outcome of an alliance between the landed aristocracies and economic and social scientists – was one of the factors responsible for the revival of agriculture after the depression. But at the same time it was a device to build a consensus among the peasants and small proprietors. The innovative capacity of the landed aristocracies was most strikingly evident when the agrarian organisations created (as in the case of the *Société des Agriculteurs de France* or the *Bund der Landwirte*) *reseaux conglomérés*, multifunctional organisations operating as political associations and trade unions and providing agricultural credit and social insurance. Other associations concentrated their activities in a particular sector; some examples being creating fiscal policy for the Central Land Association, contending with strike action for the agrarian associations of the Italian Po Valley or facilitating economic cooperation for the *Federazione Italiana dei Consorzi Agrari*.

Agrarian organisation resulted from the ability of the landed elites to adjust to change by transmitting social demands via the novel channel of the interest group. However, the assumption of new collective identities by the landed aristocracies did not radically alter the structure of their political representation. The overall aim of the agrarian associations was to increase the representation of agriculture in parliament in order to counteract pro-industrial economic policies and fiscal pressure on landed estates. The growth of interest groups changed the face of political representation in early twentieth-century Europe by replacing representation by virtue of notability (i.e., based on the accumulation of personal capital) with representation based on delegated capital (i.e., entirely in the hands of the organisation). In the late nineteenth and early twentieth centuries, this transformation had only just begun; indeed, the only country in which it was fully accomplished was Germany, where organised capitalism was already well established.[30] Unlike the landed aristocracy of Prussia, those of the other European countries were loath to abandon their individualistic mentality and to accept, at the political level, the discipline of the organisation.

In neither Eastern[31] nor Western Europe did the landowner associations transform themselves into fully-fledged agricultural parties. There were two reasons for this. Firstly, economic groups were structurally prevented from becoming political parties because they represented sectoral, rather than general, interests. The landed aristocracies of the late nineteenth and early twentieth centuries found themselves at an impasse. They claimed to represent the general interest, but could no longer claim that agriculture was the only industry capable of strengthening the national economic identity, nor could they represent the nation in the name of the middle and working classes. Secondly, the landed aristocracies never thought of creating a mass party: the *Bund der Landwirte*, for instance, was an extraparliamentary pressure group and always remained one. Instead, they used cross-party techniques to build the broadest consensus possible on agricultural policy among various parliamentary alignments. This strategy of alliancebuilding enhanced the representation of agriculture in the parliaments of late nineteenth- and early twentieth-century Europe, but it was also a signal that the age of privilege enjoyed by the landed aristocracies was past and that their survival now depended on their ability to bargain.

Notes

1. F.J. Grund, *Aristocracy in America*, (1st edn, London, 1839), 2nd edn, Gloucester, MA, 1968. The best representation of the European nobility by Henry James is to be found in his novels *The American* (1876) and *The Golden Bowl* (1904); A.J. Mayer, *The Persistence of the Old Regime: Europe to the Great War*, New York, 1981.

2. S.D. Bowman, 'Antebellum Planters and Vormärz Junkers in Comparative Perspective', *The American Historical Review*, 85 (1980), pp. 779–808. F.J. Turner, *The Frontier in American History*, New York, 1920; A.G. Bogue, *From Prairie to Corn Belt: Farming the Iowa and Illinois Pairies in the Nineteenth Century*, Chicago, 1963.

3. M. Confino, 'Some Current Problems in Comparative Social History: the Case of the European Nobility', in *Modern Age — Modern Historian: In Memorian György Ránki (1930–1988)*, ed. F. Glatz, Budapest, 1990, pp. 87–96.

4. J. Cruz Villalón, *Proprietad y uso de la tierra en la Baja Andalucia: Carmona, siglos XVIII–XX*, Madrid, 1980; W. Conze, 'The Effects of Nineteenth-Century Liberal Agrarian Reforms on Social Structure in Central Europe', in *Essays in European Economic History 1789–1914*, ed. F. Crouzet, W.H. Chaloner and W.M. Stern, London, 1969, pp. 54–69; M. Petrusewicz, *Latifondo: Economia morale e vita materiale in una periferia dell'Ottocento*, Venice, 1989.

5. P. Barral, 'Aspects régionaux de l'agrarisme français avant 1930', *Le Mouvement Social* 67 (1969), pp. 3–16; F.M.L. Thompson, 'The Social Distribution of Landed Property in

England since the Sixteenth Century', in *Third International Conference of Economic History*, Paris-La Haye, 1965, pp. 471–85.

6. N.G.F. Monteiro, *O crepsculo dos grandes: A casa e o patrimonio de aristocracia em Portugal (1750–1832)*, Lisbon, 1998.

7. D.W. Urwin, *From Ploughshare to Ballotbox: The Politics of Agrarian Defence in Europe*, Oslo, 1980, pp. 174ff.

8. V. Karady, *Une élite dominée: la bourgeoisie juive en Hongrie dans l'entre-deux-guerre (Un cas du problème de la dualité des élites dans la modernization en Europe Centrale)*, paper presented to the Colloque International Université Toulouse-Le Mirail (September 1994): 'Anciennes et nouvelles aristocraties'.

9. J.S. Donnelly Jr., *The Land and the People of Nineteenth Century Cork*, London and New York, 1975; M.D. Higgins and J.P. Gibbons, 'Shopkeepers-graziers and Land Agitation in Ireland 1895–1900', in *Ireland: Land, Politics and People*, ed. P.J. Drudy, Cambridge, 1982, pp. 93–103.

10. D. Lieven, *The Aristocracy in Europe, 1815–1914*, London, 1992, p. 91; J.D. Bell, *Peasants in Power: Alexander Stamboliski and the Bulgarian National Union, 1899–1923*, Princeton, 1979.

11. F.M.L. Thompson, *English Landed Society in the Nineteenth Century*, London, 1980, pp. 109ff.

12. Y. Hayami et al., *A Century of Agricultural Growth in Japan*, Tokyo, 1975, pp. 47ff.

13. J.M. Moriceau and G. Postel-Vinay, *Ferme, entreprise, famille: Grande exploitation et changements agricoles XVIIe–XX siècles*, Paris, 1992; J.P. Jessenne, *Pouvoir au village et Révolution: Artois 1760–1848*, Lille, 1987; R. Robledo, 'Los arrendamientos castellanos ante y después de la crisis de fines del siglo XIX', in *Historia agraria de la Espana contemporánea*, vol. 2, ed. R. Garrabou and J. Sanz, Barcelona 1985, pp. 369–441; M. Malatesta, *I signori della terra: L'organizzazione degli interessi agrari padani (1860–1914)*, Milan, 1989, chap. 2; H. Schissler, *Preussische Agrargesellschaft im Wandel*, Göttingen, 1978, p. 87.

14. W. Abel, *Congiuntura agraria e crisi agrarie*, Torino, 1976, pp. 339–57.

15. P. Ruiz Torres, 'La aristocracia en el país valenciano: la evolución dispar de un grupo privilegiado en la España del siglo XIX', in *Les noblesses européennes*, ed. G. Delille, Collection de l'Ecole française de Rome, Rome, 1988, pp. 137–63; A. Daumard, 'Noblesse et aristocratie en France au XIXe siècle', in *Les noblesses européennes*, pp. 81–104; C. Capra, 'Nobili, notabili, élites: dal modello francese al caso italiano', *Quaderni storici* 37 (1978), pp. 5–42; M.T. Perez Picazo, 'De regidor a cacique: las oligarquias municipales murcianas en el siglo XIX', in *Señores y campesinos en la Péninsula iberica, siglos XVIII–XX*, vol. 1, ed. P. Saavedra and R. Villares, Barcelona 1991, pp. 16–37.

16. A. Daumard, *Les fortunes françaises au XIXe siécle*, Paris, 1973; R. Robledo, *La renta de la tierra en Castilla la vieja y Leon (1836–1913)*, Madrid, 1984; A.M. Banti, 'Les richesses bourgeoises dans l'Italie du XIXe siècle: exemples et remarques', in *Mèlanges de l'Ecole francaise de Rome* 97 (1985), pp. 361–79.

17. J. Baz Vicente, *El patrimonio de la casa de Alba en Galicia en el siglo XIX*, Lugo, 1991.

18. R. Hubscher, *L'agriculture et la société rurale dans le Pas-de-Calais du milieu du XIXe siècle à 1914*, vols 1 and 2, Arras, 1979; D. Higgs, *Nobles in Nineteenth-Century France: The Practice of Inegalitarianism*, Baltimore and London, 1987; G.W. Pedlow, *The Survival of the Hessian Nobility 1770–1870*, Princeton, 1988.

19. H. Schissler, 'The Junkers. Notes on the social and historical signifiance of the agrarian elite in Prussia', in *Peasant and Lords in Modern Germany*, ed. R.G. Moeller, Boston and London, 1986; A. Guillemin,'Rente, famille, innovation. Contribution à la sociologie du grand domaine noble au XIXe siècle', Annales E.S.C. 1 (1985), pp. 52–67; R. Garrabou and J. Sanz Fernández, 'La agricultura española durante el siglo XIX: immobilismo o cambio?', in *Historia agraria de la España contemporánea*, vol. 2, ed. R. Garrabou and J. Sanz Fernandez, Barcelona, 1985, pp. 7–191; A.M. Banti, *Terra e denaro: Una borghesia padana dell'Ottocento*, Venezia, 1989.

20. G. Pescosolido, *Terra e nobiltà. I Borghese. Secoli XVIII e XIX*, Rome, 1979; E. Malefakis, *Agrarian Reform and Peasant Revolution in Spain*, New Haven and London, 1970; C.I. Brelot, *La noblesse réinventée: Nobles de Franche-Comté de 1814 à 1870*, vol. 1, Paris, 1992, chaps 4 and 5.

21. M. Confino, *Systèmes agraires et progrès agricole: L'assolement triennal en Russie au XVIIIe–XIXe siècles*, Paris, 1969; P. Gunst, 'Agrarian Systems of Central and Eastern Europe', in *The Origins of Backwardness in Eastern Europe*, ed. D. Chirot, Berkeley, Los Angeles and Oxford, 1989; R.H. Havens, *Farm and Nation in Modern Japan: Agrarian Nationalism 1870–1940*, Princeton, 1974.

22. D. Spring, 'English Landowners and Nineteenth Century Industrialism', in *Land and Industry: the Landed Estates and the Industrial Revolution*, ed. J.T. Ward and R.G. Wilson, Newton Abbott, 1971, pp. 16–42; J. Kocka, 'Enterpreneurs and Managers in German Industrialization', in *The Cambridge Economic History*, vol. 7, part 1, ed. P. Mathias and M.M. Postan, Cambridge, 1978; S. Clark, 'Nobility, Bourgeoisie and the Industrial Revolution in Belgium', *Past and Present* 105 (1984), pp. 150–75; G. Richard, 'La noblesse dans l'industrie textile en Haute-Normandie dans la première moitié du XIXe siècle', *Revue d'Histoire Economique et Sociale* XLVI (1968), nn. 3–4, pp. 305–38, 506–49; M. Malatesta, *Le aristocrazie terriere nell'Europa contemporanea*, Roma, Bari 1999, chaps. 2–3.

23. F.L.M. Thompson, 'The Land Market in the Nineteenth Century', *Oxford Economic Papers* 9, no. 3 (1957), 285–308; D. Cannadine, *Lords and Landlords: The Aristocracy and the Towns 1774–1967*, Leicester, 1980 ; Lieven, *The Aristocracy*, chap. 5; A.L. Cardoza, *Aristocrats in Bourgeois Italy: The Piedmontese nobility, 1861–1930*, Cambridge, 1997, chaps III, VI; Malatesta, *I signori della terra*, pp. 314–19.

24. D. Cannadine, *The Decline and Fall of the British Aristocracy*, New Haven and London, 1990; M. Levy-Leboyer, *Le revenue agricole et la rente foncière en Basse Normandie: Etude de croissance régionale*, Paris, 1972.

25. A. Bahamonde Magro, 'Crisis de la nobleza da cuna y consolidación burguesa (1840–1880)', in *Madrid en la societad del siglo XIX*, vol. 1, Madrid, 1986, pp. 326–75.

26. E. Spring, 'The Settlement of Land in Nineteenth Century England', *The American Journal of Legal History*, 8 (1964), pp. 209–23; C. Dipper, 'La noblesse allemande à l'epoque de la bourgeoisie. Adaptation et continuité', in Delille, *Les noblesses européennes*, pp. 165–97; J. Habakkuk, *Marriage, Debt and the Estate System: English Landownership 1650–1950*, Oxford, 1994, chaps 1–3.

27. G. Delille, *Famiglia e proprietà nel Regno di Napoli*, Torino, 1988, pp. 325–38; P. Macry, *Ottocento: Famiglia, élites e patrimoni a Napoli*, Torino, 1988, pp. 172–5; F. Héran, *Les bourgeois de Séville: Terre et parenté en Andalusie*, Paris, 1990; G. Montroni, *Gli uomini del re: La nobiltà napoletana nell'Ottrocento*, Rome, 1996.

28. G.W. McDonogh, *Good Families of Barcelona*, Princeton, 1986; A.M. Banti, 'Strategie matrimoniali e stratificazione nobiliare. Il caso di Piacenza', in Delille, *Les noblesses européennes*, pp. 451–71; H. Kaelble, 'Borghesia francese e borghesia tedesca 1870–1914', in *Borghesie europee dell'Ottocento*, ed. J. Kocka, Venice, 1989, 127–60.

29. H.J. Puhle, *Agrarische Interessenpolitik und preussischer Konservatismus im wilhelminischen Reich 1893–1914*, Bonn-Bad Godesberg, 1975; P. Barral, *Les agrariens français de Méline à Pisani*, Paris, 1968; M. Malatesta, 'Une nouvelle stratégie de reproduction: les organisations patronales agraires européennes (1868–1914)', *Histoire, Economie, Société* 16 (1997), pp. 203–19.

30. P. Bourdieu, 'La représentation politique', *Actes de la recherche en sciences sociales* 38 (1981), pp. 3–24; P. Ullmann, *Interessenverbände in Deutschland*, Frankfurt am Main, 1988.

31. L. Péter, 'The Aristocracy, the Gentry and their Parliamentary Tradition in Nineteenth-Century Hungary', *Slavonic and Eastern European Review* 70 (1992), pp. 9

Bibliography

Abel, W. *Congiuntura agraria e crisi agrarie*. Torino, 1976.

Bahamonde Magro, A. 'Crisis de la nobleza da cuna y consolidación burguesa (1840–1880)', in *Madrid en la societad del siglo XIX*, vol. 1. Madrid, 1986, pp. 326–75.

Banti, A.M. 'Les richesses bourgeoises dans l'Italie du XIXe siècle: exemples et remarques', in *Mélanges de l'Ecole francaise de Rome* 97 (1985), pp. 361–79.

—— 'Strategie matrimoniali e stratificazione nobiliare. Il caso di Piacenza', in *Les noblesses européennes*, ed. G. Delille, Collection de l'Ecole française de Rome. Rome, 1988, pp. 451–71.

—— *Terra e denaro: Una borghesia padana dell'Ottocento*. Venice, 1989.

—— 'Aspects régionaux de l'agrarisme français avant 1930', *Le Mouvement Social* 67 (1969), pp. 3–16.

Barral, P. *Les agrariens français de Méline à Pisani*. Paris, 1968.

Baz Vicente, J. *El patrimonio de la casa de Alba en Galicia en el siglo XIX*. Lugo, 1991.

Bell, J.D. *Peasants in Power: Alexander Stamboliski and the Bulgarian National Union, 1899–1923*. Princeton, NJ, 1979.

Bogue, A.G. *From Prairie to Corn Belt: Farming the Iowa and Illinois Prairies in the Nineteenth Century*. Chicago, IL, 1963.

Bourdieu, P. 'La représentation politique', *Actes de la recherche en sciences sociales*, no. 38, 1981, pp. 3–24.

Bowman, S.D. 'Antebellum Planters and Vormärz Junkers in Comparative Perspective', *The American Historical Review* 85 (1980), pp. 779–808.

Brelot, C.I. *La noblesse réinventée: Nobles de Franche-Comté de 1814 à 1870*, vol. 1. Paris, 1992.

Cannadine, D. *Lords and Landlords: The Aristocracy and the Towns 1774–1967*. Leicester, 1980.

—— *The Decline and Fall of the British Aristocracy*. New Haven, CT and London, 1990.

Capra, C. 'Nobili, notabili, élites: dal modello francese al caso italiano', *Quaderni storici* 37 (1978), pp. 5–42.

Cardoza, A.L. *Aristocrats in Bourgeois Italy. The Piedmontese Nobility, 1861–1930*. Cambridge, 1997.

Clark, S. 'Nobility, Bourgeoisie and the Industrial Revolution in Belgium', *Past and Present* 105 (1984), pp. 150–75.

Confino, M. *Systèmes agraires et progrès agricole: L'assolement triennal en Russie au XVIIIe–XIXe siècles*. Paris, 1969.

—— 'Some Current Problems in Comparative Social History: the Case of the European Nobility', in *Modern Age - Modern Historian. In Memorian György Ránki (1930–1988)*, ed. F. Glatz. Budapest, 1990, pp. 87–96.

Conze, W. 'The Effects of Nineteenth-Century Liberal Agrarian Reforms on Social Structure in Central Europe', in *Essays in European Economic History 1789–1914*, ed. F. Crouzet, W.H. Chaloner and W.M. Stern. London, 1969, pp. 54–69.

Cruz Villalón, J. *Propriedad y uso de la tierra en la Baja Andalucia: Carmona, siglos XVIII–XX*. Madrid, 1980.

Daumard, A. *Les fortunes françaises au XIXe siècle*. Paris, 1973.

—— 'Noblesse et aristocratie en France au XIXe siècle', in *Les noblesses européennes*, ed. G. Delille, Collection de l'Ecole française de Rome. Rome, 1988, pp. 81–104.

Delille, G. *Famiglia e proprietà nel Regno di Napoli*. Torino, 1988.

—— (ed.). *Les noblesses européennes*, Collection de l'Ecole française de Rome, Rome, 1988.

Dipper, C. 'La noblesse allemande à l'epoque de la bourgeoisie. Adaptation et continuité', in *Les noblesses européennes*, ed. G. Delille, Collection de l'Ecole française de Rome. Rome, 1988, pp. 165–97.

Donnelly, J.S. Jr. *The Land and the People of Nineteenth Century Cork*. London and New York, NY, 1975.

Garrabou, R. and Sanz Fernández, J. 'La agricultura española durante el siglo XIX: immobilismo o cambio?', in *Historia agraria de la España contemporánea*, vol. 2, ed. R. Garrabou and J. Sanz Fernandez. Barcelona, 1985, pp. 7–191.

—— (eds). *Historia agraria de la Espana contemporánea*, vol. 2. Barcelona, 1985.

Grund, F.J. *Aristocracy in America*, (1st edn., London, 1839). Gloucester, MA, 1968.

Guillemin, A. 'Rente, famille, innovation. Contribution à la sociologie du grand domaine noble au XIXe siècle', *Annales E.S.C.* 1 (1985), pp. 52–67.

Gunst, P. 'Agrarian Systems of Central and Eastern Europe', in *The Origins of Backwardness in Eastern Europe*, ed. D. Chirot. Berkeley, Los Angeles and Oxford, 1989.

Habakkuk, J. *Marriage, Debt and the Estate System: English Landownership 1650–1950*. Oxford, 1994.

Havens, R.H. *Farm and Nation in Modern Japan: Agrarian Nationalism 1870–1940*. Princeton, NJ, 1974.

Hayami, Y. et al. *A Century of Agricultural Growth in Japan*. Tokyo, 1975.

Héran, F. *Les bourgeois de Séville: Terre et parenté en Andalusie*. Paris, 1990.

Higgins, M.D. and Gibbons, J.P. 'Shopkeepers-graziers and Land Agitation in Ireland 1895–1900', in *Ireland: Land, Politics and People*, ed. P.J. Drudy. Cambridge: Cambridge University Press, 1982, pp. 93–103.

Higgs, D. *Nobles in Nineteenth-Century France: The Practice of Inegalitarianism*. Baltimore, MD and London, 1987.

Hubscher, R. *L'agriculture et la société rurale dans le Pas-de-Calais du milieu du XIXe siècle à 1914*, vols 1 and 2. Arras, 1979.

James, H. *The American* (1st edn. 1876). New York, NY, 1963.

—— *The Golden Bowl* (1st edn. 1904). New York, NY, 1972.

Jessenne, J.P. *Pouvoir au village et Révolution: Artois 1760–1848*. Lille, 1987.

Kaelble, H. 'Borghesia francese e borghesia tedesca 1870–1914', in *Borghesie europee dell'Ottocento*, ed. J. Kocka. Venice, 1989, pp. 127–60.

Karady, V. *Une élite dominée: la bourgeoisie juive en Hongrie dans l'entre-deux-guerre (Un cas du problème de la dualité des élites dans la modernization en Europe Centrale)*, paper presented to the Colloque International Université Toulouse-Le Mirail, September 1994: 'Anciennes et nouvelles aristocraties'.

Kocka, J. 'Enterpreneurs and Managers in German Industrialization', in *The Cambridge Economic History*, vol. 7, part 1, ed. P. Mathias and M.M. Postan. Cambridge: Cambridge University Press, 1978.

Levy-Leboyer, M. *Le revenue agricole et la rente foncière en Basse Normandie: Etude de croissance régionale*. Paris, 1972.

Lieven, D. *The Aristocracy in Europe, 1815–1914*. London, 1992.

Macry, P. *Ottocento: Famiglia, élites e patrimoni a Napoli*. Torino, 1988.

Malatesta, M. *I signori della terra: L'organizzazione degli interessi agrari padani (1860–1914)*. Milan, 1989.

—— 'Une nouvelle stratégie de reproduction: les organisations patronales agraires européennes (1868–1914)', *Histoire, Economie, Société* 19 (1997), pp. 213–19.

—— *Le aristocrazie terriere nell'Europa contemporanea*. Roma, Bari, 1999.

Malefakis, E. *Agrarian Reform and Peasant Revolution in Spain*. New Haven, CT, London, 1970.

Mayer, A.J. *The Persistence of the Old Regime: Europe to the Great War*. New York, NY, 1981.

McDonogh, G.W. *Good Families of Barcelona*. Princeton, NJ, 1986.

Monteiro, N.G. *O crepuscolo dos grandes: A casa e o patrimonio da aristocracia em Portugal (1750–1832)*. Lisbon, 1998.

Montroni, G. *Gli uomini del re: La nobilità napoletana nell'Ottocento*. Rome, 1996.

Moriceau, J.M. and Postel-Vinay, G. *Ferme, entreprise, famille: Grande exploitation et changements agricoles XVIIe–XX siècles*. Paris, 1992.

Pedlow, G.W. *The Survival of the Hessian Nobility 1770–1870*. Princeton, NJ, 1988.

Perez Picazo, M.T. 'De regidor a cacique: las oligarquias municipales murcianas en el siglo XIX', in *Señores y campesinos en la Península ibérica, siglos XVIII–XX*, ed. P. Saavedra and R. Villares. Barcelona, 1991, pp. 16–37.

Pescosolido, G. *Terra e nobiltà. I Borghese. Secoli XVIII e XIX*. Rome, 1979.

Péter, L. 'The Aristocracy, the Gentry and their Parliamentary Tradition in Nineteenth-Century Hungary', *Slavonic and Eastern European Review* 70 (1992), pp. 97–8.

Petrusewicz, M. *Latifondo: Economia morale e vita materiale in una periferia dell'Ottocento*. Venice, 1989.

Puhle, H.J. *Agrarische Interessenpolitik und preussischer Konservatismus im wilhelminischen Reich 1893–1914*. Bonn-Bad Godesberg, 1975.

Richard, G. 'La noblesse dans l'industrie textile en Haute-Normandie dans la première moitié du XIXe siècle', Revue d'Histoire Economique et Sociale XLVI (1968), pp. 305–38, 506–49.

Robledo, R. *La renta de la tierra en Castilla la vieja y Leon (1836–1913)*. Madrid, 1984.

—— 'Los arrendamientos castellanos ante y después de la crisis de fines del siglo XIX', in *Historia agraria de la Espana contemporánea*, vol. 2, ed. R. Garrabou and J. Sanz. Barcelona, 1985, pp. 369–411.

Ruiz Torres, P. 'La aristocracia en el país valenciano: la evolución dispar de un grupo privilegiado en la Espana del siglo XIX', in *Les noblesses européennes*, ed. G. Delille, *Collection de l'Ecole française de Rome*. Rome, 1988, pp. 137–63.

Saavedra, P. and Villares, R. (eds) *Señores y campesinos en la Península ibérica, siglos XVIII–XX*. Barcelona, 1991.

Schissler, H. *Preussische Agrargesellschaft im Wandel*. Göttingen, 1978.

—— 'The Junkers. Notes on the Social and Historical Significance of the Agrarian Elite in Prussia', in *Peasant and Lords in Modern Germany*, ed. R.G. Moeller. Boston, MA, London, 1986.

Spring, D. 'English Landowners and Nineteenth Century Industrialism', in *Land and Industry: the Landed Estates and the Industrial Revolution*, ed. J.T. Ward and R.G. Wilson. Newton Abbot, 1971, pp. 16–26.

Spring, E. 'The Settlement of Land in Nineteenth Century England', *The American Journal of Legal History*, 8 (1964), pp. 209–23.

Thompson, F.M.L. 'The Land Market in the Nineteenth Century', *Oxford Economic Papers* 9 (1957), pp. 285–308.

—— 'The Social Distribution of Landed Property in England since the Sixteenth Century', in *Third International Conference of Economic History*. Paris-la Haye, 1965, pp. 471–86.

—— *English Landed Society in the Nineteenth Century*. London, 1980.

Turner, F.J. *The Frontier in American History*. New York, NY, 1920.

Ullmann, P. *Interessenverbände in Deutschland*. Frankfurt am Main, 1988.

Urwin, D.W. *From Ploughshare to Ballotbox: The Politics of Agrarian Defence in Europe*. Oslo, 1980.

4

THE PROFESSIONS IN NINETEENTH-CENTURY EUROPE

Hannes Siegrist

In the nineteenth century, the professions belonged to the most active driving forces of the modernisation process. Professionals calculated and made use of the concomitant risks and possibilities and were able to strengthen their position among both normative and functional elites. The professions owed their ascendance to the idea of progress, the systematisation of knowledge, and the assertion of liberal and meritocratic principles, but also to the expansion of the modern state and to the nationalisation of society and culture.

For the scholarly and educated occupations of continental Europe, the nineteenth century began with a crisis. In the final decade of the eighteenth century and in the early nineteenth century, the autonomous colleges of lawyers and physicians, as well as the independent university corporations, were dissolved in most areas of the continent and the professions subordinated to state and government. Local market monopolies and privileges in education and occupational admittance were done away with. Yet in the further course of the nineteenth century, the institutional models and mentalities of old European corporative professional culture were revived in new forms adapted to bourgeois and national society – one need only think of the right of participation by lawyers and physicians in training and in occupational admittance, in the forming of ethical principles and in corporative–occupational self-administration through professional associations. In liberal society, lawyers and physicians became models for other professions:[1] notaries, pharmacists, architects, engineers and management experts emulated them in one way or another.

The character of the European professions in the 'long' nineteenth century is varied and complex.[2] They were the bearers of progress and rationalisation, and yet, at the same time, defenders of older professional cultures and corporative mentalities. They had at their disposal a rational expert knowledge, but also a ritualistic and symbolic knowledge which was difficult for outsiders to understand. They exercised power: social and political circumstances rendered some the recipients of governmental orders, while others formed into relatively free scientific elites or became rebels and the bearers of cultural, economic, social and political innovations. The professions insisted upon traditional work domains and yet created new services and products, markets and sources of income. On the one hand, they defended the monopolies and conceptions of an occupation and a lifestyle befitting one's rank or station; on the other hand, they were themselves subject to market pressures. At the beginning of the nineteenth century, most of the members of the highly educated professions were civil servants or were self-employed; at the beginning of the twentieth century, the professions were, in regard to their position, divided into state and communal civil servants, the self-employed, private employees and entrepreneurs.

The members of the professions had to subordinate themselves to the rules of a more or less closed group of self-employed or to those of a civil servant corps, even though they themselves were already regarded as bourgeois individuals. They viewed themselves as members of a community of educated Europeans which transcended national boundaries and they orientated themselves according to the universalistic scientific and ethical principles of their profession. Yet as local, state and national elites, they stood in competition with one another. As graduates of academic secondary schools and universities, the members of professions shared a similar educational background as well as a common general cultural knowledge. However, the individual professional and status groups were also rivals for the validity and hegemony of their specific knowledge in regard to the definition of meaning and to the solution of political, social and moral problems. Theologians and ministers lost their influence, while lawyers, physicians and scholars of the humanities pushed themselves into the foreground, only to find themselves under pressure from natural scientists and engineers in the late nineteenth century.

It should be noted that the history of physicians, lawyers, ministers, engineers and professors in the different European countries cannot be easily reduced to a common denominator.[3] In spite of this, I will attempt to sketch out a brief history of the professions in Europe.

Comparative research about the professions in Europe offers a particular point of access to European social and cultural history. Such
research concentrates upon professions and occupations, which form an
intersection among individuals, social structures and institutions. It takes
into account the fact that societies and cultures cannot be compared as
wholes. Rather, selected and definable phenomena must be compared
and considered within their narrower and wider contexts, namely those
of structures and processes, configurations and sequences, situations and
problems, systems of meaning and symbols.[4] The following presentation
concentrates on six selected aspects: first, an international comparison of
the construction and institutionalisation of the professions; second, the
development of knowledge and the discourse of professional experts
within bourgeois society; third, the relation of professionals to the market; fourth, the role of the state in the institutionalisation and the
representation of the professions; fifth, the interaction between experts
and laypeople; and sixth, the role of the professions in the process of
nationalisation in the nineteenth century. Our central question will be:
how and why do professions succeed in developing a specific knowledge
and a professional culture, as well as in creating authority and recognition for themselves?

Institutional history of the professions in a comparative perspective

The structures and processes, as well as the tensions and strategies out-
lined in the introduction, can be observed in all of Europe from the late
eighteenth century until 1918 – in Western and Central Europe earlier
than in Eastern Europe. The similarities within Europe can be explained,
in the first place, through the continued effect of the old-European understanding and institutionalisation of occupation and work.[5] Secondly, they
can be traced back to processes of cultural emulation and institutional
transfers, conditioned by the competition for modernisation among the
different states. Individual states and nations used the professions to
secure political dominance and order, as well as to develop their domestic economies, laws and cultures and to distinguish themselves from
other nations and to demonstrate efficiency and strength in foreign
affairs. The case of engineers may serve as an example. The model of
engineers' qualification through state institutions of higher education on
the basis of general bureaucratisation developed much earlier in France
and Germany than in England and in the United States, where training

within the 'shop culture' initially predominated. Between 1870 and 1939, the different qualification and occupational systems became increasingly similar; those elements that were held to be decisive for survival in international competition were copied.[6]

Occasionally the adoption of professional models was forced through politically by European empires. Thus, traces of the 'French lawyers' code', introduced during the Napoleonic occupation of Europe, existed for a long time, from the Rhineland to Warsaw and Naples.[7] The Habsburg monarchy shaped the system of professions in Southeastern Europe, while the Prussian model spread to the civil service and professions in northern Central Europe,[8] and the Russian model to conditions in the entire Tsarist Empire.[9] The English model of professions spread throughout the colonies worldwide.[10]

Some of the differences that existed at the time among various states, nations and regions appear, from the present perspective, merely as asynchronicities, that is, as differences between pioneer and latecomer societies which, in the course of time, levelled out. Some differences, however, hardened into institutional structures and long-lasting mentalities, so that they came to be regarded, and are still regarded, as national distinctions. In France, Germany and in the Habsburg Empire, the model of the civil servant spread to all educated occupations; in England, Switzerland and Italy, the 'gentleman professions', respectively the 'bourgeois or middle-class professions' such as barristers or advocates, became the leading model for other professions.[11] The examples suggest that national particularities could ultimately be traced back to the genesis, shaping and duration of specific political and social systems. In countries with an early liberal order and a weak civil servant tradition, the models of self-employment and entrepreneurship spread earlier and more strongly to professions than in bureaucratic authoritarian states.

On the basis of recent historical-comparative studies, we now know in detail the similarities and distinctions among the individual 'national' professions. The German Protestant minister was distinguished from the English cleric because the former was redefined by the system of state churches according to the model of the civil servant and thus removed from the patronage of the nobility and the cities.[12] The engineers from French elite colleges enjoyed more prestige than their German colleagues, who as technicians continued to have a lower status than university graduates.[13] On the basis of the greater significance of the university in Germany, the German professor had a higher status than his French colleague.[14] English and American journalists developed a specific professional image and their own professional ethic earlier than their French and, above all, their German counterparts. In the latter two countries, journalism and party politics were differentiated from one another at a later point in time and more weakly.[15] In the United States and Switzerland, women had access to university and were able to acquire the qualification necessary for academic occupations earlier than in Germany. Factors such as the influence of democratisation, bureaucratisation and the system of entitlements were responsible for these differences.[16] If women in Western and Southern European countries became teachers earlier and more frequently than in Central Europe, this was certainly influenced by the stronger tradition of religious and private schools.[17]

I will not extend this series of examples of regional and international differences with regard to selected aspects of professional life, nor will I expand the necessarily brief explanations of these distinctions and similarities. My interest here is simply to indicate that professional functions and professional knowledge existed in principle in all of Europe, but that the various European societies treated them differently and thus constructed the professions differently. The national and regional differences between professions of the same name can be explained to a large degree through differences in the political, social, cultural and scientific orders and the traditions of the various countries. Even at first glance, it is evident that in individual countries the same expert knowledge and institutional models were, in many respects, used slightly differently on the basis of specific presuppositions and conditions.

In the nineteenth century, there was a Europe-wide process of professionalisation and meritocratisation. The modern 'professions' – i.e., occupations which were characterised by scientifically and systematically grounded knowledge and capacities – were formed through diverse processes: through an exclusive theoretical and practical education, which also introduced unwritten rules and attitudes; through titles, which were supposed to indicate status and to secure trust; through a particular attitude towards the exercise of a profession (a scientific attitude, collegiality, orientation to public welfare, unselfishness); through a specific position in the social division of labour which, on the basis of its expertise, was superior to that of artisans and laypeople; through a specific mode of acquisition of income; through a greater prestige as well as through particular forms of collective control and organisation, both of which were tied to the notion of individual and occupational-corporative autonomy and honour.[18] The history of European professions shows that, within the framework of the complex processes of professionalisation, initially a few occupations, and then increasingly more of them, moved towards this ideal type. 'Professionalisation', however, proceeded with as little uniformity and linearity as the process of 'modernisation', a process with which it in many ways overlapped, but to which it at times also ran contrary.

Even when it was only a matter of minor variations and nuances of a general model, national and regional differences were often carefully registered and emphasised by contemporaries, who declared these to be the foundation of their own national and occupational identity and who stylised them in the histories of their own occupational or status group. This individualising historiography spread national professional myths and facilitated the social and cultural integration of occupational groups and of the nation as a whole. Historical-comparative investigations of usually two or three countries, as well as social-scientific comparisons, made on the basis of several variables, of a greater number of countries have been interested in the similarities and commonalities as well as in the differences. In principle, this essay follows this tendency. However, due to lack of space I must limit myself more to the presentation of general trends and similarities.

Scientific discourses and bourgeois values

The dissolution of corporative society of estates, the development of the modern state, the introduction of commercial and occupational freedom, and the change in culture, science and education meant losses for the traditional 'scholarly occupations' and 'educated classes'. Occupational-corporative privileges and monopolies were devalued; the merit system gained in significance; the contents and forms of expert knowledge as well as liberal education and occupational praxis changed. In this situation, the professional and political elite formulated new discourses and professional models. The physician was presented increasingly as a scientific and practically educated healer, helper and health expert; the lawyer as an expert of the law and a 'priest of justice', responsible for the realisation of the modern state under the rule of law and for the securing of rights, property and honour of citizens. The engineer was defined as the carrier of scientific, economic and technical progress, the university professor and the *Gymnasium* teacher as experts in education, aesthetics, ethics and morality, the Protestant minister as a scientifically educated theologian who no longer justified himself simply through the certainty of belief and through piousness.

Around 1800, these occupations were still not professions or expert occupations in the present sense. Their knowledge was incompletely systematised and their occupational culture hardly established. The discourses about hierarchy and the distribution of knowledge, tasks, symbols and jurisdictions within professional groups, as well as with regard to third parties, indicate that occupational images were in flux. Thus there were disputes about the relation between the 'scholarly physician', the practical 'surgeon', herbal healers, healing nuns, midwives and nurses. The distinctions and boundaries between expert knowledge and lay knowledge remained controversial into the second half of the nineteenth century. The new experimental knowledge was not unambiguously superior to everyday knowledge, and old mentalities and ideas about health and bodies held on tenaciously. Medical innovations and technologies, however, soon spread throughout all of Europe, although the degree of acceptance varied quite significantly.[19] These differences were determined less nationally than through factors such as the degree of urbanisation, the strength of the bourgeois middle class and the accessibility of medical services for workers and the rural populace. All of this occurred along a significant East–West and North–South divide.

Since the late eighteenth century, all of the professions and expert occupations in Europe followed a strategy of freeing themselves from patronage relations which made them dependent upon their clients, and of attaining a certain autonomy and technical superiority. With the development of a new professional culture which attempted to establish the status of the autonomous expert, they called upon professional and bourgeois, middle-class values such as a scientific attitude, autonomy, independence, distance and unselfishness. The criterion of efficiency, on the contrary, only gradually came to the foreground.

Already around 1800, 'independence' was a generally recognised bourgeois value, while 'a scientific attitude' was only recognised as such during the course of the nineteenth century. The establishment of the professional values of 'autonomy', 'disinterestedness' and 'orientation to public welfare' was more difficult. The noble, bourgeois and governmental purchasers and users of professional services were not unconditionally ready to recognise an occupational autonomy which rested upon a complex of knowledge, symbols and practices which were difficult for an outsider to understand. In order to check this resistance, the professions formulated a discourse which circled around the concepts of 'disinterestedness', 'loyalty', 'acting to the best of one's knowledge and conscience' and 'sensitivity' (tact, delicacy). With the concepts of 'autonomy' and 'disinterestedness', the professions distanced themselves, on the one hand, from the view that the bureaucratic authoritarian state alone was responsible for the general interest and public welfare, and, on the other hand, from the liberal idea that the following of private interests would automatically lead to general welfare and progress.[20] 'Sensitivity' referred to the duty and capacity of professional experts to respect, within certain boundaries, the individual peculiarities of clients with regard to taste in the use of the goods, values and symbols in question. All in all, the egoistic tendencies of the professions were supposed to be domesticated, the interests of the clients protected and the public welfare promoted. The values and criteria of behaviour were summarised into a professional ethic and a code of behaviour (laws, deontologies, occupational manuals), which often regulated not only occupational behaviour, but extraoccupational as well.

The creation of professional markets

The ascent of European professions rested not only upon a new discourse about knowledge and its applications, but also upon material, social and cultural achievements, which were demanded first in the cities and then increasingly in the countryside. In part, the professions stimulated this demand themselves by creating needs. They covered an ever-expanding need for understanding the world, for the creation of meaning, and for edification and entertainment, whether of a religious or profane nature. They ensured that questions about rights, property, health and death were considered somewhat less fatalistically. In the construction business and in commerce, in industries, banking and insurance, numerous new tasks arose. In each case, the professions profited from the growing prosperity and the cultural needs of the middle class. Professional values and ideas had an increasingly strong effect on bourgeois culture.

As opposed to merchants, businessmen and entrepreneurs, most professionals were not allowed to promote themselves openly or to advertise. This was forbidden either on the basis of a traditional occupational ethic or as a legal requirement. Thus professionals had to draw attention to themselves through other means. Often they were assisted by the state.

The role of the state in the institutionalisation and the representation of professions

In broad sections of Europe, the state – in its welfare, interventionist, cultural and constitutional guises – promoted the demand for professional services and provided professions with functional rights and symbols. While in England, as well as in several smaller, institutionally more traditional areas of the Continent, the corporative professional order survived externally, these, too, came to require governmental recognition and legal toleration as regulated 'chartered professions'.[21] In England, the regulation of professional culture and the representation of experts thus remained a matter of corporations or professional bodies which were vested with privilege – at first barristers and physicians, and then other professions as well. On the Continent, however, the position and authority of the professions was strengthened by the transition to commercial and occupational freedom, in that professionals were allowed to present themselves as occupiers of an exactly defined 'profession'. This was of great symbolic significance, contrasting with the abolishment of guilds and brotherhoods in crafts and industry, and it decisively shaped the self-understanding of professionals, as well the understanding of non-professional occupations. Within the framework of liberal reforms, states and legislatures deregulated most of the crafts, trades and commercial occupations through the introduction of commercial and occupational freedom and the free market, thus dealing a severe blow to the old-European corporative and communal conception of an occupation. Yet they also declared several kinds of employment – those concerned with central goods and values, such as property, honour, health, public order, morality and science – to be legally regulated 'occupations' or 'educated professions'. In areas in which a strategic significance was ascribed to order, freedom, security, culture and civilisation, the old-European idea of occupation and vocation was able to survive.

Monarchic and bureaucratic authoritarian states, as well as liberal republics, conferred a higher ordination and a greater authority to those occupations of strategic significance. In respect to questions of how these positions should be regulated and how the professions themselves should be constructed, however, the answers differed markedly. Bureaucratic states made professions primarily into 'civil service occupations', secondarily into 'official professions' (*Amtsprofessionen*) and only after this into 'self-employed or freelance occupations'.[22] *Professionals in civil servant positions* were to a great degree bound to the king or to the state. In cases of doubt, the individual lawyer, physician, engineer or teacher had to put aside professional criteria and follow the instructions of his superior. However, as a result of the increasing recognition of 'professional competence' and the 'immunity from dismissal' enjoyed by higher civil servants, specific conceptions and forms of professional autonomy developed within bureaucracies as well. *Official professions* such as Prussian, Bavarian and Austrian court lawyers (*Gerichtsanwälte, Prokuratoren*), Prussian district physicians and Italian communal physicians did not have the status of civil servants, but they did exercise a governmental or public office. They were admitted only in limited numbers and were controlled by the state. While political appointments strengthened expert authority externally, they relativised the inner autonomy of the professional. In the course of the nineteenth century, the model of the *'liberal' or 'self-employed' profession* gained increasing acceptance. In this case, the state or legislature provided the members of a profession, so to speak, with governmental credit, as it trained them in state universities, examined them and provided them with a title. The self-employed professional, once admitted, existed in a more or less free market. The minimal standards of a profession were indeed legally regulated, but in individual cases, the definition and control occurred through compulsory organisations of the occupation (professional associations) or through the informal control of colleagues and clients.

The official professions, which expanded into the second third of the nineteenth century above all in bureaucratic and statist countries, developed a specific occupational culture under the patronage of the state, a culture which on the one hand was characterised by a strong orientation towards the state, and on the other hand, by a considerable distance to clients and scepticism with regard to the market. With time, however, the official professions, on the basis of negative experiences internal and external to their practice, emancipated themselves from governmental protection and subordination. They connected the discourse of political freedom to the discourse of professional autonomy and attempted to become 'really self-employed' professions. In all of Europe, they orientated themselves according to an idealised notion of the English professions and French lawyers, and to the myth of the self-employed and 'liberal' occupations of the Middle Ages and of Greek and Roman antiquity. Through revised occupational laws, they negotiated for themselves a stronger dependence on the market, a dependence which led to a continual discussion – mostly without results – about 'overcrowding' and demands for restricted entry. Since the end of the nineteenth century, debates about professional protectionism in Central and Eastern Europe converged with anti-Semitic currents; the so-called overrepresentation of Jews at universities and in professions was made responsible for overcrowding and for the deterioration of professionals' working and living conditions.[24]

Compulsion and negotiation – The institutionalised and symbolic interaction between professionals and users

The process of professionalisation brought about tensions and conflicts between experts and laypeople. In practice, the contents, forms and rituals of professional knowledge and occupational culture were not always easy to mediate either cognitively or emotionally, all the more so because experts could often not predict or guarantee the results and success of their own conduct. While institutional and social trust helped here, frequently clients attempted to negotiate with experts over professional contents, procedures and forms. Professionals thus developed strategies in order to assert their knowledge and occupational culture against unwilling and uncomprehending laypeople.

Professional conduct wavered between compulsion and negotiation. Following Foucault, numerous studies have emphasised the dimension of compulsion. According to this line of argument, professionalisation was introduced during the great historical process of social disciplining: the professions thus bound together the medicalisation, legalisation, technologisation, moralisation and education of society with institutional and symbolic forms of domination.[25] From this perspective, professional-scientific culture is seen as a mixture of knowledge and power, which has penetrated into all domains of modern life and thought, with experts having thereby consolidated their social, scientific, political and cultural superiority. In contrast to this, more recent historical and cultural-anthropological studies have taken into greater consideration the interests, conceptions and independent actions of the clients and purchasers of professional services, and have thus directed their attention increasingly to the concrete interaction between experts and laypeople and to the situations in which social meanings were negotiated.[26] According to these arguments, expert culture was seldom asserted and received in pure form. From time to time, laypeople consciously avoided the experts who in principle were responsible, seeking advice and help elsewhere, for example, from ministers or priests in questions of health or from union leaders in questions of rights. According to this view, as a result of this reciprocal negotiation, the eventual outcome was always a convergence of expert and lay culture.

Those professions which were governmentally and legally regulated were, above all, able to exercise compulsion. Experts who were active in public administration, the justice system, education or the army could compel people, with relatively little room for compromise, to seek professional services and to subordinate themselves to professional procedures. Contemporary concepts such as compulsory education, curriculum, examination material, the obligation of attaining a university degree in order to practice an occupation (*Studierzwang*), the obligation of being represented in court by a lawyer (*Anwaltszwang*), as well as the obligation of using the minister in one's own parish (*Pfarrzwang*), indicate that many of the services offered by civil servants and self-employed professionals were obtained compulsorily. Experts could exert their symbolic power to the greatest degree in places where laypeople stood alone and unprotected, places such as in hospitals for the poor, insane asylums, boarding schools and barracks. In the brief visit to a physician's practice, in the office of a lawyer and in a minister's house, the client was less completely at the mercy of the expert. In spite of this, most middle-class families avoided these situations and received the physician, lawyer or minister at their own homes. While ministers in the late nineteenth century were forced, due to declining church attendance, to seek out believers, physicians increasingly summoned patients to their offices or to hospitals, where they could present their new medical culture as grounded in natural science, and give the patient a diagnosis and treatment in a distanced and urgent peremptory tone. The rule for lawyers was that one was not allowed to chase after clients like a shopkeeper. This had been the case, in principle, since the *ancien régime*, and only in special cases was this rule broken. Equipped with books, compendia of laws and diplomas in his office, the attorney constructed a quasi-religious atmosphere.

The self-employed professionals had to engage overall in a lot of persuasion and convincing. Specific forms of symbolic production and rituals were used as helpful tools. In manuals, it was consistently emphasised how important the furnishings of the workplace, clothing, ritual and rhetoric were. For many professions, rhetoric was an integral part of occupational culture – one need only think of the minister's sermon, the professor's lecture and the lawyer's plea. In the classical humanistic educational culture of the *ancien régime*, the art of speaking was taught as one of the seven artes liberales in the Latin schools and at the universities. In the course of the educational and scholastic reform of the nineteenth century, it was pushed out of the curriculum – in the German-speaking countries more completely so than in the Latin countries. It survived in the institutions of secondary education, such as the *Gymnasium*, and in the culture of bourgeois families, from which the professions predominantly recruited themselves and where poems were avidly declaimed and discussed. Many professions were careful to ensure that the prospective experts were made familiar with this art in occupational training and through advisory literature.

Rhetoric is the art which through instruction, entertaining performance and infectious appeal is aimed at the human understanding, feelings and will in order to convince, persuade or move someone to action. The use of rhetoric varied from profession to profession. On the basis of their one-sided form of address, ministers and professors could lay greater weight upon instruction than entertainment. The plea and the adversarial speech of the attorney at public trials, on the contrary, had to entertain and to move its audience. In France, Italy and Russia the rhetorically skilled defence attorney was not only 'admired by the people', but was also highly esteemed by his colleagues – for example, the attorney from Naples whose plea was compared by his colleagues to a torrent, which tore everything with it over cliffs and abysses as it thundered down to the valley; with the eruption of Vesuvius, whose lava flow tore down and devoured everything; and with the speeches of the famous French orator Mirabeau. Pleas were admired which were architectonically constructed, were enriched with technical, scientific and literary knowledge, and involved surprising turns of the argument which dramatised the case.[27]

While in France and Italy in general a cult of the speaker predominated, in Germany and the Habsburg Empire, the rhetoric of the attorney was frowned upon. Prussia's Frederick II rejected flowery speeches during trials with the words, 'I do not want a theatre troupe in the courts.' In 1814, several attorneys from Hamburg expressed the following opinion: 'Pleading is not something we Germans accept. It runs contrary to our language and to our nature. Thus, the German is earnest and more introspective, and it is both a fault and a virtue of this people that they seldom have talent for the art of speaking.'[28] Even after the transition around 1850 from written legal proceedings, in which rhetorical turns were regarded as excesses, to the oral trial, rhetoric remained suspect in Germany. While attorneys who attempted to use rhetoric to overcome the barrier between the 'educated' population and the 'people' and to bring some entertainment into the monotony of life were indeed tolerated, sober argumentation without flourishes continued to be recommended. A different development was evident with physicians: while around 1800 the physicians' advisory manuals still recommended that one speak to distinguished patients with due modesty and to listen to them, by 1900 they recommended a distanced, determined, and urgent peremptory tone.[30] A sought-after specialist could, of course, allow himself this more readily than one of the numerous general practitioners.

Outlook: professions, nations and Europe

The construction and shaping of professions by states and nations destroyed the social type of the old-European educated local profession and prevented contemporaries from imagining a new European and cosmopolitan type of professional. The nation state placed strict limits on occupational mobility and even, in many cases, connected occupational access to the presupposition of citizenship, nationality or ethnicity. The graduate of an Italian university could not simply practise in Germany, nor the English physician in France. In the Habsburg monarchy, in Tsarist Russia, and above all, in the British and French empires, restrictions were, in principle, fewer, but in each case, ethnic and national discriminations created limitations.

In the nineteenth century, European society and culture were nationalised and the perception of the professions changed. There is no national history of the nineteenth century which does not refer to the technically or politically significant achievements of a famous physician, lawyer, minister, professor, pedagogue, historian or engineer. Sooner or later, the professions became the champions of national society, science, knowledge and culture in all European countries. Professionals represented – together with the nobility and entrepreneurs, and with the literati and intellectuals, depending on the country in question – the system of dominance and opposition, knowledge and meaning of the world. In those countries which only belatedly became nation states, the prenational regional governments had already laid the foundations which were then built up either centrally or federally after national unification. In the (more or less) liberal nation states, which understood themselves as states of culture and as states under the rule of law, and which promoted progress in economics, technology and health services, academic occupations and professions gained further significance, expanding into many areas of social, political, economic and cultural life. With the rationalisation and expansion of modern institutions on a national scale, increasing numbers of professors and teachers, judges, administrative civil servants, attorneys, physicians, engineers and architects were needed. Modern elites owed to the nation state colleges and universities, modern occupational images and occupational laws, positions and market monopolies, a certain ethical autonomy and authority, a superiority with regard to nonexperts, the sanctioning of forms of knowledge and treatments as well as the repression of lay knowledge. As members of national and local elites, they developed a common interest in maintaining the connection between power, status, knowledge and livelihood.

Although the sciences or bodies of knowledge became, in principle, increasingly international and systems and procedures were developed with universal validity, the knowledge and status of professions themselves were shaped nationally. This nationalisation of knowledge was driven forward, in the case of the humanistic scholarly professions and the legal occupations, with ideological and practical justifications; in the case of medicine and the natural sciences, through a superficial symbolic aura, as was the case when contemporaries spoke of German and English chemistry. In the nineteenth century, individual national occupational groups developed a particular occupational culture in which local, regional and national characteristics came together. Occupational identity mixed with that of the citizen of the city and of the nation. At the end of the nineteenth century, the English, French, German, Italian, Swiss, Russian and Hungarian professions had their particular myths and rituals as well as their local and national bourgeois heroes, who were honoured in speeches and writing and were presented in the public sphere through busts and statues, paintings and street names.[31] European and universal similarities and commonalities were, indeed, repeatedly invoked at international congresses, but they had little effect.

For professionals, the First World War meant a functional and political increase in value as national elites – and the emergence of a radical nationalism. In 1917–18, an era began which in large parts of Europe was interpreted as a crisis or decline and the end of the heyday of middle-class professions. The nationalisation of professions by no means ended here, but rather was radicalised on the basis of fears about decline and loss, during the time between the world wars as well as during the Second World War. After 1945, the national closing-off of professions and the nationalisation of self-perceptions as well as the perceptions of others continued. Only today, in the face of the liberalisation of the European market, the realisation of the European Union and of globalisation, has this national dimension become weaker.

Notes

1. H. Siegrist, *Advokat, Bürger und Staat: Sozialgeschichte der Rechtsanwälte in Deutschland, Italien und der Schweiz (18.–20. Jh.)*, Frankfurt am Main, 1996; M. Malatesta, 'Gli ordini professionali e la nazionallizzazione in Italia', in *Dalla città alla nazione*, ed. M. Meriggi and P. Schiera, Bologna, 1994, pp. 165–80; M. Burrage, 'Unternehmer, Beamte und freie Berufe. Schlüsselgruppen der bürgerlichen Mittelschichten in England, Frankreich und den Vereinigten Staaten', in *Bürgerliche Berufe: Zur Sozialgeschichte der freien und akademischen Berufe im internationalen Vergleich*, ed. H. Siegrist, Göttingen, 1988, pp. 52–83.

2. While there are numerous individual studies about particular professions within particular countries, systematic comparative overviews are rare. The following anthologies are useful, with contributions on different professions and many countries in which the theme 'the professions in Europe' is considered in one way or another: *Bildungsbürgertum im 19. Jahrhundert. Teil I: Bildungssystem und Professionalisierung in internationalen Vergleich*, ed. W. Conze and J. Kocka, Stuttgart, 1985; *Bürgerliche Berufe: Zur Sozialgeschichte der freien und akademischen Berufe im internationalen Vergleich*, ed. H. Siegrist, Göttingen, 1988; *Professions in Theory and History*, ed. M. Burrage and J. Thorstendahl, London, 1990; *Professionen im modernen Osteuropa*, ed. C. McClelland, S. Merl and H. Siegrist, Berlin, 1995; C. Charle, *Vordenker der Moderne: Die Intellektuellen im 19. Jahrhundert*, Frankfurt am Main, 1996; *The European and American University since 1800*, ed. S. Rothblatt and B. Wittrock, Cambridge, 1993; *Università e professioni giuridiche in Europa nell'età liberale*, ed. A. Mazzacane and C. Vano, Naples, 1994; *Aux sources de la compétence professionelle: Critéres scolaires et classements sociaux dans les carriéres intellectuelles en Europe (15e–19e siècles)*, ed. D. Julia, Gent, 1994 (special edition of the journal *Paedagogica Historica* 30 (1994)); C. Charle, *La république des universitaires 1870–1940*, Paris, 1994.

3 For new anthologies and monographs on multiple professions in one country, see the following: *Professions in the French State 1700–1900*, ed. G.L. Geison, Philadelphia, 1984; *German Professions, 1800–1950*, ed. G. Cocks and K.H. Jarausch, New York, 1990; K.H. Jarausch, *The Unfree Professions: German Lawyers, Teachers and Engineers 1900–1950*, New York, 1990; C.E. McClelland, *The German Experience of Professionalization: Modern Learned Professions and their Organization from the Early Nineteenth Century to the Hitler Era*, Cambridge, 1991; *The Sociology of the Professions: Lawyers, Doctors and others*, ed. R. Dingwall and P. Lewis, London, 1983; H. Perkin, *The Rise of Professional Society: England since 1880*, London, 1989; *Le libere professioni in Italia*, ed. W. Tousijn, Bologna, 1987; *Society and the Professions in Italy 1860–1914*, ed. M. Malatesta, Cambridge, 1995; *Avvocati, medici ingegneri: Alle origini delle professioni moderne (secoli 16.–19.)*, ed. M.L. Betri and A. Pastore, Bologna, 1997.

4. See Siegrist, *Advokat*, pp. 3f., 24–32; *Geschichte und Vergleich: Ansätze und Ergebnisse international vergleichender Geschichtsschreibung*, ed. H.-G. Haupt and J. Kocka, Frankfurt am Main, 1996.

5. For the history of the concept 'occupation' (Beruf) in the German language, see W. Conze, 'Beruf', in *Geschichtliche Grundbegriffe*, ed. O. Brunner, W. Conze and R. Koselleck, vol. I, Stuttgart, 1972, pp. 490–507. For the concept in the Romance languages, see M. Meriggi, 'Arte, mestiere, professione. Problemi di lessico tra età modern

e etá contemporanea', in *Avvocati, medici, ingegneri: Alle origine delle professioni moderne*, ed. M.L. Betri and A. Pastore, Bologna, 1997, pp. 61–80.

6. P. Lungreen, 'Engineering Education in Europe and the USA 1715–1930. The Rise to Dominance of School Culture in the Engineering Profession', *Annals of Science* 47 (1990), pp. 33–75.

7. Siegrist, *Advokat*; W. Wolodkiewicz, 'La professione di avvocato nei territori polacchi tra otto e novecento', in *Università e professioni giuridiche in Europa nell'età liberale*, ed. A. Mazzacane and C. Vano, Naples, 1994, pp. 335–47.

8. The civil servant model spread to architects, engineers and management experts. See *Ingenieure in Deutschland, 1770–1990*, ed. P. Lundgren and A. Grelon, Frankfurt am Main, 1994; E. Bolenz, *Vom Baubeamten zum freiberuflichen Architekten: Technische Berufe im Bauwesen (Preußen/Deutschland 1799–1931)*, Frankfurt am Main, 1991; H. Franz, *Zwischen Markt und Profession: Betriebswirte in Deutschland im Spannungsfeld von Bildungs- und Wirtschaftsbürgertum*, Göttingen, 1998; S. Schweitzer, 'Der Ingenieur', in *Der Mensch im 19. Jahrhundert*, ed. U. Frevert and H.-G. Haupt, Frankfurt am Main, New York, 1999, pp. 67–85.

9. McClelland et al., *Professionen im modernen Osteuropa*.

10. D. Duman, *The English and Colonial Bars in the Nineteenth Century*, London, 1983.

11. See Burrage, 'Unternehmer'; Siegrist, *Advokat*; A.J. Heidenheimer, 'Professional Knowledge and State Policy in Comparative Historical Perspective. Law and Medicine in Britain, Germany, and the United States', *International Social Science Journal* 122 (1989), pp. 529–33; C. Brooks, 'Le déclin et la recréation des organisations professionelles de 'barristers' et de 'solicitors' au 19e et au 20e siècle', in *Les structures du barreau et du notariat en Europe de l'Ancien Régime à nos jous*, ed. J.-L. Halpérin, Lyon, 1996, pp. 99–112; D. Sugarman, 'Bourgeois Collectivism, Professional Power and the Boundaries of the State. The Private and the Public Life of the Law Society, 1825 to 1914', *International Journal of the Legal Profession* 3 (1996), pp. 81–135.

12. O. Janz, 'Protestantische Pfarrer vom 18. bis zum frühen 20. Jahrhundert. Deutschland und England im Vergleich', *Comparativ* 8 (1998), 2, pp. 83–111.

13. M. Späth, 'Der Ingenieur als Bürger, Frankreich, Deutschland und Rußland im Vergleich', in *Bürgerliche Berufe*, ed. H. Siegrist, Göttingen, 1988. pp. 84–105.

14. Charle, *République*.

15. J. Requate, *Journalismus als Beruf: Entstehung und Entwickung des Journalistenberufs im 19. Jahrhundert. Deutschland im internationalen Vergleich*, Göttingen, 1995.

16. I. Costas, 'Das Verhältnis von Professionen, Professionalisierung und Geschlecht in historisch vergleichender Perspektive', in *Professionen und Geschlecht*, ed. A. Wetterer, Frankfurt am Main, 1992, pp. 51–82; C. Huerkamp, 'Frauen im Arztberuf im 19. und 20. Jahrhundert, Deutschland und die USA im Vergleich', in *Was ist Gesellschaftsgeschichte? Festschrift für H.-U. Wehler*, ed. M. Hettling et al., Munich, 1991, pp. 135–45.

17. J.C. Albisetti, 'Deutsche Lehrerinnen im 19. Jahrhundert im internationalen Vergleich', in *Frauen zwischen Familie und Schule: Professionalisierungstrategien bürgerlicher Frauen im internationalen Vergleich*, ed. J. Jacobi, Cologne, 1994, pp. 28–53.

18. On the use of the concept 'profession' and 'professionalization' in history, see among others Siegrist, *Advokat*, pp. 12–18.

19. C. Huerkamp, *Der Aufstieg der Ärzte im 19. Jahrhundert: Vom gelehrten Stand zum professionellen Experten*, Göttingen, 1995; O. Faure, *Histoire sociale de la médecine 18e–20e siècle*, Paris, 1994; P. Frascani, 'Between the State and the Market: Physicians in Liberal Italy', in *Society and the Professions in Italy 1860–1914*, ed. M. Malatesta, Cambridge, 1995, pp. 145–74; J. Léonard, *La vie quotidienne du médecin de province au 19e siècle*, Paris, 1977; J. Léonard, *La médecine entre les savoirs et les pouvoirs: Histoire intellectuelle et politique de la médecine francaise au 19e siècle*, Paris, 1981; J.-P. Goubert, 'Le role social des médecins dans la France du 19ème siècle', in *Eliten in Deutschland und Frankreich im 19. und 20. Jahrhundert*, vol. 2. *Strukturen und Beziehungen*, ed. L. Dupeux, R. Hudemann and F. Knipping, Munich, 1996, pp.137–41; M. Ramsey, 'The Politics of Professional Monopoly in Nineteenth-century Medicine. The French Case and its Rivals', in *Professions and the French State 1700–1900*, ed. G.L. Geison, Philadelphia, 1984, pp. 225–305.

20. E.W. Orth, 'Interesse', in *Geschichtliche Grundbegriffe*, ed. O. Brunner, W. Conze and R. Koselleck, vol. 3, Stuttgart, 1982, pp. 305–65. Unfortunately, the article hardly deals at all with the historical counter-concept of 'disinterest'.

21. See Burrage, 'Unternehmer'.

22. On the distinction, see Siegrist, *Advokat*; P. Lundgreen, 'Akademiker und Professionen in Deutschland', *Historische Zeitschrift* 254 (1992), pp. 657–70.

23. For German, French and Italian physicians respectively, see: Huerkamp, Aufstieg; Goubert, 'Role'; Frascani, 'State and Market'.

24. For central Eastern Europe, see C. McClelland et al., 'Introduction', in *Professionen im modernen Osteuropa*, ed. C. McClelland, S. Merl and H. Siegrist, pp. 11–26, p. 24 (including further references). For Germany, see T. Krach, *Jüdische Rechtsanwälte in Preußen*, Munich, 1991.

25. See, for example, Huerkamp, Aufstieg; J. Goldstein, *Console and Classify: The French Psychiatric Profession in the Nineteenth Century*, Cambridge, 1987; J. Goldstein, 'Foucault among the Sociologists: the "Disciplines" and the History of the Professions', *History and Theory* 23 (1984), pp. 170–92.

26. See F.-J. Brüggemeier, 'Konstruktion und Wirklichkeit. Neuere Arbeit zur Geschichte von Medizin und Gesellschaft', *Archiv für Sozialgeschichte* 34 (1994), pp. 489–94.

27. See Siegrist, *Advokat*, pp. 525f.

28. Cited and depicted in Siegrist, *Advokat*, pp. 212f.

29. L. Thoma, *Erinnerungen*, 3rd edn., Munich, 1980, p. 105.

30. Huerkamp, *Aufstieg*, pp. 28, 154f.

31. Siegrist, *Advokat*, pp. 693–96, 886–88, 912–14.

Bibliography

Albisetti, J.C. 'Deutsche Lehrerinnen im 19. Jahrhundert im internationalen Vergleich', in *Frauen zwischen Familie und Schule: Professionalisierungstrategien bürgerlichen Frauen im internationalen Vergleich*, ed. J. Jacobi. Cologne, 1994, pp. 28–53.

Betri, M.L. and Pastore, A. (eds) *Avvocati, medici ingegneri: Alle origini delle professioni moderne (secoli 16.–19.)*. Bologna, 1997.

Bolenz, E. *Vom Baubeamten zum freiberuflichen Architekten: Technische Berufe im Bauwesen (Preußen/Deutschland 1799–1931)*. Frankfurt am Main, 1991.

Brooks, C. 'Le déclin et la recréation des organisations professionelles de "barristers" et de "solicitors" au 19e et au 20e siècle', in *Les structures du barreau et du notariat en Europe de l'Ancien Régime à nos jous*, ed. J.-L. Halpérn. Lyon, 1996, pp. 99–112.

Brüggemeier, F.J. 'Konstruktion und Wirklichkeit. Neuere Arbeit zur Geschichte von Medizin und Gesellschaft', *Archiv für Sozialgeschichte* 34 (1994), pp. 489–94.

Burrage, M. 'Unternehmer, Beamte und freie Berufe. Schlüsselgruppen der bürgerlichen Mittelschichten in England, Frankreich und den Vereinigten Staaten', in *Bürgerliche Berufe: Zur Sozialgeschichte der freien und akademischen Berufe im internationalen Vergleich*, ed. H. Siegrist. Göttingen, 1988, pp. 52–83.

Burrage, M. and Thorstendahl, J. (eds) *Professions in Theory and History*. London, 1990.

Charle, C. *La république des universitaires 1870–1940*. Paris, 1994.

—— *Vordenker der Moderne: Die Intellektuellen im 19. Jahrhundert*. Frankfurt am Main, 1996.

Cocks, G. and Jarausch, K.H. (eds) *German Professions, 1800–1950*. New York, NY, 1990.

Conze, W. 'Beruf', in *Geschichtliche Grundbegriffe*, ed. O. Brunner, W. Conze and R. Koselleck, vol. I. Stuttgart, 1972, pp. 490–507.

Conze, W. and Kocka, J. (eds) *Bildungsbürgertum im 19. Jahrhundert. Teil I: Bildungssystem und Professionalisierung in internationalen Vergleich*. Stuttgart, 1985.

Costas, I. 'Das Verhältnis von Professionen, Professionalisierung und Geschlecht in historisch vergleichender Perspektive', in *Professionen und Geschlecht*, ed. A. Wetterer. Frankfurt am Main, 1992, pp. 51–82.

Dingwall, R. and Lewis, P. (eds) *The Sociology of the Professions. Lawyers, Doctors and others*. London, 1983.

Duman, D. *The English and Colonial Bars in the Nineteenth Century*. London, 1983.

Faure, O. *Histoire sociale de la médécine 18e–20e siècle*. Paris, 1994.

Franz, H. *Zwischen Markt und Profession: Betriebswirte in Deutschland im Spannungsfeld von Bildungs- und Wirtschaftsbürgertum*. Göttingen, 1998.

Frascani, P. 'Between the State and the Market: Physicians in Liberal Italy', in *Society and the Professions in Italy 1860–1914*, ed. M. Malatesta. Cambridge: Cambridge University Press, 1995, pp.145–74.

Geison, G.L. (ed.) *Professions in the French State 1700–1900*. Philadelphia, PA, 1984.

Goldstein, J. 'Foucault among the Sociologists: the "Disciplines" and the History of the Professions', *History and Theory* 23 (1984), pp. 170–92.

—— *Console and Classify: The French Psychiatric Profession in the Nineteenth Century*. Cambridge: Cambridge University Press, 1987.

Goubert, J.-P. 'Le role social des médecins dans la France du 19ème siècle', in *Eliten in Deutschland und Frankreich im 19. und 20. Jahrhundert, vol. 2. Strukturen und Beziehungen*, ed. L. Dupeux, R. Hudemann and F. Knipping. Munich, 1996, pp.137–141.

Haupt, H.G. and Kocka, J. (eds) *Geschichte und Vergleich: Ansätze und Ergebnisse international vergleichender Geschichtsschreibung*. Frankfurt am Main, 1996.

Heidenheimer, A.J. 'Professional Knowledge and State Policy in Comparative Historical Perspective. Law and Medicine in Britain, Germany, and the United States', *International Social Science Journal* 122 (1989), pp. 529–33.

Huerkamp, C. 'Frauen im Arztberuf im 19. und 20. Jahrhundert, Deutschland und die USA im Vergleich', in *Was ist Gesellschaftsgeschichte? Festschrift für H.-U. Wehler*, ed. M. Hettling et al. Munich, 1991, pp. 135–45.

—— *Der Aufstieg der Ärzte im 19. Jahrhundert. Vom gelehrten Stand zum professionellen Experten.* Göttingen, 1995.

Janz, O. 'Protestantische Pfarrer vom 18. bis zum frühen 20. Jahrhundert. Deutschland und England im Vergleich', *Comparativ* 8 (1998), 2, pp. 83–111.

Jarausch, K.H. *The Unfree Professions. German Lawyers, Teachers and Engineers 1900–1950.* New York, NY, 1990.

Julia, D. (ed.). *Aux sources de la compétence professionelle: Critéres scolaires et classements sociaux dans les carriéres intellectuelles en Europe (15e–19e siècles).* Gent, 1994 (special edition of the journal *Paedagogica Historica* 30 (1994)).

Krach, T. *Jüdische Rechtsanwälte in Preußen.* Munich, 1991.

Léonard, J. *La vie quotidienne du médecin de province au 19e siècle.* Paris, 1977.

—— *La médecine entre les savoirs et les pouvoirs: Histoire intellectuelle et politique de la médecine francaise au 19e siècle.* Paris, 1981.

Lundgreen, P. 'Akademiker und Professionen in Deutschland', *Historische Zeitschrift* 254 (1992), pp. 657–70.

Lundgren, P. and Grelon, A. (eds) *Ingenieure in Deutschland, 1770–1990.* Frankfurt am Main, 1994.

Lungreen, P. 'Engineering Education in Europe and the USA 1715–1930. The Rise to Dominance of School Culture in the Engineering Profession', *Annals of Science* 47 (1990), pp. 33–75.

Malatesta, M. 'Gli ordini professionali e la nazionallizzazione in Italia', *Dalla città alla nazione*, ed. M. Meriggi and P. Schiera. Bologna, 1994, pp. 165–80.

—— (ed.) *Society and the Professions in Italy 1860–1914.* Cambridge: Cambridge University Press, 1995.

Mazzacane, A. and Vano, C. (eds). *Università e professioni giuridiche in Europa nell'età liberale.* Naples, 1994.

McClelland, C.E. *The German Experience of Professionalization: Modern Learned Professions and their Organization from the Early Nineteenth Century to the Hitler Era.* Cambridge: Cambridge University Press, 1991.

McClelland, C.E., Merl, S. and Siegrist, H. (eds) *Professionen im modernen Osteuropa.* Berlin, 1995.

—— 'Introduction', in C.E. McClelland, S. Merl and H. Siegrist (eds) *Professionen im modernen Osteuropa.* Berlin, 1995, pp. 11–26.

Meriggi, M. 'Arte, mestiere, professione. Problemi di lessico tra etá modern e etá contemporanea', in *Avvocati, medici, ingegneri, Alle origine delle professioni moderne*, ed. M.L. Betri and A. Pastore. Bologna, 1997, pp. 61–80.

Orth, E.W. 'Interesse', in *Geschichtliche Grundbegriffe*, ed. O. Brunner, W. Conze and R. Koselleck, vol. 3. Stuttgart, 1982, pp. 305–65.

Perkin, H. *The Rise of Professional Society: England since 1880.* London, 1989.

Ramsey, M. 'The Politics of Professional Monopoly in Nineteenth-century Medicine: The French Case and its Rivals', in *Professions and the French State 1700–1900*, ed. G.L. Geison. Philadelphia, PA, 1984, pp. 225–305.

Requate, J. *Journalismus als Beruf: Entstehung und Entwickung des Journalistenberufs im 19. Jahrhundert. Deutschland im internationalen Vergleich.* Göttingen, 1995.

Rothblatt, S. and Wittrock, B. (eds) *The European and American University since 1800.* Cambridge: Cambridge University Press, 1993.

Schweitzer, S. 'Der Ingenieur', in *Der Mensch im 19. Jahrhundert*, ed. U. Frevert and H.-G. Haupt. Frankfurt am Main, New York, NY, 1999, pp. 67–85.

Siegrist, H. *Advokat, Bürger und Staat: Sozialgeschichte der Rechtsanwälte in Deutschland, Italien und der Schweiz (18.–20. Jh.)*. Frankfurt am Main, 1996.

—— (ed.). *Bürgerliche Berufe: Zur Sozialgeschichte der freien und akademischen Berufe im internationalen Vergleich*. Göttingen, 1988.

Späth, M. 'Der Ingenieur als Bürger: Frankreich, Deutschland und Rußland im Vergleich', in *Bürgerliche Berufe*, ed. H. Siegrist. Göttingen, 1988, pp. 84–105.

Sugarman, D. 'Bourgeois Collectivism, Professional Power and the Boundaries of the State. The Private and the Public Life of the Law Society, 1825 to 1914', *International Journal of the Legal Profession* 3 (1996), pp. 81–135.

Thoma, L. *Erinnerungen*, 3rd edn. Munich, 1980.

Tousijn, W. (ed.). *Le libere professioni in Italia*. Bologna, 1987.

Wolodkiewicz, W. 'La professione di avvocato nei territori polacchi tra otto e novecento', in *Università e professioni giuridiche in Europa nell'età liberale*, ed. A. Mazzacane and C. Vano. Naples, 1994, pp. 335–47.

5

THE PETITE BOURGEOISIE AND COMPARATIVE HISTORY

Geoffrey Crossick

The petite bourgeoisie of shopkeepers and master artisans, a group once neglected by a social history concerned primarily with workers and by an economic history concerned primarily with large-scale enterprise and industrialisation, has at last begun to be recognised as a significant force in modern European society.[1] Recognition came not from political historians, because the political history of the petite bourgeoisie was long confined to tracing the origins of European fascism, as if the deformed instincts of a supposedly declining class might somehow satisfy the hunger for explanation. The growth of interest in the owners of small enterprise has many roots, but all lie in the concern to add nuances to a perspective on modern history too readily painted in stark contrasts. As social historians have begun to reexamine heroic conceptions of class, as economic historians have come to question the large-scale nature of European industrialisation and as political historians have sought to understand the history of petit bourgeois mobilisation, so the world of small enterprise has come to seem a more promising route than it once did for understanding the development of modern European societies. Small enterprise refused to fulfil the predictions of nineteenth-century liberal and Marxist economists alike and remained a persistent part of European economies throughout the century. Research over the last decade or so has generated a more subtle and balanced understanding of the social and political world of those small enterprises and their owners.[2]

This essay has two distinct but closely related purposes. The first is to draw upon that research to offer some reflections on the social development of the petite bourgeoisie in nineteenth- and early twentieth-century Europe. The second aim is, through the study of the petite bourgeoisie, to explore some problems involved in carrying out comparative analysis in social history. The central difficulty concerns the units upon which comparison is based, which are most commonly national, in that the object of analysis is the population of each nation state. Ought we to distinguish, however, those problems explored by the social historian whose analysis is effectively undertaken at the level of the nation state, from others where that basis is inappropriate? Furthermore, what are the difficulties presented by the use of these national-level comparisons? As we pursue the petite bourgeoisie through recent research, we encounter many of the awkward problems which comparative social historians have to confront.[3]

The character of sources confronts the social historian of the petite bourgeoisie at the outset, for characterisations of a social group frequently emerge within a framework constructed by the character of sources. The *patente* business licence and records of property left at death, prominent sources for the historian of the petite bourgeoisie where available, provide opportunities for basic research on business and wealth composition in France and Belgium that are quite absent in Britain. With respect to workplace relations, historians have too readily accepted as reality the myths of workplace harmony transmitted by those who idealised small enterprise as an alternative basis for social relations, for in small firms strikes were less common than less well-recorded forms of resistance. The archives of the *Conseil de Prud'hommes*, established in France to resolve disputes between masters and employees, enabled Haupt to uncover the character of workplace relations within Lyon's small enterprises in a way impossible where such courts did not exist.[4] Ideological and political imperatives produced some of the most striking sources for the history of small enterprise, such as the 1847/48 statistical survey of Paris industry, constructed to demonstrate the strength of small enterprise,[5] or the vast documentation produced by the Belgian *Commission nationale de la petite bourgeoisie* from 1903, brought into existence by the imperatives of political conjuncture, but which gave the (almost certainly false) impression of a petite bourgeoisie in Belgium far greater in both size and problems than that in Britain.[6] Inquiries are ideological and political projects. So too are censuses of population, an irreplaceable source yet one whose serried ranks of rows and columns evoke a scientific accuracy belied by the ideological specificities of census classification.[7] The enumeration of small enterprises and their owners was dependent on the extent to which census makers were interested in separating out such groups, and this varied so much between countries, and across time within a single country, as to render comparative analysis as well as time series of doubtful value. The census might be a fine source for exploring contemporary conceptions of the social fabric, but it is a fragile basis for comparative analyses of social structure.

The comparative social historian also needs to consider the terminologies which emerged to describe the owners of small enterprise, while refusing to see those terminologies as simply descriptive. In defining the groups concerned and inserting them within a particular conception of the social structure, the language employed constituted an act of intervention.[8] We find not only the absence of readily accepted terms in Britain, but also the differentiated terminology amongst those societies where one emerged. The term *classes moyennes* used in France and Belgium evoked the older language of bourgeois assertiveness against the nobility rather than any estate or corporate ideas, narrowing by the later nineteenth century to include only the lower sections of the bourgeois class. The parallel term in Germany was *Mittelstand*, which similarly narrowed after the mid-nineteenth century, but it was rooted in a corporatist conception of society, identifying less a specific occupational status than a position within an organically conceived social order. The common conception of the middle is vital to contemporary designations of the group,[9] but so too is the difference between *classe* in the French and Belgium term and *Stand* (estate) in the German. The problems of language, together with the belief that we can establish terms with equivalent meanings in different societies, is one of the great problems of comparative social history, exacerbated by the way that terminology was itself a matter of contest within each society.

Problems such as these make comparisons of a social group between different countries more awkward than a comparison of occupational groups such as tailors or lawyers, or of actions such as strikes or demonstrations. If the goals of comparative social history are essentially heuristic, pursued not only to demonstrate the differences between societies but also to generate structures of explanation, then the issue of units of comparison assumes primary importance. European comparative history tends to compare nation states, assuming that within their boundaries lie national societies. The unit of the comparison is thus taken for granted. Yet cohesive national phenomena can be identified more easily in some dimensions of the past than in others: the state inevitably, and by extension conflicts over the state which we call politics, as well as juridical structures such as corporations, and issues of history and language which are fundamental to the identity of national entities. However, national-level analyses become more problematic when we turn to economic and social structures. The nation state itself creates the seductive image of a national social structure – by censuses of population, by stimulating national occupational associations, and so on. When we turn to the structural level, however, the idea of a national society is more problematic, for it remains to be demonstrated that those acting and living within the territorial boundaries of a particular nation state during the nineteenth century experienced or were shaped by that national social structure and that national society. The existence of national societies and national economies are too often taken for granted by comparative historical analyses, which assume that data produced on the national level represent some underlying national phenomenon – for example that census data depict a national society or national accounts data a national economy.

These reflections, derived from research into the petite bourgeoisie in modern Europe, force us to consider other units of comparison appropriate to the study of that group. One thinks of patterns of economic development, often more readily comprehended at the regional level, and their effects on the composition and experiences of the petite bourgeoisie. They would include different regional agrarian structures, which influence both migration to urban small enterprise and cultures of small proprietorship. A further unit must be occupations, for similar characteristics linked occupations across different countries, differentiating them from other elements in their own society (one thinks, for example, of butchers, shoemakers, jewellers or general shopkeepers). Then there are types of town – distinguished less by country than by function – metropolitan centres, factory towns, mining towns, market towns and small rural *bourgs*. In many artisanal trades producing consumer goods, for example, the craft community disintegrated at about the same time – the 1830s/1840s – in London, Paris and Berlin, spreading only later through their respective national urban hierarchies. The work experiences of tailors in Paris and London were thus more like each other than they were like those of fellow tailors in smaller towns in their own country. Size of town might also prove a good basis for comparative analysis, for although the expansion of small enterprise rested on the growth of large towns, it was in small and medium-sized towns that petits bourgeois felt most at home. The absence of wealthy local elites, protection through localism of markets, more stable daily relations and more limited competition for municipal control combined to make the smaller town a more stable setting for petit bourgeois life.[10]

Units such as these often seem more relevant to a comparative analysis of the petite bourgeoisie than do national societies. There were of course national forces, which shaped a perceived national social formation, such as political organisations, legal structures, electoral systems, the relationship between state and associations. If they provide the basis for national comparisons, by their very operations they construct those national social structures which should not be taken for granted. In so far as national social structures are given form by organisations, movements and language, then forces such as law, taxation and party politics help create the sense of a national social structure and of social groups and relationships that exist at the national level, but one which social historians should approach with critical caution. Research has deepened our understanding of the petite bourgeoisie within European society, but on a great many themes national comparisons fail to yield a great deal. The experience of the petite bourgeoisie displays common features across countries, and these themes are the stuff of social historical research. This essay is not the place to offer a rounded history of the nineteenth-century petite bourgeoisie and it will not be burdened with extensive footnotes to the research and the literature on which the discussion draws. These reflections arise out of my recent experience of jointly writing a history of the petite bourgeoisie, and the essay rests upon the evidence and references which may be followed up in that book.[11] The paper will concentrate on some of the most important of these social themes.

Independence, crisis and the economic position of the petite bourgeoisie

Although independence was fundamental to the self-identity and social values of the owners of small enterprise, challenges that arose from credit, contract and crisis made independence ever more ambiguous. Independent artisanal producers were increasingly tied to merchant capitalists, who supplied raw materials on credit, advances to pay weekly costs including wages, and outlets for the goods produced. This dependency was established in tailoring, shoemaking, furniture and similar consumer goods industries in Europe's large urban centres by the 1830s and 1840s, and then in small metal and hardware trades by the 1860s in much of industrial Europe. The size of town and its integration into transport and marketing systems influenced the extent of small producer dependence on merchant capital, but by the 1860s and 1870s throughout urban Europe we find subcontract tying small producers to large industrial manufacturers and merchants. Retailers relied increasingly on wholesalers' credit, not just for regular stock but often in the initial setting up of their shops. These shopkeepers were themselves bound up in credit ties with their customers, whether middle class or working class. The customer loyalty or dependency which accompanied credit secured trade for the retailer, but many a shopkeeper struggled between the conflicting pressures of credit advanced by them and to them, in a balancing act which often ended in failure.

The changing physiognomy of independence and dependence thus provides an effective approach to the economic experience of small enterprise during the nineteenth and early twentieth centuries. So too does economic crisis, which was equally ambiguous. Industrial and retail small enterprise rapidly felt the reduction in business at times of general crisis in the economy, locked as they were into debt networks which served to exacerbate instability. Here was one reason for the high mortality among small enterprise. At times of crisis, existing small businesses on the one hand were faced with large entrepreneurs increasing productivity and lowering costs to meet the more competitive environment, while on the other hand small-scale competitors proliferated with the flight of unemployed workers into marginal independent activity as a means of survival.

Social mobility

Research from across Europe reveals the social instability that characterised the world of small enterprise. As Heinz-Gerhard Haupt and I have written, 'in comparison with other classes, a greater proportion of the petite bourgeoisie had been born into a different class; a greater proportion spent only a period of their lives as independent craftsmen or shopkeepers; and a greater proportion saw their children enter other classes. The world of small enterprise was thus a world in movement.'[12] The careers of most of those who owned a small enterprise at any one time were marked by instability through the life-cycle, difficulty in establishing a dynastic enterprise to pass on to children and frequent movement between wage labour and small enterprise. Consider, for example, the destinations of children. The petite bourgeoisie was far less able than either the substantial bourgeoisie or the working class to assure class continuity for all their children. The petite bourgeoisie was not uniform in this respect, for craft training could facilitate artisanal continuities where the trade itself was not in decline, especially when reinforced by legal or corporate controls on entry; while amongst shopkeepers financial resources were generally more important than skill in determining children's access to petit bourgeois occupations. Even for such families, however, the late nineteenth-century crisis sharpened doubts about placing children in small enterprise, doubts about the advisability of passing on the enterprise and problems in achieving that transmission even when desired. Now it was that petit bourgeois parents throughout Europe adopted what might be called a 'strategy of reconversion.'[13] Education appeared an increasingly appropriate way to invest very limited financial resources in assuring a place for their sons (and to a lesser degree their daughters) in the expanding world of white-collar and minor professional employment.

The various dimensions of instability make small enterprise an excellent testing ground for the very conception of social mobility as classically used: working with changes in occupational titles, assuming that these titles represent social as well as occupational position, assuming that occupational designation refers to something relatively homogeneous, and ranking occupations in a linear hierarchy, in which movement up and down represents social mobility. The complexity of occupational labels and their social meaning become clear when we explore the petite bourgeoisie, not least because pluriactivity characterised this class more than any other. It characterised many rural petits bourgeois, whose income over the course of a year might be constructed from a craft, say that of a shoemaker or wheelwright; a small peasant holding; a cart to do some carrying and carting work; and maybe a local office as rate collector or overseer. What occupational title would be attached to such a person in the censuses or marriage registers which provide the historian with raw data for mobility studies? Pluriactivity was often recreated in towns and not only for the owners of more marginal enterprises. In any case, the assumption that individual mobility was the key needs to be questioned, for the overall occupational and work experience of a family was more important amongst the petite bourgeoisie in defining social experience and sense of position. There is a further problem, and that is the assumption that moving from wage employment to independent enterprise represented a change of social position and with it a change of social milieu. Independence often did carry such resonances, in aspiration more often than in achievement, but it did not necessarily do so. The power of popular neighbourhood sociability, craft culture, personal values and multiple family occupations all shaped the way such change was experienced.

Small enterprise was frequently a short-lived affair for many who opened a small shop or workshop, part of a fluctuating life-cycle movement between wage-employment and a tenuous independence. Instability on this scale raises fundamental questions about how social identity might develop in a group of such fluctuating membership. One response must be to differentiate between the highly unstable sections of small enterprise, with its own personal and family identities, and the more established and long-lived layer of small enterprises which gave the petite bourgeoisie its public identity, above all through its participation in petit bourgeois organisations and politics.

The family and petit bourgeois social experience

The family was central to the European petite bourgeoisie, because of the wide range of functions it embraced. The intensity of family life is evident from autobiographical literature, but small enterprise itself was deeply bound up with the family in so many ways that it becomes a further key notion, alongside those of independence and mobility, through which to understand the distinctiveness of the petite bourgeoisie. Family labour was essential to most small enterprise, especially in retailing, where the wife and husband would take an equally active part in running the business, in addition to the many shops which were the wife's responsibility while the man worked outside the home. The ideology of domesticity might have pushed the wife into the background – keeping the books or organising orders, in households seeking to emulate more substantial bourgeois lifestyles – but such cases were not the norm. Few small enterprises could survive without family labour, not least because wife and children could be paid much less than hired employees, often nothing in formal terms. A particular relationship between family and artisanal enterprise consequently developed as the latter came under intense competitive pressures. Whether Lyonnais silk weavers from the 1840s or German master artisans during the Great Depression, the need to cut costs in a competitive environment frequently saw artisanal households turning in on themselves as their industry entered structural crisis. Journeymen were shed and the enterprise survived on family labour alone.[14]

This was only an extreme expression of the close overlapping of family and enterprise in the petit bourgeois world. Family space and business space overlapped, and even accounts were often muddled together, as the owners of small enterprise failed to distinguish household expenditure from business expenditure in the way expected by accountants and the bankruptcy courts. Accountants reporting on a drapery and millinery business in East London in 1888 were confused: 'We are informed that the amount entered as Takings is the money left in the till at the end of each day after various payments for housekeeping and other payments have been made.'[15] This rested on a genuine mixing of household and business in the minds of owners of small enterprise, reflecting a lived reality which would have escaped more conventional accounting techniques.

Beyond this material world of family and business lay the importance of the petit bourgeois family within the idealising discourse that surrounded the world of small enterprise by the later nineteenth century. In that discourse – primarily but not exclusively conservative in political and social terms – the social relationships of small enterprise were contrasted with those of class society. Harmony was set against conflict, hierarchy and order against atomisation and individualism. The small enterprise household was in this vision an integrated unit, with apprentices and employees living with the master's family, a work unit that kept this residential and familial grouping together under the watchful eye of the paterfamilias, and which mixed work, education and leisure as the wholesome alternative to large-scale employment and urban anonymity. The harmony was often illusory, and living-in was declining throughout Europe by the later nineteenth century, but the image persisted and was reflected in the new weight attached to small enterprise in conservative and Catholic thought from the 1890s.[16]

Petits bourgeois and the working-class neighbourhood

The urban neighbourhood was throughout Europe the unit linking together workers and that majority of petit bourgeois shopkeepers and workshop masters whose work went on largely in working-class districts. The consequence was a social milieu that long remained popular rather than proletarian. The relationship was not a simple one. Shopkeepers offered credit at times of family or community hardship, including strikes, but the ability to offer credit also gave them power. The shop provided a meeting place, especially for women, and the conversation there ('gossip') helped shopkeepers to distinguish customers who would ultimately repay their debts from those who might not. Shopkeeper credit – its granting and its withholding – thus helped to reinforce behavioural norms, such as those tight notions of respectability observed amongst the poor in late nineteenth-century London.

Local petits bourgeois were often the leaders in such neighbourhoods. They would take the lead in local social and political associations, head ritual occasions such as funerals or fêtes, and act as witnesses at neighbourhood weddings. The owners of small enterprise provided the framework of the neighbourhood's sociability: its pubs, cafés and bars, of course, but also the bakers' and grocers' shops, the shoemakers' and tailors' workshops or the warm smithy where people met and talked. The working-class neighbourhood of the nineteenth-century European city can be understood only after we have reinserted the local petits bourgeois who were fundamental to its identity and, having reinserted them, we will need to reinterpret the meaning of those neighbourhoods. In communities with high rates of working-class residential instability it was petits bourgeois with the more stable enterprises who provided continuity, structure and memory.[17] They framed the neighbourhood and they framed the neighbourhood's sense of itself.

Reestablishing the centrality of petits bourgeois to the working-class neighbourhood makes sense of popular political tradition as well. It helps explain the way radical politics remained for so long popular, democratic and egalitarian more than it was proletarian or socialist, and these older political traditions, bound up with the radicalism of the *menu peuple*, shaped the character of socialism itself in many countries. The ideology that thrived amongst the *menu peuple* between the 1780s and 1848 – an ideology of modest means, hard work, independence and a denunciation of oppression and privilege – shaped radical movements in Europe for much of the century. Although in the later decades of the century the petite bourgeoisie divided more clearly in its political orientation, with a shift of organised small business to the right and with it a detachment from the popular community, the continuing role of some petits bourgeois in popular politics and the persistence of older radical critiques even in those movements orientated to the right, suggests that popular and populist traditions remained of continuing relevance.

Petit bourgeois culture

There are, of course, variations in this generalised picture of the European petite bourgeoisie as it has emerged from research in recent years, for there was uniformity neither across Europe nor within individual countries, but these themes rarely permit helpful national comparisons. There are many such social and economic themes, but I shall focus finally on petit bourgeois culture, which has two principal dimensions. The first saw the emergence from the mid-nineteenth century of a distinct petit bourgeois pattern of sociability and associational life in much of Europe. The gymnastic and shooting clubs, choral societies and bands, debating and reading clubs, or simple local cercles meeting weekly in a room above the café, signal both the detachment of a section of the petite bourgeoisie from popular social milieux and the growth of internal sociability among these middling groups.

A further dimension to petit bourgeois culture was constructed around the organising experiences of petit bourgeois life: family, home and privacy, localism and property. The ambiguities of petit bourgeois culture are rooted in the ambiguities of petit bourgeois life, not least because the owners of most small enterprises found themselves pulled between the merchants and wholesalers, on whom they so depended, and their intimate daily relations with a small workforce and working-class customers. The outcome was a persistent way of life shaped by the need for correct public behaviour in order to retain credit, contracts and often customers. The outcome was a culture bound up with family, locality and property.

Here was the most localised of social groups, and the one whose links to property were the most ambiguous. Petit bourgeois conceptions of property shifted during the middle decades of the nineteenth century, becoming more precisely individualistic. With the abolition or decline of guilds and the changing nature of competition, corporatist conceptions of property, in which property was individually owned but defined by collective and social obligations, were progressively shed. The contrast between eighteenth-century Britain and France is too easily overstated in this connection for, whatever the juridical differences, British artisanal trades retained expectations traditionally associated with guild protections. Throughout industrial Europe, the conception of small property lost its collective meaning and came instead to constitute a source of individual identity, to confer upon its owners the status of property owner. This change, perhaps more than any other, marked the emergence of a petit bourgeois identity through the middle decades of the century and was reflected in investment patterns that were themselves local and immediate. The purchase of housing property for rental was the most common, as urban petits bourgeois found in bricks (or stone) and mortar the security they required of property, and in its proximity the localism which they also sought. For those who could expand their investments the same preference for security and localism prevailed, mistrustful of the chimeric visions offered by stock markets or foreign loans and clinging instead to municipal bonds and local utility company shares long after more substantial bourgeois had diversified.[18]

Ideals of independence were closely related to these conceptions of property. The petit bourgeois world was one of immediate and local personal relations, and the accompanying culture was rooted in personal independence. Independence shifted its meaning, however, from the optimistic (often utopian) assertive radical visions of the sans-culottes, Painite radicals or the followers of Proudhon, to an ideal of independence in the later nineteenth century which had become conservative and defensive, an inward-looking and at times strident vision defined against the populace and, to a degree that varied between countries, against large capital. As with many dimensions of petit bourgeois social and political culture, however, there was continuity notwithstanding this change. As Blackbourn has argued for the German petite bourgeoisie, in terms which apply more broadly, it characteristically judged the state, economic relations and public life by that vision of personal and family relations which shaped their own experience.[19] Petit bourgeois politics in many countries can be understood through this cultural perspective.

A complex physiognomy of a social group has emerged which is coloured by the national and often local focus of most research, but which does not sit easily within national boundaries. As important as any national variations were differences that cut horizontally across a Europe divided vertically by national boundaries: differences between types of town, types of regional economy, types of enterprise, levels of wealth and so on. National comparisons are above all valuable when we direct our attention towards petit bourgeois identity, consciousness and the variations in petit bourgeois public behaviour and action. There were marked national variations with respect to political mobilisation, formation of associations, political demands, and the way a petit bourgeois identity found expression in such activities and was in turn shaped by them. If national contrasts are much clearer here than in other aspects of the social history of the petite bourgeoisie, there are important implications for comparative history.

The years between 1880 and 1914 were those in which most European countries witnessed a petit bourgeois awakening in response to new economic, social and political pressures. There was a new degree of scale and capitalisation in retailing and industrial production; the emergence of organised working-class and socialist movements; the fragmentation of the popular milieux of nineteenth-century larger towns and the consolidation of more self-consciously working-class culture and sociability; and petit bourgeois difficulties in securing family status, for continuity of small enterprise was becoming even more difficult at the same time that finding suitable government and other white-collar employment for their children was under threat from both the proliferation of very marginal clerical work and from increased competition for posts, as a result of the spread of working-class state education. There was a growing overall sense for petits bourgeois that society was dividing in ways uncongenial to the middling sort. Labour and capital now provided the framework of social perception.

The form of petit bourgeois responses to these pressures varied between countries, and it is here that national comparisons come into their own. The conclusions from such an analysis partly follow the choice of countries which are to be compared, and the implications of this for comparative social history are instructive. A comparison of Germany and France would highlight the influence of the state on the organisation of the petite bourgeoisie in the former, helping explain the much higher levels of mobilisation, demands for state support and corporate consciousness of German petits bourgeois in comparison with France. It would also stress the survival of corporate expectations in Germany, due in part to the late abolition of guilds, with the result that in Germany (and also in Austria) master artisans were central to the petit bourgeois movement as it entered the twentieth century. In all other industrial countries shopkeepers were dominant. If the comparison were between France and Belgium, the historian would be struck by the fact that Belgium had an even higher level of petit bourgeois mobilisation than France, but that governmental responses were more cosmetic, whereas in France some real legislative concessions were made to petit bourgeois demands. This difference is partly explained by the sustained attempts to bind Belgian petits bourgeois into Catholic social and political institutions, in order to build a fortress against socialism, whereas the more fragmented party structure in France made legislative concessions a more necessary strategy for those seeking petit bourgeois votes. If we make the comparison between Britain and France, then the French petite bourgeoisie, so much less statist and corporatist in comparison with

Germany, appears in the British comparison to be distant from the liberal and market orientation of British petit bourgeois associations and to display a level of organisation, protest and state-directed demands much greater than that in Britain. It is, of course, in the nature of comparative perspectives that the view will change with the position of the observer and with the relationship between the objects being observed, but these comparative tableaux compel reflection about the need to unravel the issues in bilateral as opposed to multilateral comparisons, as well as about the variables involved in such comparative analysis.

I confronted these problems some years ago when considering the relationship between British shopkeepers and the state in the period between 1870 and 1914.[20] It became clear that if British shopkeepers were less vocal, less organised, less politically assertive and less demanding of the state than were those in France, Belgium or Germany, this was not because their problems were less serious. Yet when the social investigator Charles Booth sent a questionnaire to London shopkeepers inquiring about wages, he received a revealing reply still to be found in the sheaves of notes in the Booth archive. A linen draper from North London had scrawled across the form in thick blue crayon the words: 'Sorry, I cannot assist you. My business is carried on by self, wife and children. All we ask is legislative non-interference.'[21] The ideas expressed by organised British shopkeepers articulated the belief that small enterprise had no special role to play in society beyond that of business; that its survival had to depend upon commercial considerations; that the state had no role to play by supporting small enterprise or by restricting its large-scale competitors; and, above all, that small enterprises were part of the world of business and that their owners could neither claim nor express any special identity of their own. This was the voice of the more established organised shopkeepers, but so were the voices in other European countries which proclaimed different solutions. If the problems faced were neither different nor smaller than those of shopkeepers elsewhere in Europe, the explanations for the weakness of their demands and sense of identity had to be found in phenomena largely outside themselves. I was drawn towards those forces elsewhere in Europe which encouraged a sense of petit bourgeois social identity and which encouraged the possibility of state action to resolve petit bourgeois problems. The themes that emerged were various.

One was the success of British elites in integrating the petite bourgeoisie into the political and ideological framework of liberalism, helped by the fact that that ideology was the outgrowth of a movement and a body of ideas that the petite bourgeoisie had itself been involved in constructing. This required looking at the radical roots of liberal ideology, which helped explain the two traditions that made it unlikely that shopkeepers would see the state as a potentially beneficent force. Firstly, shopkeeper radicalism of the late eighteenth and early nineteenth centuries saw the state only in negative terms, as an oppressive force identified with aristocratic oligarchy. Secondly, there was economic liberalism with its vision of a noninterventionist state. Turning to the state, in other words, meant turning to a particular image of the state, and one constructed differently in different countries. The analysis also stressed the ways in which institutional, legal and fiscal structures derived from the state could direct the manner in which shopkeepers' problems were experienced, and the kind of solutions that seemed available. These combined in Britain to inhibit the growth of a distinct petit bourgeois sense of identity and to make it less likely that the state would appear as a potential solution to petit bourgeois problems. Finally, my explanation led me on to the evolving political structure in Britain, which seemed to deny the space into which organisations of small shopkeepers might insert themselves and into which they might be drawn. In other parts of Europe, shopkeepers came to matter to politicians, and politicians came to matter to shopkeepers. Not so in Britain.

In seeking to explain these different levels of petit bourgeois mobilisation, the differing ideologies, the varying willingness to look to the state for support, together with the range of government responses, we encounter those spheres where national-level comparisons do indeed seem the most effective. These spheres include the character of states and the traditional expectations of state action; the role of state activities such as law and taxation in shaping social groups and their behaviour; the character of party politics; and the political conjunctures that affect the way in which social groups and interests were able to mobilise or to be mobilised. These themes need elucidating in order to balance the stress in the earlier part of this essay on those aspects of the petite bourgeoisie where national distinctions were less relevant.

The first is *the structure of official and quasi-official institutions relating to small enterprise.* Institutions linking local business communities to the state could play a central role in developing petit bourgeois identities and in directing demands towards the state. Examples include the *tribunaux de commerce* (commercial courts) in France, where smaller business struggled to achieve representation and votes, and the demands of German small enterprise for a place in chambers of commerce. In Bremen and Hamburg they campaigned for the establishment of small retail chambers of their own.[22] The contests for access to these institutions sharpened an identity in both countries, for that identity flowed not from structural position alone, but from organising and campaigning, and from a willingness to make demands of state institutions. There were no parallels in Britain, where the absence of such state-related institutions limited petit bourgeois demands and denied them that campaigning stimulus towards petit bourgeois identity. The distinct character of these institutions also influenced the way petit bourgeois identity developed. In Germany the *Innungen*, which maintained a continuity of craft organisation after the abolition of traditional guild rights, became the focus for artisanal identities and demands, so that their rights and responsibilities were strengthened from the 1880s as the state responded to artisanal protest. In contrast stood the position of French artisans, whose place within the generalised *Chambres syndicales* was not specifically as artisans but as producers within a broader industry. The structure in France allocated artisanal enterprise no distinct organisational or legal status.

A closely related theme is the existence of informal institutions and assumptions which evoked past ideals: above all the status of *corporatist ideology*, increasingly deformed by the late nineteenth century yet retaining strong resonances even in France and Belgium. The faith in corporatist solutions to the problems of small enterprise spread widely from the 1880s, encouraged by the Austrian guild reforms of 1883 and the increasing significance attached to *Innungen* in Germany. These may have organised only a minority of master artisans but, linked to the relatively recent abolition of compulsory guilds in much of Germany, they sustained corporate expectations. Corporate controls as such had been long abolished in France, where artisan and shopkeeper commitment to republican ideals allowed no place for corporatist solutions. A corporatist spirit could nonetheless suffuse late nineteenth-century demands. The ribbon weavers' strike of 1900 in St Etienne, where the *chefs d'atelier* used corporate Catholic ideas to defend the idiosyncratic patriarchal workshop against threats from both journeymen and merchants, provides a precise example.[23] A more general articulation of this corporate spirit without corporations can be found amongst French shopkeepers. The social conceptions of the *Ligue syndicale*, which organised Parisian shopkeepers from 1888, stressed specialisation, the right of each to live by his trade, the right to control entry to the trade and the economic self-sufficiency of the *quartier*. Here was a set of ideals that was set, as elsewhere in continental Europe, against the dual challenge of the organised economy and the modern bureaucratic state, and the response was constructed with the bricks of corporatist ideas. The fate of corporate structures must not obscure the continuities of corporate assumptions.

We must also consider the impact of different fiscal structures, for systems of taxation helped shape ideology as well as demands. The principal tax which concerned petits bourgeois in Britain was the local rates levied on property. In the political mobilisation of small enterprise in Britain, an identity as ratepayers was more powerful than an identity as small business. In this context, small enterprise was unlikely to conceive of a role for taxation in discouraging the growth of forces hostile to petit bourgeois survival. Fiscal demands were fundamental, on the other hand, to the petit bourgeois movement that grew in Belgium and France in the 1890s, as they demanded that the *patente* (business licence tax) be adapted to reflect the scale of business, and then, by extension, that it be used to inhibit the growth of large enterprise in retail and artisanal trades. The *patente* in France also embedded even more deeply the notion of specialism. The *Ligue syndicale* argued that each person should have one specialist trade, and only one. That guarantee of decent rewards for honest endeavour seemed to be denied by the department stores, the force which symbolised all they hated about organised large capital. The *patente* categorised businesses by trade specialism and thus maintained in mutant form the corporate sense of the 'the trade', while reinforcing the belief that the state should help the petite bourgeoisie.[24] Consideration of the political consequences of different fiscal regimes must also take account of Europe's surviving *octroi* systems, by which goods passing through city walls were subject to special taxation. The consequence was not only to distort population distribution, as the poor gathered just beyond the old city limits to minimise their costs, but often to distort the political formation of traders. In late nineteenth-century Milan the *dazio consumo* excise tax provoked continuing protests whenever attempts were made to reform it, ensuring that until the tax districts were united in 1898 Milan's shopkeepers were divided by their location within or without the walls, more than by any other criterion. Only then could the city's retailers find common ground for action.[25]

Electoral structures and political conjunctures, and the differential role that these gave to middling groups, provide a further theme of national comparison. The 1893 suffrage reform in Belgium introduced universal manhood suffrage, but with a weighted franchise which enhanced the importance of small-propertied groups. The result was the emergence of an autonomous petit bourgeois movement that sought to create its own political party, denouncing the policies, above all in relation to cooperative traders, of both the Catholics in power and the socialist Belgian Workers' Party. The autonomous movement had only limited success, but together with the new electoral system it obliged the Catholic Party to pursue the petit bourgeois vote with new vigour. Petit bourgeois consciousness and mobilisation, as in Belgium, is partly the product of the importance of the owners of small enterprise to political parties and to governments. The conjuncture could be quite precise, as when Republicans and Nationalists fought to attract the votes of Parisian small shopkeepers at the municipal elections of 1900 and the national elections two years later. The political conjunctures that produced efforts to mobilise the owners of small enterprise are essential to an understanding of petit bourgeois consciousness. While petit bourgeois socialism and genuine progressive radicalism persisted through the period, the key focus must be on the way political parties of the centre and right sought to mobilise the owners of small enterprise: Germany in the face of socialism; France with a shifting and fragmented party structure and the effort of the *Parti radical* to maintain a constituency in the early years of this century; Belgium with a mass franchise, increasing social anxiety and a growing socialist presence. Political parties and movements in all these countries courted shopkeepers and master artisans, and proposed legislation that purported to support them. The contrast with Britain is striking, where neither party needed to mobilise the petite bourgeoisie against the other and where liberalism prevailed in both to an extent quite absent from the dominant political formations elsewhere in Europe.

These political, ideological and state structures which were fundamental to petit bourgeois development in different countries are, unlike the earlier themes in this chapter, directly susceptible to comparative analysis at the national level. These structures do not simply provide or deny the space in which petit bourgeois action can emerge but, in view of the contradictory and ambiguous position of the petite bourgeoisie as a social class, are equally important in creating and constituting a petit bourgeois identity by providing such space. In this way one can bridge the false alternatives between, on the one hand, seeing petit bourgeois movements as stirred into existence by an outside hand wielding a spoon called *Mittelstandspolitik* or nationalism or whatever, and, on the other, seeing petit bourgeois organisation as a response to predominantly autonomous forces at work within the petite bourgeoisie itself. The dichotomy between internal and external processes is a false one, for it was precisely the political space provided by state activities and by specific political conjunctures which established the context within which these petit bourgeois organisations and demands could take shape.

The relationship between structural changes affecting the petite bourgeoisie and its shifting politics cannot, of course, be denied. The experience of small shopkeepers and master artisans in much of Europe between 1840 and 1860 reveals groups which had once been bound up with a world of radical and progressive politics detaching themselves from that popular milieu, and coming to constitute more clearly the lower section of the bourgeoisie. This was no more than a trend, but a significant one, bound up with the radical politics of the 1840s and the explosive events of 1848 itself, as well as with the shifting economic imperatives that affected small enterprise. There are clear contrasts even here. The Parisian shopkeepers in the National Guard refused to put down popular protest in February 1848, whereas their London counterparts were soon to enrol as special constables against the Chartists. Such symbolic moments provide elegant examples for the historian, but can be exaggerated. By June much had changed in Paris, and it is tempting to see 1848 as the moment when a large section of the European petite bourgeoisie shifted from the democratic tradition and began to be preoccupied with the defence of property and fear of the working class. The temptation should be resisted, in light of the continuing involvement of many French petits bourgeois in republican and democratic movements through 1848/49, above all in the provinces, and in resistance to the reaction that followed. Indeed, the repressive 1850s in much of Europe reconstructed in a more fragile fashion the popular political identity that had brought workers and petits bourgeois together. The detachment was firmest in Britain, where the threat of 1848 was immediately contained and where the 1850s were characterised by liberalism rather than repression.

However, alongside the shifting character of popular politics, and obviously not unconnected with it, a process of structural change evolved, above all in small artisanal production, by which masters and journeymen were torn more decisively apart and by which masters (as well as shopkeepers) needed to present themselves more convincingly as respectable small businessmen if they were to obtain the credit and contracts upon which survival – let alone success – so often depended. A study of bankruptcy in the western French town of Niort has revealed that a family's standing in the town was far more important than the size of debts in determining which enterprises were made bankrupt.[26] In the early 1830s, a small screw manufacturer in Birmingham described the importance of his workshop being in order, and himself in control of it, when the merchant who provided both contracts and credit made his unannounced visits.[27] Here are two glimpses of the way petit bourgeois behaviour could be constructed in a changing structural context. There were other structural forces at work. Late nineteenth-century petit bourgeois political mobilisation occurred in more highly capitalised industrial economies, in which the distribution sector was now penetrated by large capital and large organisation. The petite bourgeoisie's social position was itself changing, with working-class movements assuming labour and socialist identities and with expanding workers' cooperatives threatening to undermine the remaining involvement of petits bourgeois with the popular world. In other words, if we are to identify changing political conjunctures as fundamental to petit bourgeois mobilisation, and if we are to stress the significance of political opportunity created outside the world of small enterprise itself, then we must also acknowledge the parallel importance of change within the petite bourgeoisie and changes in its own economic and social experiences.

It was not just formal party politics and the state that were crucial at the comparative level in shaping petit bourgeois social and political identity – so too were the ideological developments through which sections of social and intellectual elites turned towards the petite bourgeoisie. Here are the ideological uses of the petite bourgeoisie by movements seeking to defend and recreate a viable middle to society: social Catholicism, groups like the Le Playists and those around *la Réforme sociale*.[28] From the closing decades of the nineteenth century we find in Germany, France and Belgium an idealisation of small enterprise as the basis of family, independence, stability and continuity. The connections between the petite bourgeoisie and a stable social order were more metaphorical than real, and the idealisation of workplace relations, family traditions and permanence have too often been taken as descriptions of petit bourgeois social relations. The idealisation of the petite bourgeoisie as the embodiment of a fluid society was even less realistic. The distance from reality – even when protested by those petits bourgeois angry at being preached at rather than helped – was of no great importance. The politics of order and stability round the turn of the century was in much of Europe accompanied by the ideologies of class denial, and the world of small enterprise was given a pivotal role in those ideas. These were not alien to the petite bourgeoisie, whose own modes of thought inclined towards the denial of conflictual models of society and towards the elevation of 'the people' with small independent property at its heart. In the later nineteenth century, however, these habits were pressed by new social ideologies into a more conservative mould. There was social Catholicism in Belgium, the increasingly conservative syntheses of republicanism in France, as well as the influence of social Catholics and the followers of Le Play, and the way the *Mittelstand* in Germany was idealised as a buffer that would prevent the class polarisation of society,

a unified *Stand* whose existence denied other divisions. These Aristotelian visions identified the social world of small enterprise as the *juste
milieu*, 'a middling estate, a group of classes which form a buffer
between the rich and the poor.'[29] By bridging the extremes, by their mod-
eration, family values and harmonious work relations, the petite
bourgeoisie would provide the basis for a stable social order. As the
social Catholic economist Victor Brants observed, the *classe moyenne*
'represents the personal and moral link between employers and workers,
it is a personal link between producer and customer, it is, as one says, a
system of social peace.'[30]

    This discourse not only idealised a distorted vision of small enterprise
in many countries, but also provided much of the language with which
organisations of the petite bourgeoisie came to assert its importance. In
Britain, on the other hand, the petite bourgeoisie was rarely endowed
with the role of providing a social base for cohesion and stability. The
response to turn-of-the-century social crisis there was not to elevate the
middle as a buttress against class polarisation. The most coherent intellectual response, Liberal Idealism, was concerned primarily with
relations and obligations involving the rich and the working class. Ideas
about 'the individualisation of property' (to quote Thomas MacKay of
the Charity Organisation Society)[31] gained some popularity in Tory circles from the 1880s, but they went little further than agricultural
smallholdings and allotments. Proponents of small enterprise as a source
of social stability were politically marginal and, in the absence of a conscious small propertied sector of society on which to draw, there was no
secure footing for the kind of discourse that emerged elsewhere. Why
was it that the ideas of small property and the stabilising middle never
really took off in Britain as a source of social stability? The answer lies
partly with economic structure and the more competitive transformation
of urban small enterprise in Britain. More important was the strength of
liberal ideas, providing no purchase for the idea of a petite bourgeoisie
sustained by nonmarket assistance. An analysis must also address ideological factors – the weakness of organic or corporatist conceptions of
society, more effective in Germany and even in France than in Britain,
and for which Catholicism alone can constitute only a partial explanation. The metaphorical power of the middle – the excessive Aristotelian
weight that rested upon the small grocer – is a powerful point of comparison, as is the language of metaphor with which the petite bourgeoisie
was described.

    State and political structures, and the ideologies of political and social
concern, are thus central to effective comparisons at the national level.

Nevertheless, as I have argued in this essay, the use of national-level variables in comparative analysis works in quite precise and limited areas, and there are significant implications for the direction of comparative social history, which classically rests on nation states. It would be quite wrong to conclude from my argument that the only relevant variables in comparative social history analysis were those bound up with politics, mobilisation and the state. Such a conclusion would reinforce a current, and in my view mistaken, trend towards denying the specificity of social history and giving analytical priority to the political. The danger in such positions is that the social variables are eliminated as significant variables – especially as significant variables in comparative analysis – merely on the grounds that they lack precision as explanatory variables, that it is hard to quantify or at least systematise them. The distinctive character of social variables must not constitute the grounds for denying their significance.

The issue which I have raised is not whether comparative social history is possible, but which units of analysis are relevant, and I have urged caution about the automatic recourse to national data and assumptions about comparisons between national social structures.[32] The themes where national-level comparisons make the most sense are those that relate to such phenomena as institutions, law and taxation, political conjunctures, and political and social discourse, variables which exist on a national level in a way that others do not. National comparisons surely require variables that make more sense within, rather than across, national boundaries. Comparative social history needs a greater not lesser degree of sensitivity to the appropriate means of analysing its variables, to differences in language and institutions, and to the question of establishing the appropriate units of analysis.

Notes

1. The argument presented in this chapter first appeared in a briefer form in G. Crossick, 'L'histoire comparée et la petite bourgeoisie', *Bulletin du Centre Pierre Léon d'histoire économique et sociale*, June 1992, pp. 13–25.

2. See G. Crossick and H.-G. Haupt, *The Petite Bourgeoisie in Europe 1780–1914: Enterprise, Family and Independence*, London, 1995. Important specialist studies of recent years include S. Jaumain, *Les petits commerçants belges face à la modernité (1990–1914)*, Brussels, 1995; J. Morris, *The Political Economy of Shopkeeping in Milan, 1886–1922*, Cambridge, 1993; P. Nord, *Paris Shopkeepers and the Politics of Resentment*, Princeton, 1986; D.L. Caglioti, *Il Guadagno Difficile: Commecianti napoletani nella seconda metà dell'Ottocento*, Bologna, 1994.

3. For the practice of comparative history in Britain, see G. Crossick, 'E che cosa si può sapere dell'Inghilterra? La storia comparata in Gran Bretagna', *Passato e Presente* 28 (1993), pp. 30–41. A revised German version was published as 'And What Should They Know of England? Die vergleichende Geschichtsschreibung im heutigen Großbritannien', in *Geschichte und Vergleich: Ansätze und Ergebnisse international vergleichender Geschichtsschreibung*, ed. H.-G. Haupt and J. Kocka, Frankfurt am Main, 1996, pp. 61–75.

4. H.-G. Haupt, 'Les employés lyonnais devant le Conseil de prud'hommes du commerce (1910–1914)', *Le Mouvement Social* 141 (1987), pp. 81–99.

5. J.W. Scott, 'Statistical Representations of Work: the Politics of the Chamber of Commerce's statistique de l'industrie à Paris, 1847–48', in *Work in France: Representations, Meaning, Organization and Practice*, ed. S.L. Kaplan and C.J. Koepp, Ithaca, 1986, pp. 335–63.

6. G. Kurgan-van Hentenryk, 'A la recherche de la petite bourgeoisie: l'Enquête orale de 1902–1904', *Revue belge d'histoire contemporaine* 14 (1983), pp. 287–332; Jaumain, *Les petits commerçants belges*, pp. 103–28.

7. E. Higgs, 'The Struggle for the Occupational Census, 1841–1911', in *Government and Expertise: Specialists, Administrators and Professionals 1860–1919*, ed. R.M. McLeod, Cambridge, 1988, pp. 73–86; A. Desrosières and L. Thévenot, 'Les mots et les chiffres: les nomenclatures professionnelles', *Economies et statistiques* 110 (1979), pp. 49–65.

8. G. Crossick, 'From Gentlemen to the Residuum: Languages of Social Description in Victorian Britain', in *Language, History and Class*, ed. P. Corfield, Oxford, 1990, pp. 150–78.

9. On the concept of the middle in late nineteenth-century discourse about small enterprise, see G. Crossick, 'Metaphors of the Middle: the Discovery of the Petite Bourgeoisie 1880–1914', *Transactions of the Royal Historical Society*, 6th series, 4 (1994), pp. 251–79; G. Crossick, 'Formation ou invention des classes moyennes? Une analyse comparée: Belgique-France-Grande-Bretagne (1880–1914)', *Revue belge d'histoire contemporaine* 26 (1996), pp. 105–38; K.-P. Sick, 'Le concept de classes moyennes. Notion sociologie ou slogan politique?', *Vingtième Siècle* 37 (1993), pp. 13–33.

10. See for example the cases of Württemberg and Limousin: D. Blackbourn, *Class, Religion and Local Politics in Wilhelmine Germany: the Centre Party in Württemberg before 1914*, New Haven, 1980; A. Corbin, *Archaïsme et modernité en Limousin au XIXe siècle* (1845–1880), Paris, 1975.

11. For that see Crossick and Haupt, *The Petite Bourgeoisie*.

12. Ibid. p. 64.

13. P. Bourdieu, L. Boltanski and M. de Saint-Martin, 'Les stratégies de reconversion. Les classes sociales et le système d'enseignement', *Information sur les Sciences Sociales* 12 (1973), pp. 61–113.

14. G.J. Sheridan Jr., 'Household and Craft in an Industrializing Economy: the Case of the Silk Weavers of Lyons', in *Consciousness and Class Experience in Nineteenth-Century Europe*, ed. J.M. Merriman, New York, 1979, pp. 111–12; C. Charmettant, 'La petite industrie à Lyon', *La Réforme sociale* 3 (1882), pp. 78–83; S. Volkov, *The Rise of Popular Antimodernism in Germany: the Urban Master Artisans 1873–1896*, Princeton, 1978, pp. 73–4.

15. Mile End Vestry: Deed 5094. Tower Hamlets Library, London.

16. Crossick, 'Metaphors of the Middle' and 'Formation ou invention des classes moyennes?'

17. For a study of the role of petits bourgeois in the emergence of identity in a new quartier, see G. Massard-Guilbaud, 'The Genesis of an Urban Identity: the *Quartier de la Gare* in Clermont-Ferrand 1850–1914', *Journal of Urban History* 25 (1999), pp. 779–808.

18. G. Crossick, 'Meanings of Property and the World of the Petite Bourgeoisie', in *Urban Fortunes, Property and Inheritance in the Town, 1700–1900*, ed. J. Stobart and A. Owens, Aldershot, 2000, pp. 50–78.

19. D. Blackbourn, 'La petite bourgeoisie et l'Etat dans l'Allemagne impériale 1871–1914', *Le Mouvement Social* 127 (1984), p. 13.

20. G. Crossick, 'Shopkeepers and the State in Britain, 1870–1914', in *Shopkeepers and Master Artisans in Nineteenth-Century Europe*, ed. G. Crossick and H.-G. Haupt, London, 1984, pp. 239–69.

21. Booth Manuscripts, A20 f. 32 (at the British Library of Political and Economic Science).

22. J.-C. Martin, 'Hiérarchie et structure de la société commerçante: les listes d'électeurs au tribunal de commerce de Niort en 1864 et 1874', *Le Mouvement Social* 112 (1980), pp. 57–77; R. Gellately, *The Politics of Economic Despair: Shopkeepers and German Politics 1890–1914*, London, 1974, pp. 97–108.

23. J. Lorcin, 'Un essai de stratigraphie sociale: chefs d'ateliers et compagnons dans la grève des passementiers de Saint-Etienne en 1900', *Cahiers d'histoire* 13 (1968), pp. 179–92.

24. Nord, *Paris Shopkeepers and the Politics of Resentment*.

25. Morris, *Political Economy of Shopkeeping in Milan*.

26. J.-C. Martin, 'Le commercant, la faillite et l'historien', *Annales E.S.C.* 35 (1980), pp. 1251–68.

27. C. Behagg, 'Masters and Manufacturers: Social Values and the Smaller Unit of Production in Birmingham, 1800–50', in *Shopkeepers and Master Artisans*, ed. Crossick and Haupt, pp. 144–6.

28. For this process of discovery and idealisation see Crossick, 'Metaphors of the Middle' and 'Formation ou invention des classes moyennes?'

29. P. du Maroussem at Closing Banquet of 1910 Congress of the *Société d'économie sociale: Les Classes Moyennes dans le Commerce et l'Industrie. XXIXe Congrès de la Société d'internationale d'économie sociale*, Paris, 1910, p. 128.

30. V. Brants, *La petite industrie contemporaine*, 2nd edn, Paris, 1902, p. 30.

31. Quoted in H. Perkin, *The Origins of Modern English Society 1780–1880*, London, 1969, p. 151.

32. I was recently interested to discover the same point made with respect to urban systems before 1800 in J. de Vries, *European Urbanization 1500–1800*, London, 1984, p. 152.

Bibliography

Behagg, C. 'Masters and Manufacturers: Social Values and the Smaller Unit of Production in Birmingham, 1800–50', in *Shopkeepers and Master Artisans in Nineteenth-Century Europe*, ed. G. Crossick and H.-G. Haupt. London, 1984, pp. 144–6.

Blackbourn, D. *Class, Religion and Local Politics in Wilhelmine Germany: the Centre Party in Württemberg before 1914*. New Haven, CT, 1980.

—— 'La petite bourgeoisie et l'Etat dans l'Allemagne impériale 1871–1914', *Le Mouvement Social* 127 (1984), p. 13.

Bourdieu, P., Boltanski, L. and Saint-Martin, M. de. 'Les stratégies de reconversion. Les classes sociales et le système d'enseignement', *Information sur les Sciences Sociales* 12 (1973), pp. 61–113.

Brants, V. *La petite industrie contemporaine*, 2nd edn. Paris, 1902.

Caglioti, D.L. *Il Guadagno Difficile: Commecianti napoletani nella seconda metà dell'Ottocento*. Bologna, 1994.

Charmettant, C. 'La petite industrie à Lyon', *La Réforme sociale* 3 (1882), pp. 78-83.

Corbin, A. *Archaïsme et modernité en Limousin au XIXe siècle (1845–1880)*. Paris, 1975.

Crossick, G. 'Shopkeepers and the State in Britain, 1870-1914', in *Shopkeepers and Master Artisans in Nineteenth-Century Europe*, ed. G. Crossick and H.-G. Haupt. London, 1984, pp. 239–69.

—— 'From Gentlemen to the Residuum: Languages of Social Description in Victorian Britain', in *Language, History and Class*, ed. P. Corfield. Oxford, 1990, pp. 150–78.

—— 'L'histoire comparée et la petite bourgeoisie', *Bulletin du Centre Pierre Léon d'histoire économique et sociale*, June 1992, pp. 13–25.

—— 'E che cosa si può sapere dell'Inghilterra? La storia comparata in Gran Bretagna', *Passato e Presente* 28 (1993), pp. 30–41.

—— 'Metaphors of the Middle: the Discovery of the Petite Bourgeoisie 1880-1914', *Transactions of the Royal Historical Society*, 6th series, 4 (1994), pp. 251–79.

—— 'And What Should They Know of England? Die vergleichende Geschichtsschreibung im heutigen Großbritannien', in *Geschichte und Vergleich: Ansätze und Ergebnisse international vergleichender Geschichtsschreibung*, ed. H.-G. Haupt and J. Kocka. Frankfurt am Main, 1996, pp. 61–75.

—— 'Formation ou invention des classes moyennes? Une analyse comparée: Belgique-France-Grande-Bretagne (1880–1914)', *Revue belge d'histoire contemporaine* 26 (1996), pp. 105-38.

—— 'Meanings of Property and the World of the Petite Bourgeoisie', in *Urban Fortunes, Property and Inheritance in the Town, 1700–1900*, ed. J. Stobart and A. Owens. Aldershot, 2000, pp. 50–78.

Crossick, G. and Haupt, H.G. *The Petite Bourgeoisie in Europe 1780–1914: Enterprise, Family and Independence.* London, 1995.

Desrosières, A. and Thévenot, L. 'Les mots et les chiffres: les nomenclatures profession-nelles', *Economies et statistiques* 110 (1979), pp. 49–65.

Gellately, R. *The Politics of Economic Despair: Shopkeepers and German Politics 1890-1914.* London, 1974, pp. 97–108.

Haupt, H.-G. 'Les employés lyonnais devant le Conseil de prud'hommes du commerce (1910–1914)', *Le Mouvement Social* 141 (1987), pp. 81–99.

Higgs, E. 'The Struggle for the Occupational Census, 1841–1911', in *Government and Expertise: Specialists, Administrators and Professionals 1860–1919*, ed. R.M. McLeod. Cambridge: Cambridge University Press, 1988, pp. 73–86.

Jaumain, S. *Les petits commerçants belges face à la modernité (1990–1914).* Brussels, 1995

Kurgan-van Hentenryk, G. 'A la recherche de la petite bourgeoisie: l'Enquête orale de 1902–1904', *Revue belge d'histoire contemporaine* 14 (1983), pp. 287–332.

Lorcin, J. 'Un essai de stratigraphie sociale: chefs d'ateliers et compagnons dans la grève des passementiers de Saint-Etienne en 1900', *Cahiers d'histoire* 13 (1968), pp. 179–92.

Martin, J.C. 'Hiérarchie et structure de la société commerçante: les listes d'électeurs au tribunal de commerce de Niort en 1864 et 1874', *Le Mouvement Social* 112 (1980), pp. 57–77.

—— 'Le commercant, la faillite et l'historien', *Annales E.S.C.* 35 (1980), pp. 1251–68.

Massard-Guilbaud, G. 'The Genesis of an Urban Identity: the *Quartier de la Gare* in Clermont-Ferrand 1850-1914', *Journal of Urban History* 25 (1999), pp. 779–808.

Morris, J. *The Political Economy of Shopkeeping in Milan, 1886–1922.* Cambridge: Cambridge University Press, 1993.

Nord, P. *Paris Shopkeepers and the Politics of Resentment.* Princeton, NJ, 1986.

Perkin, H. *The Origins of Modern English Society 1780–1880.* London, 1969.

Scott, J.W. 'Statistical Representations of Work: the Politics of the Chamber of Commerce's statistique de l'industrie à Paris, 1847–48', in *Work in France: Representations, Meaning, Organization and Practice*, ed. S.L. Kaplan and C.J. Koepp. Ithaca, NY, 1986, pp. 335–63.

Sheridan, G.J., Jr. 'Household and Craft in an Industrializing Economy: the Case of the Silk Weavers of Lyons', in *Consciousness and Class Experience in Nineteenth-Century Europe*, ed. J.M. Merriman. New York, NY, 1979, pp. 111–2.

Sick, K.P. 'Le concept de classes moyennes. Notion sociologie ou slogan politique?', *Vingtième Siècle* 37 (1993), pp. 13–33.

Volkov, S. *The Rise of Popular Antimodernism in Germany: the Urban Master Artisans 1873–1896.* Princeton, NJ, 1978, pp. 73–4.

Vries, J. de. *European Urbanization 1500–1800.* London, 1984.

6

THE EUROPEAN WORKING CLASSES IN THE LATE NINETEENTH AND EARLY TWENTIETH CENTURIES

Dick Geary

In the period between 1850 and 1914 the 'working classes' intervened in the European historical process in a way that pleased some and shocked others. Their presence as an industrial and political force could no longer be overlooked, as more and more men and women took strike action against their employers, joined trade unions and formed political parties which claimed expressly to speak for and represent the interests of 'the working class'. In France there was no year between 1900 and 1914 that saw fewer than five hundred industrial disputes and some of these had become national in scale. Ever greater numbers of German employees articulated their grievances in strike action, with some 681,000 taking part in 1910 and over one million two years later. The year 1911 witnessed the first national rail strike in British history, and the next three years engulfed the country's industry in a strike wave of unprecedented numbers. The protests of working men and women were not restricted to short-term, direct action, however, but also found more permanent articulation in trade union organisation. In Britain these unions mobilised over four million employees on the eve of war, the various trade unions in Imperial Germany over three million in total and in France roughly one million at the same point in time. Workers entered the political stage, too, and with a vengeance in this period. By the end of 1910 forty-two British Labour Party MPs sat in the House of Commons, the French Socialist Party (SFIO) could command one and a half million votes in national elections and the German Social Democratic Party (SPD), which won over four million votes in 1912 and sent 110 Deputies to the *Reichs-*

tag, could boast over one million individual, fee-paying members. This massive organisation, which developed a host of ancillary organisations (choral and drama societies, cycling and chess clubs, educational associations and sports organisations) and a large party bureaucracy, provided the model for social democratic parties elsewhere in Europe, as in Denmark, Sweden, Norway, Austria-Hungary, Finland and – perhaps most famously – Russia. Strikes, trade unions, labour and socialist parties proclaimed the arrival of the European worker, and in some cases his or her actions were much more explosive and dramatic than those described thus far. Violence against employers and state authorities characterised the 'tragic week' in Barcelona in 1909, 'red week' in June 1914 in Italy, and most seriously of all, the Russian Revolution of 1905/6.[1]

It is scarcely surprising that the emergence of the European labour movement in the late nineteenth and early twentieth centuries has been associated in the minds of many historians with the famous twin processes of industrialisation and urbanisation, not so much because these occasioned unprecedented poverty, for they did not, but because they brought more and more workers together in the factories and new residential districts and because they saw an ever greater percentage of the labour force become dependent upon wage labour. (It has been argued that it was precisely this wage dependence which was crucial in the creation of class identity.)[2] At the same time some commentators, most classically Marx, believed that the development of industrial production and the modernisation of technology would iron out differences in skill and remuneration, thereby creating a more monolithic working class and one aware of its common interests.[3] Yet the relationship between these general developments and the emergence of a class identity was far from being so clear or straightforward; for class-based politics predated industrial production, modernity was often dysfunctional for labour protest, and industrial development as often fragmented as it united European labour.

Interestingly and somewhat ironically the politics and language of class emerged in Britain, France and Germany *before* factory production became widespread. The radical Chartists in Britain in the first half of the nineteenth century, the members of the revolutionary secret societies that sprang up in France in the 1830s and 1840s, especially in Paris, and those who died or were arrested on the barricades in the French capital, in Berlin, Dresden, Leipzig and in Vienna during the revolutionary upheavals of 1848/49 were not members of a new factory proletariat (in any case and as yet extremely few in numbers on the European continent), but rather practitioners of the so-called 'degraded' artisan trades of joinery, shoemaking and tailoring and in particular the journeymen of these trades. The problem encountered by such 'degraded' craftsmen was not the industrialist, the new, dynamic factory boss and owner, but the merchant capitalist, who did not labour with his hands, but possessed economic power simply through the ownership of capital. No Samuel Smiles, the enemy of these 'artisan socialists' was thus denounced as 'parasite', and the spread of 'artisan socialism', which addressed itself specifically to the problems of wage labourers, was a consequence of the increased dependence of the artisanate on merchants for raw materials and retail outlets in those industries dominated by the putting-out (domestic) system and competition, especially in tailoring, from sweated labour. Thus in most cases artisan protest was not directed at and not caused by the new factory/industrial order.[4]

The centrality of craftsmen to labour protest was a phenomenon that did not wither away in the later decades of the nineteenth century. Rather, as Bernard Moss and Michael Hanagan have shown for France, and as Jürgen Kocka, Toni Offermann, John Breuilly, Christiane Eisenberg and Wolfgang Renzsch have demonstrated in the case of the German states (later of the Second Reich), the organisations of labour, in some cases now of socialist persuasion, were primarily dependent upon journeymen artisans. In Italy, too, the idea that factory workers constituted the initial vanguard of labour politics has been displaced by a recognition of the role of artisans in the woollen industry of the Biella region, and of skilled printers and textile workers around Milan.v There is even evidence that, in their early days at least, those industries most clearly deploying mechanised factory production were oases of relative calm in societies that were otherwise turbulent. In Britain, for example, the operatives of the new factories in Halifax distanced themselves from radical politics, whereas Chartism was to prove most attractive in towns with strong craft traditions, such as Huddersfield. As the most authoritative study of industrial Lancashire has argued, there was in Britain in the middle of the nineteenth century an inverse relationship between factory production and labour protest. Patrick Joyce writes:

> The consequences of modern factory production were to be expressed in the first evidence of that reformism which has since characterised English working-class movements ... The consolidation of mechanised, factory industry in the second half of the nineteenth century was the occasion of class harmony more than class conflict.[6]

It remained the case much later – between 1910 and 1920 – that the militancy of some British engineering workers was not to be found in the most modern factories of the automobile industry, such as those in Coventry, but in the older centres of the engineering industry. A good deal of research has also shown that strikes and radical working-class politics in France between 1870 and 1914 were dominated by artisans and skilled workers, whereas involvement in activities testifying to the existence of some form of class awareness was much less common on the part of the unskilled and often female workforce of the mechanised textile industry. Michelle Perrot has even told us of the 'calm' of the large factories.[7] Significantly a not dissimilar pattern of behaviour can be detected in Imperial Germany, where the labour force of the most modern and highly mechanised factories, in which mass production by semi- or unskilled workers was the rule, was the least likely to engage in conflict with employers, join trade unions or give overt support to left-wing politics. The unskilled of the country's large textile factories, workers in the largest metal plants of the Ruhr, the employees of BASF, Bayer and Hoechst (very modern chemical firms) rarely went on strike and usually refused to participate in union or socialist activities. Strikes in Germany were much more common in the small and medium-sized concerns, whilst the Free Trade Unions (close to the SPD) and the Social Democratic Party recruited most of their support from the ranks of skilled (and male) labour.[8] The same applied to working-class organisations in virtually every European country before the outbreak of hostilities in 1914.[9] In consequence it is accurate say that commitment to class-based forms of action and organisation was no inevitable result of employment as an industrial worker.

In fact the attempt to 'read off' specific forms of working-class politics from 'objective economic interests', skill levels or occupation (the last once a hobby-horse of some labour historians) is ultimately doomed to failure. For the extent of organisational solidarity and political radicalism on the part of the same kinds of workers revealed huge national and regional variations. The idea that 'labour aristocrats' (printers, skilled engineering workers and other relatively well-placed employees in secure jobs) provide the key to an understanding of the 'reformism' of the British labour movement is thrown into doubt the minute one realises that such exemplars of sectionalism and collaborationism in the case of the UK were in Germany the very fundament of the SPD's rank and file at a time when the party espoused a Marxist ideology, and that they were disproportionately present in the revolutionary upheavals that gripped Tsarist Russia in its death throes. Even within the boundaries of a single state it remains impossible to reduce the political identity of workers to occupational factors alone. For example, around the turn of the century French miners in the Nord and Pas-de-Calais generally gave their support to reformist socialism, whereas those of the Southern Massif around

St Etienne tended to syndicalism. Similarly explanations of anarchosyn-dicalism in both France and Spain, which concentrate their attention upon small-scale artisan production, may carry some weight as far as the craft trades of Paris and the textile industry of Catalonia are concerned, and yet the French syndicalist movement also embraced unskilled porce-lain workers, whilst syndicalism in Spain did not appear to attract the operatives of the small-scale textile industry of the Basque province of Guipuzcoa.[10] Clearly it is not possible to reduce the specific political expression of working-class identity to occupational or industrial struc-tures. Rather the picture is one of massive national and regional diversity, even when we are talking about similar kinds of workers in similar industries. What this suggests in turn is that, at least as far as political identity is concerned, the most important determinants of action and organisation are to be found outside the workplace, in exogenous factors such as patterns of residence, aspects of popular culture, the attitudes and behaviour of other social groups towards the working class, and above all the nature and role of the state. We will return to these factors later.

That differences existed between the patterns of working-class forma-tion in different countries and regions, of course, does not in itself imply that it is impossible to make meaningful national and cross-national gen-eralisations about the identity and behaviour of workers. The emergence of artisan socialism amongst 'degraded' artisans was characteristic of certain similar groups in Britain, France and Germany around the middle of the century. It was also the case that skilled males dominated the organisations of all European labour movements between 1850 and 1914, as we have already seen. Everywhere the labour institutions found it difficult, in some cases almost impossible, to mobilise female and unskilled workers, though their underrepresentation was less marked when it came to strike action than it was in the case of union and party membership. It was also true that some specific working-class occupa-tions displayed marked similarities across national boundaries, at least as far as their industrial behaviour was concerned. Dock workers in most countries proved volatile and difficult to organise in any permanent way, and in many European ports syndicalism – or at least syndicalist tenden-cies – could be detected. Virtually everywhere print workers, the classic 'labour aristocrats', were the first to organise on any significant – often national – scale and they often used their strong bargaining position to achieve collective bargaining with their employers. The years between 1900 and 1914 saw skilled engineering workers become increasingly prominent in various forms of labour protest, often involving tension between the official union leadership and a more restless rank and file, in

Austria, Britain, France, Germany and Hungary. Such protest on their part was especially marked in the upheavals which followed the ending of war in 1918.[11] Miners across national boundaries displayed a powerful sense of occupational solidarity, not least because they lived in relatively isolated but monolithic communities and shared a common danger in their work below ground.[12] The relationship between such *occupational* identity and class solidarity, however, was extremely complex, especially in the case of coal miners. In Britain, for example, in the first half of the nineteenth century, most miners refused to be associated with that movement, whose radical wing espoused some degree of class identity, namely, Chartism. Furthermore the mineworkers' union was the last of all the major trade unions in Britain to affiliate to the Trades Union Congress (TUC) after the turn of the century. In Imperial Germany, and again in the revolutionary upheavals between 1918 and 1921, the concerns of miners seem to a very large extent to have concentrated on specific problems in the pits, rather than on the iniquities of the capitalist economic and social order in general. The campaign for socialisation of the mines in the Ruhr in 1919/20, for example, did not extend to a general campaign for a new social order, unlike the more general agitation for socialisation on the part of the workers of the much more diverse industries of Saxony.[13] Despite such similarities, however, it is important to recognise that common occupational activity in different countries was primarily restricted to the sphere of industrial relations, strikes and union membership, and only rarely extended to the realm of politics. Similarities in industrial behaviour, explicable in terms of a common workplace experience, did not translate into similarities in political identity, where, as we have seen, the picture is rather one of diversity and fragmentation. Solidarity along class, as distinct from trade, lines was only to be found in some places and remained relatively uncommon. One reason for such fragmentation is to be found in the nature of industrial growth itself.

The most fundamental fact about economic growth, industrial change and technological modernisation is that all of these processes take place unevenly. At the most obvious level the onset and subsequent rate and timing of those changes we have come to characterise as 'industrialisation' – significantly reference to an 'industrial *revolution*' is increasingly rare amongst economic historians – varied enormously from one European country to another. There is no doubt that the early but relatively gradual (in comparison, say, with Germany) industrialisation of Britain, where various craft associations of labour were already in existence, facilitated the development of powerful, skilled and often sectional trade unions, which in turn gave rise to a system of collective bargaining and a less confrontational relationship between workers and their employers in both the economic and the political sphere than was the case in the German Reich, where later, more rapid and more technologically intensive industrial change spawned intransigent bosses and played a part in the formation of class-based politics. Equally the different pace and timing of the process of industrialisation in different European countries produced national labour forces of very different structures, as, for example, in the size of the agricultural labour force which was massive in Russia and most of Eastern Europe, large in France and of still considerable importance in Germany. In the latter country it still employed around 30 percent of the active workforce in 1907. No less significant than these differences between nation states, however, was uneven development within national boundaries. Here British experience of *relatively* uniform urban and industrial growth was very definitely the exception rather than the rule. In many countries the industrialisation of some regions was accompanied by the marked deindustrialisation of other areas. Thus Germany's eastern and southern provinces remained largely untouched by the economic changes which characterised the large Saxon towns (Dresden, Leipzig and Chemnitz), Berlin and – most spectacularly – the Ruhr, which had been largely rural in 1850. In France much of the Midi remained unaffected by industrialisation and, if anything, Languedoc deindustrialised. The gulf that separated the rural Italian *mezzogiorno* from the industrial triangle comprising Milan, Turin and Genoa grew notoriously large and bred problems for the future; whilst Catalonia and the northern Basque provinces became much more economically developed than the rest of Spain. The sprawling Empire of prewar Austria-Hungary could contrast large, modern industrial cities such as Prague, Vienna and Budapest, and centres of manufacture such as Bohemia, with vast and often extremely primitive agrarian economies in its Eastern territories. The inevitable consequence of all this, of course, was that the different regions within a single country possessed labour forces very different in their interests and experiences; and this, in turn, may explain the persistence of oft-noted regional variations in working-class behaviour and identity.

It was not only national and regional economic growth which exhibited unevenness. The same phenomenon could also be observed in the different rates and timing of modernisation experienced by different sectors of the economy. In the case of France, for example, there existed on the eve of the First World War on the one hand an extremely large artisanal sector, especially, though not only, in the luxury trades. On the other, the same country was in the forefront worldwide of the development of artificial fibres (rayon) and the exploitation of hydroelectric power, had pioneered a whole series of initiatives in the retail trade (the large department store) and could boast one of the most advanced automobile industries of Europe on the outskirts of Paris. The German Empire of 1914 is often and quite rightly seen as an industrial giant and as being in the forefront of the deployment of new technologies, yet side by side with the modern plants of Siemens and AEG in electrotechnology, BASF, Hoechst and Bayer in chemicals and the giant iron and steel works of the Ruhr, there existed a large agricultural sector, as we have already seen, domestic manufacture characterised the production of toys and musical instruments and large parts of the Saxon textile industry, especially in the Vogtland, and even shoemaking in the Palatine town of Pirmasens. In the occupational census of 1907 around half of those listed as *Arbeiter* (workers) lived in small towns and villages of under 10,000 inhabitants, and approximately a third of those characterised as being employed in *Industrie und Handwerk* (industry and handicrafts) worked in firms employing five or fewer people.[14]

Even within a single industry the idea that technological development would create a more homogeneous workforce is open to question, especially where such modernisation is held to produce an erosion of skill, the so-called 'deskilling' or 'dequalification' of significant numbers of workers. In so far as any such process took place in Europe before 1914 it was extremely limited in extent, and this for a number of reasons. In the first place the huge expansion of the engineering industry before the First World War, though often associated with the use of new machinery, actually created more and not fewer jobs for skilled engineers, as, for example, in the town of Bielefeld, which had become a centre of bicycle manufacture. Even where the deployment of more modern machines did facilitate the employment of semiskilled labour, highly skilled men were still needed to set up, maintain, repair and supervise those machines. The opportunities for self-employment for skilled mechanics were further increased by the invention and application of gas and electric motors, as well as by the need for bicycle and motorcar repair and maintenance. Not only was deskilling often less serious than imagined, therefore; it was also the case that different sectors of the engineering industry modernised at different rates and different times. This meant that technological modernisation in this sector (and, for that matter, others) did not necessarily produce a uniformity of skills or remuneration amongst its workers. Even in the German engineering industry, which probably can be seen as the most advanced in Europe, the application of the 'American system' – the use of a single, central source of power and the systematic replacement of skilled male by less skilled female labour – remained very much the exception rather than the rule. Indeed the only real attempt to introduce such a system in Imperial Germany took place at the Bosch works in Stuttgart just before the War. Significantly it was met with considerable resistance from the firm's employees. There is yet another problem with the belief that technological modernisation necessarily leads to deskilling. In the case of the French textile industry, for example, mechanisation did not lead to the employment of former craft workers in unskilled production, for the resultant jobs were often taken by those newly recruited to industry from rural backgrounds.[15]

The uneven nature of economic growth thus militated *against* rather than *for* the creation of a homogeneous labour force. Industrial development was more likely to give rise to sectionalism and fragmentation when left to itself. There were other factors relating to the economy which could further set worker against worker. This was the case, for example, with certain forms of payment adopted by employers. The differential treatment of white- and blue-collar workers in the electrical engineering industry of Imperial Germany, for example, was at least in part the consequence of a deliberate attempt on the part of large firms such as Siemens to prevent the development of a community of interest between the two groups of workers. Similarly Rudolf Vetterli's study of the Fischer engineering company at Schaffhausen (Switzerland) before 1914 brilliantly demonstrates how the existence of numerous grievances within the plant failed to result in collective action on the part of the workforce precisely because of the existence of a multiplicity of payment hierarchies. Conflicts between skilled men and their less skilled helpers (e.g., bricklayers' mates) could also arise where the skilled were offered bonus payments or piece rates for increased productivity at the same time as their unskilled helpers remained tied to hourly rates of pay and thus had no interest whatsoever – rather the very opposite – in any intensification of labour. In the pits of the Ruhr payment by work team (*Gedinge*) could also lead to tension between older workers, who were deemed to be unfit and thus not so productive, and younger, fitter coalface men, who resented the possibility that the inclusion of older miners in their team might reduce their earning power. Once again we see that the workplace scarcely functioned as the crucible of solidarity or communal interests.[16]

It can be argued in the light of the above that workers came together across skill, occupational and industrial boundaries, therefore, not as a consequence of shared economic interest, though that doubtless constituted the *sine qua non* of all solidarity, but rather as a result of factors to be found outside the workplace. I have argued at length elsewhere that a sense of class solidarity which transcended regional, local and economic fissures within the labour force was most likely to develop where the role of the state was repressive and discriminatory, as in Russia, Austria-Hungary and Germany before the First World War; where the national bourgeoisie was weak (Tsarist Russia) or had abandoned its commitment to liberal constitutional reform (as was to a significant extent the case in Wilhelmine Germany); and where employers adopted authoritarian attitudes towards their workforce and refused to engage in collective bargaining (as was true of most of Europe outside the UK, but especially true of Continental employers in large-scale industry).[17] I will not repeat those arguments here, though I am more convinced of their veracity than ever, but I would like to stress that a sense of solidarity also had to be created, and it was precisely this task that the SFIO in France, the Italian Socialist Party (PSI) and above all the SPD allocated to themselves. The centrality of the political party to the formation of class consciousness was, of course, famously stated by Lenin in *What is to be Done?* in 1912, but significantly the quotations he used and the arguments he deployed came from German Social Democracy's arch-ideologue – Karl Kautsky.[18] However, the ability of the SPD, in contrast to any socialist sect in Britain, to recruit so many supporters before 1914 was not simply a consequence of the 'external' factors mentioned above, nor of the party's commitment to mass mobilisation along class lines. It also related to certain aspects of working-class residence and popular culture. In particular the ancillary cultural, educational and leisure associations of the SPD did not have to compete to anything like the same extent with either a commercialised leisure industry (predicated in the British case upon relatively high wages and a relatively short working week) or a 'modest domesticity' (Ross McKibbin), facilitated in the UK from the 1870s onwards by single-family working-class housing.[19] The sheer density of lower-class housing in the German Reich sent workers out of the home and into the public places (especially the pubs), where political mobilisation found its most fruitful soil.[20]

Even in Germany, however, that part of the labour movement which spoke the language of class, i.e., the Social Democratic Party, could never claim to speak for the whole of the workforce. Firstly, in most countries women and the unskilled remained largely *outside* the ranks of formal trade union and party-political organisations, and, at least in the German case, when women were enfranchised, their voting behaviour suggested that class position was not the prime determinant of their choices. In Weimar Germany many women did not bother to vote in the early years, whilst those that did tended to vote for the Catholic Centre Party (if Catholic) and for the German National People's Party, a conservative organisation close to the Evangelical Church (when Protestant). Few gave their support to the SPD, the party which had enfranchised women, and even fewer to the Communist Party (KPD), which adopted positions closest to those of the feminist movement of contemporary Europe, such as abortion on demand.[21] In the July elections of 1932 it also appears to be the case that a substantial percentage of German women gave their votes to the National Socialists.[22] Secondly, many males adopted political positions that were equally unamenable to explanation exclusively in class terms. In Britain and France a not insignificant section of the working class preferred the collaborationist politics of liberalism to class confrontation and voted respectively for the British Liberal or the French Radical Party. It was also not unusual, though it scarcely fits any class-based model of political behaviour, for some workers to give their support to conservative or nationalist candidates. This was most clearly the case in the 'working-class Tory' districts of industrial Lancashire, where anti-Irish sentiment or even hostility to the local mill-owners, who were often Liberals, played a role. This last possibility raises the spectre that a sense of class identity and political conservatism are not necessarily incompatible; and we find the same phenomenon amongst the wool-shearers of Mazamet in France, who proved themselves capable of sustained action against their employers yet gave their vote to right-wing political candidates. In the German case, too, there were industrial workers to be found, though in no great numbers, who voted for the National Liberals (the party closest to some big business interests) in the Imperial period, for the nationalist German National People's Party (DNVP) for much of the Weimar Republic and who even turned to the Nazis in the economic crisis of the early 1930s. These tended to be workers who lived in company housing, such as the 'core' employees (*Stammarbeiter*) of Krupp in Essen, who also often belonged to company insurance schemes and who were members of 'yellow', i.e., company, unions. It is also worth noting that the Nazis registered some electoral success with workers lacking previous traditions of political mobilisation, as in small towns and rural areas.[23]

A sense of class could also be countered by powerful religious/confessional identities. Areas of high religious observance in France, Spain and Italy were often to prove immune to the blandishments of socialist activity and propaganda, which conversely flourished in areas where religious observance (church attendance etc.) was low and anti-clericalism strong.

In Holland and Germany working-class organisations actually fractured along lines of religious confession. In the former case both industrial and political mobilisation was structured into three parallel and competing pillars (liberal, Catholic, socialist). In Germany most Catholics, even when they worked as industrial labourers, continued to give their votes to the Catholic Centre Party and the SPD did badly in towns that were solidly Catholic though industrial, such as Aachen and Cologne. German Catholics formed their own trade union organisations (the so-called Christian Trade Unions), and there were occasions, such as the industrial action at the steel-making Dortmunder Union in 1911 and the great miners' strike of the following year in the Ruhr, when these Christian Unions refused to collaborate with the Free Trade Unions, which were close to the SPD, thus jeopardising the chances of a successful outcome for the workers involved. There were even some – admittedly rare – cases where the Christian Unions found themselves on strike without the support of their 'Free' Union counterparts. In areas of mixed confession (i.e., where there were significant numbers of both Catholics and Protestants) such as the Ruhr, confessional identities sometimes overrode class sentiment in the case of Protestant workers, too. Where the SPD won votes from Protestant workers in some constituencies in the first round of two-stage elections, in the second ballot those same Protestants who had supported the SPD candidate in the first round actually voted for a conservative in the second, as the other candidate was a Catholic, albeit a worker![24]

At least as divisive and potentially much more explosive were the many ethnic divisions within the European working class. In Austria-Hungary Czech and German workers did not join common organisations, but formed their own, separate ones. In Germany before 1914 Poles formed a specifically Polish trade union and supported the political cause of Polish nationalism rather than Social Democracy, though it is also worth noting that the subgroup of Masurians from the Eastern provinces, who were Protestant, remained loyal to Empire and Emperor, unlike the Catholic Poles. Local employees in northeastern France registered resentment when the bosses took on relatively placid Belgian Catholics in an attempt to reduce industrial militancy, whilst Marseilles dockers displayed even greater hostility to North African (Arab) immigrants. In the United Kingdom Irish workers were often regarded as a threat to jobs and wages by the English, whilst, analogously to German Poles, Irish Catholic labourers espoused the politics of Irish nationalism at the same time as their Protestant counterparts constituted the popular backbone of conservative Unionism.[25]

So far we have seen that a sense of class identity was no automatic reflex of employment as an industrial wage-earner and, further, that any number of other factors – ethnicity, religion, region, skill – could impair and sometimes prevent the development of working-class solidarity. However, it is at this point that some words of qualification and caution are necessary. That workers were divided along lines of skill, occupation, gender, religion, ethnicity and political choice, the last of which was never simply reducible to the former elements though strongly related to them, did not mean that the men and women involved had no conception of themselves as 'workers'. Nor did it invariably prevent collective action across these various divides. Thus German industrial workers who were also Catholic, might belong to specifically Christian trade unions. However, in order to retain credibility as defenders of employee interests those unions increasingly had to behave like their socialist-orientated Free Union rivals, that is, engage in industrial conflict and distribute strike pay, even though their statutes normally contained some general commitment to social harmony. The Christian Unions also sometimes joined with the Free Trade Unions in major strikes, as in the case of the Ruhr miners in 1905. Much the same could be said of the industrial organisation of the Reich's Polish workers, which had a history of participation in conflicts with employers – in fact the Polish Union joined in that other major strike of Ruhr miners after the turn of the century (1912), when the Christian Unions refused to become involved. Indeed, in Imperial Germany being a Pole and a worker often went hand in hand, thus ethnic and class identity were far from contradictory in this case. Another aspect of ethnic tension within the working class is worth investigation at this point: hostility to foreign workers could on occasion be instrumental rather than anything else. To take an example from outside the period of this study, after 1945 Scottish coalminers exhibited considerable hostility to Poles, who had been brought over because of local labour shortages in the pits, when they first arrived. Yet, as it became clear that these foreign workers neither threatened safety at work nor depressed wage levels, that hostility subsided. Also interesting is the fact that the failure of German trade unions to integrate Polish miners before 1914 was not repeated in France after the First World War, when some who had migrated, often from the Ruhr, to the French northern coalfields became members of the native organisations, albeit with considerable autonomy, rather than forming their own separate organisations.[26]

The coexistence of various identities raises another important point: the crass historiography which claims that the events of August 1914, when the parties of organised labour supported their various national war efforts almost without exception, denoted the demise or absence of class consciousness, fails to recognise the possibility of simultaneous experiences of patriotism *and* class identity. Not only was working-class patriotism very different in nature to the jingoism of the nationalist right, but also the same Welsh miners who volunteered to fight for Britain in August 1914 were back on strike in the following year. In any case local studies in Germany and of Vienna have suggested that the working class did not demonstrate the same nationalist fervour in the very early days of the conflict as did other groups in the population.[27] More to the point, patriotism and a sense of class could go hand in hand. The German Social Democrat Bromme reports evenings spent in working-class (SPD-affiliated) choral society gatherings, at which socialist songs were sung, followed by walks home with the same colleagues at which patriotic tunes seemed to be favoured. The same source refers to a strange mixture of identities in the home of his working-class parents: for there were to be found pictures of Karl Marx, Ferdinand Lassalle and Wilhelm Liebknecht (icons of Social Democracy), of Bismarck, General von Moltke (victor of Sedan) and the Kaiser, together with even the representations of several saints.[28] A further testimony to the multiplicity of working-class identities on the part of but a single group of workers is to be found in the Museum of Labour History in Bethnall Green (London). It is a banner produced by Australian dockers in the wake of the great London dock strike of 1889. Its predictable and prime message is working-class solidarity across the oceans. But as well as the representations of heroic dock workers, the banner also depicts the Union flag of the UK and an image of Britannia. So here we have international working-class solidarity under the monarchy and within the British Empire!

That the European working classes should be divided by skill, occupation, gender, religion, region, nation and ethnicity is not surprising. Indeed what is perhaps more truly remarkable is the extent to which working men and women have overcome those matters that divide them to take on the privileged and the established orders. No less surprising is the coexistence at one and the same time of multiple identities in individual workers and groups of workers, for workers were not only socialised in the workplace or in segregated residential communities. They often lived cheek by jowl with other groups and mixed with them in their daily intercourse. They had access to popular press and media which were local, regional or even national, rather than class-specific. In the schools and through conscription (which was the norm in continental Europe) they were inculcated with the values of the nation state, especially where schools were seen as the instruments of nation building.

The teleology which leads from wage labour to class consciousness has proved mostly false, where unaided by cultural and especially political factors.

Notes

1. P. Adelman, *The Rise of the Labour Party*, London, 1972; G. Beier, *Geschichte und Gewerkschaften*, Frankfurt am Main, 1978; J. Belchem, *Industrialisation and the Working Class*, Oxford, 1970; G. Brenan, *The Spanish Labyrinth*, Cambridge, 1950; K.D. Brown, *The First Labour Party*, London, 1986; A.H. Clegg et al., *A History of British Trade Unions since 1889*, Oxford, 1964/1985; *Social Conflict and Political Order in Britain*, ed. J. Cronin and J. Schneer, London, 1982; J.A. Davis, 'Socialism and the Italian Working Classes in Italy before 1914', in *Labour and Socialist Movements in Europe before 1914*, ed. D. Geary, Oxford, 1989; E. Dolléans, *Le mouvement ouvrier*, vol. 2, Paris, 1946; D. Geary, *European Labour Protest, 1848–1939*, 2nd edn, London, 1984; D. Geary, 'Socialism and the German Labour Movement', in *Labour and Socialist Movements*, ed. Geary; D. Geary, *European Labour Politics from 1900 to the Depression*, London, 1991; *Strikes, Wars and Revolutions in International Perspective*, ed. L. Haimson and C. Tilly, Cambridge, 1989; H. Hautmann and R. Kropf, *Die österreichische Arbeiterbewegung vom Vormärz bis 1945*, Linz, 1974; P. Heywood, 'The Labour Movement in Spain', in *Labour and Socialist Movements*, ed. Geary; D.L. Horowitz, *The Italian Labour Movement*, Cambridge, MA, 1963; R. Hostetter, *The Italian Socialist Movement*, vol.1, Princeton, 1958; E.H. Hunt, *British Labour History*, London, 1981; J.L.H. Keep, *The Rise of Social Democracy in Russia*, Oxford, 1966; D. Kynaston, *King Labour*, London, 1976; T. de Lara, *El Movimento Obrero en la Historia de España*, Madrid, 1972; G. Lefranc, *Le mouvement ouvrier socialiste*, Paris, 1963; A.S. Lindemann, *The 'Red Years'*, Berkeley, 1984; L. Lotti, *La settimana rossa*, Florence, 1965; R. Magraw, *The Left in France*, London, 1986; R. Magraw, 'Socialism, Syndicalism and French Labour', in *Labour and Socialist Movements*, ed. Geary; G. Marks, *Unions in Politics*, Princeton, 1989; R. McKibbin, *The Evolution of the Labour Party*, Oxford, 1974; H. Mitchell and P.N. Stearns, *Workers and Protest*, Ithaca, 1971; *The Development of Trade Unionism in Britain and Germany*, ed. W. Mommsen and H.-G. Husung, London, 1985; J. Moses, *Trade Unionism in Germany*, London, 1982; M. Perrot, *Workers on Strike*, Leamington Spa, 1987; G. Phillips, 'The British Labour Movement before 1914', in *Labour and Socialist Movements*, ed. Geary; G. Procacci, *La lotta di classe in Italia agli inizi del secolo XX*, Rome, 1972; C. Read, 'Labour and Socialism in Tsarist Russia', in *Labour and Socialist Movements*, ed. Geary; *Der Aufstieg der deutschen Sozialdemokratie*, ed. G.A. Ritter, Munich, 1990; G.A. Ritter and K. Tenfelde, *Arbeiter im deutschen Kaiserreich*, Bonn, 1992; M. Schneider, *A Brief History of German Trade Unions*, Bonn, 1991; K. Schönhoven, *Expansion und Konzentration*, Stuttgart, 1989; M. Schwarz, *The Russian Revolution of 1905*, Chicago, 1967; R. Service, *The Russian Revolution 1900–27*, London, 1986; E. Shorter and C. Tilly, *Strikes in France*, Cambridge, 1974; P.N. Stearns, *Revolutionary Syndicalism*, New Brunswick, 1971; K. Tenfelde and H. Volkmann, *Streik*, Munich, 1981; *Arbeiter und Arbeiterbewegungen in Europa*, ed. K. Tenfelde, Munich, 1986; J.C. Ullman, *The*

'Tragic Week', Cambridge, MA, 1967; F. Venturi, Roots of Revolution, London, 1970; A.K. Wildman, The Making of a Workers' Revolution, Chicago, 1967.

2. The significance of dependent wage labour for class formation is the central theme of J. Kocka, Lohnarbeit und Klassenbildung, Berlin/Bonn, 1983.

3. K. Marx and F. Engels, Marx-Engels Gesamtausgabe, Moscow, 1927, vol. 1, pt. 3, p. 207 and pt. 6, pp. 533f.

4. See the survey of the literature in D. Geary, 'Strikes and Protest', in Arbeiter, ed. Tenfelde, p. 373. Luddism constitutes something of an exception, though even here machine-breaking was often 'bargaining by riot' (Eric Hobsbawm). Before 1950 there were only a few industrial processes (nail-making, cotton-spinning) in continental Europe which had been thoroughly mechanised and displaced skill.

5. H.D. Bell, Sesto san Giovanno, New Brunswick, 1986; J. Breuilly, 'Liberalism or Social Democracy', European History Quarterly 15 (1985), pp. 3–42; J. Breuilly, Joachim Friedrich Martens, Göttingen, 1984; Davis, 'Socialism and the Working Classes in Italy before 1914'; C. Eisenberg, Deutsche und englische Gewerkschaften, Göttingen, 1986; M. Hanagan, The Logic of Solidarity, Urbana, 1980; Kocka, Lohnarbeit; B. Moss, The Origins of the French Labour Movement, Berkeley, 1976; T. Offermann, Arbeiter und liberales Bürgertum in Deutschland, Bonn, 1979; W. Renzsch, Handwerker und Lohnarbeiter in der frühen Arbeiterbewegung, Göttingen, 1980.

6. P. Joyce, Work, Society and Politics, Brighton, 1983, pp. 50, 63.

7. Hanagan, Logic; J. Hinton, The First Shop Stewards Movement, London, 1973; M. Perrot, 'On the Formation of the French Working Class', in Working Class Formation, ed. I. Katznelson and A. Zollberg, Princeton, 1986, pp. 89ff.

8. Geary, Labour Protest, pp. 70–80 for multiple references.

9. Ibid.

10. See the articles on Britain, France and Spain by, respectively, G. Phillips, R. Magraw and P. Heywood in Labour and Socialist Movements, ed. Geary. For a survey of the relationship between miners and Chartism see R. Church, 'Chartism and the Miners', Labour History Review 56 (1991), pp. 23–36. On Ruhr Miners see F. Brüggemeier, Leben vor Ort, Munich, 1983; J. Tampke, The Ruhr and Revolution, London, 1979; K. Tenfelde, Sozialgeschichte der Ruhrbergarbeiterschaft, Bonn, 1981 and – on the specificity of miners' protests – D. Geary, 'Protest', in Sozialgeschichte des Bergbaus im 19. und 20. Jahrhundert, ed. K. Tenfelde, Munich, 1982, pp. 559–64.

11. J. Breuilly, Labour and Liberalism, Manchester, 1992, passim; Geary, Labour Protest, pp. 70–80, 123–5, 139f. On dockworkers see M. Cattaruzza, '"Organisierter Konflikt" und "Direkte Aktion"', Archiv für Sozialgeschichte 20 (1980), pp. 326–45; M. Grüttner, Arbeitswelt an der Wasserkante, Göttingen, 1984; E. Hobsbawm, Labouring Men, London, 1979, chaps 9, 10, 11; J. Lovell, Stevedores and Dockers, London, 1969; A. Lyttleton, 'Revolution and Counter-Revolution in Italy', in Revolutionary Situations in Europe: The Rebellious Century, ed. L. Charles and R. Tilly, London, 1975, pp. 97–120. For printers see G. Beier, Schwarze Kunst und Klassenkampf, Frankfurt am Main, 1966; U. Engelhardt, Nur vereinigt sind wir stark, Stuttgart, 1977; P. Ullmann, Tarifverträge und Tarifpolitik in Deutschland, Frankfurt am Main, 1977, pp. 49, 56, 163f. Engineers are treated in J.B. Jefferys, The Story of the Engineers, London, 1946; F. Opel, Der deutsche Metallarbeiterverband, Hanover, 1962.

12. For a survey of the relationship between miners and chartism see R. Church, 'Chartism and the Miners', *Labour History Review* 56 (1991), pp. 23–36. Also R. Page Arnot, *South Wales Miners*, London, 1967. On Ruhr miners Brüggemeier, *Leben vor Ort*; Hartewig, *Das unberechenbare Jahrzehnt*, Munich, 1993; Tampke, *Ruhr and Revolution*; Tenfelde, *Sozialgeschichte der Ruhrbergarbeiterschaft*. For various national and international aspects of miners' history see J. Michel, 'Le mouvement ouvrier chez les mineurs de l'Europe', Ph.D. diss., Lyons II, 1990 (and *Sozialgeschichte des Bergbaus im 19. und 20. Jahrhundert*, ed. K. Tenfelde, Munich 1992; for France, R. Trempé, *Les Mineurs de Carmaux*, Paris, 1971.

13. Geary, *Labour Protest*, p. 559.

14. A classic study of uneven development can be found in F.B. Tipton, *Regional Variations in the Economic Development of Germany*, Middleton, 1976 and is central to S. Pollard, Peaceful Conquest, Cambridge, 1983. The importance of regional variations in the nature of working-class formation is also central to the essays on France, Italy and Spain in *Labour and Socialist Movements*, ed. Geary, and is also stressed by A. Cottereau, 'The Distinctiveness of Working-Class Cultures in France', in *Working-Class Formation*, ed. Katznelson and Zollberg, pp. 111–23.

15. K. Ditt, *Industrialisierung, Arbeiterschaft und Arbeiterbewegung in Bielefeld 1850–1914*, Dortmund, 1982; D. Geary, 'Technological Change and Labour Protest before 1914', in *Technik und Industrielle Revolution*, ed. Theo Pirker et al., Opladen, 1987, pp. 211–17; Hanagan, *Logic*; H. Homburg, 'Anfänge des Taylorsystems in Deutschland', *Geschichte und Gesellschaft* 4 (1978), pp. 170ff.

16. J. Kocka, *Unternehmerverwaltung und Angestelltenschaft*, Stuttgart, 1969; R. Vetterli, *Industriearbeit, Arbeiterbewußtsein und gewerkschaftliche Organisation*, Göttingen, 1978.

17. Geary, *Labour Protest*, pp. 47–70; D. Geary, 'Class in Germany', *Bradford Occasional Papers* 9 (1988), pp. 42–61; and D. Geary, 'The State and the SPD in Imperial Germany', in D. Geary, *Hope and Impotence: Aspects of German Labour, 1870–1933*, London, 2001.

18. D. Geary, *Karl Kautsky*, Manchester, 1987, pp. 30f.

19. R. McKibbin, 'Why was there no Marxism in Great Britain?', in *English Historical Review* 99 (1984), pp. 303–9.

20. D. Geary, 'Residence and Working-Class Identity in Europe in the 19th and early 20th Century', in *The European City in the Nineteenth Century*, ed. J. Machacek and J. Ferris, Prague, 1995, pp. 106–21.

21. On the gendering of labour in general see L.R. Berlanstein, *Rethinking Labour History: Essays on Discourse and Class Analysis*, Urbana, 1993; H. Beyer, 'Die Frau in der politischen Entscheidung', in *Wählerbewegungen in der deutschen Geschichte*, ed. O. Büsch et al., Berlin, 1978, pp. 298–301; G. Jordan and L.R. Berlanstein, *Cultural Politics: Class, Gender and Race in the Post-modern World*, Oxford, 1995. Also *Women, Work and the Family*, ed. L.A. Tilly and J.W. Scott, 2nd edn, Cambridge, 1989 and J.W. Scott, *Gender and the Politics of History*, Cambridge, 1981. On women and labour in Germany see *Gender Relations in German History*, ed. L. Abrams and E. Harvey, London, 1996; S. Bajohr, *Die Hälfte der Fabrik*, Frankfurt am Main, 1983; *Women in German History*, ed. U. Frevert, Oxford, 1990. On women and the organisations of the

German labour movement see R.J. Evans, *Sozialdemokratie und Frauenemanzipation*, Bonn, 1979; U. Frevert, 'Women Workers, Workers' Wives and Social Democracy in Imperial Germany', in *From Bernstein to Brandt*, ed. R. Fletcher, London, 1986, pp. 34–44; H. Niggemann, *Emanzipation zwischen Sozialismus und Feminismus*, Wuppertal, 1981; R. Pore, *Women in German Social Democracy*, Westport, 1991; J. Quataert, *Reluctant Feminists*, Princeton, 1979; W. Thönneson, *The Emancipation of Women*, Frankfurt am Main, 1963; N. Reagin, *A German Women's Movement: Class and Gender in Hanover*, Chapel Hill, 1995.

22. Or, at least, claims H. Boak, 'Women in Weimar Germany', in *Social Change and Political Development in the Weimar Republic*, ed. R. Bessel and E.J. Feuchtwanger, London, 1981, pp. 155–73. This, however, is somewhat misleading, as there were more female than male voters in Weimar. Until 1930 relatively few women voted for Hitler. After 1930 women remained more loyal to both the Catholic Parties (Centre and Bavarian People's Party) and the SPD than their male counterparts. However between 1930 and 1932 the female Nazi vote increased more rapidly than the male; and in July 1932 in Protestant Germany the NSDAP (National Socialist German Workers Party) gained a higher percentage of the female than of the male electorate (though a much lower one in Catholic districts). Throughout Weimar very few women voted communist. For a survey of voting behaviour in the Weimar Republic see H. Boak, 'National Socialism and Working-Class Women before 1933', in *The Rise of National Socialism and the Working Classes in Weimar Germany*, ed. C. Fischer, Oxford, 1996, pp. 163–88; T. Childers, *The Nazi Voter*, Chapel Hill, 1983; *The Formation of the Nazi Constituency*, ed. T. Childers, London, 1986; J. Falter, *Hitlers Wähler*, Munich, 1991; R. Hamilton, *Who voted for Hitler?*, Princeton, 1982; P. Manstein, *Die Mitglieder und Wähler der NSDAP*, Munich, 1991; K. Rohe, *Wähler und Wählertraditionen in Deutschland*, Frankfurt am Main, 1992; J. Stephenson, 'Women and the Nazi Seizure of Power', in *The Nazi Machtergreifung*, ed. Peter D. Stachura, London, 1983, pp. 35–8.

23. K. Mattheier, *Die Gelben*, Düsseldorf, 1973, provides a history of such workers.

24. On the significance of religious observance and/or anti-clericalism for political choice see J. Bruhat, 'Anticlericalisme et mouvement ouvrier en France avant 1914', in *Christianisme et Monde Ouvrier*, ed. F. Bédarida and J. Maitron, Paris, 1978; F.R. Gibson, *A Social History of French Catholicism*, London, 1989, pp. 212–26; P.M. Jones, 'Political Commitment and Rural Society in the Southern Massif', in *European Studies Review* 10 (1980), pp. 337–56. For Italy see Lyttleton, 'Revolution and Counter-Revolution in Italy', pp. 64ff. For Spain: Brenan, *The Spanish Labyrinth*, pp. 89ff., 152; G. Jackson, *The Spanish Republic and the Civil War*, Princeton, 1965, pp. 289ff.; F. Lannon, *Privilege, Persecution and Prophecy: the Catholic Church in Spain*, Oxford, 1987; J.M. Sanchez, *The Spanish Civil War as a Religious Tragedy*, Notre Dame, Indiana, 1987; J.C. Ullmann, The 'Tragic Week'; M. Vincent, *Catholicism in the Second Spanish Republic*, Oxford, 1995. On Holland see L.H. Van Voss, 'The Netherlands', in *The Force of Labour*, ed. S. Berger and D. Broughton, Oxford, 1995, pp. 44–54. For Germany, K. Klocker, 'Konfession und sozialdemokratische Wählerschaft', in *Wählerbewegungen*, ed. Büsch et al., pp. 197–207; D. Groh, *Negative Integration und revolutionärer Attentismus*, Frankfurt am Main, 1973, pp. 282f.; G.A. Ritter, *Die Arbeiterbewegung im wilhelminischen Reich*, Berlin, 1959, pp. 73–83; Ritter and Tenfelde, *Arbeiter im deuschen Kaiserreich*, pp. 747–80; K. Rohe, 'Die Ruhr-

gebietssozialdemokratie im wilhelminischen Kaiserreich', in *Der Aufstieg der deutschen Arbeiterbewegung*, ed. G.A. Ritter, Munich, 1990, pp. 317–45; M. Schneider, *Die Christlichen Gewerkschaften*, Bonn, 1982.

25. R. Brubak, *Citizenship and Nationhood in France and Germany*, Cambridge, 1992; *Socialism and Nationalism*, ed. E. Cahm and V. Fisera, Nottingham, 1979; G. Cross, *Immigrant Workers in Industrial France*, Philadelphia, 1983; U. Herbert, *A History of Foreign Labour in Germany*, Ann Arbor, 1990; B. Jenkins, *Nationalism in France: Class and Nation since 1789*, London, 1980; C. Klessmann, *Polnische Arbeiter im Ruhrgebiet*, Göttingen, 1978; J.H. Kulczycki, *The Foreign Worker and the German Labour Movement*, Oxford, 1994; Magraw, 'French Labour', in *Labour and Socialist Movements*, ed. Geary, pp. 62ff.; R.C. Murphy, *Guestworkers in the German Reich*, Boulder, 1983.

26. D. Geary, 'Protest', in *Tenfelde, Sozialgeschichte des Bergbaus*, pp. 559–64; and J.H. Kulczycki, 'Nationalism over Class Solidarity', *Canadian Review of Studies in Nationalism* 14 (1987), pp. 261–76.

27. F. Boll, *Massenbewegungen in Niedersachsen*, Bonn, 1981, pp. 151ff.; V. Ullrich, 'Everyday Life and the German Working Class', in *From Bernstein to Brandt*, ed. R. Fletcher, London, 1987, p. 56; and more generally W. Kruse, *Krieg und nationale Integration*, Essen, 1994.

28. W. Bromme, *Lebensgeschichte eines modernen Fabrikarbeiters*, Jena, 1930, pp. 71ff.

Bibliography

Abrams, L. and Harvey, E. *Gender Relations in German History*. London, 1996.
Adelman, P. *The Rise of the Labour Party*. London, 1972.
Bajohr, S. *Die Hälfte der Fabrik*. Frankfurt am Main, 1983.
Beier, G. *Schwarze Kunst und Klassenkampf*. Frankfurt am Main, 1966.
—— *Geschichte und Gewerkschaften*. Frankfurt am Main, 1978.
Belchem, J. *Industrialisation and the Working Class*. Oxford, 1970.
Bell, H.D. *Sesto san Giovanno*. New Brunswick, NJ, 1986.
Berlanstein, L.R. *Rethinking Labour History: Essays on Discourse and Class Analysis*. Urbana, IL, 1993.
Bertrand, C. *Revolutionary Situations*. Montreal, 1977.
Beyer, H. 'Die Frau in der politischen Entscheidung', in *Wählerbewegungen in der deutschen Geschichte*, ed. O. Büsch et al. Berlin, 1978, pp. 298–301.
—— 'National Socialism and Working-Class Women before 1933', in *The Rise of National Socialism and the Working Classes in Weimar Germany*, ed. C. Fischer. Oxford, 1996, pp. 163–88.
Boak, H. 'Women in Weimar Germany', in *Social Change and Political Development in the Weimar Republic*, ed. R. Bessel and E.J. Feuchtwanger. London, 1981, pp. 155–73
Boll, F. *Massenbewegungen in Niedersachsen*. Bonn, 1981.
Brenan, G. *The Spanish Labyrinth*. Cambridge: Cambridge University Press, 1950.
—— *The Spanish Labyrinth*, Cambridge: Cambridge University Press, 1962
Breuilly, J. *Joachim Friedrich Martens*. Göttingen, 1984.
—— 'Liberalism or Social Democracy', *European History Quarterly* 15 (1985), pp. 3–42.
—— *Labour and Liberalism*. Manchester, 1992.
Bromme, W. *Lebensgeschichte eines modernen Fabrikarbeiters*. Jena, 1930.

Brown, K.D. *The First Labour Party*. London, 1986.
Brubak, R. *Citizenship and Nationhood in France and Germany*. Cambridge, MA, 1992.
Brüggemeier, F. *Leben vor Ort*. Munich, 1983.
Bruhat, J. 'Anticlericalisme et mouvement ouvrier en France avant 1914', in *Christianisme et Monde Ouvrier*, ed. F. Bédarida and J. Maitron. Paris, 1978, pp. 79–115.
Cahm, E. and Fisera, V. (eds). *Socialism and Nationalism*. Nottingham, 1979.
Cattaruzza, M. '"Organisierter Konflikt" und "Direkte Aktion"', *Archiv für Sozialgeschichte* 20 (1980), pp. 326–45.
Childers, T. *The Nazi Voter*. Chapel Hill, NJ, 1983.
—— (ed.). *The Formation of the Nazi Constituency*. London, 1986.
Church, R. 'Chartism and the Miners', *Labour History Review* 56 (1991), pp. 23–36.
Clegg, A.H. et al. *A History of British Trade Unions since 1889*. Oxford, 1964/1985.
Connelly Ullmann, J. *The Tragic Week: A Study of Anti-Clericalism in Spain, 1875–1912*. Cambridge, MA,1968.
Cottereau, A. 'The Distinctiveness of Working-Class Cultures in France', in *Working Class Formation*, ed. I. Katznelson and A. Zollberg. Princeton, NJ, 1986, pp. 111–23.
Cronin, J. and Schneer, J. (eds) *Social Conflict and Political Order in Britain*. London, 1982.
Cross, G. *Immigrant Workers in Industrial France*. Philadelphia, PA, 1983.
Davis, J.A. 'Socialism and the Working Classes in Italy before 1914', in *Labour and Socialist Movements in Europe before 1914*, ed. D. Geary. Oxford, 1989, pp. 198–207.
Ditt, K. *Industrialisierung, Arbeiterschaft und Arbeiterbewegung in Bielefeld 1850–1914*. Dortmund, 1982.
Dolléans, E. *Le mouvement ouvrier*, vol. 2. Paris, 1946.
Eisenberg, C. *Deutsche und englische Gewerkschaften*. Göttingen, 1986.
Engelhardt, U. *Nur vereinigt sind wir stark*. Stuttgart, 1977.
Evans, R.J. *Sozialdemokratie und Frauenemanzipation*. Bonn, 1979.
Falter, J. *Hitlers Wähler*. Munich, 1991.
Frevert, U. 'Women Workers, Workers' Wives and Social Democracy in Imperial Germany', in *From Bernstein to Brandt*, ed. R. Fletcher. London, 1986, pp. 34–44.
—— (ed.). *Women in German History*. Oxford, 1990.
Geary, D. 'Protest', in *Sozialgeschichte des Bergbaus im 19. und 20. Jahrhundert*, ed. K. Tenfelde. Munich, 1982, pp. 559–64.
Geary, D. *European Labour Protest, 1848–1939*, 2nd edn. London, 1984
—— 'Strikes and Protest', in *Arbeiter und Arbeiterbewegungen in Europa*, ed. K. Tenfelde. Munich, 1986, pp. 363–88.
—— *Karl Kautsky*. Manchester, 1987.
—— 'Technological Change and Labour Protest before 1914', in *Technik und Industrielle Revolution*, ed. Theo Pirker et al. Opladen, 1987, pp. 211–17.
—— 'Class in Germany', Bradford Occasional Papers 9 (1988), pp. 42–61.
—— 'Socialism and the German Labour Movement', in *Labour and Socialist Movements in Europe before 1914*, ed. D. Geary, Oxford, 1989, pp. 101–36.
—— *Labour and socialist Movements in Europe before 1914*, ed. Geary. Oxford, 1989.
—— *European Labour Politics from 1900 to the Depression*. London, 1991.
—— 'Residence and Working-Class Identity in Europe in the 19th and early 20th Century', in *The European City in the Nineteenth Century*, ed. J. Machacek and J. Ferris. Prague, 1995, pp. 106–21.
—— 'The State and the SPD in Imperial Germany', in D. Geary, *Hope and Impotence: Aspects of German Labour, 1870–1933*. London, 2001.
Gibson, F.R. *A Social History of French Catholicism*. London, 1989.
Groh, D. *Negative Integration und revolutionärer Attentismus*. Frankfurt am Main, 1973.
Grüttner, M. *Arbeitswelt an der Wasserkante*. Göttingen, 1984.

Haimson, L. and Tilly, C. (eds) *Strikes, Wars and Revolutions in International Perspective.* Cambridge, 1989.

Hamilton, R. *Who voted for Hitler?* Princeton, NJ, 1982.

Hanagan, M. *The Logic of Solidarity.* Urbana, IL, 1980.

Hartewig, K. *Das unberechenbare Jahrzehnt.* Munich, 1993.

Hautmann, H. and Kropf, R. *Die österreichische Arbeiterbewegung vom Vormärz bis 1945.* Linz, 1974.

Herbert, U. *A History of Foreign Labour in Germany.* Ann Arbor, MI, 1990

Heywood, P. 'The Labour Movement in Spain', *Labour and Socialist Movements in Europe before 1914*, ed. D. Geary. Oxford, 1989, pp. 231–65.

Hinton, J. *The First Shop Stewards Movement.* London, 1973.

Hobsbawm, E. *Labouring Men.* London, 1979.

Homburg, H. 'Anfänge des Taylorsystems in Deutschland', *Geschichte und Gesellschaft* 4 (1978), pp. 155–85.

Horowitz, D.L. *The Italian Labour Movement.* Cambridge, MA, 1963

Hostetter, R. *The Italian Socialist Movement*, vol.1. Princeton, NJ, 1958.

Hunt, E.H. *British Labour History.* London, 1981.

Jackson, G. *The Spanish Republic and the Civil War.* Princeton, NJ, 1965.

Jefferys, J.B. *The Story of the Engineers.* London, 1946.

Jenkins, B. *Nationalism in France: Class and Nation since 1789.* London, 1980.

Jones, P.M. 'Political Commitment and Rural Society in the Southern Massif', *European Studies Review* 10 (1980), pp. 337–56.

Jordan, G. and Berlanstein, L.R. *Cultural Politics: Class, Gender and Race in the Postmodern World.* Oxford, 1995.

Joyce, P. *Work, Society and Politics.* Brighton, 1983.

Keep, J.L.H. *The Rise of Social Democracy in Russia.* Oxford, 1966.

Klessmann, B. *Polnische Arbeiter im Ruhrgebiet.* Göttingen, 1978.

Klocker, K. 'Konfession und sozialdemokratische Wählerschaft', in *Wählerbewegungen in der deutschen Geschichte*, ed. O. Büsch et al. Berlin, 1978, pp. 197–207.

Kocka, J. *Unternehmerverwaltung und Angestelltenschaft.* Stuttgart, 1969.

—— *Lohnarbeit und Klassenbildung.* Berlin, Bonn, 1983.

Kruse, W. *Krieg und nationale Integration.* Essen, 1994.

Kulczycki, J.H. 'Nationalism over Class Solidarity', *Canadian Review of Studies in Nationalism* 14 (1987), pp. 261–76.

—— *The Foreign Worker and the German Labour Movement.* Oxford, 1994.

Kynaston, D. *King Labour.* London, 1976.

Lannon, F. *Privilege, Persecution and Prophecy: The Catholic Church in Spain.* Oxford, 1987.

Lara, T. de *El Movimento Obrero en la Historia de España.* Madrid, 1972.

Lefranc, J. *Le mouvement ouvrier socialiste.* Paris, 1963.

Lindemann, A.S. *The 'Red Years'.* Berkeley, CA, 1984.

Lotti, L. *La settima rossa.* Florence, 1965.

Lovell, J. *Stevedores and Dockers.* London, 1969.

Lyttleton, A. 'Revolution and Counter-Revolution in Italy', in *Revolutionary Situations in Europe: The Rebellious Century*, ed. L. Charles and R. Tilly. London, 1975, pp. 97–120

—— 'Socialism, Syndicalism and French Labour', in *Labour and Socialist Movements in Europe before 1914,* ed. D. Geary. Oxford, 1989, pp. 48–100.

Magraw, R. *The Left in France.* London, 1986.

Manstein, P. *Die Mitglieder und Wähler der NSDAP.* Munich 1991.

Marks, G. *Unions in Politics.* Princeton, NJ, 1989.

Marx, K. and Engels, F. *Marx-Engels Gesamtausgabe.* Moscow, 1927, vol. 1.

Mattheier, K. *Die Gelben.* Düsseldorf, 1973.

McKibbin, R. *The Evolution of the Labour Party*. Oxford, 1974.

McKibbin, R. 'Why was there no Marxism in Great Britain?', in *English Historical Review* 99 (1984), pp. 303–9.

Michel, J. 'Le mouvement ouvrier chez les mineurs de l'Europe', Ph.D. diss. Lyons II, 1990.

Mitchell, H. and Stearns, P.N. *Workers and Protest*. Ithaca, NY, 1971.

Mommsen, W. and Husung, H.-G. (eds) *The Development of Trade Unionism in Britain and Germany*. London, 1985.

Moses, J. *Trade Unionism in Germany*. London, 1982.

Moss, B. *The Origins of the French Labour Movement*. Berkeley, CA, 1976.

Murphy, R.C. *Guestworkers in the German Reich*. Boulder, CO, 1983.

Niggemann, H. *Emanzipation zwischen Sozialismus und Feminismus*. Wuppertal, 1981.

Offermann, T. *Arbeiter und liberales Bürgertum in Deutschland*. Bonn, 1979.

Opel, F. *Der deutsche Metallarbeiterverband*. Hanover 1962.

Page Arnot, R. *South Wales Miners*. London, 1967.

Perrot, M. 'On the Formation of the French Working Class', in *Working Class Formation*, ed. I. Katznelson and A. Zollberg. Princeton, NJ, 1986, pp. 71–110.

Perrot, M. *Workers on Strike*. Leamington Spa, 1987.

Phillips, G. 'The British Labour Movement before 1914', in *Labour and Socialist Movements in Europe before 1914*, ed. D. Geary. Oxford, 1989, pp. 11–47.

Pollard, S. *Peaceful Conquest*. Cambridge, 1983.

Pore, R. *Women in German Social Democracy*. Westport, CT, 1991.

Procacci, G. *La lotta di classe in Italia agli inizi del secolo XX*. Rome, 1972.

Quataert, J. *Reluctant Feminists*. Princeton, NJ, 1979.

Reagin, N. *A German Women's Movement: Class and Gender in Hanover*. Chapel Hill, NC, 1995.

Read, C. 'Labour and Socialism in Tsarist Russia', in *Labour and Socialist Movements in Europe before 1914*, ed. D. Geary. Oxford, 1989, pp. 137–81.

Renzsch, W. *Handwerker und Lohnarbeiter in der frühen Arbeiterbewegung*. Göttingen, 1980.

Ritter, G.A. *Die Arbeiterbewegung im wilhelminischen Reich*. Berlin, 1959.

—— (ed.). *Der Aufstieg der deutschen Sozialdemokratie*. Munich, 1990.

Ritter, G.A. and Tenfelde, K. *Arbeiter im deutschen Kaiserreich*. Bonn, 1992.

Rohe, K. 'Die Ruhrgebietssozialdemokratie im wilhelminischen Kaiserreich', in *Der Aufstieg der deutschen Arbeiterbewegung*, ed. G.A. Ritter. Munich, 1990, pp. 317–45.

—— *Wähler und Wählertraditionen in Deutschland*. Frankfurt am Main, 1992.

Sanchez, J.M. *The Spanish Civil War as a Religious Tragedy*. Notre Dame, IN, 1987.

Schneider, M. *Die Christlichen Gewerkschaften*. Bonn, 1982.

—— *A Brief History of German Trade Unions*. Bonn, 1991.

Schönhoven, K. *Expansion und Konzentration*. Stuttgart, 1989.

Schwarz, M. *The Russian Revolution of 1905*. Chicago, IL, 1967.

Scott, J.W. *Gender and the Politics of History*. Cambridge, MA, 1981.

Service, R. *The Russian Revolution 1900–27*. London, 1986.

Shorter, E. and Tilly, C. *Strikes in France*. Cambridge: Cambridge University Press, 1974.

Stearns, P.N. *Revolutionary Syndicalism*. New Brunswick, NJ, 1971.

Stephenson, J. 'Women and the Nazi Seizure of Power', in *The Nazi Machtergreifung*, ed. Peter D. Stachura. London, 1983, pp. 35–8.

Tampke, J. *The Ruhr and Revolution*. London, 1979.

Tenfelde, K. *Sozialgeschichte der Ruhrbergarbeiterschaft*. Bonn, 1981.

—— (ed.). *Arbeiter und Arbeiterbewegungen in Europa*. Munich, 1986.

—— (ed.). *Sozialgeschichte des Bergbaus im 19. und 20. Jahrhundert*. Munich, 1992.

Tenfelde, K. and Volkmann, H. *Streik*. Munich, 1981.

Thönneson, W. *The Emancipation of Women*. Frankfurt am Main, 1963.

Tilly, L.A. and Scott, J.W. (eds) *Women, Work and the Family*, 2nd edn. Cambridge, MA, 1989.

Tipton, F.B. *Regional Variations in the Economic Development of Germany*. Middleton, 1976.

Trempé, R. *Les Mineurs de Carmaux*. Paris, 1971.

Ullman, J.C. *The 'Tragic Week'*. Cambridge, MA, 1967.

Ullmann, P. *Tarifverträge und Tarifpolitik in Deutschland*. Frankfurt am Mai, 1977.

Ullrich, V. 'Everyday Life and the German Working Class', in *From Bernstein to Brandt*, ed. R. Fletcher. London, 1987, pp. 55–64.

Venturi, F. *Roots of Revolution*. London, 1970.

Vetterli, R. *Industriearbeit, Arbeiterbewußtsein und gewerkschaftliche Organisation*. Göttingen, 1978.

Vincent, M. *Catholicism in the Second Spanish Republic*. Oxford, 1995.

Voss, L.H. Van. 'The Netherlands', in *The Force of Labour*, ed. S. Berger and D. Broughton. Oxford, 1995, pp. 44–54.

Wildman, A.K. *The Making of a Workers' Revolution*. Chicago, IL, 1967.

PART 2

SOCIAL PATTERNS AND DYNAMICS

7

A 'EUROPEAN FAMILY' IN THE NINETEENTH AND TWENTIETH CENTURIES?*

Michael Mitterauer

In many respects our perception of family structures in the past is shaped by stereotypes. These stereotypes are reinforced by the use of certain typologies. Among the stereotypical terms used are 'the family of the industrial age' or 'the family of the preindustrial age', which can frequently be found both in scholarly and everyday language. It is generally taken for granted that the 'industrial revolution' fundamentally changed family structures. Similarly, this applies to specific developments within the family. The period around the turn of the nineteenth century is generally seen as an age of fundamental change, which leans, for example, towards the spread of 'bourgeois gender roles' or towards more child-orientated models of bringing up children. The clichéd distinction between the 'traditional' and the 'modern' family is a more general version of the juxtaposition of the 'family of the preindustrial age' against the 'family of the industrial age'.

This paper sets out to reconsider the following notions. Is it possible to discern a uniform pattern of the family, which arose in the process of industrialisation and modernisation and which has existed in modern industrial nations ever since? Is it thus possible – against the backdrop of this model of social change – to conceive of a 'European family' in the nineteenth and twentieth centuries?

---

* Work on the manuscript of this article was finished in 1989; the bibliography was updated again in 1995.

I shall attempt to answer these questions along the lines of the following five theses, which will subsequently be discussed at greater length:

1. The immediate effects of the 'industrial revolution' had as little impact on the development of family structures as all the other revolutions of that time. Reinhard Koselleck's concept of the 'Sattelzeit', a period of accelerated historical development around 1800, apparently does not pertain to the social history of the family.[1] Continuity across the turn of the nineteenth century prevailed over aspects of change.

2. In the nineteenth and twentieth centuries family structures were affected by various processes of accelerating social change. Given the growing dynamics of change, any concept of a stable pattern of the family is highly questionable. The model of a singular process of change at the beginning of the nineteenth century, producing a new pattern of the family that was hardly subject to any further change afterwards, cannot be sustained.

3. Never before in European history had family forms been so diverse – by region as well as by milieux – as they were during these past two centuries. This was partly due to the uneven pattern of modernisation, which affected different parts of the population at different points in time. In part, modernisation was bound to aggravate preexisting differences. Heterogeneity was probably at its greatest during the first half of the twentieth century.

4. Despite all this heterogeneity, some basic common conditions were fundamental to the development of the family in Europe, which, however, allowed for wide variation. These factors can be elucidated by comparing European and non-European family structures of the time. However, the area in which these distinct European family structures arose did not coincide with the whole of Europe in a geographical sense.

5. The climax of the diversification of family forms was achieved in the first half of the twentieth century. Thereafter, tendencies towards convergence became clearly visible. An evident example of these tendencies is a phenomenon which sociologists characterise as the 'modern family cycle' (*moderner Familienzyklus*).[2] However, the convergence mainly pertains to the formal structure of the family, whereas the ways of interaction within the family have become more diverse. Both of these tendencies apply to the development of the family beyond the geographical confines of Europe.

In order to maintain the thesis that there was an exceptional heterogeneity of European family forms in the nineteenth and twentieth century, it is necessary to consider the various criteria which were relevant to the structure of the family. The apparent differences with regard to these criteria must also be taken into account: not only the size and the composition of the family differed – whether it consisted only of relatives or also of unrelated people – but also relations within the family – whether they were stable or unstable, harmonious or conflictual. Families' central functions such as reproduction, upbringing, work, leisure or cult were organised in very different ways. There were differences in the structure of settlement and housing, which shaped the spatial conditions of living together as a family. Throughout their life-cycle families changed their composition in different ways. Moreover, the family's dependence on social institutions, which were tightly intertwined with family structures, for example, school, was rarely the same everywhere in Europe. It is impossible in this article to cover all these aspects in a European comparison stretching across centuries. Thus, the manifold differentiations by region and milieux will be illustrated by discussing the institution of the so-called 'life-cycle servants', a phenomenon typical of Europe.[3]

The inclusion of predominantly juvenile servants in the family household was a very old custom in Europe.[4] At the turn of the nineteenth century, the importance of this phenomenon was not declining – rather, it became ever more important throughout the nineteenth century, both in the countryside, where the demand for labour rose due to the agricultural revolution,[5] and in the cities, where the number of domestic servants grew.[6] In the early phase of industrialisation some artisans employed more apprentices and journeymen, who continued to live with the master's family.[7] Modernisation did not abolish these traditional concepts of the family – on the contrary, their importance grew. Only in the twentieth century was the institution of servants successively abolished across the whole of society, with the exception of some remaining domestics in a few upper-class households. Increasingly, unrelated domestics were perceived as strangers, interfering with the intimacy of the core family.

The great variety of terminology used to describe different sorts of male and female servants according to the jobs they performed shows that the inclusion of servants brought about an extraordinary heterogeneity in the family forms. Very different sorts of servants came to live and work with the family, depending on to the needs of the household or family business.[8] Among those types of servants there were the milkmaid and the groom, the nurse and the shepherd boy, the apprentice and the shop-girl, the cook and the coachman, the governess and the private tutor. Servants' roles within the family, and their social interactions with other members of the household, were greatly dependant on their job and status. On the issue of inclusion and exclusion, servants' positions varied widely. On the one hand, servants could be as tightly integrated into the family as the farm-maid, who had her meals with the family, sharing the same table, who received a dowry at marriage like a daughter and who was buried in the family's grave in the case of premature death. On the other hand, domestics could be as excluded as the urban maid, who had to use a separate servants' staircase, who was considered the 'enemy in the house' and whose oppressed situation was so bleak that she would rather terminate her life by jumping out of the window.[9]

The heterogeneity of family forms in Europe with regard to domestics was not simply a consequence of the different types of servants employed, but also whether servants were employed at all. The institution of service is typical of Europe – however, it did not exist everywhere in Europe, or had not been maintained into the nineteenth and twentieth centuries. In the Mediterranean, the position of maids had been viewed more critically than in Central or Northern Europe, due to the special appreciation of virginity.[10] Thus in many rural parts of the Mediterranean female service was all but nonexistent.[11] In areas dominated by the latifundium, neither male nor female servants were employed. Also, however, north of the Alps there were many agrarian regions in which servants were uncommon.[12] Generally this applied to wine-growing areas. Family forms including servants were especially widespread where cattle-raising was important.[13] There was an marked difference between artisan households in Northwestern and Central Europe. Well before 1800 journeymen in England and parts of Northern France no longer lived with their master, but rather had families of their own. At the same time, a master's household in Central Europe was still characterised by unmarried journeymen. These very different patterns of artisan households continued to exist well into the industrial age, causing different patterns of reproduction, thus having an impact on population growth.[14] In urban society – as opposed to rural society – it was possible to distinguish between vocational and domestic personnel.[15] Thus different family forms – with or without servants – reflected distinct ways of organising domestic work, contingent on social strata. Although family forms varied by social strata, upper-class families were also linked to different strata, through the domestic servants they employed. This brief outline illustrates how servants were an important factor in the heterogeneity of the European family. However, it also raises awareness of similar relations, which will be summarised in the following three rather general theses:

1. As the family was a unit of production, whose needs affected and shaped the family, there was an ample variety of family forms and great differences between them. Put differently, it was the specific conditions of different working environments that produced the crucial common features, which are the essential criteria for more general typologies. Even though this typology ignores certain aspects, it makes sense to distinguish between, for example, the 'peasant family', the 'agricultural labour family', the 'artisan family', the 'working-class family', the 'public servant family'.[16] The concept of the recently oft-quoted 'proto-industrial family' also fits into this context — on a more specialised level, however, comparable to the 'miner family'.[17]

2. The basic types of the family, which were moulded by the respective occupational milieux, were, however, subject to regional differentiation, especially among rural families. Distinct natural environments, resulting in different ways of organising work, are an important factor explaining regional differentiation. As a secondary factor, the so-called 'ecotypes' accounted for much of the heterogeneity of European family forms.[18] The distribution of these regional types rarely corresponded to ethnic or national units.

3. In Europe, the process of dissociation of the family from the organisation of work and production started very early. However, it was only in the nineteenth and twentieth centuries that the family underwent radical change. The initially dominant role of the family as a unit of production all but disappeared. The transition to individual wage labour was a crucial precondition for the recent tendencies towards convergence of the European family's formal structure.

Studies on the family in non-European countries do not mention that the family was similarly differentiated by occupational milieux. Perhaps this is due to the researchers' predilections and manners of approach, in which the social organisation of work is of lesser importance. It is, however, more probable that this factor only affected the patterns of family forms to a lesser degree because of the more decisive impact of other factors. It can be derived from studies on non-European family forms in the nineteenth and twentieth centuries that the structure of the family there was determined by factors very different from the ones at work in Europe.[19] In order to raise awareness of these differences, methods and categories of anthropology shall be applied to the European family. Some examples of such differences between the European and the non-European family will be examined to highlight the commonalities of the European family.

Strict marriage rules, such as anthropologists generally view as an important criterion of family types, did not exist in nineteenth- and twentieth-century Europe.[20] There were no endogamous rules, such as existed in Oriental societies. These rules implied that men preferred or were required to marry the daughter of their father's brother.[21] Exogamous rules were also not in place, as opposed to, for example, China, where it was not permitted to marry someone of the same last name, because it was suspected that they could be of common ancestry.[22] There were no patterns of widows being passed on to be remarried within the husband's family, which was common in many African and Oriental societies, for example, as levirate.[23] It was only in the Balkans where similar tendencies existed.[24] Among some of the tribes in Albania, Montenegro and parts of Serbia, it was strictly prohibited to marry someone, whose family celebrated the same 'slava' (i.e., who worshipped the same patron saint), for it was taken as an indication of common patrilinear descent. The practice of levirate and similar practices concerning a widow's remarriages within the agnatic family could also be found there. With respect to these social phenomena the Balkans and parts of Eastern Europe were an exception to the 'European rule'. In Europe, there did not exist any obligation to marry a certain relative. Modern European societies were clearly not endogamous. Local endogamy, endogamy within an occupational group or estate, which were common in Europe, are inherently different from rules based on kinship; thus they belong to a different realm. However, European societies were not clearly exogamous either. There were no rules precluding marriages within a certain group of kin or common descent. Incestuous relations were prohibited by the church or by law;[25] however, these rules applied to single related individuals, not to entire groups of common descent. These kinds of kinship had not existed in Europe for a long time. This notion is of crucial importance, ranging way beyond the rules of descent. In nineteenth- and twentieth-century Europe the idea that common descent implied common obligations was totally absent. Ancestral worship or offering to the dead was not common, unlike in China or India.[26] Defending the group's 'honour' in vendettas, which was common in some parts of the Orient or Caucasus, had long been abolished.[27] Again it was the Balkans which were the exception. It was there that vendettas were waged between groups of common descent and, furthermore, strictly patrilinear groups were obliged to practise the common cult of their ancestors – in the guise of Christian rites, however.[28] These patrilinear groups are an equivalent to the patrilinearily structured 'joint families' outside of Europe.[29] Such sorts of extended families could also be found in Europe, although only in the southeastern and eastern parts.[30] In other parts of Europe, where these 'joint families' existed, they did not comply to the notion of mutual assistance due to common descent.[31] On the whole, the notion of kinship did not dominate the individual to such an extent as was common in non-European societies. This was probably a consequence of the specifically European trend towards individualisation, which also affected the constitution of the family.

In nineteenth- and twentieth-century Europe marriage patterns were not geared towards copious offspring. Thus early marriages, polygyny or the right of divorce in case of female infertility were not common. However, in most non-European societies surviving male descendants were necessary for religious reasons. Therefore, there was an innate trend towards high levels of fertility, at times when infant mortality was also high. Consequently girls were married to their husbands shortly after they reached sexual maturity.[32] Against this backdrop, the famous 'European marriage pattern' (characterised by a relatively old age at marriage – especially of women) is very exceptional.[33] Many characteristic features of European family structures contributed to this marriage pattern, namely, less complex family forms, adolescents leaving home to work as servants in other households, a more or less balanced male and female role concerning work within the household, great importance of youth groups as opposed to the family, relative maturity and economic independence at marriage.[34] However, the 'European marriage pattern' did not apply to the whole of Europe. 'Non-European' patterns of marriage existed east of the line stretching from St Petersburg to Trieste. Again it was the Balkans where the marriage pattern was most clearly opposed to the common 'European' one.

In the Balkans, strict rules governed the choice of partner from within or without groups of kin. Complex systems of kinship ensured solidarity. There were rules governing with whom the newly-wed had to reside, and marriage patterns ensured the continuity of agnatic groups. All of this contributed to a framework of family structures which allowed little leeway for external factors. Apparently the relative homogeneity of family forms outside of Europe was a consequence of these strict rules and systems. Conversely, the relative heterogeneity of family forms within Europe may be regarded as a result of the absence of these same rules. The religious beliefs that shaped the structure of the family in other parts of the world were also missing.[35]

My thesis about what brought about the specific 'European marriage pattern' is as follows. One of the decisive preconditions of the special European development towards more heterogeneous family forms can be attributed to Christianity.[36] As opposed to Jewish religion from which it originated, Christianity was based on conversion, not on descent. Accordingly, descent was irrelevant for salvation, thus the practice of cult was not based on kinship. When religious offices were passed on to the next generation, principles of descent were consciously ignored.[37] Spiritual fathers not only came to complement but in some cases even to replace one's own father.[38] In these respects, Christianity can be regarded as hostile towards descent. Such an assertion appears irreconcilable with the common image of the old European social order ruled by consanguinity. These notions clearly require modification, for Christianity contributed strongly to the weakening of rigid ties of descent. This breakup of complex structures of descent affected different regions at different times throughout European history, varying in its extent. On the whole, it represented an effective dynamic force in the development of European family forms.

This very broad thesis requires limitations and additions. Christianity tolerated preexisting marriage rules and systems of kinship, for example, patrilinear endogamy, which was practised in some Oriental churches.[39] However, it was not legitimated by religious backing. Yet in some regions these practices were at times sanctified: in Ethiopia, Armenia and in parts of the Balkans.[40] The 'slava-festival', a Christianised ceremony in the honour of the ancestors, provides an obvious example of such a development.[41] It must be stressed that Christianity did not only influence family structures by its thrust towards the dissolution of groups of descent. Christianity also accounts for other major factors that made an impact on the development of the European family. I will provide three cases to illustrate this thesis: schools founded by the church were one of the preconditions for mass literacy and concomitant individualisation, which affected first Protestant Europe, then in a later phase the Catholic countries, and eventually, though less thoroughly, the Orthodox regions. Since men and women were considered equals in the laymen's cult this may also have influenced gender roles within the household. The relative insignificance of domestic cult – when compared to worship involving a congregation – can be regarded as a precondition conducive to the takeover of some social functions of the family by other social entities outside the sphere of religion. Even if Christian faith shaped the family in various other respects, Christianity's specific hostility towards bonds of descent appears preeminent. As a consequence, nonreligious factors were able to exert strong influence on the special European development of the family.

Since it is impossible to discuss these nonreligious factors and their impact on the positive development of the family in this article adequately, I shall mention only two conditions regarding the social organisation of work. The respective patterns of the manorial system strongly shaped rural family forms. The extension of the Frankish agrarian system spread specifically 'European' patterns of lifestyle well into Eastern Central Europe, such as the 'life-cycle servants', peasants' retirement (*Ausgedinge*) or sole inheritance.[42] Although these customs arose against the backdrop of a Christian attitude towards descent, they were not primarily generated through religion. Moreover, these customs can be used as crucial criteria to distinguish between the manifold variants of peasant family forms. The impact of these patterns on urban family forms will be briefly discussed, in terms of the guilds.[43] The special family form of the artisan family was to some extent shaped by the customs of apprenticeship. Furthermore, its existence was regulated by the guild on the basis of economic criteria, namely, a permission to marry was only given if it was expected that the market could sustain yet another producer's output. Both of these examples show the longevity of the different types of the European family, which were adapted to the needs of the organisation of work. These trends existed from their inception in the Middle Ages to well throughout the nineteenth and twentieth centuries.

The origin of the basic types of family business date back to the Middle Ages. This also applies to tendencies to overcome this way of organising work by replacing it with individual wage labour. The beginning of such processes could be observed in mining and construction.[44] In the nineteenth and twentieth centuries individual wage labour became an all but ubiquitous phenomenon.[45] Urbanisation, bureaucratisation, industrialisation, as well as other processes of modernisation, generated a situation in which earning one's living increasingly took place outside of the family. Hence it was other familial functions which became more decisive for a family's way of life. Subsequently new patterns of the family began to arise. The 'modern family cycle', which originated in the twentieth century, appears to be a common European pattern.

In the 1950s and 1960s sociologists created an idealtype of the 'modern family cycle', which can be described as follows. After marriage and establishing a neolocal home, the couple arrive at the first phase of the cycle, which can be regarded as a 'phase of preparation and organisation', before the birth of their first child. This is followed by the phase of a 'primary socialisation family' with children of preschool age; then subsequently by the phase of 'family with preadolescent children'; after that by the phase of a 'family with adolescent children'. After the last child leaves home, the parents arrive at the last phase of the cycle, namely, the 'phase of contraction' or 'postparental companionship', eventually even as a lone widow or widower in the 'phase of old age'.[46] This model is based on the results of a thorough transformation of society through various processes of modernisation.

In the sphere of work the model of the 'modern family cycle' is based on the ubiquitous spread of individual wage labour – certainly with wages high enough to pay for neolocal residency and a family. Throughout a long phase of transition in the nineteenth and twentieth century, wages were in many cases not sufficient for sustaining both housing and a family. As the model suggests at least two children already in the second phase, it is implicitly based on the idea of the husband as the single breadwinner.

The model's description of the family's reproductive function derives from the conception that the process of 'demographic transition' has already taken effect. Pregnancy can be planned; the number of children is reduced to two. The death of infants is not expected, the children are of similar age, facilitating a safe and simultaneous passage through the phases of preadolescence and adolescence.

Socialisation is considered the crucial function in the course of the family cycle. Children are at the centre of a family's life. The phases of children's life determine the needs and duties of the family. Interestingly enough, socialisation within the family is opposed to socialisation through schooling, which consequently marks another phase. Accordingly, it is implicitly expected that there is mandatory schooling for all children.

The last two phases of the cycle are implicitly based on two preconditions which have only been achieved recently. Due to risen life expectancy and earlier marriages, people may look forward to living together as a couple or alone as a widowed person for quite some time, even after all of their children have left home. Sufficiently high pensions enable the elderly to maintain their own households, even after they have stopped working. In a similar way as in the case of mandatory schooling, it is again the interference of the state which strongly influences the family cycle, in this case by legally prescribed pensions. A standardisation of the courses of life is a main goal of state intervention, and is thus also reflected in the family cycle.

The model of the 'modern family cycle' may have been an adequate description of social realities in the 1950s and 1960s. However, it cannot be expected to describe a basic new stable form of familial structure in Europe which is a result of the processes of modernisation and industrialisation. Dynamic processes of social change have rapidly generated new diversity.[47]

Even the model's point of departure has become questionable during the last few decades: leaving the parent's family, taking up neolocal residency and committing to marriage no longer pertain to one single process. After leaving home, many youngsters – whether male or female – live in their own households or share a flat with one permanent partner or at times changing partners or with a group of people. Initially flatsharing was viewed as an ephemeral new lifestyle typical of young people; however, it has become a permanent phenomenon. Marriage and starting a family have come to be only one option among others after leaving the parental household.

It has become increasingly difficult to distinguish between formally married couples and cohabiting couples. Cohabitation can involve various degrees of commitment, for example sharing a common flat, a common purse, and so on. Therefore, it is very difficult to establish exact statistical data about cohabiting couples. However, a rough approximation can be provided which reflects regional differences. In Europe, cohabitation is more widespread in the North than in the South. It is similarly difficult to estimate the number of people who remain single throughout their whole lives. The models of the family cycle from the 1950s and 1960s does not include this option, which is becoming ever more relevant. Given that the phases which include being single, cohabitation and formal marriage no longer necessarily follow this order, it is impossible to establish a new model of a family cycle. In all European countries a rising number of divorcées take up residence in more or less permanent single-person households. Divorce is not included in the model of the family cycle or is considered as an exception from the normal path, although it was already a common phenomenon at the time when the model was proposed. By now, it has become impossible to ignore this factor with regard to family forms.

Demographic transition resulted in the emergence of a 'normal family', with the number of children per family limited to two. However, the process of change did not stop thereafter. The percentage of married couples with just one child or no children at all has risen steeply in most European countries during the last few decades. These family forms are qualitatively different from larger families. In families with only one child, no relations to siblings can be established. If there are no children at all, the family does not fulfil its major function, namely, the socialisation of children. Moreover, a rising number of births out of wedlock in many European countries is no longer an indication of societal problems, as it was in the past. Nowadays, 'new illegitimacy' simply is a consequence of the decline of marriage as an institution. The social situation of children born out of wedlock is generally hardly different from that of legitimate children. However, the situation of the so-called 'new stepchildren' – after their divorced parents' remarriage – involves a more complex relationship between parents and siblings.

The model of the 'modern family cycle' must be modified to fit recent developments. Not only do families have fewer children, but the phase of bearing and raising children is often postponed. Many women continue to pursue a career after their wedding, deferring the bearing of children to a later stage. The increasing participation of women in the labour market is an important variable affecting the phases of the family cycle. It also affects children's socialisation. Again, there is a marked difference in the level of women's employment between the North and the South of Europe, as a consequence of traditional patterns.[48] The large proportion of women working outside their homes in Eastern Europe is a result of more recent communist policies.

The final phases of the 'modern family cycle' have not been subject to major change, except for the fact that they last longer and are achieved more frequently. 'Empty-nest' families – virtually unknown in the nineteenth century – have become a widespread phenomenon in European societies in recent decades.[49] As life expectancy has risen by ten to twelve years since the 1950s, the average duration of marriages has also increased. Because the life expectancy of women has become much higher everywhere, the number of widows' single households is growing. As most families in modern Europe are neolocal, rising life expectancy did not bring about an increasing number of extended families, which might include three or four generations. Families consisting of four generations, which can still be found in some rural areas, are a rare and negligible phenomenon. More importantly, there are increasingly tight relationships between the generations, even though they live separately. Monetary or in-kind transfers from grandparents to their grandchildren – a very recent phenomenon in European history – illustrate these changes. Yet, growing regional mobility militates against the rise of such family relations across households.

With an eye solely on statistics, the development of the European family could be cynically portrayed as converging to a single-person household. Indeed, in many European metropoles this type already accounts for more than 50 percent of the total number of households.[50] However, single households can involve the most different of lifestyles and family relations. This includes youngsters who have left home, without having yet started a relationship; 'singles' proper, who consciously avoid any firm relationship; male or female divorcées without children; and widows and widowers. All differences considered, this development can be understood as a certain trend towards individualisation. This trend has become visible within families, too. Increasingly individuals claim personal spaces within a common dwelling. This is only conceivable as a result of drastic housing improvements. People have much more space at their disposal – even having a second flat has become a mass phenomenon in Western industrialised nations.

Generally, there has been a trend towards shrinking household size. However, the combination of people living together as a family has become more dissimilar. The sequence of ways of living together has become ever more disparate. If family relations across households are included, the picture becomes even more diverse. The homogeneous pattern of the European family as reflected in the concept of the 'modern family cycle', which may have adequately described the average family's situation in the 1950s and 1960s, has been dissolved.

In order to characterise the 'European family', it may be more important to consider the plurality of lifestyles, the various common activities in the family and the different ways of dealing with common problems –

rather than simply enumerating the various combinations of people form-ing a 'family'. The functions of the family have been reduced to leisure times, to maintaining a common household, and – if there are any – to the raising of children. The possibilities of spending free time individually or together as a family have increased greatly. Surveys about how families spend their free time suggest that the members of the same families engage in very different activities – involving particular kinds of inter-actions with other members of the family.[51] Rather than uniformity, diversity seems to be the rule among families at times of leisure. This similarly applies to lifestyles – for example, how homes are decorated. Given the decline of traditions, the distribution of domestic chores has also become more diverse – both among the generations and between the sexes. There is a strong trend towards greater choice between different ways of life. These choices, however, always imply the decision between living with a family or being alone. The thrust towards individualisation does not spare the internal relations within the family.

As a conclusion, the basic ideas of my initial thesis shall be reconsid-ered within the greater perspective of the process of individualisation. Historians can only make certain statements about the family in the European past, basically limited to the size, the structure and the func-tions of the family. Considering these aspects, there seems to have been a great process of convergence in the twentieth century, followed by signs of new diversity. Yet, this is not the whole of the picture. Rigid rules regulated the roles of family members, their mutual relations and their living together as a family in the various family forms of the past. Conversely, the apparently homogeneous family forms of the latter half of the twentieth century allow much more flexibility. The most obvious example is the decline of traditional gender roles. If all this is taken into account, the process towards a greater variety of family forms appears as a linear, and moreover, an irreversible one. It is no longer limited to Europe and the Western civilisation. However, its origins can be traced back in European history even beyond the processes of industrialisation and modernisation.

NOTES

1. R. Koselleck, *Vergangene Zukunft: Zur Semantik geschichtlicher Zeiten*, Frankfurt am Main, 1979; W. Schulze, *Einführung in die Neuere Geschichte*, Stuttgart, 1987, p. 18.

2. R. König, 'Soziologie der Familie', in *Handbuch der empirischen Sozialforschung vol. 7. Familie, Alter*, ed. R. König, Stuttgart, 1976, pp. 1–217, p. 115; following P.C. Glick, 'The Life Cycle of the Family', *Marriage and Family Living* 17 (1955), pp. 3–9.

3. P. Laslett, 'Characteristics of the Western Family Considered over Time', in *Family Life and Illicit Love in Earlier Generations*, ed. P. Laslett, Cambridge, 1977, pp. 12–49, p. 34; P. Laslett, 'Family and Household as Work Group and Kin Group: Areas of Traditional Europe Compared', in *Family Forms in Historic Europe*, ed. R. Wall, J. Robin and P. Laslett, Cambridge, 1983, pp. 513–64, p. 534; J. Hajnal, 'Two Kinds of Pre-industrial Household Formation', in *Family Forms in Historic Europe*, eds R. Wall, J. Robin and P. Laslett, Cambridge, 1983, pp. 65–104, p. 95; M. Mitterauer, 'Europäische Familienformen im interkulturellen Vergleich', in *Historisch-anthropologische Familienforschung: Fragestellungen und Zugangsweisen*, ed. M. Mitterauer, Vienna, 1990, pp. 25–40, p. 26.

4. L. Kuchenbuch, *Bäuerliche Gesellschaft und Klosterherrschaft im 9. Jahrhundert*, Wiesbaden, 1978, p. 78; G. Duby, *Rural Economy and Country Life*, London, 1968, p. 221; C. J. Hammer jr., 'Family and "familia" in early-medieval Bavaria', in *Family Forms in Historic Europe*, ed. R. Wall, J. Robin and P. Laslett, Cambridge, 1983, pp. 217–48, p. 246; M. Mitterauer, 'Gesindedienst und Jugendphase im europäischen Vergleich', *Geschichte und Gesellschaft* 11 (1985), pp. 177–204, p. 197.

5. A. Kußmaul, *Servants in Husbandry in Early Modern England*, Cambridge, 1981, p. 124; M. Mitterauer, 'Auswirkungen der Agrarrevolution auf die bäuerliche Familienstruktur in Österreich', in *Historische Familienforschung*, ed. M. Mitterauer and R. Sieder, Frankfurt am Main, 1982, pp. 241–70, p. 255.

6. R. Engelsing, 'Das häusliche Personal in der Epoche der Industrialisierung', in R. Engelsing, *Zur Sozialgeschichte deutscher Mittel- und Unterschichten (Kritische Studien zur Geschichtswissenschaft 4)*, Göttingen, 1973, pp. 225–61, pp. 235, 239, 249.

7. M. Mitterauer, 'Auswirkungen von Urbanisierung und Frühindustrialisierung auf die Familienverfassung an Beispielen des österreichischen Raums', in *Sozialgeschichte der Familie in der Neuzeit Europas*, ed. W. Conze, Stuttgart, 1976, pp. 53–146, p. 112; J. Ehmer, *Familienstruktur und Arbeitsorganisation im frühindustriellen Wien*, Vienna, 1980, p. 78; J. Ehmer, *Heiratsverhalten, Sozialstruktur, ökonomischer Wandel. England und Mitteleuropa in der Formationsperiode des Kapitalismus*, Göttingen, 1991, p. 199.

8. Engelsing, 'Das häusliche Personal', p. 225; Mitterauer, 'Gesindedienst', p. 177; R. Sieder, *Sozialgeschichte der Familie*, Frankfurt am Main, 1987, p. 50.

9. L. Stone, *The Family, Sex and Marriage in England 1500–1800*, London, 1977, p. 27; L. Fairchilds, *Domestic Enemies: Servants & Their Masters in Old Regime France*, Baltimore, London, 1984; J.-L. Flandrin, *Familles: Parenté, maison, sexualité dans l'ancienne societé*, Paris, 1984, p. 138; A. Arru, 'I servi e le serve ', *Quaderni storici* NS

68 (1988), pp. 341–572, p. 341; H. Rosenbaum, *Formen der Familie: Untersuchungen zum Zusammenhang von Familienverhältnissen, Sozialstruktur und sozialem Wandel in der deutschen Gesellschaft des 19. Jahrhunderts*, Frankfurt am Main, 1982, pp. 102, 367; Sieder, *Sozialgeschichte*, p. 48; H. Müller, *Dienstbare Geister: Lebens- und Arbeitswelt städtischer Dienstboten (Schriften des Museums für Deutsche Volkskunde, Berlin 5)*, Berlin, 1981, p. 189; M. Tichy, *Alltag und Traum, Leben und Lektüre der Dienstmädchen im Wien der Jahrhundertwende (Kulturstudien 3)*, Vienna, 1984, p. 28; T. Weber, ed. *Mägde, Lebenserinnerungen an die Dienstbotenzeit bei Bauern*, Vienna, 1985, p. 12; N. Ortmayr, ed. *Knechte: Autobiographische Dokumente und sozialhistorische Skizzen*, Vienna, 1992, p. 328.

10. J. Schneider, 'Of Vigilance and Virgins', Ethnology 9 (1971), pp. 1–24; J.G. Peristiany, 'Introduction', in *Mediterranean Family Structures*, ed. J.G. Peristiany, Cambridge, 1976, pp. 1–26, p. 12; J. Davis, *People of the Mediterranean: An Essay in Comparative Social Anthropology*, London, 1977, p. 100.

11. M. Barbagli, *Sotto lo stesso tetto: Mutamenti della famiglia in Italia dal XV al XX secolo*, Bologna, 1984, p. 236; M. Barbagli, 'Three Household Formation Systems in Eighteenth and Nineteenth-Century Italy', in *The Family in Italy from Antiquity to the Present*, ed. D.J. Kertzer and R.P. Saller, New Haven, London, 1991, pp. 250–70, pp. 255, 267.

12. A. Fitz, *Familie und Frühindustrialisierung in Vorarlberg*, Dornbirn, 1985, p. 139; Ehmer, *Heiratsverhalten*, p. 133; A. Tanner, *Spulen–Weben–Spinne: Die Industrialisierung in Appenzell – Außerrhoden*, Zurich, 1982, p. 222; R. Braun, *Das ausgehende Ancien Régime in der Schweiz*, Göttingen, Zurich, 1984, p. 51; U. Pfister, 'Haushalt und Familie auf der Zürcher Landschaft des Ancien régime', in *Schweiz im Wandel: Studien zur neueren Gesellschaftsgeschichte (Festschrift für Rudolf Braun zum 60. Geburtstag)*, ed. S. Brändli et al., Basle, Frankfurt am Main, 1990, pp. 19–42, p. 41.

13. M. Mitterauer, 'Formen ländlicher Familienwirtschaft', in *Familie und Arbeitsorganisation in ländlichen Gesellschaften*, ed. J. Ehmer and M. Mitterauer, Vienna, 1986, pp. 185–324, p. 190; M. Mitterauer, 'Peasant and Non-Peasant Family Forms in Relation to the Physical Environment and the Local Economy', *Journal of Family History* 17 (1992), pp. 139–60, p. 144.

14. Ehmer, *Heiratsverhalten*, pp. 19, 163, 173, 185, 225, 233.

15. Mitterauer, 'Auswirkungen von Urbanisierung', p. 112.

16. Rosenbaum, Formen der Familie, pp. 47, 121, 251, 381; Sieder, *Sozialgeschichte*, pp. 12, 103, 146; M. Segalen, *Sociologie de la famille*, Paris, 1981, pp. 190, 195, 197; P. Melograni, ed., *La famiglia Italiana dall'ottocento a oggi*, Rome, 1988, pp. 3, 61.

17. Rosenbaum, *Formen der Familie*, p. 189; Sieder, Sozialgeschichte, p. 73; following H. Medick, 'Die proto-industrielle Familienwirtschaft', in *Industrialisierung vor der Industrialisierung*, ed. P. Kriedte et al., Göttingen, 1977, pp. 90–154, p. 90. Cf. Mitterauer, 'Peasant and Non-Peasant Family Forms', p. 154.

18. O. Löfgren, 'Peasant Ecotypes: Problems in the Comparative Study of Ecological Adaption', *Ethnologia Scandinavica* 6 (1976), pp. 100–29, p. 100; Mitterauer, 'Formen ländlicher Familienwirtschaft', p. 185.

19. W.J. Goode, *World Revolution and Family Patterns*, Glencoe, 1963; J. Goody, *The Oriental, the Ancient and the Primitive: Systems of Marriage and the Family in the Preindustrial Societies of Eurasia*, Cambridge, 1990.

20. C. Lévy-Strauss, *Les structures élémentaires de la parenté*, Paris, 1949, p. 216; *Segalen, Sociologie de la famille*, p. 80.

21. R. Patai, 'Cousin-Right in Middle Eastern Marriage', in *Readings in Arab Middle Eastern Societies and Cultures*, ed. A.M. Lutfiyya and C.W. Churchill, Paris, 1970, pp. 535–53, p. 535; F. Khuri, 'Parallel Cousin Marriage Reconsidered', *Man* 5 (1970), pp. 597–618, p. 599; G. W. Kressel, 'Prescriptive Patrilateral Parallel Cousin Marriage: the Perspective of the Bride's Father and Brothers', *Ethnology* 25 (1986), pp. 163–80, p. 163; P. Bourdieu, *Entwurf einer Theorie der Praxis*, Frankfurt am Main, 1979, p. 66; E. Todd, *La troisième planète: Structures familiales et systèmes ideologiques*, Paris, 1983, p. 152; P. Guichard, *Structures sociales "orientales" dans l'Espagne musulmane*, Paris, 1977, p. 19; J. Goody, *The Development of the Family and Marriage in Europe*, Cambridge, 1983, p. 10.

22. G. Linck-Kesting, 'China: Geschlechtsreife und Legitimation zur Zeugung', in *Geschlechtsreife und Legitimation zur Zeugung*, ed. E.W. Müller, Freiburg, Munich, 1985, pp. 85–176, p. 128.

23. Goode, *World Revolution*, pp. 199, 161; Goody, *The Oriental*, pp. 120, 152, 206, 352, 379, 476.

24. K. Kaser, *Hirten, Helden, Stammeskämpfer: Ursprünge und Gegenwart des balkanischen Patriarchats*, Vienna, 1992, pp. 245, 252, 267, 272; K. Kaser, 'Ahnenkult und Patriarchalismus auf dem Balkan', *Historische Anthropologie* 1 (1993), pp. 93–122, p. 117; K. Kaser, *Familie und Verwandtschaft auf dem Balkan: Analyse einer untergehenden Kultur*, Vienna, 1995.

25. Summarising Goody, *Development*. Criticisms of Goody's thesis in: *Continuity and Change* 6 (1991), and J. Martin, 'Zur Anthropologie von Heiratsregeln und Besitzübertragung. 10 Jahre nach den Goody-Thesen', *Historische Anthropologie* 1 (1993), pp. 149–62, p. 149.

26. Goody, *The Oriental*, 42; Linck-Kesting, 'Geschlechtsreife', pp. 86, 101, 113; D. Rosenast, 'Strukturen der Reproduktion im Universum des vedischen Kults', in *Geschlechtsreife und Legitimation zur Zeugung*, ed. E.W. Müller, Freiburg, Munich, 1985, pp. 177–212, p. 188.

27. Goode, *World Revolution*, p. 134; Peristiany, 'Introduction', p. 7; E. Sarkisyanz, *Geschichte der orientalischen Völker Rußlands bis 1917*, Munich, 1961, pp. 56, 96, 116.

28. Kaser, *Hirten*, pp. 272, 275; Kaser, 'Ahnenkult und Patriarchalismus', p. 119; M. Durham, *Some Tribal Origins, Laws and Customs of the Balkans*, London, 1928, p. 162; J. Whitaker, 'Familial Roles in the Extended Patrilineal Kin-group in Northern Albania', in *Mediterranean Family Structures*, ed. J.G. Peristiany, Cambridge, 1976, pp. 195–203, p. 198; W. Peinsipp, *Das Volk der Shkypetaren: Geschichte, Gesellschafts- und Verhaltensordnung. Ein Beitrag zur Rechtsarchäologie und zur soziologischen Anthropologie des Balkan*, Vienna, 1985, p. 149; J.K. Campbell, *Honour, Family and Patronage*, Oxford, 1964, p. 193.

29. R. Wheaton, 'Family and Kinship in Western Europe. The Problem of the Joint Family Household', *Journal of Interdisciplinary History* 4 (1975), pp. 601–28, p. 625.

30. M. Mitterauer and A. Kagan, 'Russian and Central European Family Structures: A Comparative View', *Journal of Family History* 7 (1982), pp. 103–31, p. 127; M. Mit-

terauer, 'Komplexe Familienformen in sozialhistorischer Sicht', in M. Mitterauer, *Historisch-anthropologische Familienforschung. Fragestellungen und Zugangsweisen*, Vienna, 1990, pp. 87–130, pp. 102, 118; Kaser, Hirten, p. 227.

31. Mitterauer, 'Komplexe Familienformen', pp. 109, 112, 115, 117.

32. E.g. in India; see Goody, *The Oriental*, p. 207.

33. J. Hajnal, 'European Marriage Patterns in Perspective', in *Population in History: Essays in Historical Demography*, ed. D.V. Glass and D.E.C. Eversley, London, 1965, pp. 101–43; J. Hajnal, 'Two kinds', p. 69; Laslett, 'Characteristics', p. 12.

34. Hajnal, 'Two kinds', p. 69; Laslett, 'Characteristics', p. 13; M. Mitterauer, *A History of Youth*, Cambridge, 1993, pp. 20, 154; Mitterauer, 'Gesindedienst', p. 198; M. Mitterauer, 'Geschlechtsspezifische Arbeitsteilung und Geschlechterrollen in ländlichen Gesellschaften Mitteleuropas', in M. Mitterauer, *Familie und Arbeitsteilung: Historisch vergleichende Studien*, Vienna, 1992, p. 141.

35. M. Mitterauer, 'Die Toten und die Lebenden. Jenseitsvorstellungen und Sozialentwicklung', *Beiträge zur historischen Sozialkunde* 21 (1991), pp. 99–106.

36. Mitterauer, 'Europäische Familienformen im interkulturellen Vergleich', p. 25.

37. M. Mitterauer, 'Christentum und Endogamie', in *Historisch-anthropologische Familienforschung: Fragestellungen und Zugangsweisen*, ed. M. Mitterauer, Vienna, 1990, pp. 41–86, pp. 62, 76.

38. M. Mitterauer, *Ahnen und Heilige: Namengebung in der europäischen Geschichte*, Munich, 1993, pp. 115, 121, 148, 153, 175.

39. Patai, 'Cousin-Right', p. 551; Khuri, 'Parallel Cousin Marriage Reconsidered', p. 599, R. Cresswell, 'Lineage Endogamy among Maronite Mountaineers', in *Mediterranean Family Structures*, ed. J.G. Peristiany, Cambridge, 1976, pp. 101–14, p. 101.

40. L.L. Luzbetak, *Marriage and the family in Caucasia (Studia instituti Anthropos)*, Vienna, 1951, p. 50; Kaser, 'Ahnenkult'.

41. M. Mitterauer, 'Ein archaisches Relikt? Die Balkanfamilie in Diskussion', *Balkanistic Forum* 2 (1995), pp. 15–32.

42. W. Rösener, *Die Bauern in der europäischen Geschichte*, Munich, 1993, pp. 53–8; W. Rösener, *Bauern im Mittelalter*, Munich, 1985, pp. 177, 185, 197; Kuchenbuch, *Bäuerliche Gesellschaft*, p. 78; Mitterauer, 'Gesindedienst', p. 197.

43. M. Mitterauer, 'Familie und Arbeitsorganisation in städtischen Gesellschaften', in M. Mitterauer, *Familie und Arbeitsteilung: Historisch vergleichende Studien*, Vienna, 1992, pp. 256–300, p. 283, Ehmer, *Heiratsverhalten*, p. 159, Rosenbaum, *Formen der Familie*, pp. 128, 145, 175; Sieder, *Sozialgeschichte der Familie*, p. 103.

44. Mitterauer, 'Auswirkungen', p. 111.

45. Rosenbaum, *Formen der Familie*, pp. 378, 381, 470, 447; Sieder, *Sozialgeschichte*, pp. 146, 282.

46. C. Mühlfeld, *Familiensoziologie: Eine systematische Einführung*, Frankfurt am Main, 1976, pp. 147–54. A table with different phase models can be found in König, *Familie*, p. 124. See also Segalen, *Sociologie de la famille*, p. 168, with interesting criticisms of the family cycle approach.

47. Sieder, *Sozialgeschichte*, p. 243; K. Boh, 'European Family Life Patterns – a Reappraisal', in *Changing Patterns of European Family Life: A Comparative Analysis of 14 European Countries*, ed. Katja Boh et al., London, New York, 1989, pp. 265–96; ed. K. Lüscher et al., *Die 'postmoderne' Familie. Familiale Strategien und Familienpolitik in einer Übergangszeit*, Konstanz, 1988; R. Nave-Herz and M. Markefka, eds, *Handbuch der Familien- und Jugendforschung*, Vol. 1: *Familienforschung*, Neuwied, Frankfurt, 1989, especially pp. 211–40, 361–432.

48. M. Bak, 'Introduction', in *Changing Patterns of European Family Life: A Comparative Analysis of 14 European Countries*, ed. K. Boh et al., London, New York, 1989, pp. 1–16, p. 8.

49. J. Ehmer, *Sozialgeschichte des Alters*, Frankfurt am Main, 1990, p. 187.

50. In Berlin the 50 percent threshold was surpassed in the 1970s: W.H. Hubbard, *Familiengeschichte, Materialien zur deutschen Familie seit dem Ende des 18. Jahrhunderts*, Munich, 1983, p. 126.

51. M. Mitterauer, '"Single" oder Familienmensch. Zu Entwicklungstendenzen der Freizeitgestaltung', in M. Mitterauer, *Familie und Arbeitsteilung. Historisch vergleichende Studien*, Vienna, 1992, pp. 333–55.

Bibliography

Arru, A. 'I servi e le serve', *Quaderni storici* NS 68 (1988), pp. 341–572.

Bak, M. 'Introduction', in *Changing Patterns of European Family Life: A Comparative Analysis of 14 European Countries*, ed. K. Boh et al. London, New York, NY, 1989, pp. 1–16.

Barbagli, M. *Sotto lo stesso tetto: Mutamenti della famiglia in Italia dal XV al XX secolo*. Bologna, 1984.

—— 'Three Household Formation Systems in Eighteenth and Nineteenth-Century Italy', in *The Family in Italy from Antiquity to the Present*, ed. D.J. Kertzer and R.P. Saller. New Haven, CT, London, 1991, pp. 250–70.

Boh, K. 'European Family Life Patterns – a Reappraisal', in *Changing Patterns of European Family Life: A Comparative Analysis of 14 European Countries*, ed. K. Boh et al. London, New York, 1989, pp. 265–96.

Bourdieu, P. *Entwurf einer Theorie der Praxis*. Frankfurt am Main, 1979.

Braun, R. *Das ausgehende Ancien Régime in der Schweiz*. Göttingen, Zurich, 1984.

Campbell, J.K. *Honour, Family and Patronage*. Oxford, 1964.

Cresswell, R. 'Lineage Endogamy among Maronite Mountaineers', in *Mediterranean Family Structures*, ed. J.G. Peristiany. Cambridge: Cambridge University Press, 1976, pp. 101–14.

Davis, J. *People of the Mediterranean: An Essay in Comparative Social Anthropology*. London, 1977.

Duby, G. *Rural Economy and Country Life*. London, 1968.

Durham, M. *Some Tribal Origins, Laws and Customs of the Balkans*. London, 1928.

Ehmer, J. *Familienstruktur und Arbeitsorganisation im frühindustriellen Wien*. Vienna, 1980.

—— *Sozialgeschichte des Alters*. Frankfurt am Main, 1990.

—— *Heiratsverhalten, Sozialstruktur, ökonomischer Wandel: England und Mitteleuropa in der Formationsperiode des Kapitalismus*. Göttingen, 1991.

Engelsing, R. 'Das häusliche Personal in der Epoche der Industrialisierung', in R. Engelsing, *Zur Sozialgeschichte deutscher Mittel- und Unterschichten (Kritische Studien zur Geschichtswissenschaft 4)*. Göttingen, 1973, pp. 225–61.

Fairchilds, L. *Domestic Enemies: Servants & Their Masters in Old Regime France*. Baltimore, MD, London, 1984.

Fitz, A. *Familie und Frühindustrialisierung in Vorarlberg*. Dornbirn, 1985.

Flandrin, J.-L. *Familles: Parenté, maison, sexualité dans l'ancienne societé*. Paris, 1984.

Glick, P.C. 'The Life Cycle of the Family', *Marriage and Family Living* 17 (1955), pp. 3–9.

Goode, W.J. *World Revolution and Family Patterns*. Glencoe, 1963.

Goody, J. *The Development of the Family and Marriage in Europe*. Cambridge: Cambridge University Press, 1983.

—— *The Oriental, the Ancient and the Primitive: Systems of Marriage and the Family in the Pre-industrial Societies of Eurasia*. Cambridge: Cambridge University Press, 1990.

Guichard, P. *Structures sociales 'orientales' dans l'Espagne musulmane*. Paris, 1977.

Hajnal, J. 'European Marriage Patterns in Perspective', in *Population in History: Essays in Historical Demography*, ed. D.V. Glass and D.E.C. Eversley. London, 1965, pp. 101–43.

—— 'Two Kinds of Pre-industrial Household Formation', in *Family Forms in Historic Europe*, ed. R. Wall, J. Robin and P. Laslett. Cambridge: Cambridge University Press, 1983, pp. 65–104.

Hammer, C.J. Jr. 'Family and "Familia" in Early-medieval Bavaria', in *Family Forms in Historic Europe*, ed. R. Wall, J. Robin and P. Laslett. Cambridge: Cambridge University Press, 1983, pp. 217–48.

Hubbard, W.H. *Familiengeschichte, Materialien zur deutschen Familie seit dem Ende des 18. Jahrhunderts*. Munich, 1983.

Kaser, K. *Hirten, Helden, Stammeskämpfer: Ursprünge und Gegenwart des balkanischen Patriarchats*. Vienna, 1992.

—— 'Ahnenkult und Patriarchalismus auf dem Balkan', *Historische Anthropologie* 1 (1993), pp. 93–122.

—— *Familie und Verwandtschaft auf dem Balkan: Analyse einer untergehenden Kultur*. Vienna, 1995.

Khuri, F. 'Parallel Cousin Marriage Reconsidered', *Man* 5 (1970), pp. 597–618.

König, R. 'Soziologie der Familie', in *Handbuch der empirischen Sozialforschung vol. 7. Familie, Alter*, ed. R. König. Stuttgart, 1976, pp. 1–217.

Koselleck, R. *Vergangene Zukunft: Zur Semantik geschichtlicher Zeiten*. Frankfurt am Main, 1979.

Kressel, G.W. 'Prescriptive Patrilateral Parallel Cousin Marriage: the Perspective of the Bride's Father and Brothers', *Ethnology* 25 (1986), pp. 163–80.

Kuchenbuch, L. *Bäuerliche Gesellschaft und Klosterherrschaft im 9. Jahrhundert*. Wiesbaden, 1978.

Kußmaul, A. *Servants in Husbandry in Early Modern England*. Cambridge: Cambridge University Press, 1981.

Laslett, P. 'Characteristics of the Western Family Considered Over Time', in *Family Life and Illicit Love in Earlier Generations*, ed. P. Laslett. Cambridge: Cambridge University Press, 1977, pp. 12–49.

—— 'Family and Household as Work Group and Kin Group: Areas of Traditional Europe Compared', in *Family Forms in Historic Europe*, ed. R. Wall, J. Robin and P. Laslett. Cambridge: Cambridge University Press, 1983, 513–64.

Lévy-Strauss, C. *Les structures élémentaires de la parenté*. Paris, 1949.

Linck-Kesting, G. 'China: Geschlechtsreife und Legitimation zur Zeugung', in *Geschlechtsreife und Legitimation zur Zeugung*, ed. E.W. Müller. Freiburg, Munich, 1985, pp. 85–176.

Löfgren, O. 'Peasant Ecotypes: Problems in the Comparative Study of Ecological Adaption', *Ethnologia Scandinavica* 6 (1976), pp. 100–29.

Lüscher, K. et al. (eds) *Die 'postmoderne' Familie: Familiale Strategien und Familienpolitik in einer Übergangszeit*. Konstanz, 1988.

Luzbetak, L.L. *Marriage and the Family in Caucasia (Studia instituti Anthropos)*. Vienna, 1951.

Martin, J. 'Zur Anthropologie von Heiratsregeln und Besitzübertragung. 10 Jahre nach den Goody-Thesen', *Historische Anthropologie* 1 (1993), pp. 149–62.

Medick, H. 'Die proto-industrielle Familienwirtschaft', in *Industrialisierung vor der Industrialisierung*, ed. P. Kriedte et al. Göttingen, 1977, pp. 90–154.

Melograni, P. (ed.), *La famiglia Italiana dall'ottocento a oggi*. Rome, 1988.

Mitterauer, M. 'Auswirkungen von Urbanisierung und Frühindustrialisierung auf die Familienverfassung an Beispielen des österreichischen Raums', in *Sozialgeschichte der Familie in der Neuzeit Europas*, ed. W. Conze. Stuttgart, 1976, pp. 53–136.

—— 'Auswirkungen der Agrarrevolution auf die bäuerliche Familienstruktur in Österreich', in *Historische Familienforschung*, ed. M. Mitterauer and R. Sieder. Frankfurt am Main, 1982, pp. 241–70.

—— 'Gesindedienst und Jugendphase im europäischen Vergleich', *Geschichte und Gesellschaft* 11 (1985), pp. 177–204.

—— 'Formen ländlicher Familienwirtschaft', in *Familie und Arbeitsorganisation in ländlichen Gesellschaften*, ed. J. Ehmer and M. Mitterauer. Vienna, 1986, pp. 185–324.

—— 'Christentum und Endogamie', in *Historisch-anthropologische Familienforschung. Fragestellungen und Zugangsweisen*, ed. M. Mitterauer. Vienna, 1990, pp. 41–86.

—— 'Europäische Familienformen im interkulturellen Vergleich', in *Historisch-anthropologische Familienforschung: Fragestellungen und Zugangsweisen*, ed. M. Mitterauer. Vienna, 1990, pp. 25–40.

—— 'Komplexe Familienformen in sozialhistorischer Sicht', in M. Mitterauer, *Historisch-anthropologische Familienforschung: Fragestellungen und Zugangsweisen*. Vienna, 1990, pp. 87–130.

—— 'Die Toten und die Lebenden. Jenseitsvorstellungen und Sozialentwicklung', *Beiträge zur historischen Sozialkunde* 21 (1991), pp. 99–106.

—— 'Geschlechtsspezifische Arbeitsteilung und Geschlechterrollen in ländlichen Gesellschaften Mitteleuropas', in M. Mitterauer, *Familie und Arbeitsteilung: Historisch vergleichende Studien*. Vienna, 1992, pp. 58–148.

—— 'Familie und Arbeitsorganisation in städtischen Gesellschaften', in M. Mitterauer, *Familie und Arbeitsteilung: Historisch vergleichende Studien*. Vienna, 1992, pp. 256–300.

—— 'Peasant and Non-Peasant Family Forms in Relation to the Physical Environment and the Local Economy', *Journal of Family History* 17 (1992), pp. 139–60.

—— '"Single" oder Familienmensch. Zu Entwicklungstendenzen der Freizeitgestaltung', in M. Mitterauer, *Familie und Arbeitsteilung: Historisch vergleichende Studien*. Vienna, 1992, pp. 333–55.

—— *A History of Youth*. Cambridge, MA, 1993.

—— *Ahnen und Heilige: Namengebung in der europäischen Geschichte*. Munich, 1993.

—— 'Ein archaisches Relikt? Die Balkanfamilie in Diskussion', *Balkanistic Forum* 2 (1995), pp. 15–32.

Mitterauer, M. and Kagan, A. 'Russian and Central European Family Structures: A Comparative View', *Journal of Family History* 7 (1982), pp. 103–31.

Mühlfeld, C. *Familiensoziologie: Eine systematische Einführung.* Frankfurt am Main, 1976.

Müller, H. *Dienstbare Geister: Lebens- und Arbeitswelt städtischer Dienstboten (Schriften des Museums für Deutsche Volkskunde, Berlin 5).* Berlin, 1981.

Nave-Herz, R. and Markefka, M. (eds). *Handbuch der Familien- und Jugendforschung, Vol. 1: Familienforschung.* Neuwied, Frankfurt, 1989.

Ortmayr, N. (ed.). *Knechte: Autobiographische Dokumente und sozialhistorische Skizzen.* Vienna, 1992.

Patai, R. 'Cousin-Right in Middle Eastern Marriage', in *Readings in Arab Middle Eastern Societies and Cultures*, ed. A.M. Lutfiyya and C.W. Churchill. Paris, 1970, pp. 535–53.

Peinsipp, W. *Das Volk der Shkypetaren: Geschichte, Gesellschafts- und Verhaltensordnung. Ein Beitrag zur Rechtsarchäologie und zur soziologischen Anthropologie des Balkan.* Vienna, 1985.

Peristiany, J.G. 'Introduction', in *Mediterranean Family Structures*, ed. J.G. Peristiany. Cambridge: Cambridge University Press, 1976, pp. 1–26.

Pfister, U. 'Haushalt und Familie auf der Zürcher Landschaft des Ancien régime', in *Schweiz im Wandel: Studien zur neueren Gesellschaftsgeschichte (Festschrift für Rudolf Braun zum 60. Geburtstag)*, ed. S. Brändli et al. Basle, Frankfurt am Main, 1990, pp. 19–42.

Rosenast, D. 'Strukturen der Reproduktion im Universum des vedischen Kults', in *Geschlechtsreife und Legitimation zur Zeugung*, ed. E.W. Müller. Freiburg, Munich, 1985, pp. 177–212.

Rosenbaum, H. *Formen der Familie: Untersuchungen zum Zusammenhang von Familienverhältnissen, Sozialstruktur und sozialem Wandel in der deutschen Gesellschaft des 19. Jahrhunderts.* Frankfurt am Main, 1982.

Rösener, W. *Bauern im Mittelalter.* Munich, 1985.

—— *Die Bauern in der europäischen Geschichte.* Munich, 1993.

Sarkisyanz, E. *Geschichte der orientalischen Völker Rußlands bis 1917.* Munich, 1961.

Schneider, J. 'Of Vigilance and Virgins', *Ethnology* 9 (1971), pp. 1–24.

Schulze, W. *Einführung in die Neuere Geschichte.* Stuttgart, 1987.

Segalen, M. *Sociologie de la famille.* Paris, 1981.

Sieder, R. *Sozialgeschichte der Familie.* Frankfurt am Main, 1987.

Stone, L. *The Family, Sex and Marriage in England 1500–1800.* London, 1977.

Tanner, A. *Spulen-Weben-Spinnen: Die Industrialisierung in Appenzell – Außerrhoden.* Zurich, 1982.

Tichy, M. *Alltag und Traum, Leben und Lektüre der Dienstmädchen im Wien der Jahrhundertwende (Kulturstudien 3).* Vienna, 1984.

Todd, E. *La troisième planète: Structures familiales et systèmes ideologiques.* Paris, 1983.

Weber, T. (ed.). *Mägde, Lebenserinnerungen an die Dienstbotenzeit bei Bauern.* Vienna, 1985.

Wheaton, R. 'Family and Kinship in Western Europe: The Problem of the Joint Family Household', *Journal of Interdisciplinary History* 4 (1975), pp. 601–28.

Whitaker, J. 'Familial Roles in the Extended Patrilineal Kin-group in Northern Albania', in *Mediterranean Family Structures*, ed. J.G. Peristiany. Cambridge: Cambridge University Press, 1976, pp. 195–203.

8

THE HISTORY OF CONSUMPTION IN WESTERN EUROPE IN THE NINETEENTH AND TWENTIETH CENTURIES

Some Questions and Perspectives for Comparative Studies

Heinz-Gerhard Haupt

Looking back over the last forty years, one cannot but be struck by the relatively little attention the field of social history has given to consumption, especially when compared with the importance that analyses of production have had and continue to have. Numerous monographs on the subject have been written recently; but in general studies of the last two centuries, greater emphasis has been placed on the structures and mechanisms of industrial production than on consumer behaviour and venues of consumer activity. Indeed, in none of the broadly conceived studies of nineteenth- and twentieth-century social history has consumption played a significant role. In Eric Hobsbawm's influential studies, consumption remained peripheral, nor did Pierre Léon focus much attention on the phases of consumer history in his *Histoire économique et sociale du monde*. Hartmut Kaelble, in his social history of Western Europe, did not examine the consumer behaviour of Europeans or the creation of a consumer society in Europe with an eye towards understanding their specific role in creating a unified Europe.[1] Social historiography on the national level shows this same void. In Hans-Ulrich Wehler's social history, consumers disappear at the moment when he chronicles the transition to the consumer family from the 'in house' family, in which both consumption and production took place. Jürgen Kocka did not explicitly include consumption among the subjects he set out to treat in the third volume of his study of class formation among nineteenth-century German workers; nor was any attention given to consumption, consumers and forms of consumption in Fernand Braudel and Ernest Labrousse's *Histoire économique et sociale de la France*, in Yves Lequin's *Histoire des français*, or in the more recent *Histoire sociale de la France du 19e siècle* by Christophe Charle. F.M.L. Thomson's *Cambridge Social History of Britain* does deal with consumption – however, only tangentially.[2]

In the last decade or more, a number of social histories have refined our understanding of Europe and its constituent societies in the nineteenth and twentieth centuries, but have paid almost no attention to the history of consumption either in their definition of periods or in their interpretation. Given that consumption has received equally little attention in social histories of individual nations, I think it is fair to say the subject is one that social history as a discipline has largely ignored. Several reasons account for this neglect. It is the natural result of a structural perspective more predisposed to take collective rather than individual processes as its point of departure. In the nineteenth century, historians tended to focus on the historically powerful formative processes of industrialisation and its dominant, dynamic sectors, namely, production and the capital-goods industry. It follows, too, from an implicit or explicit theoretical assumption about modernisation that perceives advanced forms of social organisation as resulting primarily from changes in methods of production rather than in the sphere of consumption.[3] Moreover, consumption has not been a major concern for the theoreticians who have exerted the greatest influence on social historiography. It does not occupy a central place in the work of Karl Marx or Max Weber. For Marx – and in *Das Kapital* in particular – reproduction of capital remained secondary to the production of surplus value. Use value is of primary interest in consumer research, but for Marx it was subordinate to exchange value. And in Marxist political writing, such as Friedrich Engels' essay on housing, changes in the housing sector were presented as intimately linked to social and economic conditions. Conditions of life were presented as subordinate and secondary to the terms dictated by capital. Max Weber's theory of class did attribute importance to those goods that each social group offered in the marketplace and that gave each group a specific role in society, depending on whether that group was able to maintain a monopoly on those goods or not. Yet, in Weber's theory, the act of buying and consuming those goods played no constituent role in the formation of classes. Consumer goods were rather understood as indicators of collective circumstances than as factors in

social relationships. They were rather associated with the old estate concept of 'honour', which could, as a value, either be at odds with class
circumstances or aligned with them and which became increasingly
important in times of slow economic growth.[4] Authors such as Pierre
Bourdieu, who elucidated how strategies of differentiation in the consumer field can be formative of class, have only relatively recently been
receiving a similar kind of attention as theoreticians like Marx and
Weber.[5]

Unlike those masters, who have been the major inspiration behind
research in social history, there are, however, other theoreticians in the
nineteenth century who placed greater emphasis on consumption and did
more to stimulate research on it. Among them were representatives of
subjective value theory, such as Léon Walras, William St. Jevons, and
Carl Menger. They deviated sharply from both the classic theory of economic balance and from Marxist thinking, by placing the satisfaction of
human needs at the centre of their considerations. Menger formulated
this perspective succinctly: 'goods as our discipline defines them are ...
things useful for satisfying human needs and available for that purpose.'[6]
Further, sociologists like Emil Durkheim and, especially, Maurice Halbwachs emphasised the necessities of life over production because of their
greater formative influence on social life. In a 1912 study that compared
conditions in different countries, Maurice Halbwachs tried to use the
'hiérarchie des besoins' within the working class as a key for understanding the formation of classes. After a detailed analysis based on
household budgets, he came to the following rather disheartening conclusion: 'il n'existe pas de séparations dans la classe ouvrière en raison
d'une diversité de niveaux de vie' ('there is no separation by means of
lifestyle inside the working class'). Halbwachs stressed the relatively
minor role that the level of consumption and the standard of living
played in shaping the consciousness of the working class. The mind of
the working man, Halbwachs found, continued to be influenced primarily by his work experience: 'les habitudes contractées à l'usine se sont
révélées trop durables' (the habitus developed at the workplace persist).[7]

Ever since the early nineteenth century, bourgeois reformers sought
possible solutions to the social problems of working-class families not in
analyses of production but in the conduct of working-class family life.
Frédéric Le Play and his followers tried to use household budgets to
plumb the secrets of proletarian domestic economics and to devise sug-
gestions for improving the lot of the working classes. Towards the end of
the nineteenth century, unions and municipal authorities conducted similar studies to define the societal parameters of working-class actions,

demands and negotiations. The value of these studies was by no means lost on contemporary observers. In 1905, Paul Mombert pointed out: 'We can say without exaggeration that the statistical surveys conducted by the unions continue to be one of our most important sources and, often, our only source of quantitative information on the economic and social circumstances of the working-class population.'[8]

Social history in recent decades has neither been significantly influenced by these studies nor by other historical studies on consumer behaviour that have been only peripheral to social history. Among the latter are the anthropological studies undertaken by the French *Annales* School that inquired into changes in human physical characteristics and changes in food habits. As Jacques Revel put it, the focus of these studies was the 'longue durée des habitudes culturelles et des structures bio-économiques'. Social differentiation and cultural interpretation of foods and consumption were not, however, central concerns in these studies.[9] Nor did studies based on an economic theory of household conduct exert any significant influence on sociohistorical analyses, focusing, as they did, on how household behaviour affected the family and the marketplace. Even when these studies did make it possible to reconstruct the different patterns of consumption displayed by individual family members, these patterns did not constitute the central concern of these studies.[10] However, these early forays into the history of consumer behaviour, which examined consumer goods as reflecting consumer desires, longings and projections and saw them primarily as manifestations of an escapist dream world, drew more criticism than approval from social historians. Because these studies tended to drift off into speculation or because they remained in the realm of intellectual history, they have not proved particularly attractive to researchers in social history. What apparently made these studies even more problematic was the fact, that they were based on a premise, that is, the acquisition of consumer goods, which the theories and analyses of the Frankfurt School claimed to be distorting social interpretation.[11]

Three factors helped to make research on consumer issues more appealing: studies done on the history of the early modern period, studies conducted in the United States and studies based on careful observation of the present. Even at times when little work on consumer issues was done, there were still occasional studies on standard of living and food habits, on retail trade and consumer societies. However, the coalescing of such studies into a weak branch of social-historical research is a relatively recent development in Western Europe. Evidence has been found, primarily in the Netherlands and in Great Britain, for example, that even before 1800 societies existed in which consumption shaped social relationships and was not limited exclusively to the upper classes. It therefore comes as no surprise that Fernand Braudel gave considerable attention to food, living quarters and clothing in his study of premodern society in Europe, and called them 'structures of everyday life.'[12]

A second important impulse for research in this field came from the United States. There, the subject became one of pressing interest when modern consumer society matured a good thirty years before it did in Europe and when consumption itself became a central element in the ideology undergirding American society. In this society, the individual's acquisition of consumer goods assumed greater importance than the collective organisation of individual and social life, and the individual's standard of living became the measure of successful social organisation. As the reality and ideology of the consumer society grew ever more prominent in the United States, followed quickly by an awareness of consumer goods as vehicles of cultural values and political organisation, political and scholarly criticism and analysis of the consumer society increased correspondingly.[13]

In Western Europe, the triumph of consumer society, which took place in those post-1950s decades known in France as 'Les Trois Glorieuses', is a major event not only in the memories of the postwar generations but also among the social and economic changes that still await scholarly description and explanation. Despite all the differences within Europe, the period 1950 to 1973 was marked not only by extraordinary economic growth but also by increases in nominal and real wages. The increasing importance of the service sector and of product advertising, the widespread distribution and possession of consumer goods, and the standardisation of patterns of life and behaviour in the societies of Western Europe — and, to some extent, of Southern Europe as well — in the 1960s, 1970s and 1980s both accompanied and embodied this change. The authors of a survey of the period therefore come to the following conclusion: 'In meno di mezzo secolo i modi di vita si sono massificati, unificati e globalemente omogenizzati. A prezzo di una notevole riduzione della differenza dei modi di vita, l'Europa sembra essere definitàvamente passata alla "cultura del consumo"' (During less than half a century the way of life been characterised by the mass society, by unification and global homogenisation. By the means of reducing the differences between national lifestyles Europe seems to have developed towards a 'culture of consumption').[14]

Against the backdrop of these historical changes, which appear to be slowing down at the present time, sociologists and, in their footsteps, historians as well have turned their attention to the phases of this development, to the role of individual goods, to the impact of consumption on social classes and groups, on relationships between the sexes, on hierarchies of power, on political parties, and on national policies. Initial work in this new research field has stayed, however, within the context of national historiography, and even studies like Fraser's *The Coming of the Mass Market*, which raise expectations of a general approach, remain focused on individual countries – in Fraser's case, on Great Britain.[15] Comparative international studies on styles of consumption, consumer goods and consumer behaviour are the exception. Studies on the transfer of American models of consumption to Europe have drawn attention to international connections to some degree, but at the same time placed greater emphasis on the assimilation of these influences within national societies.[16] A comparative analysis of consumption in Europe would prove a difficult task even if its scope were limited to those West European countries that have already been subject to considerable research, with occasional glances at South European countries as well. The danger of interpreting a national development as paradigmatic is particularly great. Given the uneven state of research, our approach should be the reverse. We should be asking what contribution studies of consumption patterns in individual countries could make to a comparative social history of European countries. Ripe for discussion, then, are analyses that take as their point of departure a 'European model of a consumer society' and that see this model being increasingly realised, especially from 1950 on. In this period, as Hartmut Kaelble has shown, consumer goods became increasingly standardised, expenditures for food and clothing in private households declined, consumption became commercialised, the forms of commerce changed, social and territorial differences became less pronounced, and both the modes and content of discourse about consumption underwent change. All these processes have, according to Kaelble, 'led to a notable convergence of European societies'.[17]

There is no question about the value of such macrostructural analysis. It points out the central dimensions of consumption, notes important turning points in its development, and is based on a detailed evaluation and comparison of national statistics. There is an underlying model of mass consumer society that is grounded in clear criteria, the successive development of which is described. Kaelble's study evokes methodical reservations, however, if it takes West European developments as its point of departure, notes deviating patterns of development in Southern and

Eastern Europe, but then fails to take the latter into account in formulating its hypotheses. In overemphasising similarity of development, international historical comparison runs the risk of glossing over differences. It focuses so exclusively on the process of mass consumption's emergence that variations in temporal stages of development, structural disparities, and resistance against consumer society are pushed to the periphery. If, however, we follow the German economist Ernst Engels' lead in measuring the material well-being of societies by whether expenditures for basic foodstuffs per household decline or remain high, then in 1988 Italy, Spain, Portugal, Greece and Ireland have to be counted among the comparatively poorer regions. In these countries, on the average, more than 25 percent of income was spent on food compared to 15 or less in rich countries.[18] The structural dissimilarities within Europe were obviously reflected in the area of consumption. Nevertheless, a perspective that insists on seeing similarities tends to dismiss divergent data. The advance of the mass consumer society and its institutions has, for example, sometimes encountered massive resistance, which even took violent form in the Poujade movement and in Gérard Nicoud's populism in the Fourth Republic. Also, the resistance of French intellectuals to Americanisation, a phenomenon Robert Kuisel has studied, belongs in this context.[19]

We also have to ask whether a macrostructural approach does not, by its very nature, ignore many aspects of consumption, and whether the focus on processes of European unification downplays the significance of other regions as units for analysis and as locales of consumption. Or, put differently, if we regard consumption as a process involving the utilisation of goods, their commercialisation, and endowing them with symbolic value, what are social actors' – men's, women's, and children's – experiences concerning consumption and in what contexts? Clearly, a local or regional context is a more appropriate one for studying various aspects of consumption defined in this way. An international, comparative historiography should thus place greater emphasis on consumption in specific locales.

Consumption as part of family economics can be analysed only in a local context. Roman Sandgruber's studies on the division of labour in Lower Austrian farmers' families make clear that the men were in charge of marketing cattle and grain, whereas it was the women's job to sell poultry, eggs and vegetables. The women thus earned their own income, which they then usually used, however, within the framework of traditional gender roles, to buy clothing for their children.[20] In an urban context, the analysis of such locale-specific patterns would focus on the composition of family income and therefore on the question of who contributed to income by what means and to what extent. It is no coincidence that contemporary and historical studies of this kind normally focus either on certain occupational groups or on a city. In 1904, the statistical office of the city of Dresden published *Inventories of Eighty-seven Working-Class Households in Dresden*, adding the following self-critical comment: 'In terms of the size and composition of households, of the occupations and incomes of the breadwinners, and of the location, size and rental cost of living quarters, the eighty-seven inventories presented here are very diverse.'[21] If our focus in examining rural and urban households in the nineteenth and early twentieth centuries is on family strategies and on the connection between family size and consumer behaviour, then local surveys are indispensable and may also be able to contribute to our understanding of larger connections and structures. However, generalising from such particulars is not without its problems, as the heterogeneity of the examples gathered by Frédéric Le Play demonstrates.[22] Maurice Halbwachs, who gave careful study to contemporary surveys, stated this problem as follows: 'trop peu nombreux et trop hétérogènes pour autoriser des inductions scientifiques, ses budgets et ses monographes demeurent, pour l'histoire, des *documents* de tout premier ordre' ('too rare and too heterogeneous for any scientific conclusion the budgets and individual studies remain, however, for history first rate documents').[23]

The allocating of resources also took place within households. In normal times, the disposition of income and savings was a matter for debate. According to Martine Segalen's study of rural proverbs, money management was a highly controversial subject between husband and wife. The population of a village even claimed it could determine from certain rituals how a conflict in a farmer's family had been resolved. If the husband had to give in, his prestige declined accordingly.[24] In other locales, control of money was not open to question. Conflicts over consumption could arise, however, at times of shortages or famine if rules governing allocation were not firmly in place. Both in the German bourgeoisie and in the Madrid working class at the end of the nineteenth century, the male breadwinner was the privileged member of the family, but if we can believe Salvadore Satta, the first piece of meat served in middle-class Sardinian families went to the lady of the household. 'Even at times of bitter family strife, there was not the slightest danger that she would serve herself first at table; for by tradition the platter was placed before him to carve and distribute the meat. The first piece went to Donna Vicenza, and he would have stood up and left the table if she had refused it, as she sometimes felt moved to do.'[25]

As contemporary studies of consumption deal with individual cases, it is difficult to generalise from them. This is true not only of farmers and workers but of middle-class families as well. Convincing studies of the consumer behaviour of bourgeois women and men, such as Marguerite Perrot's, strongly focus on individual published budgets or concentrate on a single city.[26] While, in the first case, it remains uncertain how representative the results are of bourgeois families, in the second, the concrete context within which goods and practices take on meaning is vividly clear. Research to date would seem to support the idea that local studies are the most productive for the analysis of the social significance and symbolic value of consumption. One needs the anthropological imagination and the detailed knowledge of a Marguerite Perrot to be able to derive a convincing and multifaceted picture of the worker as consumer from an overall understanding of the French working-class struggles before 1890.[27]

If the history of consumption focuses on changing household economies, includes household behaviour and strategies of saving, and also intends to keep domestic struggles for power in mind, it also has to conduct local case studies. In order to be able to compare, the contexts and significance of the local cases will have to be precisely established. A history of consumption adhering to these conditions is bound to be utterly thorough and will provide detailed insight into the mechanisms of consumptive behaviour, yet it will be all but impossible to ensure that these case studies will be nationally representative.

Local focus is just as important in studying the symbolic value of consumer goods as it is in studies of household structures. Using Laichlingen as an example, Hans Medick has shown how a 'culture of prestige' was meant to cement existing social differences. He has also shown how prescribed dress codes were subverted and former limits overstepped. In a local context, different perceptions and uses for clothing and colours become evident.[28] In Fabrizio Montebello's dissertation on the cinema culture of the western French steel city of Longwy in the twentieth century, passages based on interviews show how significantly local conditions can influence perception. Montebello is able to demonstrate how much Italian steelworkers' experience of migration and of the workplace influenced their interpretation and assimilation of American films of the 1950s. The specific milieu of this city created a special context that influenced how these films were perceived.[29]

Similarly, commercialisation can be studied better in a local context than in a national one, even though national structures and stages of development may be extremely important. For instance, retail trade in nineteenth-century England was more widespread than it was in Germany.[30] Urbanisation which took place in England in the first half of the nineteenth century separated city dwellers from their means of subsistence and therefore increased their dependence on retailers. In Germany, this development did not come about until after the 1860s. The dependency of trade on structures of urbanisation makes local studies all the more crucial, as the history of department stores shows. The growth of these stores is linked to specific stages of urban development. Once broad boulevards were laid out and built in big cities, department stores offering a wide range of goods found their ideal setting for making their appeal to the eye of anyone out for a stroll and to the acquisitiveness of a well-to-do public. Paris led the way in Europe. It was there that Aristide Boucicaut founded the Bon Marché, the first modern department store. London, Vienna, Berlin, and, a bit later, Turin and Rome followed suit.[31] In cities with a large and often politically organised working population, but also in those where workers' real income had improved, consumer cooperatives were formed. They flourished in England in the 1880s, in Belgium and Germany in the 1890s, and gradually established a foothold in France as well after 1900. By contrast, the development of chain stores, which opened from the 1880s onwards, seems to have been predicated not only on a broad market with purchasing power increased by rising wages, but also on an already existing network of retail stores that the chains sought to rationalise by means of centralised purchasing, standardised products and similar marketing strategies. Chains assumed a prominent role in food and shoe retailing and in ready-made clothing. *Les Docks Rémois* and *Kaiser's* Coffee Shops, Lipton's and *Delhaize-Frères* (in Belgium) are names that come readily to mind. Though they tended to spread out nationally, they originated in urban centers: *Kaiser's* Coffee Shops in Berlin, the Casino chain in St Etienne.[32]

If our focus is the nonsimultaneity of developments or the connection between structures of urbanisation, levels of income and entrepreneurial strategies, then studies on a national level are necessary and meaningful. They can highlight the different paths of development the consumer society has followed in different countries and discuss hypotheses on the factors responsible for those different paths. Yet, if our focus is on modes of buying and selling, on the social physiognomy of merchants and customers, local studies are needed. Only within the local context can we see whether payment in kind or in cash was preferred, whether buyers and sellers shared a common social origin, and what social practices were an integral part of buying and selling. In the nineteenth century, payment in kind remained widespread in rural areas for a long time.

Because rural people earned their livings by a number of different activities, they wanted to keep their cash expenditures down and pay with products or services that let them circumvent the monetarised economy. This form of payment limited the scope of retail businesses, of course, and obliged small retailers to engage in other activities (farm work, trades) to make ends meet. The number of occupational designations that Ronald Hubscher found in the census lists of the Northern French *département* Pas-de-Calais reflects this survival strategy, which did, however, decline in importance in the last third of the nineteenth century. In the cities, the money economy dominated, but that is not to say that cash payment was the rule. Borrowing and lending were so widespread in working-class neighbourhoods in particular that retailers there were even called the 'bankers of the poor'. Because grocers carried so much debt, their future was dependent on the income of their customers. Consequently, they sometimes supported strikers and were happy to see them get wage increases. However, to what extent these practices existed, which concrete forms they adopted and what conflicts of loyalties they precipitated, all these questions can be answered only by micro studies. A lot of these topics still await thorough examination through case studies.[33]

The social situation of buyers and sellers cannot be described on a national level, either. It surely made a difference whether a sale was negotiated by two women or by a man and a woman, whether it took place within a national minority, such as Northern French or Belgian Poles, or whether it was carried out by an ambitious apprentice serving a middle-class woman, not to mention the transactions that pedlars conducted on the street or door-to-door. The social situations that determined the atmosphere of sales transactions differed in different cities, in different quarters of a given city and in different historical periods. Those situations can be reconstructed only by means of detailed studies based on local sources, not through national surveys. Inquiry into the social practices inherent to consumption also leads inevitably to the need for local studies. Whether shops served as social gathering places where political and private matters were discussed or whether this function was limited strictly to cafés and restaurants, whether department stores in 1914 were visited only for shopping or also for family gatherings and coffee *klatsches*, whether there were separate areas in sales emporia reserved for gatherings of men and of women — all these questions can be reasonably studied and discussed only within local contexts.[34]

Uprisings caused by shortages and famines were always locally determined, too, and have to be analysed from a local perspective. It is, of course, rational to categorise them systematically, as Charles Tilly has done for other forms of protest; but their causes, the courses they took, the participants, and their outcomes all have to be studied locally. In such studies, the situation of food distribution in a locality, local traditions, and the specific political measures implemented, have to be considered as well as the events precipitating an uprising. Whether and to what extent both men and women took part in an uprising can be determined only through local sources, and only local court, police and administrative files can reveal whether the situation was resolved by repression or negotiation. And if our focus is the symbolic value the protesters placed on certain foodstuffs, if, that is, our focus is on the protesters' value system with its concomitant sympathies and antipathies, a cultural-historical analysis, if it is not to remain speculative, is obliged to study the integration of values into local social, economic and political practices.[35]

The study of consumption obliges us to look at small local units. From such factors as traditional costumes and food habits, we can derive a geography of consumption. Well into the twentieth century, these geographies were defined by local communities. At this level, we can conduct meaningful studies of family economy, of venues of consumption, of consumer protests, and of governing ideas and concepts bearing on consumption. Such studies also lead us inevitably to gender and class relations. Also, it is only in such a context that we can analyse the symbolic value of foods: 'il faudrait, pour comprendre parfaitement toute la thêmatique symbolique inhérente aus faits culinaires, reconstruire le système des morphologies alimentaires qui constituaient le répetoire de chaque communauté, de chaque village, de chaque commune, de chaque unité ethnique, groupe ou corporation' ('for understanding entirely the symbolic theme inherent in food one would have to reconstruct the morphology of food in each community, each village, each district, each ethnic unit, group and corporation').[36]

The regional level, too, is important for the history of consumption. The dominance of particular products changes from region to region. Regions can be distinguished from each other according to whether they use wine or beer, oil or butter, potatoes or chestnuts. Thus, in Italy, for a long time and until the massive twentieth-century shifts in populations and tastes, Lombardy's use of butter set it apart from the regions of central Italy where oil was favoured; and these areas differed in turn from the Emilia Romagna where lard predominated. If a region wanted to create a certain image and attract tourists, then it would tout regional specialties and use them to distinguish itself from other regions. Thus, Bavarian beer, Tuscan cuisine and

Bordeaux wine came to epitomise an entire region. Nevertheless, well into the twentieth century, local and regional preferences held their own in a market that had not yet become nationwide. Regional tastes continued to dominate until the transportation system could easily ship goods into the most remote corners of the country, until advertising created uniform tastes nationwide and until major distributors could saturate the entire national territory with the same products. To the extent that advertising promoted regional specialties, it contributed to their continuing viability. Before 1939, small and mediumsized enterprises in France operated primarily on regional rather than local bases. Research on consumption has, to date, given little attention to regional factors affecting consumption and to regional experiences in this area. This is a void that future research should attempt to fill.[37]

Studies on the national level would be those that trace trends in prices, wages and income. Existing data, however, caution us against assuming that the majority of the rural population was necessarily consigned to lagging behind on the path towards a modern consumer society. The proto-industrialisation debate has demonstrated that rural areas prior to 1800 were not excluded from commercialisation. Mercantile activity reached them, and it was common for rural people to engage in some kind of trade as a sideline. Also, studies that have pointed out the influence of markets, travelling salesmen, and mail-order trade on rural consumer habits have suggested that in the nineteenth and twentieth centuries, too, the urban consumer market reached segments of the rural population, although, as Maurice Levy-Leboyer has emphasised for France, the arrival of commercial activity came later and took different forms in rural areas than it did in the city: 'il est visible que la consommation n'a pu se développer, selon un processus continu, par diffusion d'un même modèle, des villes vers les campagnes' ('one can see that the consumption did not develop in a continuous process by the diffusion of the same model in cities and rural areas').[38]

Levy-Leboyer's point is a reminder to us to take more fully into account local and regional differences in the decline of subsistence agriculture, in the integration of agriculture into commerce and in structural changes in rural areas. John Benson finds England's situation unusual in that the cities had a disproportionate amount of purchasing power as opposed to the country, a situation clearly explicable by the fact of England's early and extensive urbanisation. In Southern European societies, just the opposite holds true. As late as the end of the nineteenth century, the persistence of rural self-sufficiency remained an obstacle to modernisation.[39]

Estimates of industrial workers' real wages reflect patterns of change at the national level. According to these estimates, only in Serbia did real wages decline almost constantly in the long period from 1850 to 1939. In Turkey, the decline was limited to the period 1913 to 1939, and in this same period wages appear to have been stagnant in France as well. In Northern and Western Europe, for example, in Belgium and Germany, in the Netherlands and Norway, and in Sweden and Great Britain, real wages experienced a long-term increase. However, the times of obvious rise do differ. Only in France, Sweden, Great Britain, and Turkey did real wages rise between 1870 and 1890 – that is, relatively early. In the other five countries, they rose markedly between the two World Wars. But even in the view of the estimates' authors, the significance of these estimates should not be exaggerated because they take into neither account unemployment, nor the wages of female workers, nor income from self-employment in the trades and in commerce. Moreover, they do not include pensions and other social-support payments, which varied considerably from country to country.[40] Nonetheless, the numbers reflect a clear tendency towards higher real wages in all European societies, although Southern and east-central European societies are underrepresented in these figures. As early as 1870, industrial workers in some countries began shopping for foodstuffs and, increasingly, for clothing as well; in most countries, however, this was not the case until the twentieth century. In any case the amount of disposable income available to proletarian households remained minimal, as Klaus Tenfelde has demonstrated for Imperial Germany. Throughout this period, the subsistence household suffered from a lack of resources. The improvements in the situation of the working class that did take place still had no influence on the basic class differences in spending, food consumption, and the relative significance of expenditures and budgeting.[41]

The nation state assumed a role in consumer affairs. By establishing norms for goods offered for sale, it tried to ensure the quality of the national food supply; by imposing special taxes, such as those on department stores, it tried to guide the development of the commercial network; by intervening in cases of famine, it sought to maintain law and order. Different governments intervened in consumer affairs at different times and to different degrees. The Belgian government of 1914, for example, controlled by the Catholic Party, relied strongly on the initiative of producers and consumers, while the German government exerted considerable control over the economy and society. These differing degrees of government intervention influenced consumer initiative and organisation, both of which remained of minor significance in Germany well into the twentieth century.[42]

The national level is important, however, not only for describing and explaining the socioeconomic structures as a backdrop of legislative measures; it is also important for reflecting changes in mentality. For instance, segments of English, French and German society responded to the growth of department stores and to the attraction they held for women shoppers by claiming that this new method of offering goods for sale encouraged kleptomaniac tendencies. Kleptomania as a new pathology primarily affecting middle-class women arose in connection with strategies for using rumour to reduce department stores' chances of succeeding and for exonerating middle-class women from the charge of shoplifting. Although it is not always clear which social groups originated and spread these ideas, they nonetheless appear to have been discussed in medical circles and among social observers.[43] Especially in periods regarded as times of national crisis and trial, the national aspect of consumption gained in importance. This phenomenon is particularly evident during the revolution of 1848. In May and June 1848, women in Prague wore Czech national costumes to demonstrate their loyalty and their resistance against the intervention of Austrian troops. In Germany, especially in Baden-Württemberg, and in Vienna, the call to boycott foreign luxury goods, particularly French ones, was motivated not only by national loyalty but also by economic interests that wanted to retain control of the domestic market themselves. Even before the revolution, German gymnasts had touted the virtues of German goods and clothing, as the example of the master cooper Ferdinand Lang at the Heilbronn Gymnastics Festival of 1846 shows:

> German linen, spun by German women
> clothes us well;
> so pay heed, you women,
> and shun the frippery of foreign lands.[44]

Consumption took on national significance for a short time at the beginning of the First World War, too. In several French cities, German chain stores like 'Salamander', or stores with German-sounding names, were attacked in early August 1914. Shop windows were smashed and the goods on display were sometimes stolen. Ostracising the national enemy and the fear of spies fuelled these excesses to some extent, but the primary motives behind them were the economic interests of competitors. After a short while, most French newspapers served up some lukewarm condemnation of this vandalism. Concerning the nationalist defences of this plundering, the exact extent and significance of them will have to be determined by detailed microstudies.[45]

The international European level should be studied not only from the perspective of structural analogies but also in terms of networks of relationship. Fashion was surely an area in which international influences made themselves felt across national borders. French fashion set the style of ready-made clothing and remained dominant until after the Second World War, when it yielded to Italian fashion. *La culture des apparances*, as Daniel Roche aptly termed this form of display, was determined by France. Buyers from the major boutiques and department stores in Germany's large and mediumsized cities travelled to French cities, if not to Paris itself, to buy new materials and acquaint themselves with the latest styles.[46] World Fairs can also be interpreted as venues where a new aesthetic of commercial goods was developed and from which it was then disseminated to European countries. Certain representations of the consumer culture can also be studied in terms of their European dimensions. In the discussion of the special qualities and the repercussions of department stores in various European countries, Emile Zola's depiction of developments in France in his *Au bonheur des dames* is an important reference text. The characteristics of these new temples of consumption described there appear repeatedly as leitmotifs outside France, too. An analysis of the dissemination and reception of this text remains yet to be done.[47]

Nevertheless, a history of European consumption would lack important aspects and perspectives if it remained limited entirely to the European level. The practices and symbolic values as well as the strategies and conflicts associated with consumer goods can be better analysed at the local level, where contextual circumstances can be precisely determined. Taking an international and comparative perspective, a comparative history of consumption in Europe could inquire, for example, into the significance of bread as a basic food and as a symbol for certain social groups within a surveyable area. A comparative study of consumer protests could also be meaningful if it did not reduce such protests to their national characteristics but fully acknowledged the diversity of local forms. Finally, an analysis focusing on all of Europe would be appropriate because within Europe relationships between consumers and salespeople were formed, because certain styles of consumption developed there, and because those styles came to play a specific role as markers of social distinctions. The focus would be either

on individual social groups and classes – e.g., the aristocracy and the
haute bourgeoisie – or on certain periods of time, for instance, the last
thirty years.

Notes

1. E.J. Hobsbawm, *Europäische Revolutionen*, Zurich, 1962; E.J. Hobsbawm, *Die
    Blütezeit des Kapitals: Eine Kulturgeschichte der Jahre 1848–1875*, Munich, 1977; E.J.
    Hobsbawm, *Das imperiale Zeitalter 1875–1914*, Frankfurt am Main, 1989; P. Léon,
    ed., *La domination du capitalisme: Histoire économique et sociale du monde*, vol. 4,
    Paris, 1978; H. Kaelble, *Auf dem Weg zu einer europäischen Gesellschaft: Eine
    Sozialgeschichte Westeuropas 1880–1980*, Munich, 1987; see also, with special refer-
    ence to consumption: H. Kaelble, *Nachbarn am Rhein: Entfremdung und Annäherung
    der französischen und deutschen Gesellschaft seit 1880*, Munich, 1991, p. 164ff.; with-
    out particular reference to consumption, H. van Dijk, *De modernising van Europa:
    Twee eeuwen Maatschappijgeschiedenis*, Utrecht, 1994. In P. Bairoch and E.J. Hobs-
    bawm, eds, *Storia d'Europa, vol V: L'età contemporanca: Secoli XIX–XX*, Turin, 1996,
    the discussion of consumption remains limited to the period after 1945, pp. 467–90.

2. H.-U. Wehler, *Deutsche Gesellschaftsgeschichte*, vols 1, 2 and 3, Munich, 1987–95; J.
    Kocka, *Arbeitsverhältnisse und Arbeiterexistenzen*, Bonn, 1990; F. Braudel and E.
    Labrousse, eds, *Histoire économique et social de la France*, vols 3,1 and 3,2; vol. 4
    (v,1; 4,2, 4,3), Paris, 1976–82; Y. Lequin, ed., *Histoire des Français XIXe–XXe siècles*,
    3 vols, Paris, 1984; C. Charle, *Histoire sociale de la France*, Paris, 1990; D.J. Oddy,
    'Food, Drink, and Nutrition' in *The Cambridge Social History of Britain*, 1750–1950,
    ed. F.M.L. Thompson, 3 vols, Cambridge, 1990, vol. 2, pp. 251–78.

3. See H.-U. Wehler, *Modernisierungstheorien*, Göttingen, 1976; W. Zapf, ed., *Theorien
    des sozialen Wandels*, Cologne and Berlin, 1969.

4. Cf. e.g., V. Bader et al., *Einführung in die Gesellschaftstheorie: Gesellschaft, Wirtschaft
    und Staat bei Marx und Weber*, Frankfurt am Main, New York, 1976; R. Williams,
    Problems in Materialism and Culture, London, 1980.

5. P. Bourdieu, *La distinction: Critique sociale du jugement*, Paris, 1979; see also: I.
    Gilcher-Holtey, 'Kulturelle und symbolische Praktiken: Das Unternehmen Pierre Bour-
    dieu', in *Kulturgeschichte heute*, ed. W. Hartwig and H.-U. Wehler, Göttingen, 1996,
    pp. 11–130; M. de Certeau, *L'invention du quotidien*, vol. 1: Arts de faire, Paris, 1980,
    has received little attention to date.

6. Cited in: W. Hoffmann, ed., *Sozialökonomische Studientexte: Wert und Preislehre*,
    Berlin, 1971, p. 131.

7. M. Halbwachs, *La classe ouvrière et les niveaux de vie: Recherches sur la hiérarchie
    des besoins dans les sociétés industrielles contemporaines*, Paris, 1913; M. Halbwachs,
    L'evolution des besoins dans les classes ouvrières, Paris, 1933.

8. See T. Pierenkemper, ed. *Zur Ökonomik des privaten Haushalts: Haushaltsrechnungen
    als Quellen historischer Wirtschafts- und Sozialforschung*, Frankfurt am Main, New
    York, 1991; Mombert quotation in: D. Dowe, ed. *Erhebungen von Wirtschaftsunter-*

suchungen minderbemittelter Familien im Deutschen Reich (1909) und 320 Haushalts-srechnungen von Mitarbeitern (1909), reprint, Berlin, 1981.

9. J. Revel, 'Consommation', in La nouvelle Histoire, ed. J. Le Goff, Paris, 1986, p. 321.

10. See Pierenkemper, Ökonomik des privaten Haushalts.

11. See the critique by V. de Grazia, 'Changing Consumption Regimes', in The Sex of the Things: Gender and Consumption in Historical Perspective, ed. V. de Grazia, Berkeley, Los Angeles, London, 1996, p. 11–24.

12. For a summary, see J. Brewer, 'Was können wir aus der Geschichte der frühen Neuzeit für die moderne Konsumgeschichte lernen?' in Europäische Konsumgeschichte: Zur Gesellschafts- und Kulturgeschichte des Konsums (18. bis 20. Jahrhundert), ed. H. Siegrist et al., Frankfurt am Main, New York, 1997, pp. 51–74; J. Brewer and R. Porter, eds, Consumption and the World of Goods, London, 1993; N. McKendrick et al., The Birth of a Consumer Society, London, 1982; S. Schama, The Embarrassment of Riches: An Interpretation of Dutch Culture in the Golden Age, London, 1987; F. Braudel, 'Les structures du quotidien', in Civilisation matérielle, Economie et Capitalisme XVe–XVIIIe siècle, ed. F. Braudel, Paris, 1979, pp. 81–290.

13. S. Mintz, Sweetness and Power: The Plan of Sugar in Modern History, New York, 1985; S.P. Benson, Counter Cultures: Saleswomen, Managers and Customers in American Department Stores, 1890–1940, Urbana, 1986; D. Horrowitz, The Morality of Spending: Attitudes towards the Consumer Society in America, 1875–1940, Baltimore, 1985; M. Featherstone, Consumer Culture and Postmodernism, London, 1991; see, too, on influences: V. de Grazia, 'Amerikanisierung und wechselnde Leitbilder der Konsum-Moderne (consumer-modernity) in Europa', in Europäische Konsumgeschichte: Zur Gesellschafts- und Kulturgeschichte des Konsums (18. bis 20. Jahrhundert), ed. H. Siegrist et al., Frankfurt am Main, New York, 1997, pp. 109–37; also, J. Tanner, 'Industrialisierung, Rationalisierung und Wandel des Konsum- und Geschmacksverhaltens im europäisch-amerikanischen Vergleich', in Europäische Konsumgeschichte: Zur Gesellschafts- und Kulturgeschichte des Konsums (18. bis 20. Jahrhundert), ed. H. Siegrist et al., Frankfurt am Main, New York, 1997, pp. 583–614.

14. A. Beltran et al., 'Nascita, crescita e dominio della società dei consumi', in Storia d'Europa, vol V: L'età contemporanca: Secoli XIX–XX, ed. P. Bairoch and E. J. Hobsbawm, Turin, 1996, pp. 467–490, p. 487.

15. H. Fraser, The Coming of the Mass Market, 1890–1914, Hamden, 1981.

16. V. de Grazia, 'Mass Culture and Sovereignty: the American Challenge to European Cinemas, 1920–1960', Journal of Modern History 61 (1989), pp. 53–87; R. Kuisel, Seducing the French, Berkeley, 1992.

17. H. Kaelble, 'Europäische Besonderheiten des Massenkonsums, 1950–1990', in Europäische Konsumgeschichte: Zur Gesellschafts- und Kulturgeschichte des Konsums (18. bis 20. Jahrhundert), ed. H. Siegrist et al., Frankfurt am Main, New York, 1997, pp. 169–203.

18. Beltran et al., 'Nascita', p. 474.

19. Kuisel, Seducing the French; S. Hoffmann, Le mouvement Poujade, Paris, 1956; M. Roy, Les commerçants entre la révolte et le modernisation, Paris, 1971; see, too, Beltran et al., 'Nascita', pp. 481ff.

20. R. Sandgruber, *Die Anfänge zur Konsumgesellschaft: Konsumgüterverbrauch, Lebens-standard und Alltagskultur in Österreich im 18. und 19. Jahrhundert*, Munich, 1982; R. Sandgruber, 'Interfamiliale Einkommens- und Konsumaufteilung', in *Ehe, Liebe, Tod*, ed. P. Borscheid and H.-J. Teuteberg, Münster, 1983, pp. 135–49.

21. *Mitteilungen des Statistischen Amtes der Stadt Dresden, 13. Heft, Inventarien von 87 Dresdner Arbeiterhaushalten, aufgenommen im November 1903*, ed. Statisches Amt der Stadt Dresden, Dresden, 1904, p. 6; on this same subject, see T. Pierenkemper, 'Das Rechnungsbuch der Hausfrau – und was wir daraus lernen können: Zur Verwendbarkeit privater Haushaltsrechnungen in der historischen Wirtschafts- und Sozialforschung', *Geschichte und Gesellschaft*, 14 (1988), pp. 38–63; for a critique, see U. Spiekermann, 'Haushaltsrechnungen als Quellen der Ernährungsgeschichte: Überblick und method-ischer Problemaufriß', in *Neue Wege zur Ernährungsgeschichte: Kochbücher, Haushaltsrechnungen, Konsumvereinsberichte und Autobiographien in der Diskussion*, ed. D. Reinhardt et al., Frankfurt am Main, 1993, pp. 51–85.

22. F. Le Play, *La méthode sociale*, reprint, Paris, 1989; on Le Play, see A. Gueslin, *L'in-vention de l'Economie Sociale: Le XIXe siècle français*, Paris, 1987; B. Kalaora and A. Savoye, *Les inventeurs oubliés*, Paris, 1989.

23. Halbwachs, *Niveaux de vie*, p. 487; similarly, S. Zanielli, *I Consumi a Milano nell'otto-cento*, Rome, 1974, p. 108.

24. M. Segalen, *Maris et femmes dans la société paysanne*, Paris, 1980; see also Sandgru-ber, *Anfänge*, passim.

25. See S. Satta, *Der Tag des Gerichts*, Frankfurt am Main, 1996, p. 50; see also S. Heym, *Nachruf*, Frankfurt am Main, 1991, p. 10; A. Lüdtke, 'Hunger, Essens-Genüsse und Politik bei Fabrikarbeitern und Arbeiterfrauen: Beispiele aus dem rheinisch-westfälis-chen Industriegebiet, 1910–1940', in A. Lüdtke, *Eigen-Sinn: Fabrikalltag, Arbeitererfahrungen und Politik vom Kaiserreich bis zum Faschismus*, Hamburg, 1993, pp. 194–209, also, pp. 81–89.

26. See M. Perrot, *Le mode de vie des familles bourgeoises, 1873–1953*, Paris, 1961; M. Wakounig, 'Konsumverhalten des Wiener Bürgertums im 19. und 20. Jahrhundert', *Jahrbuch des Vereins für die Geschichte der Stadt Wien* 44/45 (1989), pp. 154–86; P. Sarasion, 'Une coutume barbare, les fonctions significatives de l'argent dans une société bourgeoise vers 1900', *Genèses* 15 (1994), pp. 84–102; T. Pierenkemper, 'Der bürger-liche Haushalt in Deutschland an der Wende zum 20. Jahrhundert – im Spiegel von Haushaltsrechnungen', in *Zur Geschichte der Ökonomik der Privathaushalte*, ed. D. Petzina, Berlin, 1991, pp. 149–85.

27. M. Perrot, *Les ouvriers en grève: France 1871–1890*, Paris, 1974, vol. 2, pp. 201–40.

28. H. Medick, 'Eine Kultur des Ansehens: Kleider und Kleiderfarben in Laichingen 1750–1820', *Historische Anthropologie* 2 (1994), pp. 193–212.

29. F. Montebello, 'Spectacle cinématographique et classe ouvrière Longwy 1944–1960', diss., Lyon II, 1997; see, too, R. Hoggart, *La culture du pauvre*, Paris, 1970.

30. See G. Crossick and H.G. Haupt, *The Petite Bourgeoisie in Europe 1780–1914: Enter-prise, Family, and Independence*, London, New York, 1995, pp. 38ff.

31. See M.B. Miller, *Au bon marché 1869–1920: Le consommateur apprivoisé*, Paris, 1987; R. Laermans, 'Learning to Consume: Early Department Stores and the Shaping

of the Modern Consumer Culture, 1880–1914', *Theory, Culture and Society* 10 (1993), pp. 70–102.

32. See M. Prinz, *Brot und Dividende: Konsumvereine in Deutschland und England von 1914*, Göttingen, 1996; J. Benson and G. Shaw, eds, *The Evolution of Retail Systems ca. 1800–1914*, Leicester, 1992.

33. See, for instance, R. Hubscher, *L'Agriculture et la Société rurale dans le Pas-de-Calais du XIXe siècle à 1914*, Arras, 1980, 2 vols; J.P. Burdy, *Le Soleil noir: Un quartier de Saint-Etienne, 1840–1940*, Lyon, 1989; G. Jacquement, *Belleville au XIXe siècle: Du faubourg à la ville*, Paris, 1984; J.C. Martin, 'Commerce et commerçantes à Niort au XIXe siècle: Les faillites', *Bulletin de la Société Historique et Scientifique des Deux-Sèvres* 13 (1980), pp. 337–501; S. Jaumain, *Les petits commerçants belge face à la modernité (1880–1914)*, Brussels, 1995; D.L. Cagliotti, *Il Guadagno difficle: Commercianti Napoletani nella Seconda Metà dell'Ottocento*, Bologna, 1994.

34. See the discussion in Crossick and Haupt, *The Petite Bourgeoisie*, pp. 112ff.; also, H.-G. Haupt, 'Kleinhändler und Arbeiter in Bremen zwischen 1890 und 1914', *Archiv für Sozialgeschichte* 22 (1982), pp. 95–134.

35. See M. Gailus, *Straße und Brot: Sozialer Protest in den deutschen Staaten unter besonderer Berücksichtigung Preußens, 1847–1849*, Göttingen, 1990; S. Goetsch, 'Hungerunruhen – Verhandlungen im traditionellen Protestverhalten', *Zeitschrift für Volkskunde 80 (1984)*, pp. 169–82; C. Tilly et al., *The Rebellious Century 1830–1930*, Cambridge, 1975; I. Bohstedt, *Riots and Community: Politics in England and Wales, 1790–1810*, Cambridge, MA, 1983.

36. P. Camporesi, *La terre et la lune: Alimentation, folklore, société*, Paris, 1993, p. 57; see also, although very general, J. Tanner, 'Der Mensch ist, was er ißt: Ernährungsmythen und Wandel der Eßkultur', *Historische Anthropologie* 4 (1996), pp. 399–419; and, especially, S.W. Mintz, 'The Changing Role of Food in the Study of Consumption', in *Consumption and the World of Goods*, ed. J. Brewer and R. Porter, London, 1993, pp. 261–73.

37. On this, see H.J. Teuteberg and G. Wiegelmann, *Unsere tägliche Kost: Geschichte und regionale Prägung*, Münster, 1986; R. Sandgruber, 'Knödel, Nudel, Topfenstrudel: Österreichische Ernährungsgewohnheiten und regionale Unterschiede in Mitteleuropa', in *Nord-Süd-Unterschiede in der städtischen und ländlichen Kultur Mitteleuropas*, ed. G. Wiegelmann, Münster, 1985, pp. 265–97; Camporesi, *La terre et la lune*, pp. 81ff.; M.E. Chessel, *La publicité: Naissance d'une profession 1900–1940*, Paris, 1998, p. 102ff.

38. M. Levy-Leboyer and F. Bourguignon, *L'economie française au XIX siècle: Analyse macro-économique*, Paris, 1985, p. 26; see, too, Jaumain, *Les petits commerçants belges*, pp. 71ff.; D. Margairaz, 'La formation du réseau des foires et des marchés', *Annales E. S. C.* 40 (1986), pp. 1215–42; L. Fontaine, *Histoire du colportage en europe, XVe–XIXe siècle*, Paris, 1993.

39. J. Benson, *The Rise of Consumer Society in Britain 1880–1920*, London, 1994; also, V. Zamagni, *La distribuzione commerciale in Italia fra le due guerre*, Milan, 1981; V. Zamagni, 'Die langsame Modernisierung des italienischen Einzelhandels: Die Geschichte eines Sonderfalls in vergleichender Perspektive', in *Europäische Kon-*

sumgeschichte: Zur Gesellschafts- und Kulturgeschichte des Konsums (18. bis 20. Jahrhundert), ed. H. Siegrist et al., Frankfurt am Main, New York, 1997, pp. 705–16.

40. P. Scholliers and V. Zamagni, eds, *Labour's Reward: Real Wages and Economic Change in 19th and 20th Century Europe*, Aldershot, 1995; P. Scholliers, ed., *Real Wages in 19th and 20th Century Europe: Historical and Comparative Perspectives*, New York, Oxford, 1989; Y.S. Brenner et al., *Income Distribution in Historical Perspective*, Cambridge, Paris, 1991; on social support payments, see D.F. Crew, '"Wohlfahrtsbrot ist bitteres Brot": The Elderly, the Disabled, and Local Welfare. Authorities in the Weimar Republic 1924–1933', *Archiv für Sozialgeschichte* 30 (1990), pp. 217–95.

41. K. Tenfelde, 'Klassenspezifische Konsummuster im Deutschen Kaiserreich', in *Europäische Konsumgeschichte: Zur Gesellschafts- und Kulturgeschichte des Konsums (18. bis 20. Jahrhundert)*, ed. H. Siegrist et al., Frankfurt am Main, New York, 1997, pp. 245–66, and specifically pp. 256ff. For a similar treatment, see Perrot, *Ouvriers*.

42. See Crossick and Haupt, *The Petite Bourgeoisie*, pp. 133ff.; Jaumain, *Les petits commerçants belge*, pp. 99ff.; M. van der Linden, 'Working-Class Consumer Power', in *International Labor and Working Class History* 46 (1994), pp. 109–21; E. Fourlough, *Consumer Cooperation in France: The Politics of Consumption 1834–1930*, Ithaca, 1991.

43. P. O'Brien, 'The Kleptomnia Diagnosis – Bourgeois Women and Theft in Late 19th Century France', *Journal of Social History* 17 (1983–84), pp. 65–77; E.S. Abelson, *When Ladies Go A-Thieving: Middle Class Shoplifters in the Victorian Department Store*, New York, 1989; see, too, W.R. Leach, 'Transformations in a Culture of Consumption: Women and Department Stores 1890–1925', *Journal of American History* 71 (1984), pp. 319–42.

44. See D. Langewiesche, '"… für Volk und Vaterland künftig zu wirken." Zur politischen und gesellschaftlichen Rolle der Turner zwischen 1811 und 1871', in *Kulturgut und Körperkultur? Sport und Sportwissenschaft im Wandel*, ed. O. Grube, Tübingen, 1990, pp. 22–61, pp. 45f.; I. Belting, *Mode und Revolution: Deutschland 1848/49*, Hildesheim, 1997; M. Moravcovà, 'Die tschechischen Frauen im revolutionären Prag 1848/49', in *1848–49 Revolutionen in Ostmitteleuropa*, ed. R. Jaworski and R. Luft, Munich, 1996, pp. 72–91, p. 83; G. Hauch, *Frau Biedermeier auf den Barrikaden: Frauenleben in der Wiener Revolution 1848*, Vienna, 1990, pp. 223f.; S. Kienitz, 'Aecht deutsche Weiblichkeit, Mode und Konsum als bürgerliche Frauenpolitik', in *Schimpfende Weiber und patriotische Jungfrauen – Frauen im Vormärz und in der Revolution 1848–49*, ed. C. Lipp, Moos, Baden-Baden, 1986, pp. 76–88.

45. See J.J. Becker, *Comment les français sont entrés dans la guerre*, Paris, 1977, pp. 497ff.

46. D. Roche, *La culture des apparences: Une histoire du vêtement XVIIe–XVIIIe siècle*, Paris, 1989; see, too, on the role of France and of Paris in the formation of taste, I. Cleve, *Geschmack, Kunst und Konsum: Kulturpolitik als Wirtschaftspolitik in Frankreich und Württemberg (1805–1845)*, Göttingen, 1986, pp. 296ff.

47. E. Zola, *The Ladies' Paradise*, Berkeley, 1992, translation of *Au bonheur des dames*, Paris, 1927; see, too, E. Zola, *Carnets d'enquêtes: Une ethnographie inédite de la France*, ed. H. Mitterand, Paris, 1986; R. Boulby, *Just Looking: Consumer Culture in Dreiser, Gissing, and Zola*, New York, 1985, pp. 66ff.

Bibliography

Abelson, E.S. *When Ladies Go A-Thieving: Middle Class Shoplifters in the Victorian Department Store*. New York, NY, 1989.

Bader, V. et al. *Einführung in die Gesellschaftstheorie: Gesellschaft, Wirtschaft und Staat bei Marx und Weber*. Frankfurt am Main, New York, NY, 1976.

Bairoch, P and Hobsbawm, E.J. (eds) *Storia d'Europa*, vol V: *L'età contemporanca: Secoli XIX–XX*. Turin, 1996.

Becker, J.J. *Comment les français sont entrés dans la guerre*. Paris, 1977.

Belting, I. *Mode und Revolution: Deutschland 1848/49*. Hildesheim, 1997.

Beltran, A. et al. 'Nascita, crescita e dominio della società dei consumi', in *Storia d'Europa, vol V: L'età contemporanca: Secoli XIX–XX*, ed. P. Bairoch and E.J. Hobsbawm. Turin, 1996, pp. 467–90.

Benson, J. *The Rise of Consumer Society in Britain 1880–1920*. London, 1994.

Benson, J. and Shaw, G. (eds) *The Evolution of Retail Systems ca. 1800–1914*. Leicester, 1992.

Benson, S.P. *Counter Cultures: Saleswomen, Managers and Customers in American Department Stores*, 1890–1940. Urbana, IL, 1986.

Bohstedt, I. *Riots and Community: Politics in England and Wales, 1790–1810*. Cambridge, MA, 1983.

Boulby, R. *Just Looking: Consumer Culture in Dreiser, Gissing, and Zola*. New York, NY, 1985.

Bourdieu, P. *La distinction: Critique sociale du jugement*. Paris, 1979.

Braudel, F. 'Les structures du quotidien', in *Civilisation matérielle, Economie et Capitalisme XVe–XVIIIe siècle*, ed. F. Braudel. Paris, 1979, pp. 81–290.

Braudel, F. and Labrousse, E. (eds) *Histoire économique et social de la France*, vols 3,1 and 3,2; vol. 4 (v,1; 4,2, 4,3). Paris, 1976–82.

Brenner, Y.S. et al. *Income Distribution in Historical Perspective*. Cambridge, Paris, 1991.

Brewer, J. and Porter, R. (eds) *Consumption and the World of Goods*. London, 1993.

Brewer, J. 'Was können wir aus der Geschichte der frühen Neuzeit für die moderne Konsumgeschichte lernen?', in *Europäische Konsumgeschichte: Zur Gesellschafts- und Kulturgeschichte des Konsums (18. bis 20. Jahrhundert)*, ed. H. Siegrist et al. Frankfurt am Main, New York, NY, 1997, pp. 51–74.

Burdy, J.P. *Le Soleil noir: Un quartier de Saint-Etienne, 1840–1940*. Lyon, 1989.

Cagliotti, D.L. *Il Guadagno difficle: Commercianti Napoletani nella Seconda Metà dell'Ottocento*. Bologna, 1994.

Camporesi, P. *La terre et la lune: Alimentation, folklore, société*. Paris, 1993.

Certeau, M. de *L'invention du quotidien*, vol. 1: *Arts de faire*. Paris, 1980.

Charle, C. *Histoire sociale de la France*. Paris, 1990.

Chessel, M.E. *La publicité: Naissance d'une profession 1900–1940*. Paris, 1998.

Cleve, I. *Geschmack, Kunst und Konsum: Kulturpolitik als Wirtschaftspolitik in Frankreich und Württemberg (1805–1845)*. Göttingen, 1986.

Crew, D.F. '"Wohlfahrtsbrot ist bitteres Brot": The Elderly, the Disabled, and Local Welfare. Authorities in the Weimar Republic 1924–1933', *Archiv für Sozialgeschichte* 30 (1990), pp. 217–95.

Crossick, G. and Haupt, H.G. *The Petite Bourgeoisie in Europe 1780–1914: Enterprise, Family, and Independence*. London, New York, NY, 1995.

Dijk, H. van *De modernising van Europa: Twee eeuwen Maatschappijgeschiedenis*. Utrecht, 1994.

Dowe, D. (ed.). *Erhebungen von Wirtschaftsuntersuchungen minderbemittelter Familien im Deutschen Reich (1909) und 320 Haushaltsrechnungen von Mitarbeitern (1909)*, reprint. Berlin, 1981.

Featherstone, M. *Consumer Culture and Postmodernism*. London, 1991.

Fontaine, L. *Histoire du colportage en Europe, XVe–XIXe siècle*. Paris, 1993.

Fourlough, E. *Consumer Cooperation in France: The Politics of Consumption 1834–1930*. Ithaca, NY, 1991.

Fraser, H. *The Coming of the Mass Market, 1890–1914*. Hamden, 1981.

Gailus, M. *Straße und Brot: Sozialer Protest in den deutschen Staaten unter besonderer Berücksichtigung Preußens, 1847–1849*. Göttingen, 1990

Gilcher-Holtey, I. 'Kulturelle und symbolische Praktiken: Das Unternehmen Pierre Bourdieu', in *Kulturgeschichte heute, ed. W. Hartwig and H.-U. Wehler*. Göttingen, 1996, pp. 11–130.

Goetsch, S. 'Hungerunruhen – Verhandlungen im traditionellen Protestverhalten', *Zeitschrift für Volkskunde* 80 (1984), pp. 169–82.

Grazia, V. de. 'Mass Culture and Sovereignty: the American Challenge to European Cinemas, 1920–1960', *Journal of Modern History* 61 (1989), pp. 53–87.

—— 'Changing Consumption Regimes', in *The Sex of the Things: Gender and Consumption in Historical Perspective*, ed. V. de Grazia. Berkeley, CA, Los Angeles, CA, London, 1996, p. 11–24.

—— 'Amerikanisierung und wechselnde Leitbilder der Konsum-Moderne (consumer-modernity) in Europa', in *Europäische Konsumgeschichte: Zur Gesellschafts- und Kulturgeschichte des Konsums (18. bis 20. Jahrhundert)*, ed. H. Siegrist et al. Frankfurt am Main, New York, NY, 1997, pp. 109–37.

Gueslin, A. *L'invention de l'Economie Sociale: Le XIXe siècle français*. Paris, 1987.

Halbwachs, M. *La classe ouvrière et les niveaux de vie: Recherches sur la hiérarchie des besoins dans les sociétés industrielles contemporaines*. Paris, 1913.

—— *L'evolution des besoins dans les classes ouvrières*. Paris, 1933.

Hauch, G. *Frau Biedermeier auf den Barrikaden: Frauenleben in der Wiener Revolution 1848*. Vienna, 1990.

Haupt, H.G. 'Kleinhändler und Arbeiter in Bremen zwischen 1890 und 1914', *Archiv für Sozialgeschichte* 22 (1982), pp. 95–134.

Heym, S. *Nachruf*. Frankfurt am Main, 1991.

Hobsbawm, E.J. *Europäische Revolutionen*. Zurich, 1962.

—— *Die Blütezeit des Kapitals: Eine Kulturgeschichte der Jahre 1848–1875*. Munich, 1977.

—— *Das imperiale Zeitalter 1875–1914*. Frankfurt am Main, 1989.

Hoffmann, S. *Le mouvement Poujade*. Paris, 1956.

Hoffmann, W. (ed.). *Sozialökonomische Studientexte: Wert und Preislehre*. Berlin, 1971.

Hoggart, R. *La culture du pauvre*. Paris, 1970.

Horrowitz, D. *The Morality of Spending: Attitudes towards the Consumer Society in America, 1875–1940*. Baltimore, MD, 1985.

Hubscher, R. *L'Agriculture et la Société rurale dans le Pas-de-Calais du XIXe siècle à 1914*. Arras, 1980, 2 vols.

Jacquement, G. *Belleville au XIXe siècle: Du faubourg à la ville*. Paris, 1984.

Jaumain, S. *Les petits commerçants belge face à la modernité (1880–1914)*. Brussels, 1995.

Kaelble, H. *Auf dem Weg zu einer europäischen Gesellschaft. Eine Sozialgeschichte Westeuropas 1880–1980*. Munich, 1987.

—— *Nachbarn am Rhein: Entfremdung und Annäherung der französischen und deutschen Gesellschaft seit 1880*. Munich, 1991.

—— 'Europäische Besonderheiten des Massenkonsums, 1950–1990', in *Europäische Konsumgeschichte: Zur Gesellschafts- und Kulturgeschichte des Konsums (18. bis 20. Jahrhundert)*, ed. H. Siegrist et al. Frankfurt am Main, New York, NY, 1997, pp. 169–203.

Kalaora, B. and Savoye, A. *Les inventeurs oubliés*. Paris, 1989.

Kienitz, S. 'Aecht deutsche Weiblichkeit, Mode und Konsum als bürgerliche Frauenpolitik', in *Schimpfende Weiber und patriotische Jungfrauen – Frauen im Vormärz und in der Revoution 1848–49*, ed. C. Lipp. Moos, Baden-Baden, 1986, pp. 76–88.

Kocka, J. *Arbeitsverhältnisse und Arbeiterexistenzen*. Bonn, 1990.

Kuisel, R. *Seducing the French*. Berkeley, CA, 1992.

Laermans, R. 'Learning to Consume: Early Department Stores and the Shaping of the Modern Consumer Culture, 1880–1914', *Theory, Culture and Society* 10 (1993), pp. 70–102.

Langewiesche, D. '"... für Volk und Vaterland künftig zu wirken." Zur politischen und gesellschaftlichen Rolle der Turner zwischen 1811 und 1871', in *Kulturgut und Körperkultur? Sport und Sportwissenschaft im Wandel*, ed. O. Grube. Tübingen, 1990, pp. 22–61.

Le Play, F. *La méthode sociale*, reprint. Paris, 1989.

Leach, W.R. 'Transformations in a Culture of Consumption: Women and Department Stores 1890–1925', *Journal of American History* 71 (1984), pp. 319–42.

Léon, P. (ed.). *La domination du capitalisme, Histoire économique et sociale du monde*, vol. 4. Paris, 1978.

Lequin, Y. (ed.). *Histoire des Français XIXe–XXe siècles*, 3 vols. Paris, 1984.

Levy-Leboyer, M. and Bourguignon, F. *L'economie française au XIX siècle: Analyse macroéconomique*. Paris, 1985.

Linden, M. van der. 'Working-Class Consumer Power', in *International Labor and Working Class History* 46 (1994), pp. 109–21.

Lüdtke, A. 'Hunger, Essens-Genüsse und Politik bei Fabrikarbeitern und Arbeiterfrauen: Beispiele aus dem rheinisch-westfälischen Industriegebiet, 1910–1940', in A. Lüdtke, *Eigen-Sinn: Fabrikalltag, Arbeitererfahrungen und Politik vom Kaiserreich bis zum Faschismus*. Hamburg, 1993, pp. 194–209.

Margairaz, D. 'La formation du réseau des foires et des marchés', *Annales E. S. C.* 40 (1986), pp. 1215–42.

Martin, J.C. 'Commerce et commerçantes à Niort au XIXe siècle: Les faillites', *Bulletin de la Société Historique et Scientifique des Deux-Sèvres* 13 (1980), pp. 337–501.

McKendrick, N. et al. *The Birth of a Consumer Society*. London, 1982.

Medick, H. 'Eine Kultur des Ansehens: Kleider und Kleiderfarben in Laichingen 1750–1820', *Historische Anthropologie* 2 (1994), pp. 193–212.

Miller, M.B. *Au bon marché 1869–1920: Le consommateur apprivoisé*. Paris, 1987.

Mintz, S. *Sweetness and Power: The Plan of Sugar in Modern History*. New York, NY, 1985.

—— 'The Changing Role of Food in the Study of Consumption', in *Consumption and the World of Goods*, ed. J. Brewer and R. Porter. London, 1993, pp. 261–73.

Montebello, F. 'Spectacle cinématographique et classe ouvrière Longwy 1944–1960', diss., Lyon II, 1997.

Moravcovà, M. 'Die tschechischen Frauen im revolutionären Prag 1848/49', in *1848–49 Revolutionen in Ostmitteleuropa*, ed. R. Jaworski and R. Luft. Munich, 1996, pp. 72–91.

O'Brien, P. 'The Kleptomnia Diagnosis – Bourgeois Women and Theft in Late 19th Century France', *Journal of Social History* 17 (1983–84), pp. 65–77.

Oddy, D.J. 'Food, Drink, and Nutrition', in *The Cambridge Social History of Britain, 1750–1950*, ed. F.M.L. Thompson, 3 vols. Cambridge: Cambridge University Press, 1990, vol. 2, pp. 251–78.

Perrot, M. *Le mode de vie des familles bourgeoises, 1873–1953*. Paris, 1961.

—— *Les ouvriers en grève: France 1871–1890*. Paris, 1974, vol. 2, pp. 201–40.

Pierenkemper, T. 'Das Rechnungsbuch der Hausfrau – und was wir daraus lernen können: Zur Verwendbarkeit privater Haushaltsrechnungen in der historischen Wirtschafts-und Sozialforschung', *Geschichte und Gesellschaft*, 14 (1988), pp. 38–63.

—— 'Der bürgerliche Haushalt in Deutschland an der Wende zum 20. Jahrhundert – im Spiegel von Haushaltsrechnungen', in *Zur Geschichte der Ökonomik der Privathaushalte*, ed. D. Petzina. Berlin, 1991, pp. 149–85.

—— (ed.). *Zur Ökonomik des privaten Haushalts: Haushaltsrechnungen als Quellen historischer Wirtschafts- und Sozialforschung*. Frankfurt am Main, New York, NY, 1991.

Prinz, M. *Brot und Dividende: Konsumvereine in Deutschland und England von 1914*. Göttingen, 1996.

Revel, J. 'Consommation', in *La nouvelle Histoire*, ed. J. Le Goff. Paris, 1986, p. 321.

Roche, D. *La culture des apparences: Une histoire du vêtement XVIIe–XVIIIe siècle*. Paris, 1989.

Roy, M. *Les commerçants entre la révolte et le modernisation*. Paris, 1971.

Sandgruber, R. *Die Anfänge zur Konsumgesellschaft: Konsumgüterverbrauch, Lebensstandard und Alltagskultur in Österreich im 18. und 19. Jahrhundert*. Munich, 1982.

—— 'Interfamiliale Einkommens- und Konsumaufteilung', in *Ehe, Liebe, Tod*, ed. P. Borscheid and H.-J. Teuteberg. Münster, 1983, pp. 135–49.

—— 'Knödel, Nudel, Topfenstrudel: Österreichische Ernährungsgewohnheiten und regionale Unterschiede in Mitteleuropa', in *Nord-Süd-Unterschiede in der städtischen und ländlichen Kultur Mitteleuropas*, ed. G. Wiegelmann. Münster, 1985, pp. 265–97.

Sarasion, P. 'Une coutume barbare, les fonctions significantes de l'argent dans une société bourgeoise vers 1900', *Genèses* 15, (1994), pp. 84–102.

Satta, S. *Der Tag des Gerichts*. Frankfurt am Main, 1996.

Tanner, J. 'Der Mensch ist, was er ißt: Ernährungsmythen und Wandel der Eßkultur', *Historische Anthropologie* 4 (1996), pp. 399–419.

Schama, S. *The Embarrassment of Riches: An Interpretation of Dutch Culture in the Golden Age*. London, 1987.

Scholliers, P. (ed.). *Real Wages in 19th and 20th Century Europe: Historical and Comparative Perspectives*. New York, NY, Oxford, 1989.

Scholliers, P. and Zamagni, V. (eds) *Labour's Reward: Real Wages and Economic Change in 19th and 20th Century Europe*. Aldershot, 1995.

Segalen, M. *Maris et femmes dans la société paysanne*. Paris, 1980.

Spiekermann, U. 'Haushaltsrechnungen als Quellen der Ernährungsgeschichte: Überblick und methodischer Problemaufriß', in *Neue Wege zur Ernährungsgeschichte: Kochbücher, Haushaltsrechnungen, Konsumvereinsberichte und Autobiographien in der Diskussion*, ed. D. Reinhardt et al. Frankfurt am Main, 1993, pp. 51–85.

Statistisches Amt der Stadt Dresden (ed.). *Mitteilungen des Statistischen Amtes der Stadt Dresden, 13. Heft, Inventarien von 87 Dresdner Arbeiterhaushalten, aufgenommen im November 1903*. Dresden, 1904.

Tanner, J. 'Industrialisierung, Rationalisierung und Wandel des Konsum- und Geschmacksverhaltens im europäisch-amerikanischen Vergleich', in *Europäische Konsumgeschichte: Zur Gesellschafts- und Kulturgeschichte des Konsums (18. bis 20. Jahrhundert)*, ed. H. Siegrist et al. Frankfurt am Main. New York, NY, 1997, pp. 583–614.

Tenfelde, K. 'Klassenspezifische Konsummuster im Deutschen Kaiserreich', in *Europäische Konsumgeschichte: Zur Gesellschafts- und Kulturgeschichte des Konsums (18. bis 20. Jahrhundert)*, eds H. Siegrist et al. Frankfurt am Main, New York, NY, 1997, pp. 245–66.

Teuteberg, H.J. and Wiegelmann, G. *Unsere tägliche Kost: Geschichte und regionale Prägung*. Münster, 1986.

Tilly, C. et al. *The Rebellious Century 1830–1930*. Cambridge, MA, 1975.

Wakounig, M. 'Konsumverhalten des Wiener Bürgertums im 19. und 20. Jahrhundert', *Jahrbuch des Vereins für die Geschichte der Stadt Wien* 44/45 (1989), pp. 154–86.

Wehler, H.-U. *Modernisierungstheorien*. Göttingen, 1976.

—— *Deutsche Gesellschaftsgeschichte*, vols. 1, 2 and 3. Munich, 1987–95.

Williams, R. *Problems in Materialism and Culture*. London, 1980.

Zamagni, V. 'Die langsame Modernisierung des italienischen Einzelhandels: Die Geschichte eines Sonderfalls in vergleichender Perspektive', in *Europäische Konsumgeschichte: Zur Gesellschafts- und Kulturgeschichte des Konsums (18. bis 20. Jahrhundert)*, ed. H. Siegrist et al. Frankfurt am Main, New York, NY, 1997, pp. 705–16.

—— *La distribuzione commerciale in Italia fra le due guerre*. Milan, 1981.

Zanielli, S. *I Consumi a Milanonell'ottocento*. Rome, 1974.

Zapf, W. (ed.). *Theorien des sozialen Wandels*. Cologne, Berlin, 1969.

Zola, E. *The Ladies' Paradise*. Berkeley, CA, 1992 (original: *Au bonheur des dames*, Paris, 1927).

—— *Carnets d'enquêtes: Une ethnographie inédite de la France*, ed. H. Mitterand. Paris, 1986.

9

INTELLECTUALS IN EUROPE IN THE SECOND HALF OF THE NINETEENTH CENTURY

Elements for a Comparison

Christophe Charle

The new term '*intellectuels*' first appeared in France in the 1890s and, largely as a result of the Dreyfus affair, quickly spread not only throughout France but indeed throughout the whole of Europe. What was at stake in this crisis was not only a political problem but the affirmation of a new group, one which saw itself as the defender of universal values against the reason of the state.[1] These values justified the collective intervention of writers, artists, scholars, students, members of the liberal professions and others in political debates, despite the fact that most were not professional politicians. The other specificity of this moment on which I will focus my comparison is that this same cause, or other similar ones, also encouraged the intervention of intellectuals in other countries. Nevertheless, the emergence of intellectuals does not represent the appearance of a new social group during the nineteenth and twentieth centuries, as other historians or sociologists have argued. Intellectuals, especially in France at the end of the last century, present a double specificity:

1. The emergence of *intellectuels* resulted from a struggle between two different groups of intellectuals, the Dreyfusards and the anti-Dreyfusards, each of whom embraced and defended a different definition of the social, ideological or political role of intellectuals. Prior to that time, there had been only singular personalities who defended general or individual causes, like Voltaire in the case of Calas or Victor Hugo in that of the Republic against the coup d'état.

2. The second peculiarity of this conjuncture is its broad echo outside of France. Zola, for example, received letters from America and Romania. Russian, Austrian, Spanish and Belgian intellectuals also expressed their solidarity with the French Dreyfusards.[2]

The thesis that I shall defend here is that a convergence of trends in social and cultural fields prepared the ground for this success story throughout Europe. These transformations of intellectual life will be described at three levels: the social evolution of intellectual life, the changing status of intellectual professions and the new relationships between the intellectual and political fields. Nevertheless, although they had been taking place in all European countries since the 1860s, these transformations played themselves out in different ways depending on the social, cultural and political inheritance of each nation or, in the case of multiethnic states, of each region. The aim of the present comparison is to weigh the relative importance of these factors of differentiation to explain why the French conception of *intellectuels* succeeded at that time while some others did not. To make it possible to compare such different social contexts, I will here employ a minimalist definition of intellectuals as 'those claiming autonomy'. Autonomy might be understood in economic, social, cultural or political terms. The difficulty in this comparison lies in the fact that the various European states were at very different stages of economic, social and political development during this period, resulting in very case-specific conditions of affirmation for the new group of intellectuals.

The transformation of intellectual professions after the 1860s

After the 1860s, all European countries underwent dramatic changes in the various spheres of intellectual life. These changes were linked in part to the general economic transformation of Europe and in part represented an autonomous trend. They manifested themselves primarily in general expansion of education at all levels: elementary, secondary and university. Even if there are obvious time lags between Western and Eastern and between Northern and Southern Europe, the evolution was everywhere leading in the same direction.

The first consequence of this development was the broad expansion of the potential readership of printed matter. A new demand for new types of cultural products arose, giving rise to new economic opportunities for newcomers in the intellectual field (e.g., schoolbooks, books for young people, books and magazines for women, inexpensive and popular literature). Free intellectual activities became far more differentiated, requiring new and more subtle classifications.[3]

The second consequence of this change was the expansion of the intellectual professions, both in the economic market (e.g., journalists, writers, publishers, editors, freelance teachers, etc.) and in the civil service (e.g., teachers, academics, cultural agents of the state, etc.). It is very difficult to make a full evaluation of this expansion, but indirect figures, such as the expansion of university enrolments (see Table 9.1) or statistics of printed titles (see Table 9.2), can give us a rough idea of its importance.

Table 9.1: Student enrolments in Europe (in thousands) (1860–1910)[4]

	UK	Germany	Russia	France	Austria	Italy	Spain
1860	3	12	5	8	9		
1870	5	13	6	11	5.6	12	
1880	10	21	8	12	5.5	12.1	
1890	16	28	13	20	7.1	18.5	
1900	17	44.2	16	29	10	24.6	8
1910	26	66.8	37	41	12.6	24.4	16

In Germany, the expansion of the universities occurred in the 1870s, and in France and in England the 1880s. Student figures also first reached significant levels in Austria-Hungary, Italy and Russia at this time. For example, in Austria (in its actual limits) and Hungary (in its former ones) the 10,000 mark was reached. In Italy, university enrolments more than doubled (from 12,021 in 1870–1 to 24,430 in 1910–11). In Russia, the increase was even more dramatic, moving from 5000 students in 1860 to 37,000 in 1910, with significant intermediate fluctuations.

This academic expansion changed the status of the intellectual professions; it multiplied the number of intellectual professions and conferred a new importance on teachers at the secondary or university level as the academic degrees they bestowed increasingly became keys to social success. Universities, now linked with research and innovation following the spread of the German academic ideal to France, England, Italy, Russia and Central Europe, also created a special audience for learned or elitist intellectual productions through the multiplication of disciplinary journals and learned societies. Avant-garde circles in the literary and artistic capitals revolted against mass or philistine literary and artistic productions.

The diversification of cultural products

The diversification of cultural products may be grasped thanks to some quantitative data such as the number of printed titles. Figures for printed titles show an increase by the factor 1.5 to 1.8 in France, Germany and Italy (1875–1900), by more than the factor 2 in Great Britain and by almost the factor 4 in Russia (see Table 9.2). Numbers of periodicals underwent a parallel and sometimes even stronger development: in Britain from 1,855 in 1872–4 to 3,803 in 1882–5, then declining to 2,902 in 1900 due to a movement of capitalist concentration. In France, the figures indicate an even sharper rise during the same period: from 2,074 to 6,736. Expansion was also faster in more backward countries like Italy (with a twofold growth) and Austria (with a sixfold one).[6]

Table 9.2: Number of printed titles in Europe[5]

	Germany	France	Italy	U.K.	Russia
1850	9,053	9,891	1,646 (1846)	2,600	?
1876	13,556	19,068 (1875)	5,096 (1878)	?	7,366 (1878)
1891	21,279	24,472	8,340	5,706	?
1901	25,331	28,143 (1900)	7,993	6,000	10,318
1911	32,998	32,834 (1913)	?	12,379	27,400 (1912)

New intellectual professions

These new audiences, products and media created new intellectual jobs. The official figures drawn from census data may be subject to debate (for, as in the first part of nineteenth century, intellectual professions could be combined with other social activities), but it is meaningful that censuses now included the category of literary activities at large within the general classification of professions (see Table 9.3). This shows that the activities of 'journalists, publicists, authors, scientists' and so on were no longer seen as merely partial, secondary or intermittent. They ought to be distinguished from the classical liberal professions. In 1881 the English census counted 6,893 people who claimed to be 'authors, editors, journalists, and so on'; thirty years later, in 1911, this group was twice as large (13,786). At the earlier date, the corresponding item in France ('savants, hommes de lettres, publicistes') already included 7,372 people.

Table 9.3: Growth of the free intellectual professions (writers, journalists, scientists, publicists) in Europe (1880–1910)

	Germany	Growth rate %	France	Growth rate %	England and Wales	Growth rate %	Austria	Growth rate %
1876	?		4,173		?			
1881	c.5,004	?	7,372	76.6	6,893		734*	
1896	5,507 (1895)	10	6,354	-13.8	8,272 (1891)	20	1,589* (1890)	116
1906	8,753 (1907)	58.9	9,148	43.9	11,060	33.7	1,920	20.8
1910					13,786 (1911)	24.6	1,864	-2.9

Sources: Censuses of different countries

The gap between Western and Central Europe is far more visible. We may estimate the number of professional writers and journalists to have been 5,094 in 1882 in the German *Reich* and 734 in Cisleithania in 1880 (these results are based on an evaluation, as the census still confused this category with a more general one). Compared to France and Britain, this is a low level and shows a moderate growth in the first decade for Germany (plus 10 percent); it indicates that the professionalisation of authors and journalists in Central Europe was still at a different stage of development due to lingering juridical and political barriers restraining freedom of opinion. Although the autonomisation of the free literary professions took place here in the 1890s, Germany did not surpass France and England in this respect as it did in terms of book production.

In Cisleithania, on the contrary, where the book market was strongly dependent on Germany, positions with newspapers and periodicals experienced a faster growth rate, affirming the diversity of public opinion in the Empire. Vienna, with its newspapers and theatres, played an even greater role than Berlin in attracting young and ambitious literary professionals from all the German-speaking countries in the Double Monarchy.[7]

State intellectuals

By way of compensation, intellectual civil service positions were far more developed in the Eastern part of Europe than in the Western part (Table 9.4).

Table 4: University teachers in Europe (1864–1910)[8]

	Germany	France	Italy	U.K.	Spain	Austria	Hungary	Russia
1864	1,468	c. 900	?	c. 330	?	624 (1871)	137 (1874)	528 (1855)
1894	2,526	1,400	946	1,261	444	1,176	353	923
1909	3,807	2,200	1,141	2,355	480	1,618	589	

Germany had developed its universities earlier. In spite of the creation of new universities in England after 1850 (civic universities) and the expansion of academic positions in France during the Third Republic, German levels were still higher at the beginning of the twentieth century. The 900 French scholars teaching in university departments in 1865 look few in number compared to the 1,468 German academics thus employed in 1864. In Britain, the figures are even lower for the 1860s (with fewer than 400 scholars, of whom seventy-seven were at Oxbridge) and despite Britain's economic wealth were still at the same level as in France on the eve of the First World War. In comparison, France's academic effort appears impressive, with a twofold growth in the 1880s and a threefold one in 1914. Nor did the English academic expansion have the same symbolic value as the French. The new English universities were founded in industrial or commercial towns such as Manchester, Sheffield, Birmingham, Cardiff, Leeds, Liverpool and Newcastle. These new universities were strongly orientated towards concrete and practical disciplines, whereas the classical universities (Oxbridge), reformed only at the end of the century, retained their leading positions in the humanities and pure sciences and experienced only a moderate expansion due to their social elitism. Compared to France, academia in England still played a less important role in the public sphere in spite of its expansion and diversification. In sum, we see that opposite developments took place in the Western and Eastern parts of Europe. In the first half of the century, Western Europe's dominant intellectual figures came mainly from the free intellectual field, while in Central Europe the academic world enjoyed the stronger symbolic position. Expansion in the second half of the century reshifted this balance. In Central Europe, intellectuals were now not only subjected to state power but increasingly to the laws of the market. In France and, to a lesser degree, in Britain, particularly in Scotland, academic and public issues became more central to the intellectual field. This provided a basis for the convergence I mentioned in the introduction; however, persisting differences also offer evidence of typological differentiations among the European nations.

Centre and periphery

Another strong factor of differentiation within Europe was the inherited contrast between a centralised and a polycentric Europe. On the one hand, we find nations like France, Hungary, England, Russia (and, to a lesser degree, Spain and Austria) and, on the other hand, a geographical space extending from Hamburg to Palermo and from Strasbourg to Eastern Poland. In the first Europe, intellectual positions were mainly concentrated in the metropolises or in a few larger cities, whereas, in the second one, intellectual competition was less fierce, as intellectuals were distributed among a greater number of cities. In as much as avant-gardes and innovators were more strongly attracted by larger towns and capitals and have played an important role in the emergence and mobilisation of contemporary intellectuals, it is not surprising that the French model of the *intellectuel* strongly predominates in centralised countries while remaining weak in polycentric ones.

France provides the ideal example of such intellectual concentration, since 51 percent of its men of letters and journalists lived in Paris in 1876 and a far greater proportion in 1896, namely, 65 percent. Eighty percent of books were published in Paris. Vienna played a similar leading role in Cisleithania, housing 52.7 percent of the Empire's writers and journalists in 1880.

Despite London's huge population centralisation in England is not so striking, with only 39.7 percent of writers and journalists living in the metropolis in 1881 (this figure is even lower for 1910: 32.4 percent).

In Germany, in spite of the economic and demographic dynamism of Berlin, the centralising trend remained understated, with only 20 percent of printed titles published in the 'Athens on the Spree' as opposed to 17.3 percent in Leipzig. Of the addresses mentioned in the *Kuerschners Gelehrtenkalender* (which represented a kind of *Who's Who* in German intellectual life) 23 and 24 percent are in Berlin for 1883 and 1907 respectively, far ahead of Munich, Leipzig or Dresden.[9] This long-term stability shows that the new imperial capital did not increasingly attract intellectuals, apart from those working for newspapers.

Intellectual professions and social fear: the academic proletariat

These quantitative and structural transformations of intellectual life were not universally perceived in the way in which historians may perceive them now. Nevertheless, the emergence of a new social – and, in some cases, political – representation of intellectuals was first acknowledged in the public sphere in the context of a general discussion about a supposed excess of intellectuals. This discussion was not a new one,[10] but was now based not only on impressions, but on the use of quantitative arguments, in particular university enrolments, the easiest statistics for contemporary publicists to acquire. The other source of unease was the perception of increasing competition on the free market, of harsher conditions of payment for authors' royalties, and, in some countries, of growing difficulties in obtaining academic positions with the development of an academic proletariat. Yet this pessimistic view is not general. Other intellectuals, thanks to the growing prestige of science and scholarship and/or to the impressive profits earned by a minority working for newspapers, in the theatre or publishing best-sellers, boasted of their role as a social model of meritocratic success or as leaders of public opinion on the basis of their massive audiences. This Janus-faced image of the intellectual professions was unevenly present in the different regions of Europe.

Complaints about an excess of intellectuals began in Germany and Russia in the 1880s with the denunciation of academic overproduction. According to Bismarck, students without job prospects, whom he referred to as the *Abiturientenproletariat*, would become leaders of revolutionary parties, as the populist intelligentsia had in Russia.[11] The same problem was also discussed in Italy. Italian writers noted that, despite its poverty, backwardness and illiteracy, Italy educated proportionally far more *laureati* than other advanced countries in Europe; namely 51.3 students per 100,000 inhabitants in 1886–91 as opposed to 48 in Germany and 42.6 in France.[12]

In France, conservative writers such as Barrès or Taine developed similar arguments a little later, stating them as a critique of the Republic and of democracy, which encouraged excessive social ambitions among lower classes (see *Les Déracinés* [1897])[13]; in Germany, defenders of existing social order spoke of a growing mob of bohemian journalists exciting popular and vulgar political passions.[14] England, by contrast, where, as we saw earlier, the expansion of intellectual professions was as important as in continental Europe, was remarkably absent from this debate. While such pessimistic discourse did exist there, it had less impact because of the general expansion of the anglophone population all over the world and the possibility for unsuccessful intellectuals to get a second chance in the United States, Canada or in other dominions under British rule. The opposition between a professional discourse – of English type – and a more social and political one – of the Continental type – sums up relatively well one of the great divisions of intellectual typology at the end of the century.

Typological sketch of intellectual roles

These general transformations explain to a very large extent the changing aspect of the social representations of intellectual professions. However, we must now introduce more specific conditions, depending on historical, political and cultural factors to explain the different European types of intellectuals and public modes of intervention. Due to lack of space, I will now limit the comparison to three cases: France, England and Germany. Russia, Italy and Spain would also be interesting variants.[15] Russia and Spain are more akin to France in view of the centralisation public life there and of important connections between religion and politics. Italy is closer to Germany in terms of its polycentric intellectual life, but also presents some national and intellectual similarities to France (the opposition between Church and State, the liberal tradition of governing elites, the reduced role of the nobility and importance of professions and the general defeatist mood of a late-comer nation).[16]

Political conditions in France and England might appear to be quite similar, with a parliamentary 'democracy', extensive liberties and the importance of intellectual debates in the public sphere. Because of this relative freedom of expression, the main front of opposition in these countries lay within the intellectual field, between those who, holding to an elitist image of themselves, rejected modernity, democracy and militant action, and the minority who, in both countries, believed in a strong continuity between older and newer struggles. In France, the Dreyfus affair embodied this opposition. On the other side of the Channel, the struggles were more pragmatic and focused primarily on social and international questions.

Liberal Europe: The French model

In France, the birth of the *intellectuels* was precipitated by the growing inadequacy of old patterns in the new situation created by the cultural expansion of the 1880s and 1890s.[17] Intellectual professions were becoming more common, resulting in the appearance within this individualistic milieu of collective attitudes in defence of their social and symbolic status.

This defence could rest on intellectual and 'pure' values or on professional and pragmatic ones. The first use of the term *intellectuels* is credited to avant-garde circles. It would be the germ of its political transformation, as for the Russian intelligentsia. As in Russia, the reformed universities played a great role in the emergence and mobilisation of intellectuals.

The second paradoxical factor of this ideological and political change is the precocious crisis of parliamentary democracy in France. After the establishment of the Third Republic, apoliticism predominated among intellectuals, as if the end of history had already been reached. A new politicisation occurred with the crisis of the official parties and the emergence of extremist factions, with which avant-garde writers sympathised (in particular anarchism). This new trend prepared what would be the specificity of the Dreyfus affair: the invention of a new relationship to politics beyond the traditional political channels. The new *intellectuels* claimed to have an autonomous way of practising politics, different from both the official way and their own former political practice. This was possible because the legitimacy of the Republican elites rested on the same bases as that of the intellectuals themselves, that is, on merit and individual talent.

But in so far as these elites appeared to be incompetent or corrupt after various crises and scandals (Boulangism, the Panama scandal, and so on), intellectuals could claim to represent an alternative elite, and one better suited a true democracy. Before the Dreyfus affair, students, avant-garde writers and even younger generations of academics articulated these new claims of being the true representatives of the people vis-à-vis politicians. The state itself, through its increasing intolerance of literary audacities and extremist parties (in particular anarchism), contributed to the mobilisation of authors against juridical prosecutions by means of collective manifestos.

In this respect, the Dreyfus affair represents at once a true continuity with preceding years and a break from them. Henceforth, the great mobilisations of intellectuals would hold on the same collective rites and values. Its novelty was that it proved that this type of mobilisation could have real political consequences and not only at a symbolic level, in that the debate opposed two types of intellectual roles, two systems of values and two visions of politics. This twofold mobilisation (of Dreyfusards and anti-Dreyfusards) was new and established, at both ends of the political spectrum – a general definition of intellectuals which was not limited to leftist intellectuals. In other countries, on the contrary, the corresponding equivalent of the *intellectuels* was confined to one camp.

Liberal Europe: The peculiarities of English intellectuals

In contrast with France, the traditional view is that there were no intellectuals in the Continental sense at all in Britain. For one or two decades, British historians and sociologists reacted against this strong anti-intellectual bias. Some authors spoke of an intelligentsia, i.e., an elitist avant-garde, others of 'public moralists' (a term which enhances the role of dominant and academic intellectuals) or of a 'professional class' (one which assimilates the intellectual professions into a new class).[18] A comparative approach does not claim to propose a new terminology or to find approximate analogies. Rather, it seeks to identify what specific factors may explain the strong dissimilarity with France, in spite of the similarity of the economic and political conditions of intellectual life in the two countries. I have already mentioned some of these in the first part of this essay: the elitism of university life and its separation from free intellectual life. Apart from the specific history of the educational system (private versus public, aristocratic versus relatively democratic), another difference is the relative proximity between the intellectual professions and the political elites. The established elites, even if they were obliged to reform and enlarge the political system, were not challenged in their role as the legitimate holders of power, as they were in France. In fact, the dominant English intellectuals for the most part shared the same values and background as gentlemen and political leaders, because they had attended the same public schools and universities.

Apart from these dominant intellectuals, there did appear, in the last decades of the century, new types of intellectuals with outsiders' profiles. The best-known of these are the Fabians, who could not attend the best colleges and universities and had to make their own way through journalism, literature or militant politics.

Yet this avant-garde is very different from the contemporary French avant-gardes. Firstly it was limited to one field: for the Fabians, social and political questions; for aesthetes, aesthetic life, and so on. They claimed that they had created a voluntary structure which was designed to influence the official sphere indirectly, not to destroy or confront it directly. Sidney Webb's strategy was to influence the leading group in British society, which he estimated to have included 2,000 persons.[19]

Even when mobilisation occurred on a larger scale, as during the Boer War, English intellectuals continued to use and respect the officially sanctioned modes of action and legal frameworks.[20] Finally, the main difference lay in the very different functions of the state in England and in continental Europe. In England, militant intellectuals endeavoured to enlarge its role in order to correct social injustice, whereas in France and Germany, intellectuals struggled first to curb its authoritarian tendencies.

Authoritarian Europe: The case of Germany

My third comparative sketch will focus upon Germany and, more generally, Central Europe. The situation in this region is usually described only negatively in comparison with England and France, being characterised by incomplete liberalism, unfinished democracy, an authoritarian state and rapid economic development, a high level of intellectual legitimacy and limited autonomy of the intellectual field. However, this view is an oversimplification.

From my point of view, more emphasis should be placed on the fragmentation of the intellectual field (along geographical or corporatist lines). This fragmentation impeded the organisation of local or professional struggles for autonomy.

Nevertheless this remains compatible with an early emergence of the question of 'intellectuals', even before it arose in France, as has been shown in the above-mentioned discussion about the academic proletariat, as well as with the ideological struggles within German Social Democracy about the place of the *Intelligenz* in the party and also within the *Antisemitismusstreit* of 1879. The latter, a well-known debate about the position of Jews in German society between the conservative historian Treitschke and his liberal colleague Mommsen, a former 'forty-eighter', very closely resembles in its argumentation that between the French Dreyfusards and anti-Dreyfusards.[21] As in France twenty years later, the rights of minorities and, in particular, those of the individual and of Jews were at the centre of the debate. Other cases inside universities, like those of Arons or Spahn, or outside of them, like the mobilisation against the *lex Heinze* (1900), also show that debates about intellectual autonomy were just as crucial in Germany as in France and several times succeeded in mobilising certain types of intellectuals. Aron's case (the dismissal on political grounds of a *Privatdozent* (outside lecturer) from the University of Berlin despite the opposition of a majority of the professors) shows the limits of academic *Lehrfreiheit* (freedom of academic teaching), even for *Privatdozenten*, who were not officially *Beamte* (civil servants); in the Spahn case the direct political interventions of the government into the process of academic nominations can clearly be seen. Finally, the debate about *lex Heinze* (a law specifically directed against pornography, but in practice applicable to nonconformist artistic or literary expressions) forged an alliance between writers, journalists, artists, a few academics and progressive parties against the most conservative trends in German society.[22]

Nevertheless, in all cases, mobilisation inside the intellectual field was limited to certain regions, specific groups and limited issues, which did not call into question the structure of the state itself, as happened in France. A mere political explanation (that Germany was part of an Empire as opposed to a Republic) is not enough. What was specific and new in the Dreyfus case was the convergence of different intellectual groups about common values. In Germany, the corporatist ethos remained stronger even about general issues; free intellectuals and state intellectuals despised each other. Academics avoided the political sphere and indeed defended the state from within various associations. Only a small minority in the free intellectual field and a small number of academics challenged the very authority of the dominant elites or involved themselves in national causes.

Like Goethe in his relationship with the Grand Duke of Saxe-Weimar, the *Gebildete* (the educated) assumed that they represented true public opinion and were the best interpreters of national issues; however, they preferred to serve their country from within their own areas of specialisation.

Conclusion

In spite of the specificities of the different parts of Europe, the different types of intellectuals that emerged during the last century illustrate some sort of convergence at a transnational level. Most significant for the argument for a European cultural way is that each national debate had some European echo outside its national borders, at the end of the nineteenth century as well as in the Romantic period.

An important question (which I was not able to address here) is that of the influence of the relations between state and religion and of the persisting role of clerical models, which were a precursor and an alternative to intellectuals in both Catholic and Protestant countries.

Another question for future research is that of competition between intellectual and nonintellectual professions. My hypothesis for France, where the question has been better investigated, is that this precipitated the emergence of *intellectuels*, since the dominant positions within the political elite of the Third Republic were held by lawyers. The same situation existed in Italy, although in countries where the position of intellectuals was weak, the older professions remained dominant or were themselves dominated by civil servants, as in Germany.

Notes

1. This theme is developed in my book, C. Charle, *Naissance des 'intellectuels' (1880–1900)*, Paris, 1990, and in my paper C. Charle, 'Intellectuals in France around 1900 in a Comparative Perspective', in *Vanguards of Modernity, Society, Intellectuals and the University*, ed. N. Kauppi and P. Sulkunen (Publications of the Research Unit for Contemporary Culture, University of Jyväskylä, Finland, 32), Jyväskylä, 1992, pp.19–32.

2. See the spectrum of views on and reactions to the Dreyfus affair in: *L'Affaire Dreyfus de A à Z*, ed. M. Drouin, Paris, 1994.

3. There is a vast literature on this subject. See in particular F. Barbier, *L'Empire du livre*, Paris, 1995 (for Germany); *Histoire de l'édition française*, ed. R. Chartier and H.-J. Martin, vol. 3, 2nd ed., Paris, 1990; M. Plant, *The English Book Trade*, (1st edn 1939), London, 1974.

4. F.K. Ringer, *Fields of Knowledge*, Paris, Cambridge, 1992, pp. 48–9 and F.K. Ringer, *Education and Society in Modern Europe*, Bloomington, 1979 (NB: the dates are approximate; they correspond to the data available for each decade). Sources: United Kingdom, Germany, Russia: *The Transformation of Higher Learning (1860–1930)*, ed. K.H. Jarausch, Stuttgart, 1983, p. 13; France: The estimate for 1860 follows from G. Weisz, *The Emergence of Modern Universities in France 1863–1914*, Princeton, 1983, p. 46 (medicine and law extended with an evaluation for other minor faculties); other

lines: ibid., p. 23; Austria: Those universities are only considered here within the actual boundaries of Austria, excluding the Technischen Hochschulen. H. Engelbrecht, *Geschichte des österreichischen Bildungswesens*, vol. 4, Vienna, 1986, p. 236; Italy: M. Barbagli, *Disocupazione intellettuale et sistema scolastico in Italia*, Bologna, 1974, pp. 134 and 204 (American translation: *Educating for Unemployment: Politics, Labour Markets, and the School System. Italy, 1859–1973*, New York, 1982) and A. Cammelli, 'Universities and professions', in *Society and the Professions in Italy, 1860–1914*, ed. M. Malatesta, Cambridge, 1995, pp. 27–79, p. 65; Spain: J.-L. Guereña, 'L'Université espagnole à la fin du XIXe siècle', in *L'Université en Espagne et en Amérique latine du Moyen Age à nos jours. I. Structures et acteurs, Tours*, eds J.-L. Guereña, E.-M. Fell, J.-R. Aymes, Tours, 1991, pp. 225–49 and *Minerva* 1910/11, vol. 20, Leipzig, 1911.

5. Sources: Germany: N. Bachleitner, 'Übersetzungsfabriken. Das deutsche Übersetzungswesen in der ersten Hälfte des 19. Jahrhunderts', *Internationales Archiv für Sozialgeschichte der deutschen Literatur* 14 (1989), pp. 1–48, p. 8 and Barbier, *L'Empire du livre*, p. 64; France: F. Barbier, 'Une production multipliée', in *Histoire de l'édition française*, ed. Chartier and Martin, pp. 105–30, p. 109; Italy: G. Ragone, 'La letteratura e il consumo: un profilo dei generi e dei modelli nell'editoria italiana (1845–1925)', in *Letteratura italiana*, ed. A. Asor Rosa, vol. 2, Turin, 1983, pp. 687–772, pp. 700 and 719; England: Plant, *The English Book Trade*, pp. 445–7 and N. Cross, *The Common Writer: Life in Nineteenth-Century Grub Street*, Cambridge, 1985, p. 3; Russia: I.E. Barenbaum, *Geschichte des Buchhandels in Russland und der Sowjetunion*, Wiesbaden, 1991, pp. 100 and 125.

6. Ragone, 'La letteratura e il consumo', p. 725. There were 2,400 periodicals in Germany in 1870 and 4,221 in 1914 (T. Nipperdey, *Deutsche Geschichte*, vol. 1, Munich, 1990, p. 798). In Spain their number increased from 1,128 in 1887 to 1,980 in 1913 (J.-F. Botrel and J.M. Desvois, 'Les conditions de la production culturelle', in *1900 en Espagne*, ed. C. Serrano and S. Salaün, Bordeaux, 1988, pp. 23–45, p. 31).

7. M. Pollak, *Vienne 1900*, Paris, 1984, p. 73. The most important daily (*die Neue Freie Presse*) increased its circulation from 40,000 copies in 1890 to 55,000 in 1900. In 1902, twenty-six dailies existed in Vienna, but none sold 100,000 copies like the main Berlin newspapers (E. Walter, 'Les bases financières de la presse viennoise à l'époque de Schnitzler', in *Les journalistes de Arthur Schnitzler, satire de la presse et des journalistes dans le théâtre allemand et autrichien contemporain*, ed. J. Le Rider and R. Wentzig, Tusson, 1995, pp. 211–49, pp. 214–15).

8. For 1894 and 1909, *The Statesman's Yearbook*, London, 1896 and 1910, except for Italy for which figures are calculated by myself with *Minerva*, 1910/11, vol. 20; other dates: France: Weisz, *The Emergence of Modern Universities in France*, p. 318 and C. Charle, 'Paris – Zentrum der französischen Elite. Eine kommentierte Datensammlung', in *Metropolis Berlin*, ed. G. Brunn and J. Reulecke, Bonn, 1992, pp. 293–325, pp. 299–302; Germany: A. Busch, *Die Geschichte der Privatdozenten*, Stuttgart, 1959, p. 76; Spain: J.-L. Guereña, 'L'université en Espagne vers 1900', in *A la recherche de l'espace universitaire européen*, ed. C. Charle, E. Keiner and J. Schriewer, Frankfurt am Main, 1993, pp. 113–31, p. 120; Great Britain: figures quoted by J. Demogeot and H. Montucci, *L'Enseignement supérieur en Grande-Bretagne*, Paris, 1870 (teachers at the universities of Oxford, Cambridge, Durham, London and at the Scottish universities), pp. 100–4, 248, 306, 327, 408–19; 'Austria 1871/72' (teachers at the six universities of Vienna, Graz, Prague, Innsbruck, Lemberg and Cracow), in A. Ficker, *Bericht über österreichisches Unterrichtswesen aus Anlass der Weltausstellung 1873*, Vienna, 1873;

Hungary: *Statistisch-administratives Jahrbuch der Haupt- und Residenzstadt Budapest*, Budapest, 1928; Russia: A. Besançon, *Education et société en Russie*, Paris, The Hague, 1974, p. 61.

9. Barbier, *L'Empire du livre*, pp. 64 and 253; D. Briesen, 'Berlin, die überschätzte Hauptstadt', in *Metropolis Berlin*, ed. Brunn and Reulecke, Bonn, 1992, pp. 39–77, pp. 51–6.

10. See L. O'Boyle, 'The Problem of an Excess of Educated Men in Western Europe, 1800–1850', *Journal of Modern History* 42 (1970), pp. 471–95.

11. Letter of 7 March, 1889 to *Kultusminister* von Gossler, quoted by H. Titze, *Der Akademikerzyklus*, Göttingen, 1990, pp. 234–5.

12. Barbagli, *Disocupazione intellettuale*, p. 22. U. Ojetti, *Alla scoperta dei letterati* (1st edn 1895), Florence, 1946, in particular pp. 286–9.

13. For a more detailed analysis for France, see Charle, *Naissance des 'intellectuels'*, pp. 59–63.

14. J. Requate, *Journalismus als Beruf : Entstehung und Entwicklung des Journalistenberufs im 19. Jh. Deutschland im internationalen Vergleich*, Göttingen, 1995.

15. They are analysed in my book C. Charle, *Les intellectuels en Europe au XIXème siècle*, Paris, 1996, chap. 6.

16. See A.M. Banti, *Storia della borghesia italiana, l'età liberale*, Rome, 1996.

17. See Charle, *Naissance des 'intellectuels'* and C. Charle, *A Social History of France in the XIXth Century*, Oxford, 1994.

18. S. Collini, *Public Moralists: Political Thought and Intellectual Life in Britain 1850–1930*, Oxford, 1991; P. Allen, 'The Meanings of "an Intellectual": Nineteenth- and Twentieth-century English Usage', *University of Toronto Quarterly* 55 (1986), pp. 342–58; H. Perkin, *The Rise of Professional Society, England since 1880*, London, New York, 1989.

19. W. Wolfe, *From Radicalism to Socialism: Men and Ideas in the Formation of Fabian Socialist Doctrines 1881–1889*, New Haven, 1975; E. Hobsbawm, 'The Fabians Reconsidered', in *Labouring Men. Studies in the History of Labour*, ed. E. Hobsbawm, London, 1964, pp. 250–71; *The Letters of S. and B. Webb*, ed. N. MacKenzie, vol. I, Cambridge, 1978, p. 101 quoted by Collini, *Public Moralists*, p. 50.

20. *The Pro-Boers: the Anatomy of an Anti-War Movement*, ed. S. Koss, Chicago, 1973. These very general remarks ought to be nuanced in light of national differences within the United Kingdom: Scottish and Irish intellectuals, due to the opening of the educational sytem in the case of the former and to English cultural domination in that of the later adopted more radical or nonconformist strategies during the nineteenth and twentieth centuries (see the examples of G.B. Shaw and O. Wilde). For a comparative analysis of Britain in the twentieth century, see S. Collini, 'Intellectuals in Britain and France in the Twentieth Century: Confusions, Contrasts and Convergence?', in *Intellectuals in Twentieth Century France, Mandarins and Samurais*, ed. J. Jennings, London, New York, 1993, pp. 199–225, and *Intellectuals in Politics: From the Dreyfus Affair to Salman Rushdie*, ed. J. Jennings and A. Kemp-Welch, London, 1997.

21. *Der Berliner Antisemitismusstreit*, ed. W. Boehlich, Frankfurt am Main, 1965.

22. D. Fricke, 'Der Fall Leo Arons', *Zeitschrift für Geschichtswissenschaft* 8 (1960), pp. 1069–1107; J. Craig, *Scholarship and Nation Building: The Universities of Strasbourg*

and Alsatian Society 1870–1939, Chicago, 1984, pp. 145–58; R.J.V. Lenman, 'Art, Society and the Law in Wilhelmine Germany: the Lex Heinze', *Oxford German Studies*. 8 (1973), pp. 86–113 (new edition in R. Lenman, Artists and Society in Germany, 1850–1914, Manchester, New York, 1997); P. Jelavitch, *Munich and Theatrical Modernism, Politics, Playwriting, and Performance, 1890–1914*, Cambridge, 1985, pp. 143–9.

Bibliography

Allen, P. 'The Meanings of "an Intellectual": Nineteenth- and Twentieth-century English Usage', *University of Toronto Quarterly* 55 (1986), pp. 342–58.

Bachleitner, N. 'Übersetzungsfabriken. Das deutsche Übersetzungswesen in der ersten Hälfte des 19. Jahrhunderts', *Internationales Archiv für Sozialgeschichte der deutschen Literatur* 14 (1989), pp. 1–48.

Banti, A.M. *Storia della borghesia italiana, l'età liberale*. Rome, 1996.

Barbagli, M. *Disocupazione intellettuale et sistema scolastico in Italia*. Bologna, 1974. (American translation: *Educating for Unemployment: Politics, Labour Markets, and the School System. Italy, 1859–1973*. New York, NY, 1982.)

Barbier, F. 'Une production multipliée', in *Histoire de l'édition française*, ed. R. Chartier and H.J. Martin, vol. 3, 2nd edn. Paris, 1990, pp. 105–30.

—— *L'Empire du livre*. Paris, 1995.

Barenbaum, I.E. *Geschichte des Buchhandels in Russland und der Sowjetunion*. Wiesbaden, 1991.

Besançon, A. *Education et société en Russie*. Paris, The Hague, 1974.

Boehlich, W. (ed.). *Der Berliner Antisemitismusstreit*. Frankfurt am Main, 1965.

Botrel, J.-F. and Desvois, J.M. 'Les conditions de la production culturelle', in *1900 en Espagne*, ed. C. Serrano and S. Salaün. Bordeaux, 1988, pp. 23–45.

Briesen, D. 'Berlin, die überschätzte Hauptstadt', in *Metropolis Berlin*, ed. G. Brunn and J. Reulecke. Bonn, 1992, pp. 39–77.

Busch, A. *Die Geschichte der Privatdozenten*. Stuttgart, 1959.

Cammelli A., Universities and professions', in *Society and the Professions in Italy, 1860–1914*, ed. M. Malatesta. Cambridge: Cambridge University Press, 1995, pp. 27–79.

Charle, C. *Naissance des 'intellectuels' (1880–1900)*. Paris, 1990.

—— 'Intellectuals in France around 1900 in a Comparative Perspective', in *Vanguards of Modernity, Society, Intellectuals and the University*, ed. N. Kauppi and P. Sulkunen (Publications of the Research Unit for Contemporary Culture, University of Jyväskylä, Finland, 32). Jyväskylä, 1992, pp.19–32.

—— 'Paris – Zentrum der französischen Elite. Eine kommentierte Datensammlung', in *Metropolis Berlin*, ed. G. Brunn and J. Reulecke. Bonn, 1992, pp. 293–325.

—— *A Social History of France in the XIXth Century*. Oxford, 1994.

—— *Les intellectuels en Europe au XIXème siècle, essai d'histoire comparée*. Paris, 1996.

Chartier, R. and Martin, H.J. (eds) *Histoire de l'édition française*, vol. 3, 2nd edn. Paris, 1990.

Collini, S. 'Intellectuals in Britain and France in the Twentieth Century: Confusions, Contrasts and Convergence?' in *Intellectuals in Twentieth Century France, Mandarins and Samurais*, ed. J. Jennings. London, New York, NY, 1993, pp. 199–225.

—— *Intellectuals in Politics: From the Dreyfus Affair to Salman Rushdie*, eds J. Jennings and A. Kemp-Welch. London, 1997.

Collini, S. *Public Moralists: Political Thought and Intellectual Life in Britain 1850–1930*. Oxford, 1991.

Craig, J. *Scholarship and Nation Building: The Universities of Strasbourg and Alsatian Society 1870–1939*. Chicago, 1984.

Cross, N. *The Common Writer: Life in Nineteenth-Century Grub Street*. Cambridge, 1985.

Demogeot, J. and Montucci, H. *L'Enseignement supérieur en Grande-Bretagne*. Paris, 1870.

Drouin, M. (ed.). *L'Affaire Dreyfus de A à Z*. Paris, 1994.

Engelbrecht, H. *Geschichte des österreichischen Bildungswesens*, vol. 4. Vienna, 1986.

Ficker, A. *Bericht über österreichisches Unterrichtswesen aus Anlass der Weltausstellung 1873*. Vienna, 1873.

Fricke, D. 'Der Fall Leo Arons', *Zeitschrift für Geschichtswissenschaft* 8 (1960), pp. 1069–1107.

Guereña, J.-L , 'L'Université espagnole à la fin du XIXè siècle', in J.-L. Guereña, E.-M. Fell and J.-R. Aymes (eds) *L'Université en Espagne et en Amérique latine du Moyen Age à nos jours. I. Structures et acteurs, Tours*. Tours, 1991, pp.225–49.

—— 'L'université en Espagne vers 1900', in *A la recherche de l'espace universitaire européen*, eds C. Charle, E. Keiner and J. Schriewer. Frankfurt am Main, 1993, pp. 113–31.

Hobsbawm, E. 'The Fabians Reconsidered', in *Labouring Men: Studies in the History of Labour*, ed. E. Hobsbawm. London, 1964, pp. 250–71.

Jarausch, K.H. (ed.). *The Transformation of Higher Learning (1860–1930)*. Stuttgart, 1983.

Jelavitch, P. *Munich and Theatrical Modernism: Politics, Playwriting, and Performance, 1890–1914*. Cambridge, MA, 1985.

Koss, S. (ed.). *The Pro-Boers: the Anatomy of an Anti-War Movement*. Chicago, IL, 1973.

Lenman, R.J.V. 'Art, Society and the Law in Wilhelmine Germany: the Lex Heinze', *Oxford German Studies* 8 (1973), pp. 86–113 (new edn in R. Lenman, *Artists and Society in Germany, 1850–1914*. Manchester, New York, NY, 1997).

MacKenzie, N. (ed.). *The Letters of S. and B. Webb*, vol. I. Cambridge: Cambridge University Press, 1978.

Minerva 1910/11, vol. 20. Leipzig, 1911.

Nipperdey, T. *Deutsche Geschichte*, vol. 1. Munich, 1990.

O'Boyle, L. 'The Problem of an Excess of Educated Men in Western Europe, 1800–1850', *Journal of Modern History* 42 (1970), pp. 471–95.

Ojetti, U. *Alla scoperta dei letterati* (1st edn. 1895). Florence, 1946.

Perkin, H. *The Rise of Professional Society: England since 1880*. London, New York, NY, 1989.

Plant, M. *The English Book Trade* (1st edn 1939). London, 1974.

Pollak, M. *Vienne 1900*. Paris, 1984.

Ragone, G. 'La letteratura e il consumo: un profilo dei generi e dei modelli nell'editoria italiana (1845–1925)' in *Letteratura italiana*, ed. A. Asor Rosa. Turin, 1983, vol. 2, pp. 687–772.

Requate, J. *Journalismus als Beruf: Entstehung und Entwicklung des Journalistenberufs im 19. Jh. Deutschland im internationalen Vergleich*. Göttingen, 1995.

Ringer, F.K. *Education and Society in Modern Europe*. Bloomington, IN, 1979.

—— *Fields of Knowledge*. Paris, Cambridge: Cambridge University Press, 1992.

Statistisch-administratives Jahrbuch der Haupt- und Residenzstadt Budapest. Budapest, 1928.

The Statesman's Yearbook. London, 1896 and 1910.

Titze, H. *Der Akademikerzyklus*. Göttingen, 1990.

Walter, E. 'Les bases financières de la presse viennoise à l'époque de Schnitzler', in *Les journalistes de Arthur Schnitzler, satire de la presse et des journalistes dans le théâtre allemand et autrichien contemporain*, ed. J. Le Rider and R. Wentzig. Tusson, 1995, pp. 211–49.

Weisz, G. *The Emergence of Modern Universities in France 1863–1914*. Princeton, NJ, 1983.

Wolfe, W. *From Radicalism to Socialism: Men and Ideas in the Formation of Fabian Socialist Doctrines 1881–1889*. New Haven, CT, 1975.

10

NATIONALISM AND FEMINISM IN EUROPE

Ida Blom

Since the nineteenth century, a number of nation states have emerged. The process of nation building and the awareness of national identities ran parallel to what has often been termed 'first-wave feminism', that is, the growth in women's organisations and discussions of gender identities, discussions of how to understand femininity and masculinity. These two historical processes have been studied separately until very lately. Now, some historians have taken an interest in unravelling the interaction of the two ideologies, nationalism and feminism.[1]

My own fascination with this question grew out of my work as the main editor of a three-volume women's world history, written by Norwegian and Danish scholars.[2] Working on the chapters covering the eighteenth and nineteenth centuries, I was struck by what to me were unexpected parallels in Asian and Western women's history; I was less surprised, however, by the huge differences. The wish to compare some central historical aspects resulted in a few smaller studies that I shall summarise in this paper.

But first, a few words on comparative gender history.

Comparative gender history is a new field, not least since much of the knowledge about the history of gender is new and much knowledge is still lacking. Women's and gender history is, however, well versed in discussions of theory and of the precise meaning of concepts, important presuppositions for comparative research. Theories of patriarchy have been used to explain gender hierarchies, systematic differences between women and men and changes in gender relations. Patriarchal theories have gradually been broadened or even sometimes replaced by theories on interaction of cultural and physiological givens. Many historians now set out from theories of a 'gender system' or a 'gendered order'. According to this way of thinking, gender is a basic social structure, built into all other social structures, be it class, race, religion, etc. In any culture, in any society, gender will have an impact on the socialisation of the individual, on distribution of work, on responsibilities and rights in the family and in society. Gender relations are at work in politics, in economics; they influence inheritance rules, etc. When society changes, so do gender relations, and changes in gender relations influence other social relations.[3]

The theory of a gender system makes it possible to analyse conflicts as well as cooperation between women and men. The theory may be applied to all areas of historical research, political, economic, social or cultural history. It means that the importance of gender as an analytical category should always be investigated.

I shall attempt to do just that in this analysis of the interaction of nationalism and feminism around the turn of the century. The analysis first involves two nation states, Norway and Sweden. They represent the cultures that I have studied most intensively, and this is therefore also where I will look for patterns to be compared. Subsequently, comparisons will be made between these results and the interaction of nationalism and feminism in two Asian countries, Japan and India. Finally, I shall look both at similarities and differences in the ways nationalism and feminism interacted in European as well as in Asian cultures, as they are represented by these four nations.

Of course, broad comparisons such as these will to some extent neglect important nuances. What will be compared are broad social groups and central political problems, important in many countries around the turn of the century. In this process the historian will run the risk of losing the specific and of disregarding strict chronology. But the gain may be an understanding of general patterns in the interaction of feminism and nationalism, as well as a better awareness of the importance of gender to historical processes. Finally, the gender-specific conditions and possibilities of historical actors will come clearly to the forefront.

Feminism, nationalism and national identities

Let me start by attempting to define the two -isms, nationalism and feminism, and sketching out the nature of one of the central areas of interaction between them.

To define *feminism* is not an easy task, and there are reasons for insisting that to use the concept at all for the turn of the century is an anachronism. Nevertheless, I have chosen to use the concept as a collective denomination of a political ideology, which served as the base for political actions.

The main goal of feminism was – and is – to combat gendered injustices.[4] Political action to reach this goal can be discerned in at least three areas. One was to gain the same rights for women as for men. In this paper this would translate into seeing women accepted as members of the nation on the same conditions as men, for instance through the vote. The second area was to work to secure women's physical and psychological integrity, for instance through changes of laws, regulations and traditions that had to do with sexuality and family. The third area was to strengthen women's position in the labour market, for instance through better wages and working conditions, better education and so on. Although this is certainly a very important area, I shall not include it in my analysis.[5]

Feminism rested on the basically essentialist assumption of women as a distinct group with visibly common physical characteristics. These common characteristics would distinguish women from men within any other social group, be it class, caste, ethnic group or groups formed on the basis of colour of skin. Many feminists also maintained that women had special psychological characteristics that would distinguish them from men, yet sometimes this was a disputed point.

Nationalism is also a multifaceted concept. Two main forms have traditionally been distinguished.[6] One was rooted in the desire to create or support a strong state with a leading international position. It was externally aggressive and internally authoritarian and hierarchical. Imperial Germany has been seen in this light. In my paper, the extreme-conservative Swedish nationalists and the Japanese policies after the Meiji Revolution in 1868 will be the examples.

The other form of nationalism sprang out of the French revolution, built on ideas of democracy and self-determination as a reaction against absolutism. It formed the basis of nationalist liberation movements, starting in the Western world and later expanding to Asian and African fighters against colonialism. In my paper, Norway and India will serve as examples of this form of nationalism.

Like feminism, nationalism also had an essentialist core – the idea that a certain group of individuals made up the nation. This group would ideally share a common language, a common history and a common religion. It was also seen as embodying common psychological characteristics that would distinguish the group from other groups. Such ideas could lead to discrimination against 'the others'. Both forms of nationalism in this respect showed a hierarchical tendency, putting one's own nation in the highest position.

On top of this, conservative nationalism also explicitly ordered the members of the nation in an inner hierarchy, in a well-disciplined pyramid with an elite at the top. But closer analysis reveals that class and gender hierarchies (in some nations also hierarchies built on colour of skin) were innate even to democratic nationalism. Any national identity could therefore split along lines of class, gender and colour of skin.

I shall revert to the problem of identity at the end of my paper. For the moment, it suffices to say that the feeling of belonging to the nation, of individual national identity, could depend on whether or not the individual possessed certain political rights.

Certain criteria were implemented to decide who had the right to take part in the political process of making decisions with implications for the whole nation. This is where I find a major point of interaction between nationalism and feminism. Physical characteristics such as reproductive capacities were important criteria. In no nation state, except for Finland in 1906, were women given the vote at the same time as men. Although women's capacity to bear children was highly valued, it was never a criterion for granting them political rights. In the USA another physical criterion was long decisive, that of colour of skin. One might say that physical characteristics, such as the capacity to bear children and colour of skin, acted as what Eric Hobsbawn has called 'visible ethnicity', dividing individuals in more or less worthy, more or less influential members of the nation.

But criteria were not formulated as physical characteristics. What was made decisive were questions of economic self-sufficiency and intellectual abilities. Such criteria initially also excluded many men – servants, some workers and black men – and all women. All these individuals were in different ways seen as economically dependent. Add to this that women and blacks were regarded as reigned by emotions and intuition, not by rational reasoning, and consequently also fell short when it came to intellectual abilities, the second criterion for being included in the nation through political rights.

Political rights as a sign that an individual belonged to the nation were first bestowed on white men of the upper social strata, then on white male workers and peasants. Coloured men and all women, regardless of colour of skin, were – in that order – the last groups to be accepted as full citizens. The growth of democratic nation states was clearly influenced by the gender system, as well as by class and race. This was also the case in Scandinavia – as well as in Japan and India.

With these considerations in mind, let us turn to the comparison between Norway and Sweden.

Comparing nation states – Norway and Sweden

The political union between Norway and Sweden was a result of the Napoleonic wars and lasted until 1905 when, after increasing problems with the viability of the union, the two countries formed independent nation states.

Comparing Swedish and Norwegian nation building makes it obvious that the two forms of nationalism were decisive for which groups were accepted as responsible members of the nation. The most conservative and aggressive Swedish nationalists were against incorporating all men in the nation through general suffrage. For them, women's right to vote was not even on the agenda.

Norwegian nationalists, on the contrary, whether they were conservative or liberal, for or against a military solution, had all accepted general male suffrage around the turn of the century. Some of the liberals even worked for women's suffrage.

In both countries, the Social Democrats were opposed to the use of military force. The Swedish Socialists saw general male suffrage as one of their important goals, but did not care much about women's suffrage. The Norwegian Socialists won general male suffrage in 1898, and were positive to women's suffrage, although male suffrage had been more important also to them.

One could establish a gliding scale with the Swedish Conservatives at one end, and the Norwegian Social Democrats at other. In Sweden, Conservatives, men and women alike, agreed that only men, and not even all men, should be accepted as members of the nation through enfranchisement. The hierarchical thinking was clear. The Norwegian Social Democrats at the other end of the scale fought for the widest possible definition of citizenship, including also all women. The liberal nationalists, who were very pronounced in Norway, ranged somewhere in the middle.

How should such national differences be understood? Despite all the resemblance between the two Scandinavian countries, Norway and Sweden, historical differences are important. The political developments in the two nations must be taken into consideration. The nineteenth century saw a more democratic system emerge in Norway than in Sweden. Norway had a one-chamber parliament, as opposed to the Swedish two-chamber system. Parliamentarianism became an accepted ideal in Norway in 1884, in Sweden not until 1911. General male suffrage was introduced in Norway in 1898, in Sweden in 1909, and general female suffrage followed in Norway in 1913, in Sweden in 1921.

The differences mirror the stronger Swedish upper classes, consisting partly of an aristocratic nobility with traditions of an important European power. An increasingly industrialised economy there also marked a difference to Norway. The still mainly agrarian Norwegian economy was the basis for a poorer, but socially more homogeneous population than in Sweden. In Norway, due to centuries of political union, first with Denmark, later with Sweden, the nobility had long lost all importance. Businessmen and academics formed a very small upper class, with less of a distance from the rest of the population than in Sweden.

It should be stressed that citizenship through the vote is, of course, not the only way to be accepted as a member of the nation. Neither is it enough to safeguard democracy. Economic resources and other means of social prestige have kept up social hierarchies within nations. But as long as suffrage was not universal, it was seen as an important key to membership in the nation. In the debate around general male suffrage in 1898, one of the Norwegian members of parliament put it this way: 'Also people who own nothing and who are in a subordinate position in society are important parts of the nation, whom the constitution should guarantee participation in the legislative power.' Another example: in 1905, Norwegian women who had not yet gained the vote, were excluded from the important plebiscite deciding the abrogation of the union with Sweden. The response of one woman, writing in the most influential feminist journal, was to ask: 'Are we women not part of the Norwegian nation?' Without the vote, anybody, in this case women, might feel excluded from the nation.

Two strategies

To understand the gendered character of the nation-building process better, we may analyse the strategies applied to have women accepted as responsible members of the nation.

I have found two strategies, a strategy of equal rights, and a strategy of difference. These strategies should be understood as analytical tools, not as mutually exclusive entities. In fact, the two strategies often coexisted, not just within a certain group, but also within one and the same individual. They were primarily, but not exclusively, rooted in two different understandings of gender. Let us look first at the difference strategy.

The difference strategy built on the dichotomous understanding of gender, propagated with success by Jean Jacques Rousseau in his influential work *Emile*, of 1762. Women and men were understood as individuals with different, but complementary, potentials. Consequently, they also belonged to the nation in different ways, and did not need the same duties and the same rights in the nation. Different functions in family and society should lead to different rights, but different rights should form the foundation of equally important membership in the nation.

This strategy was very easy to locate in both nations. In the cultural component of nationalism, it was visible in the language of symbols. The nation was seen as a home. According to the Norwegian national hymn this home was defended by a strong father and a steadfast mother. Although the hymn ascribed the mother a tendency to sit down and weep, and found men to be the more courageous of the two, the common fight and the democratic character of the Norwegian nation was underlined.

Conservative Swedish women also saw women as national mother figures. Their role was to protect the weak, especially the children. Women were also responsible for bringing up future generations to love their country and for preparing young boys to become soldiers to defend the nation. Conservative Swedish women very clearly stated that even without the vote, they felt completely accepted members of the nation. As one of them wrote in 1903: 'with or without the vote, we are responsible for the fate of our country. We – the one half, and the numerically biggest part of the nation – have a responsibility that is no less important than the responsibility resting on the shoulders of a small group of men who are statesmen and representatives of the people. We are responsible for maintaining the feeling of national belonging and for keeping this feeling on the right track' (Dagny, 1905, no. 12, p. 238).

The idea of the nation as a home, a family, with men and women as strong father- and mother-figures, could further feminist goals. The implicit idea of protecting the weak could arouse and support demands for important feminist causes like protections against the sexual and economic exploitation of women. While the education of the young was stressed as women's special responsibility, this, however, did not change the fact that girls' education did not prepare them to become independent citizens, but to fulfil their role as good housewives and mothers. Seeing boys as future soldiers also underlined gender differences.

When the nation was symbolised by the family and different responsibilities along the lines of gender were emphasised, the limitation of women to the private, of men to the public was implicit. This division was more outspoken in the Swedish than in the Norwegian discourse. Married Swedish women were, until 1921, legally represented by their husbands, while married Norwegian women were already seen as independent legal subjects in 1888. The difference strategy easily lead to a gender hierarchy.

Yet a dichotomous understanding of gender might also, and in fact often did, lead to the other strategy, the equal rights strategy. The logic behind the claim that women and men should have the same rights was that feminine elements were needed in society, in the public, to complement masculine influence. In this thinking, the very difference between women and men was the reason for claiming equal rights.

However, the more clear-cut strategy for equal rights, of course, built on natural rights ideas, understanding women and men as individuals with the same potentials, and therefore with a claim to the same rights and the same functions within the nation. This led among other things to claiming the vote for women on the same conditions as for men. In this way of reasoning, unprivileged individuals were seen as spearheads for a progressive democracy, and the alliance with the Social Democrats was a solution.

Both Norwegian and Swedish Social Democrats mobilised the masses by promoting the idea of democracy as the best defence for the nation. In both countries, the Social Democrats supported the formation of nation states, accepting and showing respect for other nation states. An analysis of the Swedish Social Democratic Party maintains that members saw the working class as the true national class, which worked to strengthen the nation by reforms from within. Capitalism, to these Social Democrats, appeared as the expression of a reactionary internationalism and the disregard for national identities.

Such ideas manifested themselves in the Swedish fight for the male vote until 1909. Women's right to vote was hardly mentioned, not even by Swedish Socialist women.

In Norway, where the male vote was won in 1898, the Social Democrats now worked for women's enfranchisement; however, it was women who were more engaged in this than their male comrades. Their fight paralleled that of the liberal bourgeois women and some men, who were also using the national crises to fight for women's suffrage. Social Democratic women saw women's vote as a better defence for the nation than a strong army and navy, because women, according to this opinion, would avert war. They also pointed to the fact that women, in a number of ways, to which I shall shortly revert, had shown their desire and ability to assume national responsibility and therefore deserved the vote. In

1907 limited female suffrage was obtained, among other factors owing to the political rationality women had shown during the national crises of 1905. In 1913 general female suffrage was achieved.

The strategy to form a spearhead for democratic reform had a gender perspective. In Sweden it favoured men's vote, in Norway women's vote. Although time differences were small, the interaction of feminism and nationalism yielded earlier results where liberal nationalism prevailed.

In Sweden, where the more conservative nationalism was strong, national crises did not have any effect on women's suffrage. Women, as we have seen, had to wait for the vote until 1921.

Gendered political activities

Finally, the gendered *forms* of political activities come to the fore in a comparative analysis. In both countries, men gave voice to their political opinions through membership in political parties, through the vote and by supporting the nation also as soldiers. They formed voluntary organisations to act as pressure groups for their convictions.

Women also formed voluntary organisations. Conservative women in both countries created organisations to strengthen the military defence, but they did not work in the same way as men in similar organisations. Women would arrange bazaars and organise other funding activities to collect money for defence. Norwegian women financed a new motor-torpedo boat, appropriately named the 'Valkyrie'. (A valkyrie was a heathen northern goddess who decided over life and death on the battle fields.) Through their organisations conservative Swedish women also worked to promote enthusiasm for the military among young boys. Liberal Norwegian women started the education of nurses to serve at the front in case the crises over the political union should lead to war between the two nations. When, in 1905, a plebiscite was arranged in Norway to decide over the abrogation of the union, women were excluded because they did not yet have the right to vote. Norwegian women's organisations thus arranged a petition, gathering around 300,000 signatures to support the decision to abrogate the union. Using the means at their disposal women showed the intent to take responsibility for the future of the nation.

This part of the paper can be summed up thus: nationalism and feminism interacted in complicated ways in the process of nation building. The gender system stamped national symbols as well as political activities to reach national goals. Although class and political convictions seemed more important than gender when political *opinions* were concerned, gender was decisive for the *forms of political activity*.

However, there was not one single feminist strategy to build a democratic nation. The difference strategy was more acceptable to conservative aggressive nationalism than the equal rights strategy. For this latter strategy, an alliance with the Social Democrats was the most favourable, although gender decided the priority given to this question within the Social Democratic Party as well. In short, central concepts like nation and class were clearly gendered.

Nationalism and feminism in Asian cultures

Is it possible to make comparisons as to the interaction of feminism and nationalism if we extend this study to Asian cultures, such as Japan and India? Would the categories used to study these phenomena in Scandinavia yield any meanings in a very different cultural setting?[8]

To begin with, there is no doubt that in Asia we also find the two forms of nationalism. At the turn of the century Japan was characterised by conservative and aggressive nationalism. If we move to the 1920s and the early 1930s, we do, however, find a short period when moderately liberal nationalism had the upper hand. It seems no surprise that during that span of years women had better opportunities than before. Yet it was a short period that was silhouetted against the general impression of authoritarian Japanese regimes. The fact that from 1890 to 1945 Japanese women were legally prohibited from taking part in party politics, confirms the correlation between conservative nationalism and a negative attitude to feminist politics that we found in Sweden.[9]

In India, nationalism aimed at loosening, even breaking with, British domination, and may, with all due reservations, be compared to the Norwegian confrontation with Sweden. The cultural component of Indian nationalism had a clearly gendered aspect. When the British pointed to the subjugated position of Indian women as a sign of the uncivilised character of Indian culture, Indian nationalists would cite old Hindu traditions – the 'shakti' – where powerful goddesses invested women with strength and steadfastness. Also national policies comprised gendered problems. Reforms, such as the abolition of 'suttee' – the burning of widows – and of child-marriages, were proposed by Indian liberal nationalists and partly carried through with the assistance of British authorities. Such reforms belonged to the set of feminist goals mentioned at the beginning: to secure women's physical and psychological integrity.

Gender-specific realities were also expressed in the language of national symbols. Both in Japan and in India, good housewives and mothers were used as symbols for the strong and healthy nation. Indian nationalists used the term 'Mother India', just like the Scandinavians who talked about the national home with a father and a mother. But it must not be forgotten that where the family functioned according to a patriarchal model, such symbols were prone to uphold women's subordination and men's domination. Although we find conservative as well as liberal nationalism and shared national symbols in European as well as in Asian cultures, comparisons across cultural divides must take cultural differences into account. The same concepts do not necessarily have the same meaning in different cultures.

Nevertheless, the two strategies found in Norway and Sweden may also be located in a Japanese and an Indian setting. There is a parallel between the importance Swedish conservative women attributed to the education of boys to become soldiers, and the Aikoko Fujinkai, the biggest Japanese women's organisation. This organisation worked around the turn of the century to support Japanese authorities, among other things by trying to make women see their sons as the sons of the Japanese emperor and to prepare mothers to proudly sacrifice their sons for the fatherland. The Japanese tradition of the subservient wife may be seen not just as an expression of the patriarchal family model, but also of conservative Japanese nationalism.

Indian nationalists put forth the argument that women had a special role as guardians of the old Hindu traditions, so important to the national movement. The 'swadeshi' movement, expressing its criticism of British sovereignty just after the turn of the century through boycott of British goods, recruited many women who worked hard to give priority to Indian products by organising meetings and boycott activities. If we move into the interwar years, Gandhi's ideas of femininity are easily translated into the difference strategy. Women should take part in the national struggle, but preferably in other ways than men. They were not welcome in the public protest marches, but all the more welcomed when they were seen busily producing Indian cotton cloth and wearing Indian costumes. Gandhi saw the goddess Sita, the faithful, self-sacrificing wife, as the ideal woman. He also found women especially well prepared for 'satyagraha', that is, nonviolent resistance.

In both countries we also find examples of the equality strategy. This was no doubt the strategy applied by the 23-year-old Japanese woman Fukuda Hideko, when, in 1883, she spoke to an auditorium about women's right to the same education as men and suggested the same economic, legal and moral rights for women as for men. Hideko envisaged what she termed 'a civilised democratic Japan'. The Japanese reform organisations of the 1880s also saw liberal feminist politics as part of their programme. But Hideko was soon arrested, and the Liberal Party was dissolved. Japanese women had to wait until 1945 to get the vote.

In India, women's organisations such as the All India Muslim Women's Conference and the Women's Indian Association, formed in 1914 and 1917 respectively, may be seen as examples of the equal rights strategy. The support given to limited women's suffrage in some Indian provinces in the 1920s and for all India in 1935, as well as women's active participation in Gandhi's civil disobedience strategies, may testify to the existence of equal rights strategies in the formation of the Indian nation. So would the fact that – although Gandhi disapproved – many women took part in the big salt march of 1930 after Gandhi was arrested.

In Asian cultures, too, political activities appeared in gender-specific forms. Women could not participate in politics in the same ways as men and therefore they would build their gender-specific organisations. In Japan, they were lawfully excluded from party politics. Although, in India, they were not forbidden to take part in politics, women were only slowly accepted as partners in political processes.

Parallels between Asian and European cultures

Let me sum up the similarities between Asian and European cultures in the interaction of feminism and nationalism.

First, gender has everywhere been important for nation building. National symbols were imbued with gendered meanings. Central concepts like 'political rights' were not gender neutral, and purposeful political action was needed to make this concept include women.

Political actions mostly took on different forms for men and women. This happened even in cases where political opinions were gender neutral, such as in the question of resistance to Western culture in India and Japan and in Norwegian discontent with the union with Sweden.

Everywhere there is reason to believe that part of national identity had a gender-specific connotation.

The comparison also shows different patterns in the interaction of feminism and nationalism. The contrast that may be discerned between conservative and liberal nationalism in Scandinavia becomes much more prominent in the case of Japan and India.

Further, two feminist strategies are found in all of the four nations under study. One understood women as basically different from men, but nevertheless as important as men to the nation. The other saw reforms, including women in the nation through the same rights as men, as an expression of the equal potential of the two sexes. Although the difference strategy could also lead to this conclusion, there was a tendency for this strategy to uphold existing gender hierarchies. Difference strategy consequently was the preference of conservative nationalism.

How may we explain these parallels? If we see them as expressions of a universal gender system, how may that system be explained?

The cross-cultural parallels may point to universalisms in human behaviour. Gender identities seem to rest on deep mental structures, regulating feminine and masculine behaviour and changing only very slowly. Consciously or unconsciously, these mental structures may influence expectations as to acceptable thoughts, actions and strategies by the two sexes. Basic gender relations, the very understanding of feminine and masculine identities, seem to transcend cultural differences. A universal gender hierarchy has given rise to theories of patriarchy, seeing the dichotomies 'man–woman', 'public–private', 'strong–weak', and so on, as universalisms.

Does this mean that gender was more important than class or nationality?

My answer is, sometimes yes, sometimes no. The interaction of feminism and nationalism created identity conflicts everywhere and in every individual. One may also speak of competing loyalties. In some situations, gender identities were stronger than national identities. In Scandinavia, for a long time, and despite the national crises, middle-class feminists cooperated in a sisterly fashion across the Norwegian–Swedish border. For women and men of the Social Democratic Parties, the national conflict brought no problems for their cooperation. Gender – and class – proved more important than nationality.

Alliances across national borders were also important in Asian nations. Japan found inspiration for political reform in Western cultures, among other things for a modern education for middle-class women. The All India Women's Conference cooperated with the British suffragists.

Yet the harder the national conflicts grew, the more problematic became alliances across national divides. Increasingly it turned out to be a problem for different identities to coexist. Conflicts of loyalty arose. As I understand, at some point cooperation between Indian and British feminists in the question of female suffrage became extremely difficult. The heated atmosphere between the two nations made national identity prevail over gender identity. No doubt, Western inspiration for changes in the situation of Japanese women was short-lived, and even for one of the leading Norwegian feminists, Gina Krog, national identity outweighed gender identity in 1905. Swedish feminists were appalled when Krog called Sweden 'a sly, malignant robber'. Scandinavian sisterly cooperation entered an extremely chilly period.

The varying reactions, in some cases based on gender identity, in some cases on national identity or in other cases on class identity, may be explained by the concept of fractured identities. Seeing identity as a prism, reflecting varying situations, helps understand changing priorities. The Finnish philosopher Tuija Pulkkhinen maintains that one part of a person's identity will come to the foreground the moment this part is threatened or otherwise activated.[10] This will explain the changing reactions charted by my comparisons. A national crisis activated national identities, gender conflicts activated gender identities, just as class conflicts brought class identities to the forefront.

No doubt, there were a number of parallels between European and Asian cultures in the interaction of feminism and nationalism. But there were certainly also obvious differences.

Cultural differences between Asian and European Cultures

My research has shown that when similar strategies were applied within different cultures, variations between cultures were striking. Despite many similarities, the interaction of feminism and nationalism was basically different in European and Asian cultures.

One of the main differences were the very dissimilar feminist goals. In Asia, priority was given to safeguard women's physical and psychic integrity, what I have identified as one of the important goals of feminism at the beginning of my paper. Asian feminist politics were enacted within a culture where the fight was about child-marriages, about concubinage, about the total submission under husband and mother-in-law, about the prohibition of widow marriages, etc. In this setting, to see women as members of the nation in the same way as men was a distant goal for a very small part of the population.

Gender relations in Scandinavia were totally different. Feminist goals were the same education for women as for men, the right of married women to have an economic activity of their own outside the family, etc. The idea of including women in the nation by giving them the vote on the same conditions as men was not a distant one.

Consequently, despite common deep-seated ideas of gender differences, cultural variations were decisive in the interaction of feminism and nationalism.

What may be seen as central elements in these cultural differences? Cultural and economic structures should be examined, and I would especially highlight the very different importance given to collective and to individualism.

In Japan and India, the Confucian, the Hindu as well as the Muslim religion strengthened the concept of a stable and strongly patriarchal family and a submissive wife. In Asian cultures, the family was the only safety net in case of need, when sickness, accidents, poverty or old age threatened the individual. Consequently, the family was the most important centre of all loyalties. This would put an obstacle in the way of any desire for individual rights. In many cases such a wish would not even arise. With a patriarchal family system, individual rights would certainly be a more far-fetched idea for women than for men.

In Europe, on the other hand, and especially in Northern Europe, the Lutheran religion had been stressing individual freedom for a long time. Industrialisation had also loosened the ties between family and individual. At the end of the nineteenth century the first steps towards the welfare state were taken, gradually providing a public safety net around the individual to secure basic needs. This added to the weakening of collective family ties and made the road to individualism easier. But, even in Scandinavia, this road had higher barriers for women than for men.

However, it is important not to see cultures as absolute entities. Internal fractures and conflicts over values and ideas characterise any culture, among these conflicts over gender relations. Comparative studies may help us to understand cultures as multifaceted entities, and to seek parallels between groups of similar opinions within different cultures.

Also, in Western culture there were regional differences, which might sometimes be more or less the same as the differences between Western and Asian cultures. The question of loyalty to the family, of collectivism versus individualism, as well as religious and economic circumstances, differed widely from Northern to Southern Europe. Around the turn of the twentieth century Catholic religion and the agrarian economy of Southern Europe could result in tendencies towards collectivism and family loyalty that would impede the fight for equal rights for women in similar, although not as drastic ways, as in Asian cultures. An indication of the regional differences may be the much later date of women's enfranchisement in most Southern European countries, that is, after the Second World War (except for Spain). In Northern Europe female suffrage was obtained around the First World War.

Within Asian cultures, also, there were important variations. The fight for women's physical and psychic integrity was extremely important for some groups in Japanese and Indian societies, and shows that collectivism would not necessarily lead to less respect for individual rights. Consequently, the historian should be careful not to talk about cultures as monolithic entities. Studies of internal differences are important to understand the working of any cultural system, as well as to make meaningful comparisons between cultures.

Conclusion

Comparing fractured cultures and fractured identities may make the image of 'the other' more nuanced, and build bridges of understanding, not just between seemingly very different cultures such as Asian and European cultures, but also between women and men within the same cultures. Seeing individual identities as fractured and contextual and applying the theory of the gender system to the complicated interaction of nationalism and feminism, elicits knowledge that would otherwise remain concealed.

Comparative gender history, like any comparative history, may indicate general patterns and hint at major problems and tendencies. To acquire a deeper understanding of special cultures, the historian will have to analyse the culture in question more thoroughly – at the regional, the national or even local level. Such analysis will add nuances to general patterns, give them more precise meanings and probably also sometimes falsify them.

Cross-cultural perspectives on the interaction between nationalism and feminism should, therefore, rest on intimate knowledge of the cultures involved. What I have done in this paper – sketching common strategies and certain patterns of interaction between two ideologies – is, of course, only a small and uncertain start. Comparative gender history, just like most other comparative history, needs a multitude of studies clarifying similarities and differences between the phenomena that are being compared. Results, I think, will nevertheless tend to be patterns of thinking rather than verifiable knowledge.

However, I would maintain that my comparison highlights the importance of gender to central historical processes and the gender-specific circumstances and possibilities for historical actors. I would also contend that these comparisons add many nuances to theories of patriarchal subjection of women. Women and men often shared understandings of femininity and masculinity, and such understandings might be very stable through long periods. But when important changes in society occurred, such as the formation of nation states, this also affected gender relations. Finally, the often suggested polarisation of women and men as actors within the private and the public arenas respectively, does not hold true. Although political action took gendered forms, both sexes were actively engaged in the process of nation building. This process comprised the home and family as well as public parliaments and political parties.

Consequently, to fully understand a phenomenon such as nationalism and nation building – in fact, I think, to fully understand most historical phenomena – the analytical category of gender should be taken into account.

Notes

1. See for instance K. Jayawardena, *Feminism and Nationalism in the Third World*, London, 1986; C. Hall, *White, Male and Middle Class: Explorations in Feminism and History*, Cambridge, 1991; Special issue on 'Gender, Nationalisms and National Identities', *Gender and History* 5 (1993); A. McClintock, 'No Longer in a Future Heaven: Nationalism, Gender and Race', in *Becoming National*, ed. G. Eley, Oxford, 1996, pp. 260–84; N. Yuval-Davis and F. Anthias, eds, *Women – Nation – State*, London, 1990; N. Yuval-Davis, *Gender and Nation*, London, 1997; C. Pateman, 'Equality, Difference, Subordination: the Politics of Motherhood and Women's Citizenship', in *Beyond Equality and Difference: Citizenship – Feminist Politics – Female Subjectivity*, ed. G. Bock and S. James, London, New York, 1992, pp. 17–31; I. Blom, K. Hagemann and C. Hall, *Gendered Nations: The Long Eighteenth Century*, Oxford, New York, 2000.

2. I. Blom, ed, *Cappelens kvinnehistorie*, vols. 1–3, Oslo, 1992–3. This article is based on a number of my earlier publications: 'Feminism and Nationalism in the Early Twentieth Century: A Cross-Cultural Perspective', *Journal of Women's History* 7, 4 (1995), pp. 82–94; 'Das Zusammenwirken von Nationalismus und Feminismus um die Jahrhundertwende – Ein Versuch zur vergleichenden Geschlechtergeschichte', in *Geschichte und Vergleich: Ansätze und Ergebnisse international vergleichender Geschichtsschreibung*, ed. H.G. Haupt and J. Kocka, Frankfurt am Main, New York, 1996, pp. 315–38; 'Nation – Class – Gender: Scandinavia at the Turn of the Century', *Scandinavian Journal of History* 21 (1996), pp. 1–16; 'World History and Gender History: The Case of the Nation State', in *Between National Histories and Global History: Konferanserapport til 23. det nordiske historikermøte*, ed. S. Tønnessen, Helsingfors, 1997, pp. 71–92; 'Gender and Nation States: An International Comparative Perspective' in *Gendered Nations: The Long Eighteenth Century*, ed. I. Blom, K. Hagemann and C. Hall, Oxford, New York, 2000, pp. 3–26.

3. For useful introductions to the development of women's and gender history, see J.W. Scott, 'Women's History' and 'Gender: A Useful Category of Historical Analysis', in J.W. Scott, *Gender and the Politics of History*, New York, 1988, pp. 15–50. See also J. Kelly, 'The Social Relations of the Sexes: Methodological Implications of Women's History', *Signs* 1 (1975–76) (also published in J. Kelly, *Women, History and Theory*,

Chicago, 1984, pp. 1–18); E. Fox Genovese, 'Placing Women in History', *New Left Review* 133 (1982), pp. 5–29; G. Bock, 'Challenging Dichotomies: Perspectives on Women's History', in *Writing Women's History: International Perspectives*, ed. K.Offen, J. Rendall and R. Roach Pierson, London, Bloomington, 1991, pp. 1–23. For an introduction to similar developments in Norway, see I. Blom, 'Women's History', in J.E. Myhre, ed., *The Making of a Historical Culture*, Oslo, 1995, pp. 289–310. On comparative gender history, see Blom, 'Das Zusammenwirken von Nationalismus und Feminismus'; Blom, 'Gender and Nation States'.

4. The notion of a critique of the subordination of women is central to the concept of feminism, although feminists may differ in strategies adopted to gain better control of their own lives. See K. Offen, *European Feminisms 1700–1950: A Political History*, Stanford, 2000; O. Banks, *Faces of Feminism: A Study of Feminism as a Social Movement*, New York, 1981; N. Cott, *The Grounding of Modern Feminism*, New Haven, London, 1987; K. Offen, 'Defining Feminism: A Comparative Historical Approach', *Signs* 14 (1988), pp. 119–57; N. Cott and E. Dubois, 'Comments on Karen Offen's Article "Defining Feminism: A Comparative Historical Approach"', and K. Offen, 'Reply to Cott', *Signs* 15 (1989), pp. 195–209 (reprinted in an abbreviated and slightly reversed form in *Beyond Equality and Difference*, ed. G. Bock and S. James, London, New York, 1992, pp. 89–109); K. Offen, 'Feminism and Sexual Difference in Historical Perspective', in *Theoretical Perspectives on Sexual Difference*, ed. D.L. Rhode, New Haven, London, 1990, pp. 13–20; K. Melby, 'Women's Ideology: Difference, Equality or a New Femininity?' in *Moving On: New Perspectives on the Womens Movement*, ed. T. Andreasen et al. (Acta Jutlandica 67, no. 1, Humanities Series 6), Aarhus, 1991, pp. 138–54.

5. I am well aware of the difficulties involved in such compartmentalisation, but hope they may serve to highlight the broad scope of activities pursued by first-wave feminists. In my own study of the interplay of feminism and nationalism, I have emphasised the second goal, bearing directly on the perception of who constituted the nation. But the other two goals are also crucial to the development of a democratic nation state. Policies to safeguard women's personal, physical and psychic integrity, the respect of their bodies and minds, of women as individuals, often seem to activate deeply rooted perceptions of hierarchical gender relations, easily excluding women from the public and from the nation. Such perceptions may explain why inclusion in the nation by the vote, where it was obtained, after a long time proved to have limited practical consequences.

6. For an excellent introduction, see G. Eley and R.G. Suny, *Becoming National: A Reader*, Oxford, New York 1990; B. Anderson, *Imagined Communities: Reflections on the Origin and Spread of Nationalism*, London, 1983; E.J. Hobsbawm, *Nations and Nationalism since 1780: Programme, Myth, Reality*, Cambridge, 1990; R. Samuel, ed., *Minorities and Outsiders vol. 2, Patriotism – The Making and Unmaking of British National Identity*, London, New York, 1989, esp. chap. 24; M. Lake, 'Mission Impossible: How Men Gave Birth to the Australian Nation – Nationalism, Gender and Other Seminal Acts', *Gender and History* 4 (1992), pp. 305–22; K. Offen, 'Exploring the Sexual Politics of Republican Nationalism', in *Nationhood and Nationalism in France: From Boulangism to the Great War 1889–1918*, ed. R. Tombs, London, 1991, pp. 195–209.

7. All information on Norway and Sweden may be found in Blom, 'Nation – Class – Gender'.

8. This part of the paper is built on I. Blom, ed., *Cappelens Kvinnehistorie*, vol. III, Oslo, 1992–3, pp. 170–228. See also Jayawardena, *Feminism and Nationalism*; B. Ramusak, 'Women in South and South East Asia', in *Restoring Women to History: Teaching Packets for Integrating Women's History into Courses on Africa, Asia, Latin America, The Caribbean and the Middle East*, ed. I. Berger et al., Bloomington, 1988, pp.1–63; S.L. Sievers, 'Women in China, Japan and Korea', in *Restoring Women to History: Teaching Packets for Integrating Women's History into Courses on Africa, Asia, Latin America, The Caribbean and the Middle East*, ed. I. Berger et al., Bloomington, 1988, pp. 63–118; S.L. Sievers, *Flowers in Salt: The Beginnings of Feminist Consciousness in Modern Japan*, Stanford, 1983; L. Kasturi and V. Macumdar, *Women and Indian Nationalism*, New Delhi, 1994; A. Basu, 'Women in Politics. India', in *Women's Politics and Women in Politics*, ed. S. Sogner and G. Hagemann, Oslo, 2000, pp. 165–72.

9. Another interesting comparison would be between Japan and Germany. There were a number of German states, where from 1852 until 1908 women were also prohibited from participating in party politics.

10. These considerations rest on T. Pulkinen, 'Citizens, Nations and Women: The Transition from Ancient Regime to Modernity and Beyond', Paper for the International Federation for Research in Women's History Symposium, 'Rethinking Women and Gender Relations in the Modern State', Bielefeld, April 1993. See also P. Pascoe, 'Introduction' and 'Race, Gender and Intercultural Relations: The Case of Interracial Marriages', *Frontiers* 12 (1991), pp. 1–18; Catherine Hall's excellent discussion of the interplay of class, race, and gender in Hall, *White, Male and Middle Class*, pp. 199, 205–54; G. Lerner, 'Reconceptualizing Differences Among Women', *Journal of Women's History* 1 (1990), pp. 106–22.

Bibliography

Anderson, B. *Imagined Communities: Reflections on the Origin and Spread of Nationalism.* London, 1983.

Banks, O. *Faces of Feminism: A Study Of Feminism as a Social Movement.* New York, NY, 1981.

Basu, A. 'Women in Politics. India', in *Women's Politics and Women in Politics*, ed. S. Sogner and G. Hagemann. Oslo, 2000, pp. 165–72.

Blom, I. 'Feminism and Nationalism in the Early Twentieth Century: A Cross-Cultural Perspective', *Journal of Women's History* 7, 4 (1995), pp. 82–94.

—— 'Women's History', in *The Making of a Historical Culture*, ed. J.E. Myhre. Oslo, 1995, pp. 289–310.

—— 'Das Zusammenwirken von Nationalismus und Feminismus um die Jahrhundertwende – Ein Versuch zur vergleichenden Geschlechtergeschichte', in *Geschichte und Vergleich: Ansätze und Ergebnisse international vergleichender Geschichtsschreibung*, ed. H.G. Haupt and J. Kocka. Frankfurt am Main, New York, NY, 1996, pp. 315–38.

—— 'Nation — Class — Gender: Scandinavia at the Turn of the Century', *Scandinavian Journal of History* 21 (1996), pp.1–16.

—— 'World history and Gender History: The Case of the Nation State', in *Between National Histories and Global History. Konferanserapport til 23. det nordiske historikermøte*, ed. S. Tønnessen. Helsingfors, 1997, pp. 71–92.

—— 'Gender and Nation States: An International Comparative Perspective', in *Gendered Nations: The Long Eighteenth Century*, ed. I. Blom, K. Hagemann and C. Hall. Oxford, New York, NY, 2000, pp. 3–26.

—— (ed.). *Cappelens kvinnehistorie*, Vol. 1–3, Oslo, 1992–93.

Blom, I., Hagemann, K. and Hall, C. (eds). *Gendered Nations: The Long Eighteenth Century*. Oxford, New York, NY, 2000.

Bock, G. 'Challenging Dichotomies: Perspectives on Women's History', in *Writing Women's History: International Perspectives*, ed. K. Offen, J. Rendall and R. Roach Pierson. London, Bloomington, IN, 1991, pp. 1–23.

Cott, N. *The Grounding of Modern Feminism*. New Haven, CT, London, 1987.

Cott, N. and Dubois, E. 'Comments on Karen Offen's Article "Defining Feminism: A Comparative Historical Approach"' and K. Offen, 'Reply to Cott', *Signs* 15 (1989), pp. 195–209. (Reprinted in an abbreviated and slightly reversed form in *Beyond Equality and Difference*, ed. G. Bock and S. James. London, New York, NY, 1992, pp. 89–109.)

Eley, G. and Suny, R.G. *Becoming National: A Reader*. Oxford, New York, NY, 1990.

Fox Genovese, E. 'Placing Women in History', *New Left Review* 133 (1982), pp. 5–29.

'Gender, Nationalisms and National Identities' (special issue), *Gender and History* 5 (1993).

Hall, C. *White, Male and Middle Class: Explorations in Feminism and History*. Cambridge: Cambridge University Press, 1991.

Hobsbawm, E.J. *Nations and Nationalism since 1780: Programme, Myth, Reality*. Cambridge: Cambridge University Press, 1990.

Jayawardena, K. *Feminism and Nationalism in the Third World*. London, 1986.

Kasturi, L. and Macumdar, V. *Women and Indian Nationalism*. New Delhi, 1994.

Kelly, J. 'The Social Relations of the Sexes: Methodological Implications of Women's History', in J. Kelly, *Women, History and Theory*. Chicago, IL, 1984, pp. 1–18.

Lake, M. 'Mission Impossible: How Men Gave Birth to the Australian Nation — Nationalism, Gender and Other Seminal Acts', *Gender and History* 4 (1992), pp. 305–22.

Lerner, G. 'Reconceptualizing Differences Among Women', *Journal of Women's History* 1 (1990), pp. 106–22.

McClintock, A. 'No Longer in a Future Heaven: Nationalism, Gender and Race', in *Becoming National*, ed. G. Eley. Oxford, 1996, pp. 260–84.

Melby, K. 'Women's Ideology: Difference, Equality or a New Femininity?', in *Moving On: New Perspectives on the Womens Movement*, ed. T. Andreasen et al. (Acta Jutlandica 67, no. 1, Humanities Series 6). Aarhus, 1991, pp. 138–54.

Offen, K. 'Defining Feminism: A Comparative Historical Approach', *Signs* 14 (1988), pp. 119–57.

Offen, K. 'Feminism and Sexual Difference in Historical Perspective', in *Theoretical Perspectives on Sexual Difference*, ed. D.L. Rhode. New Haven, CT, London, 1990, pp. 13–20.

—— 'Exploring the Sexual Politics of Republican Nationalism', in *Nationhood and Nationalism in France: From Boulangism to the Great War 1889–1918*, ed. R. Tombs. London, 1991, pp. 195–209.

—— *European Feminisms 1700–1950: A Political History*. Stanford, CA, 2000.

Pascoe, P. 'Introduction' and 'Race, Gender and Intercultural Relations: The Case of Interracial Marriages', *Frontiers* 12 (1991), pp. 1–18.

Pateman, C. 'Equality, Difference, Subordination: the Politics of Motherhood and Women's Citizenship', in *Beyond Equality and Difference: Citizenship – Feminist Politics – Female Subjectivity*, ed. G. Bock and S. James. London, New York, NY, 1992, pp. 17–31.

Pulkinen, T. 'Citizens, Nations and Women: The Transition from Ancient Regime to Modernity and Beyond', Paper for the International Federation for Research in Women's History Symposium, 'Rethinking Women and Gender Relations in the Modern State'. Bielefeld, April 1993.

Ramusak, B. 'Women in South and South East Asia', in *Restoring Women to History: Teaching Packets for Integrating Women's History into Courses on Africa, Asia, Latin*

America, The Caribbean and the Middle East, ed. I. Berger et al. Bloomington, IN, 1988, pp. 1–63.

Samuel, R. (ed.). *Minorities and Outsiders vol. 2, Patriotism – The Making and Unmaking of British National Identity*. London, New York, NY, 1989.

Scott, J.W. 'Women's History' and 'Gender: A Useful Category of Historical Analysis', in *Gender and the Politics of History*, ed. J.W. Scott. New York, NY, 1988, pp.15–50.

Sievers, S.L. *Flowers in Salt: The Beginnings of Feminist Consciousness in Modern Japan*. Stanford, CA, 1983.

—— 'Women in China, Japan and Korea', in *Restoring Women to History: Teaching Packets for Integrating Women's History into Courses on Africa, Asia, Latin America, The Caribbean and the Middle East*, ed. I. Berger et al. Bloomington, IN, 1988, pp. 63–118.

Yuval-Davis, N. *Gender and Nation*. London, 1997.

Yuval-Davis, N. and Anthias, F. (eds). *Women — Nation – State*. London, 1990.

11

THE JEWISH PROJECT OF MODERNITY: DIVERSE OR UNITARY?

Shulamit Volkov

Diversity – Voluntary and Involuntary

With the Assyrian conquest of the Northern Jewish Kingdom of Samaria (*Shomron*) in 722 BC, and the subsequent destruction of the Kingdom of Judea by the Babylonians some 150 years later, the Jews – though never *all* Jews – were expelled from their land. They were taken eastward as captives and slaves, according to common practice at that time, and although they were later allowed to return, many preferred to stay back, often pushing on to further shores. In addition, a trickle of Jewish emigration from the new Kingdom in Jerusalem, beleaguered and internally split, made up a string of small, but distinct Jewish communities, spread across the entire ancient world. Thereafter, between the destruction of the Second Temple in Jerusalem and the establishment of the state of Israel in the aftermath of the Second World War, there was no political or territorial centre for Jewish life. Nevertheless, while living in the Diaspora, Jews continued to uphold a separate, distinct identity. The memory of destruction and expulsion remained alive among them, and their centuries-old form of minority existence may have weakened, but never seemed to destroy their inner sense of cohesion. Collective and individual interests – religious, social and economic – sustained a network of Jewish communities across Europe. A sense of solidarity in the face of a hostile world was preserved among them everywhere, while an internal hierarchy among religious authorities institutionalised existing ties, even in times of relatively sparse contacts. Young Talmudic scholars moved among the various centres of learning with relative ease, and common social welfare institutions served Jews regardless of their place of origin – a true rarity in premodern Europe. A super-local *Kehila* (Congregation), clearly more than a mere 'imagined community', was the self-evident reference group for all of them.[1] Only under the new circumstances of legal equality and the partial entry of Jews into the social fabric of their close-by environment, beginning in Central and Western Europe by the later part of the eighteenth century, did their joint identity begin to show signs of disintegration. Finally, on the eve of the First World War, the Jewish world seemed disunited as never before. Even the prospect of having to fight on opposing fronts as soldiers in the various national armies aroused no particular outcry among them. At least on the face of it, modernisation seemed to have proven a fatal blow to Jewish unity.[2]

This in itself is not surprising. The historical and sociological literature is full of examples describing the disintegrative effect of modernisation.[3] One is repeatedly presented with cases in which urbanisation, new social and occupational stratification, as well as the revolution in transport and communication, are all seen as reasons for the break-up of traditional forms of social cohesion. These have, of course, had their effect on Jews, too. An upper stratum of wealthy Jews pushed their way into new occupations in Western and Central Europe as early as the mid-eighteenth century. At the same time, a rapidly developing economy opened up new opportunities for a somewhat larger, upward-striving Jewish middle class. By then even the poor were beginning to abandon old ties and habits in order to try and form new and presumably more promising ones.[4] Thus, by the turn of that century, especially in the countries of early modernisation, Jews were moving up and out of their old limited environment. They acquired norms and habits usually associated with non-Jewish bourgeois society, and discarded old loyalties, not necessarily out of any ideological conviction but as a (presumably inevitable) side effect of their upward mobility.

Such spectacular socio-economic improvement was practically unknown in Eastern Europe. Well into the nineteenth century, the social situation of East European Jews continued to deteriorate. Everywhere in Galicia and in the 'Pale of Settlement' under Russian domination, Jews suffered from chronic unemployment and a debilitating underemployment.[5] The general backwardness of Eastern Europe and the special restrictions on the movement of Jews there and on their choice of occupation greatly retarded their modernisation. They were disadvantaged not only in comparison with the Jews in the West, but also with respect to parallel strata of the general population in the East. Jews continued to concentrate in petty trade and in the growing but backward clothing industry, and many of them endured the most extreme poverty. Thus, during much of the modern age, the gap between the Jews in the various European regions steadily widened. Furthermore, socioeconomic differentiation had its cultural counterpart, so that it often resulted in a great deal of social estrangement and cultural alienation, too. Indeed, the hostility between Western Jews and the so-called *Ostjuden* became truly proverbial and needs no further elaboration.[6]

Modernisation also accentuated differentiation within the various European regions, even within each nation state. Urbanisation and the creation of great metropolitan areas, for instance, deepened the gap between rural and urban Jews everywhere. In France, Alsatian Jews held on to traditional forms of life much longer and much more tenaciously than Parisians or the Sephardic communities in Bordeaux. Within the southeastern French provinces, considerable differences developed between Jews living in villages and small towns and those living in Metz or in Strasbourg.[7] Modernisation had different effects on Jews in the various states and regions of Germany, too. Their response to the challenge of modernity, like that of non-Jews, greatly depended on local peculiarities,[8] and even in Eastern Europe, a belated but highly differentiated pattern of modernisation affected Jews and non-Jews alike. Recently three distinct regions were diagnosed within the Pale itself, each with its own historical background, ethnic composition, the peculiar size of its Jewish population, the degree of their urbanisation and industrialisation – all combining to increase inner variations.[9] Modernisation, being an essentially uneven process, first operated to accentuate previous differences – in economic, social and cultural terms. It then added its own parameters to the existing landscape of diversity. By the early twentieth century, so it seems, not much remained of the basically unitary lifestyle and experience characteristic of European Jewry.

Turning away from the uncontrolled and at that time fully unforeseen consequences of modernisation to the self-conscious, deliberate aspects of this process, diversity seems to remain just as striking. Of course, the distinction between intended and unintended processes of change is rather arbitrary. For instance, developments which are unintentional on a collective basis may be the upshot of carefully planned action on the part of individuals and vice versa. Often very clearly goal-orientated activity, such as railway building, for instance, has a multitude of unexpected side effects. In modern Jewish history one can easily detect strategies of assimilation which have inadvertently brought about new kinds of ties among Jews, or ideologies of separation and uniqueness which actually reflected successful integration in non-Jewish society.[10] Nevertheless, it is possible to deal separately with the conscious ways by which Jews endeavoured to modernise their religion, their lifestyle, and their social and cultural milieu. This was a unique process, which may be named, paraphrasing Habermas, 'the Jewish Project of Modernity'.[11] Jews have intensively talked and written about it. They discussed the matter, argued and quarrelled about it. Above all, they made it a major theme of their self-reflection in modern times.

By the late eighteenth century, the disharmonious consequences of the efforts to introduce some of the principles of the Enlightenment into the Jewish milieu quickly became apparent. A socially rather homogeneous Jewry in Europe had by then enjoyed a considerable measure of unity and autonomy. Soon, however, a combination of external and internal causes resulted in gradual disintegration.[12] Contemporary enlightened monarchs in the various German states began to encroach upon *all* autonomous social bodies, and Jews, of course, could not for long be exempted. At the same time, as a result of internal conflict and the growing attraction of enlightened society for the better-off Jews, the conservative rabbinate was losing some of its power, while growing social mobility made it a matter of self-interest for successful Jews to mingle with non-Jews and emulate their daily habits. Popular literature and theatre often fascinated these Jews. They sought ways to evade the control of religious authority and were beginning to articulate a modernising ideology in defence of their social and cultural preferences. Differentiation and internal strife inevitably followed.

Paradoxically, indeed, religion – the major integrative force among Jews for centuries – turned out to be the most divisive element at this stage of their history.[13] To be sure, religious discord among Jews had not been unknown before. Under the backward conditions of Galicia and pre-partition Poland, for instance, Chassidism (a revivalist Jewish movement with mystical characteristics) aroused enormous enthusiasm as well as a great deal of opposition. But the split between its followers and those who radically opposed them remained primarily an *internal* affair, while the controversy over the early *Haskalah* (Jewish Enlightenment) was at least partially motivated by external trends and was, at least partially again, a response to the challenge of the outer world. Clearly, the rising interest of Jews in the scientific and rational discourse of the Enlightenment initially grew out of older Jewish traditions, but eventually everywhere – in Eastern as well as in Western Europe – it turned out to be predominantly based on borrowing from the intellectual environment of the *non-Jewish* world.

The *Haskalah* ushered in numerous new trends.[14] The *Maskilim*, its followers, were open to an unprecedented degree to the intellectual trends prevalent in the world around them, and were often concerned with the aesthetisation of Jewish religious practices, especially with regard to synagogue services. They endeavoured to adjust liturgical practices to the presumably more civilised taste of the local bourgeoisie, and occasionally even propagated reforms of the praying book texts, too. They advocated change in dress and in burial customs, rejecting – as a matter of principle – everything they judged outmoded or superstitious. But reform always brought with it bitter internal conflicts. Foremost among them was the principled struggle between orthodox and liberals. In fact, not only was Reform Judaism slowly taking shape then, but Jewish Orthodoxy too was formed and formulated in the process. Conservative rabbis were at first reluctant to respond when reformers introduced change in the style of synagogue praying or even in the liturgy; when they promoted preaching in the vernacular, or included choir singing or even organ music as part of the services.[15] They first managed a joint response only after the publication of the new prayer book in Hamburg, in 1819. But despite their intransigence, they – as well as the liberals – were at first reluctant to pursue matters. Instead they usually sought ways to accommodate each other and avoid open enmity. Even Chatam Sofer of Preßburg (present-day Bratislava), known for using the dictum that 'Nothing new is permitted by the Torah', a battle cry of the Orthodox offensive, was less strict in practice than in theory. It was finally in Hungary, during the second half of the century, that Ultra-Orthodoxy formulated an uncompromising position, preferring split to cooperation with those it considered 'like Gentiles'.[16] By canonising the *Shulchan-Aruch* (a sixteenth-century book, summarising the daily practice of Jewish law) and even by 'investing the non-confessional elements of Judaism with religious value', as for instance in the case of traditional Jewish dress or the use of the Yiddish language, they actually departed from mainstream trends in Judaism. They thus formed a *separate* religious camp, *insisting* upon internal schism and taking great pains to legitimise it.

In Eastern Europe, too, conservative Judaism sought ways to protect itself from the effects of religious modernisation. Though the struggles *inside* Eastern Orthodoxy did not abate, the *Haskalah*, first considered an intractable enemy only by Galician Chassidism, gradually turned into a major threat, worthy of the outspoken opposition of the traditional hierarchy, too.[17] From the outset, Russian *Maskilim* lived in 'spiritual estrangement', rejected by all prominent rabbinic authorities, as well as by the lay *Melamdim* (school teachers) and the great majority of Jewish artisans and petty merchants. Worse still, during a brief period in the 1830s and 1840s, while the *Maskilim* initiated cooperation with the Tsarist government, hoping to harness it to their fight against what they considered Jewish backwardness, 'free traffic between the *Haskalah* and loyalty to tradition' was 'gradually but systematically blocked.'[18] Religious reformers found themselves increasingly isolated from conservative Judaism. The latter was ever more strictly and systematically closing its ranks against the effects of change, codifying and canonising whatever it now came to consider a 'sacred tradition'.

Yet, perhaps more interesting than the schism between conservatives and modernisers were the rifts within liberal Judaism itself. By the mid-nineteenth century the initial Reform movement in Germany was practically split into at least three factions. Disregarding the extreme margins for a moment, it included reformers of more and less radical varieties and a third group, known as Neo-Orthodoxy, insisting on both the strict adherence to Jewish law and the partaking in the civil culture of bourgeois Germany.[19] The battle among them was no less acrimonious than that between Reformers on the one hand and Orthodox on the other. In this case, too, the more traditional camp, that of Neo-Orthodoxy, eventually turned out to be more uncompromising, urging a *formal* split within the Jewish community. The Neo-Orthodox congregation in Frankfurt am Main, for instance, excluded both the more outspoken, radical reformers in town, and the more conservative traditionalists, the so-called Old Orthodox.[20] Thus, religion, indeed, the strongest bond among Jews for generations, while continuing to play an important role in defining them vis-à-vis Christians, was no longer a force of cohesion – neither within the various European nation states nor across their borders. More often than not, it was now a force of division.

Jewish unity, moreover, suffered from an even deeper schism – a result of another kind of differentiation, outside the strictly religious sphere. Note for instance the string of events, about a century ago, during the year 1897. At the end of August, the Zionists convened their first congress in Basle and launched the new Jewish national movement, with chapters in practically every major centre of Jewish life. In October of that same year, the 'General Jewish Labour Union in Russia and Poland', known as the *Bund*, was founded, soon to become the most powerful Socialist party in Tsarist Russia. At about the same time, the New York *Vorwärts* began to appear, a Yiddish newspaper, combining socialism and Jewish nationalism in a special mix, fit for the immigrant population of the Lower East Side. In that same year, this time in Odessa, Ahad

Ha'Am, among the outstanding Jewish intellectuals in Russia, launched the *Hashiloach*, mouthpiece of cultural Zionism, eventually the best Hebrew literary periodical for years to come. And finally, in 1897 too, the historian and Jewish activist Simon Dubnow published his *Letters on Judaism – Old and New*, articulating the principles of Jewish autonomism.[21]

Eastern Europe, where much of all this was taking place, was particularly ripe for internal strife. In response to the pressures of poverty, overpopulation and repeated waves of violent anti-Semitism, radical Jewish youths, fresh from the experience of breaking away from their strictly traditionalist environment, developed a great number of ideological options. They were often dedicated to them with revolutionary, messianic zeal. Some were attracted to internationalist socialism, developing it into an alternative subculture within an exclusively Jewish, usually Yiddish-speaking milieu. Others slowly developed various forms of Jewish nationalism – Zionist or territorialist. Some started out from an idealist, even romantic position; others were positivists and utilitarians. Within each strand, some propagated a materialist, even Marxist version of Jewish nationalism; others were idealists with liberal tendencies. Some were more revolutionary than others, more influenced by Russian populism, more dedicated to the revival of Hebrew or of Yiddish, etc. As it is often the case, close ideological affinity did not diminish the heat of controversy but only further increased it. The various factions were constantly in battle and minor controversies often seemed a matter of life or death. Many changed camps; some were forever trying new syntheses. In any case, for them unity was no more than a dim memory.[22]

In the West, unity fared no better. Above all, it was the 'Ideology of Emancipation',[23] primarily developed in Germany, that defined the parameters of modernisation for European Jews. But discord among modernists soon overshadowed their sense of sharing in a common 'project'. By 1893, 'German Citizens of the Mosaic Faith', as many liberal German Jews now wished to be perceived, established their own organisation, the so-called *Centralverein*, often known simply as the CV. On top of the internal conflicts within late nineteenth-century Judaism, one must therafter add the constant tension, occasionally breaking into real animosity, between the new organisation and the later Zionists.[24] The sense of disintegration within Judaism, and of progressively losing all previous components of cohesion within the Jewish community, was surely becoming ever more widespread. Following the First World War, ideological contention among Jews – in the East and in the West, in the Old and in the New World – showed no sign of waning. Surprisingly enough, this remained virtually unchanged even after the Second World War. In *Eretz-Ysrael*, too, party strife within the small Jewish settlers' community – the *Yshuv* – reflected what seemed at the time a fundamental ideological diversity, both within the labour movement and between itself and the so-called bourgeois parties. Outside Palestine, the struggle between Zionism and the heirs of the German CV, upholding the principles of prewar Liberalism and the ideals of complete Jewish integration, never lost its rancour.

Mainstream historiography continues to give much attention to these internal disputes, and in many ways it merely reflects, or even unwittingly perpetuates them. Zionist historiography has for long kept up the distinction between centrifugal forces in Jewish history – destructive, negative elements and the contrary cohesive and constructive forces – reshaping the Jewish nation, invigorating Jewish identity. The so-called Liberal historiography, reasserting its position after the Second World War, was now forging a new Diaspora conception of Jewish history, cementing it with the newest tools of the profession. Following the general historiographical tendency everywhere at this time to concentrate on well-defined topics and mistrust large, all-encompassing historical works, the history of the Jews living within a single nation state seemed perfectly suitable for serious, professional research. A multitude of studies on Jews in the various host countries, with emphasis on their relations with and their assimilation into the general, non-Jewish society, was the result. Even Israeli historians followed suit.[25] All finally seemed to agree that one ought to beware of overgeneralisation and avoid sacrificing the 'individuality of historical phenomena' in the search for an overarching, general reading of Jewish history.[26]

Consequently, a picture of Jewish multiplicity now reigns supreme. And while methodologically this trend may be a blessing, it has its dangers too. In fact, it may eventually lead to a complete breakdown of Jewish historiography as such. It was Jonathan Frankel, a historian of Russian Jewry, who recently articulated his bewilderment vis-à-vis such far-reaching historiographical fragmentation: 'Order has been replaced by flux', he sums up, 'one law of motion – by a myriad of contexts and a multiplicity of responses.'[27] Clearly, there is an undertone of unease in this comment, an implicit desire to hold on to at least some kind of a unified view of Jewish history. Yet while this may only be a wish characteristic of Zionist historians, who may otherwise have to admit the limits of their nationalist historiography, others too seem to find that 'broken glass view of Jewish history' somewhat unsatisfactory. Do we really have to abandon any claim of commonality between the Jews during modernisation? Does a closer look at the 'Jewish Project of Modernity' really justify a complete swing from a unified conception of modern Jewry to a multifaceted image, offering only a mosaic of different stories, independent of each other, stressing internal diversity at each and every level of analysis? Perhaps the distance, or rather that much-acclaimed historical perspective we now possess, may finally allow us to disregard some of the old disputes and reassert a new measure of unity, even if only a relative unity? Could that peculiar 'Jewish Project of Modernity', the source of so much strife and division, also reveal a new type of cohesion?

Unity – Parallels and Similarities

Let us turn back to the beginning, and that beginning is, once more, the Jewish *Haskalah*. Indeed, its history is a classic case for discussing the differences between West-Central European Jewry on the one hand and Eastern Jews on the other, that single, fundamental division, only rarely challenged by historians. Sometime during the late eighteenth century, runs the argument, European Enlightenment has given birth to a Jewish *Haskalah*, and this unique Jewish movement quickly developed two distinct branches, a Western and an Eastern one. The first branch grew mainly in Berlin. Its towering figure was Moses Mendelssohn.[28] It stressed the need to familiarise Jews with the intellectual trends of the non-Jewish world and to prepare them to join the liberal civil society, emerging in their immediate non-Jewish environment as full and equal members. The second, the Eastern branch, presumably had more authentic Jewish origins, relying more heavily on the rational, scientific tradition of medieval Judaism and always keeping close to the sources – to the ancient Hebrew tongue and Jewish literary legacy. It did receive, no doubt, a powerful momentum from Berlin, but then, developing in the face of strong Orthodox opposition, managed to turn into an independent spiritual force – the ideological background for Jewish modernisation in the East. Thus, while in the West the *Haskalah* was a pioneering movement with radical implications, it soon ran into a dead end.[29] In contrast, it hardly represented a true revolution in the East, but soon proved powerful enough to transform local Judaism in various direct and indirect ways. Mendelssohn's disciples in the West often turned to conversion, lost interest in Judaism and prepared the way for a thoroughgoing process of assimilation. In the East, the *Haskalah* turned out to be the source of both Jewish socialism and Jewish nationalism – the main ideological strands of a secularised, modern Jewry.

Much of this is unquestionably true. Nevertheless, the *Haskalah* was a single movement, fundamentally the same in West and East. Such a division was surely meaningless for its early proponents. Nearly all of them came to Germany from the East, or at least from the remote eastern borders of Prussia. Mendelssohn came only from Dessau, but Isaac Eichel came from Königsberg, and Salomon Maimon made the journey all the way from Lithuania to Berlin. Distance, in any case, had little cultural implication at that time, since no noticeable gap had existed then between Jews in the various provinces of the Ashkenazi Jewish world. Furthermore, despite their persistent 'bad press', nowhere did the *Maskilim* intend a full abandonment of Judaism, nor did they advocate a full acceptance of non-Jewish bourgeois values by contemporary Jews. They sought a proper synthesis, fit for a new age. At first 'enlightened' Jews, in Germany as well as in Russia, all considered the revival of Hebrew a prerequisite for such a synthesis. It was meant to provide Jews with the main tool for cultural revival – a 'pure', unadulterated language, a common goal among all 'enlightened' men everywhere in Europe.[30] Soon enough, it is true, the *Maskilim* in Germany felt compelled to use German ever more frequently, finally up to the exclusion of Hebrew. They began by publishing *Ha'Meassef*, the first modern Hebrew journal, and ended by editing the German-language *Sulamith*.[31] And while this was to some degree a response to the pressure from the authorities, it was also an internal strategic decision. The *Maskilim* were thus addressing a growing Jewish public, fluent enough in the language of its surroundings and having no more use for texts that soon seemed only second-rate and provincial, randomly translated into Hebrew.[32] Developments in Russia were similar, though by no means identical. The *Maskilim* in that country gradually turned, in addition to their use of German or Russian – often indeed of both – to the use of Yiddish. They were searching for the most effective way of reaching their potential readers.[33] Clearly, the decision to prefer German in Germany had different consequences than the decision to prefer Yiddish in the East. However, the motive force in both cases was the same. The aim was to reach as many people as possible. The message, finally, was deemed more important than the medium.

Furthermore, the hopelessness of the *Haskalah* project in Germany, as well as its steadfastness in the East, have been greatly exaggerated. In fact, the *Haskalah* left a rich and highly significant legacy in the West. It opened the way for Jewish educational improvements, for the launching of the German synagogue-reform movement and for the development of a new kind of Jewish scholarship, the *Wissenschaft des Judentums*. It pioneered a Jewish public sphere, an *Öffentlichkeit*, that later was essential in the process of modernising Jewish life in Germany and provided a model for an ideology of secularisation. It thus helped delegate religion to a private, domestic function, still cherished but limited in its effect.[34] From this perspective, the role of the *Haskalah* in the East was not all that different. Historiography has particularly neglected the role of the Western-style liberal 'ideology of emancipation' in Russia, initially formulated by Western *Maskilim*, but later adopted and developed by various spokesmen of a modernised Judaism in the East, too. A new biography of the Hebrew Poet Yudah-Leib Gordon (Yalag) stresses his faith in the principles of the early Berlin-based *Haskalah*: a combination of cultural Hebrew revival and a process of absorbing Western liberalism.[35] Despite the fact that in the years following the pogroms of 1881/82 it was difficult to support a faith in the 'path of Western civilisation and progress', as Yalag had named it, this did remain for decades the hope entertained by 'millions of Jews, who strove to bridge the gap between traditional Judaism and the modern world'.[36] At least until the early 1880s, it was this conglomerate of Hebrew revival, moderate reform and liberal politics which animated many Jews between Vilnius and St Petersburg, no less than between Berlin and London.

By that time, to be sure, Jewish cultural modernisation had found other routes, too. In Germany it was the Reform movement that first came to the fore. While the accompanying ideology, playing such an important role in the German-Jewish discourse, had only little effect elsewhere, reform itself was by no means limited to Germany. Its first manifestation, in fact, came from France and its practical manifestations could be found almost everywhere in Europe. As early as 1819, a group of Viennese Jews wished to reform their services by introducing organ music and a weekly sermon held in German. At first, they were restrained by the Austrian authorities, but by 1826 Vienna did have its new *Stadttempel* (city temple) and somewhat later also its *Synagogenordnung* (synagogue regulations), though always along a rather moderate line.[37] In Bordeaux, to take another example, a choir was introduced into the service in 1821, and some fifteen years later the Jews in Prague also had weekly German sermons in their new synagogue, choir singing and even organ music – though not on the Sabbath, of course.[38] Everywhere, with or without direct influence from the ideological centre in Germany, the project of synagogue reform focused around the same issues, chiefly around matters of aesthetics and decorum. By the early nineteenth century many Jews in Western and Central Europe did not feel at ease with the appearance of their synagogue and with the style of praying within it, in what now seemed to them an unacceptable chaos and a blatant lack of elegance. Everywhere this was clearly a measure of their *embourgeoisement*, an expression of their need to adopt the outer signs of middle-class civility.

It is, therefore, not surprising that it was in Odessa, where a considerable number of middle-class Jews, some originally from Brody, achieved an unusual measure of acculturation, that the first new synagogue in the East was finally established in 1841.[39] As elsewhere, reformed services were quickly institutionalised, stressing a dignified and orderly behaviour here, too. East-European Jews, who sometimes constituted up to 20 percent of the population in the towns of the Pale, usually showed less interest in matters of representation. Yet in Galicia and Russia, in Tarnopol or even in Vilnius, synagogue reformers always placed a great emphasis on these matters. 'The dignity of synagogue services was viewed as a barometer of the moral character of a community', writes the historian of the Jewish community in Odessa, and everywhere the newly established 'temples' were conceived as no less than agents of moral education.[40] Jewish habits outside the synagogue were also targets of reform. Abandoning traditional dress, for instance, had the same kind of effect – and it was always accomplished, in the East and in the West, as Jews sought to modernise through the adoption of bourgeois taste. Even the matter of covering one's head was tampered with and it was not only radical reformers who admitted the need for change in such age-old customs. Even Neo-Orthodoxy, as anxious to uphold bourgeois standards as its more liberal contenders, agreed to practical reforms in this sphere.[41] Jewish dignity, thus defined, seemed now more critical than blindly insistent on traditional details.

Reform occasionally also went beyond form. In this respect, the issues were the same everywhere. Repeatedly under scrutiny were texts expressing hopes of vengeance and denigrating Israel's enemies – in the past and in the present. Crucial, too, was the controversy over the messianic aspects of Jewish prayers and the validity of the hope of return to Zion, repeatedly expressed in them. Relevant texts were, however, only seldom changed. In Eastern Europe, where prospects of emancipation and real social integration were dim, hope for the end of the exile seemed as relevant as ever. But in the West, too, such passages were only rarely deleted. In France and England, in fact, no textual change, except for some abridgements, was normally admitted, and in Germany, only some cuts were made in some of the reformed synagogues, especially during the early radical phase of the movement. Later on, old texts were often reintroduced. Hebrew prayers had the same fate. Following a short period of radicalism, even liberal German rabbis usually settled for a German sermon and an almost entirely Hebrew prayer-book. In Vienna, in London and in Paris such a compromise was achieved at the outset, and it was only in the United States, from about the 1890s onwards, that more far-reaching alterations were attempted once again.[42]

On the whole, even in Germany, the fervour of European synagogue reform was more or less spent by the last third of the nineteenth century. Its almost exclusive interest in external gesture might have delegated it from the outset to the margin, had it not been given so much attention by the Orthodox opposition. While modernisers were ready to admit that some aspects of Jewish tradition were more important than others, the Orthodox turned the preservation of every external detail into a matter of principle. Eventually, it became quite clear: selection was the prime strategy of the modernisers; insistence on all and everything – that of the traditionalists. Indeed, the 'Jewish Project of Modernity', meant at no point abandoning *everything* Jewish, neither in Eastern Europe, of course, nor in the West. It was never merely a matter of giving Judaism 'a proper burial', to use Gershom Scholem's critical phrase in his attack against the *Wissenschaft des Judentums*.[43] Everywhere modernisers were absorbed in selection, distinguishing between main and side issues, essentials and externalities, the core and the shell.

Reformers of Jewish education were most particularly busy with this kind of choice. Here matters were more complicated, since a solution had to be found not only by borrowing from the non-Jewish world but also by changing the hierarchy within Judaism and making decisions about the relative value of its components. Clearly, where the *Cheder*, that old-style informal institution for teaching small children, was still generally prevalent, as in much of Eastern Europe, more had to be done in order to achieve any measure of change. Indeed, the old *Melamdim*, the staff of *Cheder* – teachers – were criticised there for their ignorance and their teaching methods – their apathy and their cruelty.[44] Beyond that, consensus was also easy to achieve as far as the introduction of some *non*-Jewish subject matter was concerned. Everywhere – in Germany as well as in the East – the new schools taught the local vernacular and rudimentary courses in mathematics and science, deemed useful for mercantile and professional careers. Later on, some history and literature were added – always making sure to leave time for Jewish studies. At this point, of course, selection became inevitable and, interestingly enough, the decisions taken were usually the same. Faith in 'pure' language dictated emphasis on Hebrew grammar, and a critique of traditional Talmudic learning led to much greater stress on biblical scholarship. The Pentateuch was of prime significance everywhere, particularly for its historical chapters and the exposition of the basic Mosaic legal code.

Everywhere stress was placed on the Psalms and on the late Prophets, with special attention to what was considered their ethical message and their universal moral teaching.

Such common preferences extended to other spheres, too. Jews of all modern trends took extraordinary interest in the Jewish legacy of medieval Spain, for instance. They were everywhere fascinated by the Spanish-Jewish Golden Age, often conceived as an antecedent of their own.[45] At that time, too, Jews were apparently deeply involved in science and philosophy, contributing significantly to European culture. They mastered the vernacular as well as the scholarly languages, Latin and Greek. Most importantly, they were creative in their own ancient tongue, producing a fascinating anthology of Hebrew poetry, sacred and secular, epic and lyrical, within a short period of time.[46] This widespread fascination with medieval Spanish Jewry publicly manifested itself in the almost invariable adoption of the Moorish-Spanish architectural style for the construction of new synagogues all over the European continent. New synagogues were rich in Moorish decorations, elegant arches and typical domes. Even the so-called Brody Synagogue in Odessa followed this pattern, as did the temples in Hamburg and in Berlin, later even in New York.

Beyond the purely cultural and intellectual spheres, the 'Jewish Project of Modernity' was manifested in other areas too. Most important was the rapid development of a new kind of Jewish public life everywhere in nineteenth-century Europe. It was the *Maskilim*, once more, who sought to spread their word through a 'new journalism'. Having first placed great emphasis on the education of the young, they strove to cultivate the Jewish adult world, too. This, they believed, could only be done through an intensive use of the printed word. There is nothing particularly Jewish about that. It was a common feature of the European Enlightenment. But Jews had had even less of a secular public sphere in earlier times than non-Jews, and a systematic network of public communication had previously been unknown among them. Significantly, even *Ha'Meassef*, beginning in the 1780s, aspired to become an international journal. Its subscribers – very few, to be sure – were spread between Amsterdam, Metz and Strasbourg in the West and Vilnius, Lublin and Prague in the East.[47] *Ha'Zfira*, yet another enlightened journal, first published in Galicia, beginning in 1823, was likewise an international Jewish project, and later on journals like the Ha'Magid, published since 1856 in the remote border town of Lyck (Polish: Ełk), between Prussia and Russia, had a worldwide influence through its Hebrew-language readership across the Continent.[48]

Soon, however, Jews were also producing newspapers in the languages of their host societies. Most wellknown was the German *Allgemeine Zeitung des Judentums*, published since 1837, giving voice to the newly politicised Jewish community in Germany. Ludwig Philippson, its chief editor for almost half a century, initially may have been more interested in presenting Jewish involvement in all things German than in strengthening Jewish solidarity. But he finally found himself the mouthpiece of Jewish interests and, through a network of foreign correspondents, his newspaper offered ongoing information on Jewish issues throughout the world. Similar Jewish papers were then beginning to appear, first in France, and later on in England and in the United States, in Galicia and in Russia. In fact, by the late 1850s Jewish newspapers in Russia, no less than those in Germany and in the West, became the platform upon which all public controversies in the Jewish world were staged. The influence of this press was so far-reaching that even the Orthodox felt compelled to join battle. As early as 1848, Rabbi Jakob Ettlinger of Altona initiated the publication of his *Zionwächter*, in both Hebrew and in German,[49] and some of the more conservative newspapers in Eastern Europe, too, occasionally published articles by rabbis belonging to the Orthodox camp.[50] Gradually, the various Jewish newspapers, in whatever language, created a rudimentary Jewish public opinion, conscious of its interests and preserving a sense of solidarity despite all internal conflicts. The *Archive Israélite* in Paris reported on Jewish affairs worldwide, as did the *Jewish Chronicle* in London, and both debated extensively on matters of Jewish modernisation in Eastern Europe, or on legal and educational matters concerning the Jewish world as a whole. Finally, in Russia too the Jewish press reported and discussed a wide range of worldwide Jewish affairs, all the more so as Russian Jewish immigrant communities multiplied across the globe. Prominent in this respect was the Hebrew *Ha'Magid*, but Yiddish and Russian-language newspapers also followed the same trend. Obviously there was an interest among the readers. Modernity – a source of discord and division – also provided new techniques of communication, thus helping, paradoxically perhaps, to make old links stronger rather than weaker, more rather than less effective.[51]

Beyond journalism, modern Jews developed other forms of public action. With growing integration they were naturally drawn into the politics of their respective countries, but they also formed new political ties among themselves. Even where social acceptance was as far advanced as in England, Jews found it necessary to establish their own political bodies. The Board of Deputies was established in 1828 for the purpose of 'completing the process of Jewish emancipation', and later on the Anglo-

Jewish Association explicitly made it its policy to deal with 'the international affairs of our people', knitting ever more closely 'the bond of brotherhood' among Jews.[52] In France, too, the *Consistoire*, established in response to the pressure of the French government in 1808, was soon deemed insufficient, both culturally and politically, for reaffirming Jewish bonds 'beyond religion and beyond the borders of France'.[53] The *Alliance Israélite Universelle* was then launched, manifesting these special ties by its social welfare and educational programmes, but above all by its national and international political activities. In Germany, the organisation of a central Jewish body was repeatedly blocked by the Prussian government. It was there, too, that leading liberal Jews occasionally expressed their complete lack of interest in matters Jewish outside their *Vaterland*.[54] But at the time of their full legal emancipation, in 1869, Jews in Germany too finally formed a central organisation, the *Deutsch-Israelitischer Gemeindebund*, and while this was not a very effective or powerful body, it was yet another voice reasserting Judaism as 'a community of fate'.[55] By 1878, during the deliberations of the Congress of Berlin, these bodies were capable of organising a concerted political campaign in support of the emancipation of the Romanian Jews. By then they had established themselves as an independent political force, long before the second wave of Jewish politicisation brought about fully-fledged Jewish political movements, for example, Zionism and the Jewish socialist parties in Eastern Europe.

Indeed, in the East, too, politicisation preceded the revolutionary phase.[56] The *Maskilim* repeatedly fought for political leadership, addressing demands for social and economic reform both to the Russian government and to 'their own people'. The break-up of traditional communal ties, together with circumstances of poverty and discrimination, forced Russian Jews to develop new political approaches and various 'ideologies of survival'. The type of political organisation adopted by Russian Jews differed markedly, to be sure, from that of their Jewish counterparts in the West, due both to their fundamentally different social stratification and to the unique Russian circumstances of the late nineteenth century. But in both parts of Europe, despite the disparity, the 'Jewish Project of Modernity' proceeded in a similar way. It included the creation of a secularised public sphere, dedicated to a political fight for greater equality and against discrimination and anti-Semitism. While not all politicised Jews kept their interest in the fight for specific Jewish causes, others – in different countries and on various occasions, continued to focus upon such matters.

At the background of all that was yet another aspect of Jewish modernisation – less tangible, perhaps, than formal education or political action, but not less important. It was the consistent effort of Jews everywhere in nineteenth-century Europe to reshape their tradition in new, more or less secular terms.[57] In the sphere of what anthropologists often call 'Great Tradition', modern Jews developed their own scholarship. It included a modern philosophy of Judaism and a new historical discipline, based on the principles of historicism and the rules of modern research.[58] In terms of a 'Little Tradition' – more popular and less highbrow – Jews likewise produced an immense body of literary texts in Hebrew, in Yiddish or in their so-called 'third languages'. They were thus replacing ancient cultural sources with a new literary world of reference, designing for themselves the new parameters of a modern identity. The Judaica Catalogue of the renowned *Stadtbibliothek* (city library) of Frankfurt am Main lists thousands of titles, mostly published before 1914, related to all possible aspects of Judaism, mostly written *by* and *for* Jews. Especially impressive are some 120 volumes of collected sermons – available for those who wished to refresh their memory concerning the moral and practical lessons of Jewish religion and history. Equally popular were the various Jewish yearbooks, almanacs and calendars of various kinds. These included typical assortments of the 'new Judaism': historical essays, usually on a single Jewish community or, even more often, on a particular Jewish personality of the past or present, a few poems, sometimes in Hebrew, often with adjacent translation, and short stories, most commonly based either on a tale from the arsenal of medieval Spanish-Jewish literature or on ghetto life and folklore from Eastern Europe. This complex modern Jewish literary world also included the more famous literary works depicting Jewish life, from the pen of a Berthold Auerbach or a Jacob Wassermann; works by men less wellknown today but very popular at the time, such as Karl Emil Fransoz or Georg Hermann; and finally also a bit of Heinrich Heine's poetry – a new Jewish cosmos of cultural references.

This was no less true for Eastern Europe than it was for Germany. Significantly, from the outset Jewish creativity in Eastern Europe was mainly channelled into literary production in Hebrew and in Yiddish. Though later some outstanding authors were absorbed into the Russian intelligentsia, the majority of first-rate Jewish writers in Russia continued to operate exclusively as part of the Jewish subculture. In fact, within an extremely short period, Jews in Eastern Europe produced an amazing gallery of outstanding literary men. By the end of the century, they were further sustained by a diverse publishing establishment, a number of first-rate literary-political journals and a growing readership. It was, indeed, this budding literature that played a major role in constructing a modern Jewish consciousness in Eastern Europe. The Jewish literary world supplied a 'new ground for Jewish existence', a new and complex 'fictional consciousness', a reshaped world view for Jews in the age of modernity.[59]

Clearly, the specific content of the new Jewish literary production in the various Jewish centres in Europe was not the same everywhere. But the strategy, so to speak, was very similar. Moreover, a lot of interchange took place within and between these centres. Heine, for instance, perhaps exerted greater influence in the East than in the West, while German-Jewish journals on their part laboured to translate and publish works by major Russian-Jewish authors. During the last decade of the nineteenth century, Western Jewry seemed eager to consume as much of the cultural production of Jews in the East as possible. Jewish periodicals were swamped by serialised stories of Y.L. Peretz, Shoylem Aleichem and other less well-known authors. Martin Buber's introduction of Chassidic tales into the German-Jewish milieu was truly sensational. Finally, the search for an authentic popular Jewish culture became prevalent among acculturated East European Jews, too. In 1901, Marek Ginzburg published the first 'Anthology of Jewish Folks Songs', and a number of collections of Yiddish proverbs and poetry appeared during the first decade of the century. A 'Jewish Historic-Ethnographic Society' was founded in 1908, as well as a 'Society for Folk Music' and various literary associations, propagating an intellectual version of a romantic Jewish nationalism.[60] Russian-Jewish intellectuals, like their counterparts among German Jews, were also engaged in creating a new Jewish tradition, 'a Judaism of [their] own remaking'.[61]

To be sure, both in Germany and in Russia the momentum of these trends did not only come from within. In Russia, no doubt, the *Narodniki* had a considerable influence on Jewish intellectuals, and in Germany the *Völkisch* movement had its own Jewish interpreters. Nevertheless, everywhere in Europe at that time there was a true need among Jews to partake in the invention of a secular Jewish culture and thereby recapture the 'spiritual power of Judaism'.[62] Jews were seeking out elements of their age-old cultural tradition in order to provide their lives with unique content. Nonliterary components of this tradition were also sought out. By the second half of the nineteenth century, a number of Jewish artists focused upon the peculiarities of Jewish life, and their work clearly fed into the general trend at the time.[63] Moritz Oppenheimer's 'Scenes from a Traditional Jewish Family Life' were reprinted in many editions, photographed and reproduced on pewter plates, porcelain trays, etc. Other Jewish artists, too, aroused great interest among contemporaries, since nostalgia was shared by Jews of the most varied religious schools and ideological persuasions. Liberal anti-nationalists were no less interested in thus appropriating their tradition than Zionists.

All these are elements of what may be considered a joint 'Jewish Project of Modernity'. Even in the heyday of internal splits and fundamental controversies, during the years prior to the First World War, a measure of uniformity could be found within European Jewry. Later on, some of the old lines of division were losing their importance, too. Political developments in Soviet Russia helped decimate the unique Jewish socialist milieu, which had flourished in the East. The Holocaust brought about the violent end of all other Eastern European Jewish alternatives. Local uniqueness – such as that typical of British Jewry, for instance – may have survived, but these should not blind us to the fact that since the late eighteenth century, Jews in all parts of Europe were basically concerned with a single cultural project. It had many different manifestations, but everywhere the questions were similar and – surprisingly enough – the answers often pointed in the same direction. Internal differences seemed more striking and more consequential at the time. Now, however, observing the parallels and the similarities becomes much easier. A new emphasis may thus allow us to rethink much of modern Jewish history, making it in turn both more coherent in itself and more evidently a part of European history as a whole.

Notes

* A Hebrew version of this essay was published in *Zionism and the Return to History*, ed. S.N. Eisenstadt and M. Lissak, Jerusalem, 1999, pp. 279–305.

1. See J. Katz, *Tradition and Crisis: Jewish Society at the End of the Middle Ages*, New York, 1960, especially part I.

2. I have previously dealt with this issue, with an emphasis on German Jewry, in: S. Volkov, 'Juden und Judentum im Zeitalter der Emanzipation. Einheit und Vielfalt', in *Die Juden in die europäischen Geschichte*, ed. W. Beck, Munich, 1992, pp. 86–108.

3. See e.g., S.N. Eisenstadt, *Modernization: Protest and Change*, Englewood Cliffs, 1966.

4. See D. Sorkin, *The Transformation of German Jewry 1780–1840*, Oxford, 1987; J. Toury, *Soziale und politische Geschichte der Juden in Deutschland 1847–1871*, Düsseldorf, 1977; the essays collected in: S. Volkov, *Jüdisches Leben und Antisemitismus im 19. und 20. Jahrhundert*, Munich, 1990, especially pp. 111–541, and *Deutsche Juden und die Moderne*, ed. S. Volkov, Munich, 1994.

5. Simon Dubnow, Raphael Mahler, Benzion Dinur and Salo Baron all treated this matter. Of the more modern historiography see: E. Mendelsohn, *Class Struggle in the Pale: The Formative Years of the Jewish Workers' Movement in Russia*, Cambridge, 1970; I. Rubinow, *Economic Conditions of Jews in Russia*, New York, 1975, as well as a somewhat less well-known contribution from Germany: G. Schramm, 'Die Ostjuden als soziales Problem des 19. Jahrhunderts', in *Gesellschaft, Recht und Freiheit*, ed. H. Maus, Neuwied, 1968, pp. 353–80, and G. Schramm, *Die Juden im osteuropäischen Osten um das Jahr 1900: Zwischenbilanz eines Minderheitenproblems (Historische und Landeskundliche Ostmitteleuropa-Studien 3)*, Marburg, 1989, pp. 3–19. See also Y. Peled and G. Shapir, 'From Caste to Exclusion: The Dynamics of Modernization in the Russian Pale of Settlement', *Studies in Contemporary Jewry* 3 (1987), pp. 98–114.

6. On this issue see especially S. Aschheim, *Brothers and Strangers: The East European Jew in German and German-Jewish Consciousness 1800–1923*, Madison, 1982, and J. Wertheimer, *Unwelcome Strangers: East European Jews in Imperial Germany*, Oxford, 1987.

7. See P.E. Hyman, 'The Social Context of Assimilation: Village Jews and City Jews in Alsace', in *Assimilation and Community: The Jews in 19th Century Europe*, ed. J. Frankel and S.J. Zipperstein, Cambridge, 1992, pp. 110–29; and P.E. Hyman, 'Traditionalism and Village Jews in 19th Century Western and Central Europe: Local Persistence and Urban Nostalgia', in *The Uses of Tradition: Jewish Continuity in the Modern Era*, ed. J. Wertheimer, New York, 1992, pp. 191–201.

8. For an example of regional effects on Jewish modernisation see A. Barkai, *Jüdische Minderheit und Industrialisierung: Demographie, Berufe und Einkommen in Westdeutschland, 1850–1914*, Tübingen, 1988. For local differentiations in Germany on the whole, see F. Tipton, *Regional Variations in the Economic Development of Germany during the Nineteenth Century*, Middletown, 1976; S. Pollard, ed., *Region und Industrialisierung: Studien zur Rolle der Region in der Wirtschaftsgeschichte der letzten zwei Jahrhunderte*, Göttingen, 1980; R. Fremdling and R. Tilly, eds, *Industrialisierung und Raum: Studien zur regionalen Differenzierung im Deutschland des 19. Jahrhunderts*, Stuttgart, 1979.

9. See S.J. Zipperstein, *The Jews of Odessa: A Cultural History 1794–1881*, Stanford, 1985, p. 31.

10. See my introduction in: *Deutsche Juden und die Moderne*, ed. Volkov, pp. vi–xxiii. More specifically: A. Barkai, 'German Jewish Migration in the Nineteenth Century, 1830–1910', *Leo Baeck Institute Yearbook* (LBIYB) XXX (1985), pp. 301–18.

11. See J. Habermas, 'Die Moderne – ein unvollendetes Projekt', in J. Habermas, *Kleine politische Schriften I–IV*, Frankfurt am Main, 1981, pp. 444–64, and compare S. Volkov, 'Die Erfindung einer Tradition. Zur Entstehung des modernen Judentum in Deutschland', *Historische Zeitschrift*, 253 (1991), pp. 603–29.

12. The first to stress the importance of external factors was Isaac Marcus Jost, as early as the first half of the nineteenth century. Of the more modern literature see: S. Stern, *Der preussische Staat und die Juden*, 7 vols, Tübingen, 1962–71, as well as J. Katz, *Out of the Ghetto: The Social Background of the Jewish Emancipation 1770–1880*, Cambridge, MA, 1973. Gershom Schalom lent his authority to the interpretation that stressed internal influences. See also A. Shohet, 'Beginning of the Haskalah among German Jewry', [Hebrew] (diss., Jerusalem, 1950), and now Sorkin, *The Transformation*, pp. 14–26.

13. This has already been noted by Benzion Dinur in an essay first published 1939. See 'New Eras in Jewish History, [Hebrew], in B. Dinur, *Historical Writings*, vol. 1, *Jerusalem*, 1954, pp. 19–68. Also see J. Katz, 'Religion as a Uniting and Dividing Force in Modern Jewish History', in *The Role of Religion in Modern Jewish History*, ed. J. Katz, Cambridge, 1975, pp. 1–17.

14. In addition to the works of Katz and Sorkin above, see also M.A. Meyer, *The Origins of the Modern Jew: Jewish Identity and European Culture in Germany, 1749–1824*, Detroit, 1967; A. Altman, *Moses Mendelssohn: A Biographical Study*, London, 1979; S.M. Lowenstein, *The Berlin Jewish Community: Enlightenment, Family and Crisis, 1770–1830*, Oxford, 1994.

15. See Katz, *Out of the Ghetto*, chap. IX.

16. M. Silber, 'The Emergence of Ultra-Orthodoxy', in *The Uses of Tradition*, ed. J. Wertheimer, New York, 1992, pp. 25–84.

17. The struggle between *Maskilim* and 'Chassidism' is described by I. Bartal in 'The Heavenly City of Germany and Absolutism a la Mode d'Autriche: The Rise of the Haskalah in Galicia', in *Toward Modernity: The European Jewish Model*, ed. J. Katz, New Brunswick, Oxford, 1987, pp. 33–42. On the eventual hostility against the *Haskalah* everywhere in Eastern Europe, see *The East European Jewish Enlightenment* [Hebrew], ed. I. Etkes, Jerusalem, 1993.

18 Etkes, *The East European Jewish Enlightenment*, p. 131.

19. On the Reform Movement see M.A. Meyer, *Response to Modernity: History of the Reform Movement in Judaism*, Oxford, 1988. On the moderate camp: I. Schorsch, 'Zacharias Frankel and the European Origins of Conservative Judaism', *Judaism* 30 (1981), pp. 344–54; and on Neo-Orthodoxy: M. Breuer, *Jüdische Orthodoxie im Deutschen Reich 1871–1918*, Frankfurt am Main, 1986.

20. See R. Liberles, *Religious Conflict in Social Context: The Resurgence of Orthodox Judaism in Frankfurt am Main*, Westport, 1985.

21. This remarkable coincidence was noticed and analysed by B. Harshav, 'The Revival of the Land of Israel and the Modern Jewish Social Revolution', in *Culture and Society in the Land of Israel*, [Hebrew], ed. N. Govrin, Tel Aviv, 1988, pp. 7–31.

22. On all these factions see J. Frankel, *Prophecy and Politics: Socialism, Nationalism and the Russian Jews 1862–1917*, Cambridge, 1981.

23. This useful concept was introduced by Sorkin, *The Transformation*, esp. Part I.

24. There is rich literature on the various ideological camps among German Jews at that time. Specifically on the conflict between the CV and Zionism, see J. Reinharz, *Fatherland or Promised Land: The Dilemma of the German Jew 1893–1914*, Ann Arbor, 1975.

25. For a more detailed discussion of this issue see S. Volkov, 'Jews among the Nations: A Unique National Narrative or a Chapter in National Historiographies', [Hebrew], *Zion. A Quarterly for Research in Jewish History* LXI (1996), pp. 91–111.

26. The quote is from T.M. Endelman, 'The Englishness of Jewish Modernity in England', in *Toward Modernity*, ed. J. Katz, New Brunswick and Oxford, 1987, pp. 225–47, p. 243.

27. J. Frankel, 'Assimilation and the Jews in Nineteenth Century Europe: Toward a New Historiography', in *Assimilation and Community*, ed. J. Frankel and S.J. Zipperstein, Cambridge, 1992, pp. 1ff., 31.

28. Mendelssohn's significance as a 'founding father' of the Jewish *Haskalah* has recently been doubted by S. Feiner in his essay 'Mendelssohn and "Mendelssohn's Disciples". A Reexamination', *LBIYB* XL (1995), pp. 133–68.

29. See S. Feiner, 'The Pseudo-Enlightenment and the Question of Jewish Modernization', *Jewish Social Studies*, N.S. 3 (1966), pp. 62–88.

30. For a case study of the similarity between Jews and non-Jews in this respect, see P. Freimark, 'Language Behaviour and Assimilation. The Situation of the Jews in Northern Germany in the First Half of the Nineteenth Century', *LBIYB*, XXIV (1979), pp. 157–77.

31. On the beginnings of the Jewish press in Germany, see J. Toury, 'Das Phänomen des jüdischen Presse in Deutschland', *Qesher*, special issue [in German] (1989), pp. 4d–13d. On *Ha'Meassef*: Z. Zmarion, *Ha'Meassef*, [Hebrew], Tel Aviv, 1988. On *Sulamith* see Sorkin, *The Transformation*, pp. 81–2, and S. Stein, 'Die Zeitschrift Sulamith', *Zeitschrift für die Geschichte der Juden in Deutschland* VII (1937), pp.193–226.

32. See J. Toury, 'Die Sprache als Problem der jüdischen Einordnung im deutschen Kulturraum', in *Gegenseitige Einflüsse Deutscher und Jüdischer Kultur*, ed. W. Grab (Beiheft 4, Jahrbuch des Instituts für deutsche Geschichte), Tel Aviv, 1982, pp. 75–96. Also Y. Shavit, 'A Duty too Heavy to Bear: Hebrew in the Berlin Haskalah: 1783–1819: Between Classic, Modern and Romantic', in *Hebrew in Ashkenaz: A Language in Exile*, ed. L. Glinert, New York, 1993, pp. 111–28.

33. See I. Bartal, 'From Traditional Bilingualism to National Monolingualism', in *Hebrew in Ashkenaz*, ed. L Glinert, New York, 1993, pp. 141–50; and in a wider context, Y. Slutski, 'The Growth of Jewish-Russian Intelligentsia', in *East European Jewish Enlightenment*, ed. Etkes, pp. 269–99.

34. Some consider even the Reform Movement itself as yet another way of trying to hold back secularisation. See J. Toury, 'The Revolution that Did Not Happen. A Reapparaisal of Reform-Judaism', *Zeitschrift für Religions- und Geistesgeschichte* XXXVI (1984), pp. 193–203.

35. M. Stanislawski, *For whom Do I Toil? Judah Leib Gordon and the Crisis of Russian Jewry*, New York, 1988.

36. Ibid., p. 170.

37. See M.L. Rozenblit, 'Jewish Assimilation in Habsburg's Vienna', in *Assimilation and Community*, ed. Frankel and Zipperstein, pp. 225–45.

38. See Meyer, *Response to Modernity*, pp. 179–80.

39. See Zipperstein, *The Jews of Odessa*, pp. 56–69.

40. Ibid., p. 56.

41. See Breuer, *Jüdische Orthodoxie*, pp. 232–33.

42. See Meyer, *Response to Modernity*, pp. 320–21.

43. The relevant text was first published in Hebrew in 1945. A German version appeared as G. Scholem, 'Wissenschaft vom Judentum einst und jetzt', *Bulletin des Leo Baeck Instituts*, IX (1961), pp. 10–20.

44. Much of the literature on the *Cheder* is antiquated and written in the spirit of the *Haskalah* itself. See, for instance, the entry 'Jewish Education', in *Encyclopaedia of Religion and Ethics*, vol. V, Edinburgh, 1912, p. 197; or even the more balanced view in E. Gamoran, *Changing Conceptions of Jewish Education*, New York, 1925. On developments in Germany see M. Eliav, *The Jewish Education in Germany during Haskalh and Emancipation*, [Hebrew], Jerusalem, 1961, especially pp. 148–61, and J. Carlebach, 'Deutsche Juden und der Säkularisierungsprozeß in der Erziehung', in *Das Judentum in der deutschen Umwelt 1800–1850*, ed. H. Liebeschütz and A. Paucker, Tübingen, 1977, pp. 55–94.

45. For the details given here see I. Schorsch, 'The Myth of the Sephardic Supremacy', LBIYB, XXXIV (1989), pp. 47–66; now also in I. Schorsch, *From Text to Context: The Turn to History in Modern Judaism*, Hanover, 1994, pp. 71–92.

46. In fact, the first to deal with this topic was Franz Delitzsch. Among Jewish authors, see M. Sachs, *Die religiöse Poesie der Juden in Spanien*, Berlin, 1845, and M. Kayserling, *Sephardim: Romanische Poesien der Juden*, Leipzig, 1859. Compare also Schorsch, From Text to Context, pp. 83–5.

47. See W. Röll, 'The Kassel Ha-Meassef of 1799: An Unknown Contribution to the *Haskalah*', in *The Jewish Response to German Culture from the Enlightenment to the Second World War*, ed. J. Reinharz and W. Schatzberg, Hanover, 1985, pp. 32–50.

48. See J. Shalmon, 'David Gordon and the Newspaper Ha'Magid: Changing Attitudes towards Jewish Nationalism', [Hebrew], *Zion* 47 (1982), pp. 145–64.

49. See J. Bleich, 'The Emergence of Orthodox Press in Nineteenth-Century Germany', *Jewish Social Studies* 42 (1980), pp. 323–44.

50. See I. Etkes, 'The "Official Haskalah" and the Change in the Status of the Haskalah in Russia', [Hebrew], in *The East European Jewish Enlightenment*, ed. Etkes, pp. 167–216, esp. pp. 215–16, and E. Lederhendler, 'Modernity without Emancipation or Assimilation? The Case of Russian Jewry', in *Assimilation and Community*, ed. J. Frankel and S.J. Zipperstein, Cambridge, 1992, pp. 324–42.

51. This point was clearly made by Dinur, in his Historical Writings, I, pp. 37–38.

52. Quoted by R. Liberles, 'Emancipation and the Structure of the Jewish Community in the Nineteenth Century', *LBIYB* XXXI (1986), pp. 51–67, p. 51.

53. This is Liberles' formulation, ibid., p. 61.

54. On the extreme case of Abraham Geiger during the Damascus affair, see Meyer, *Response to Modernity*, [Hebrew], p. 119.

55. Liberles, 'Emancipation', p. 64, and Toury, *Soziale und Politische Geschichte*, pp. 258–76.

56. See especially E. Lederhendler, *The Road to Modern Jewish Politics*, New York, 1998, and on Europe in general also M. Graetz, 'Jewry in the Modern Period: The Role of the "Rising Class" in the Politicization of the Jews in Europe', in *Assimilation and Community*, ed. J. Frankel and S.J. Zipperstein, Cambridge, 1992, pp. 156–76.

57. I have elaborated upon this theme, mainly with respect to German Jewry, in Volkov, 'Die Erfindung einer Tradition'.

58. On the historicisation of Judaism see also Schorsch, *From Text to Context*; Y.H. Yerushalmi, *Zakhor: Jewish History and Jewish Memory*, Seattle, 1982; and A. Funkenstein, *Perceptions of Jewish History*, Berkeley, 1993.

59. These phrases are quoted from Harshav, 'The Revival of the Land of Israel', pp. 13, 28.

60. See D.J. Ruskies, 'S. Ansky and the Paradigm of Return', in *The Uses of Tradition*, ed. J. Wertheimer, New York, 1992, pp. 243–60.

61. Ibid., p. 260.

62. See P. Mendes-Flohr, 'The Retrieval of Innocence and Tradition: Jewish Spiritual Renewal in an Age of Liberal Individualism', in *The Uses of Tradition*, ed. J. Wertheimer, New York, 1992, pp. 279–301, especially p. 290.

63. For this issue see Schorsch, 'Art as Social History: Motitz Oppenheim and the German Jewish Vision of Emancipation', in Schorsch, *From Text to Context*, pp. 93–117, and now especially R.I. Cohen, *Jewish Icons: Art and Society in Modern Europe*, Berkeley, 1998, as well as his essays, R.I. Cohen, 'Nostalgia and "Return to the Ghetto": A Cultural Phenomenon in Western and Central Europe', in *Assimilation and Community*, ed. J. Frankel and S.J. Zipperstein, Cambridge, 1992, pp. 130–55, and R.I. Cohen, 'The Visual Image of the Jew and Judaism in Early Modern Europe', [Hebrew] in *Zion* LVII (1992), pp. 275–340.

Bibliography

Altman, A. *Moses Mendelssohn: A Biographical Study*. London, 1979.

Aschheim, S. *Brothers and Strangers: The East European Jew in German and German-Jewish Consciousness 1800–1923*. Madison, WI, 1982.

Barkai, A. 'German Jewish Migration in the Nineteenth Century, 1830–1910', *Leo Baeck Institute Yearbook (LBIYB)* XXX (1985), pp. 301–18.

——— *Jüdische Minderheit und Industrialisierung. Demographie, Berufe und Einkommen in Westdeutschland, 1850–1914*. Tübingen, 1988.

Bartal, I. 'The Heavenly City of Germany and Absolutism a la Mode d'Autriche: The Rise of the Haskalah in Galicia', in *Toward Modernity: The European Jewish Model*, ed. J. Katz. New Brunswick, NJ, Oxford, 1987, pp. 33–42.

——— 'From Traditional Bilingualism to National Monolingualism', in *Hebrew in Ashkenaz. A Language in Exile*, ed. L. Glinert. New York, NY, 1993, pp. 141–50.

Bleich, J. 'The Emergence of Orthodox Press in Nineteenth-Century Germany', *Jewish Social Studies* 42 (1980), pp. 323–44.

Breuer, M. *Jüdische Orthodoxie im Deutschen Reich 1871–1918*. Frankfurt am Main, 1986

Carlebach, J. 'Deutsche Juden und der Säkularisierungsprozeß in der Erziehung', in *Das Judentum in der deutschen Umwelt 1800–1850*, ed. H. Liebeschütz and A. Paucker. Tübingen, 1977, pp. 55–94.

Cohen, R.I. 'Nostalgia and "Return to the Ghetto": A Cultural Phenomenon in Western and Central Europe', in *Assimilation and Community: The Jews in 19th Century Europe*, ed. J. Frankel and S.J. Zipperstein. Cambridge: Cambridge University Press, 1992, pp. 130–55.

——— 'The Visual Image of the Jew and Judaism in Early Modern Europe', [Hebrew], *Zion. A Quarterly for Research in Jewish History* LVII (1992), pp. 275–340.

——— *Jewish Icons: Art and Society in Modern Europe*. Berkeley, CA, 1998.

Dinur, B. 'New Eras in Jewish History', [Hebrew], in B. Dinur, *Historical Writings*, vol. 1. Jerusalem, 1954, pp. 19–68.

Eisenstadt, S.N. *Modernization: Protest and Change*. Englewood Cliffs, NJ, 1966.

Eliav, M. *The Jewish Education in Germany during Haskalh and Emancipation* [Hebrew], Jerusalem, 1961.

Endelman, T.M. 'The Englishness of Jewish Modernity in England', in *Toward Modernity*, ed. J. Katz, New Brunswick, NC, and Oxford, 1987, pp. 225–47.

Etkes, I. 'The "Official Haskalah" and the Change in the Status of the Haskalah in Russia', [Hebrew], in *The East European Jewish Enlightenment* [Hebrew], ed. I. Etkes. Jerusalem, 1993, pp. 167–216.

——— (ed.). *The East European Jewish Enlightenment* [Hebrew]. Jerusalem, 1993.

Feiner, S. 'The Pseudo-Enlightenment and the Question of Jewish Modernization', *Jewish Social Studies*, N.S. 3 (1966), pp. 62–88.

——— 'Mendelssohn and "Mendelssohn's Disciples". A Reexamination', *LBIYB* XL (1995), pp. 133–68.

Frankel, J. *Prophecy and Politics: Socialism, Nationalism and the Russian Jews 1862–1917*. Cambridge: Cambridge University Press, 1981.

——— 'Assimilation and the Jews in Nineteenth Century Europe: Toward a New Historiography', in *Assimilation and Community: The Jews in 19th Century Europe*, ed. J. Frankel and S.J. Zipperstein. Cambridge: Cambridge University Press, 1992, pp. 1ff.

Freimark, P. 'Language Behaviour and Assimilation. The Situation of the Jews in Northern Germany in the First Half of the Nineteenth Century', LBIYB, XXIV (1979), pp. 157–77.

Fremdling, R. and Tilly, R. (eds) *Industrialisierung und Raum: Studien zur regionalen Differenzierung im Deutschland des 19. Jahrhunderts*. Stuttgart, 1979.

Funkenstein, A. *Perceptions of Jewish History*. Berkeley, CA, 1993.

Gamoran, E. *Changing Conceptions of Jewish Education*. New York, NY, 1925.

Glinert, L. (ed.) *Hebrew in Ashkenaz: A Language in Exile*. New York, NY, 1993.

Graetz, M. 'Jewry in the Modern Period: The Role of the "Rising Class" in the Politicization of the Jews in Europe', in *Assimilation and Community: The Jews in 19th Century Europe*, ed. J. Frankel and S.J. Zipperstein. Cambridge: Cambridge University Press, 1992, pp. 156–76.

Habermas, J. 'Die Moderne – ein unvollendetes Projekt', in J. Habermas, *Kleine politische Schriften I–IV*. Frankfurt am Main, 1981, pp. 444–64.

Harshav, B. 'The Revival of the Land of Israel and the Modern Jewish Social Revolution', in *Culture and Society in the Land of Israel*, [Hebrew], ed. N. Govrin. Tel Aviv, 1988, pp. 7–31.

Hyman, P.E. 'The Social Context of Assimilation: Village Jews and City Jews in Alsace', in *Assimilation and Community: The Jews in 19th Century Europe*, ed. J. Frankel and S.J. Zipperstein. Cambridge: Cambridge University Press, 1992, pp. 110–29.

——— 'Traditionalism and Village Jews in 19th Century Western and Central Europe: Local Persistence and Urban Nostalgia', in *The Uses of Tradition: Jewish Continuity in the Modern Era*, ed. J. Wertheimer. New York, NY, 1992, pp. 191–201.

'Jewish Education', in *Encyclopaedia of Religion and Ethics*, vol. V. Edinburgh, 1912, p. 197.

Katz, J. *Tradition and Crisis: Jewish Society at the End of the Middle Ages*. New York, NY, 1960.

——— *Out of the Ghetto: The Social Background of the Jewish Emancipation 1770–1880*. Cambridge, MA, 1973.

——— 'Religion as a Uniting and Dividing Force in Modern Jewish History', in *The Role of Religion in Modern Jewish History*, ed. J. Katz. Cambridge, MA, 1975, pp. 1–17.

Kayserling, M. *Sephardim: Romanische Posien der Juden*. Leipzig, 1859.

Lederhendler, E. 'Modernity without Emancipation or Assimilation? The Case of Russian Jewry', in *Assimilation and Community: The Jews in 19th Century Europe*, ed. J. Frankel and S.J. Zipperstein. Cambridge: Cambridge University Press, 1992, pp. 324–42.

—— *The Road to Modern Jewish Politics*. New York, NY, 1998.

Liberles, R. *Religious Conflict in Social Context: The Resurgence of Orthodox Judaism in Frankfurt am Main*. Westport, CT, 1985.

—— 'Emancipation and the Structure of the Jewish Community in the Nineteenth Century', *LBIYB* XXXI (1986), pp. 51–67.

Lowenstein, S.M. *The Berlin Jewish Community: Enlightenment, Family and Crisis, 1770–1830*. Oxford, 1994.

Mendelsohn, E. *Class Struggle in the Pale: The Formative Years of the Jewish Workers' Movement in Russia*. Cambridge: Cambridge University Press, 1970.

Mendes-Flohr, P. 'The Retrieval of Innocence and Tradition: Jewish Spiritual Renewal in an Age of Liberal Individualism', *The Uses of Tradition: Jewish Continuity in the Modern Era*, ed. J. Wertheimer. New York, NY, 1992, pp. 279–301, esp. p. 290.

Meyer, M.A. *The Origins of the Modern Jew: Jewish Identity and European Culture in Germany, 1749–1824*. Detroit, MI, 1967.

—— *Response to Modernity: History of the Reform Movement in Judaism*. Oxford, 1988.

Peled, Y. and Shapir, G. 'From Caste to Exclusion: The Dynamics of Modernization in the Russian Pale of Settlement', *Studies in Contemporary Jewry* 3 (1987), pp. 98–114.

Pollard, S. (ed.) *Region und Industrialisierung: Studien zur Rolle der Region in der Wirtschaftsgeschichte der letzten zwei Jahrhunderte*. Göttingen, 1980.

Reinharz, J. *Fatherland or Promised Land: The Dilemma of the German Jew 1893–1914*. Ann Arbor, MI, 1975.

Röll, W. 'The Kassel Ha-Meassef of 1799: An Unknown Contribution to the Haskalah', in *The Jewish Response to German Culture from the Enlightenment to the Second World War*, ed. J. Reinharz and W. Schatzberg. Hanover, 1985, pp. 32–50.

Rozenblit, M.L. 'Jewish Assimilation in Habsburg's Vienna', in *Assimilation and Community: The Jews in 19th Century Europe*, ed. J. Frankel and S.J. Zipperstein. Cambridge: Cambridge University Press, 1992, pp. 225–45.

Rubinow, I. *Economic Conditions of Jews in Russia*. New York, NY, 1975.

Ruskies, D.J. 'S. Ansky and the "Paradigm of Return"', in *The Uses of Tradition: Jewish Continuity in the Modern Era*, ed. J. Wertheimer. New York, NY, 1992, pp. 243–60.

Sachs, M. *Die religiöse Poesie der Juden in Spanien*. Berlin, 1845.

Scholem, G. 'Wissenschaft vom Judentum einst und jetzt', *Bulletin des Leo Baeck Instituts*, IX (1961), pp. 10–20.

Schorsch, I. 'Zacharias Frankel and the European Origins of Conservative Judaism', *Judaism* 30 (1981), pp. 344–54.

—— 'The Myth of the Sephardic Supremacy', *LBIYB*, XXXIV (1989), pp. 47–66.

—— 'Art as Social History: Motitz Oppenheim and the German Jewish Vision of Emancipation', in I. Schorsch, *From Text to Context: The Turn to History in Modern Judaism*. Hanover, 1994, pp. 93–117.

—— *From Text to Context: The Turn to History in Modern Judaism*. Hanover, 1994.

Schramm, G. 'Die Ostjuden als soziales Problem des 19. Jahrhunderts', in *Gesellschaft, Recht und Freiheit*, ed. H. Maus. Neuwied, 1968, pp. 353–80.

—— *Die Juden im osteuropäischen Osten um das Jahr 1900: Zwischenbilanz eines Minderheitenproblems, (Historische und Landeskundliche Ostmitteleuropa-Studien 3)*. Marburg, 1989.

Shalmon, J. 'David Gordon and the Newspaper Ha'Magid: Changing Attitudes towards Jewish Nationalism', [Hebrew], *Zion* 47 (1982), pp. 145–64.

Shavit, Y. 'A Duty too Heavy to Bear: Hebrew in the Berlin Haskalah: 1783–1819: Between Classic, Modern and Romantic', in *Hebrew in Ashkenaz: A Language in Exile*, ed. L. Glinert. New York, NY, 1993, pp. 111–28.

Shohet, A. 'Beginning of the Haskalah among German Jewry', [Hebrew], diss., Jerusalem, 1950.

Silber, M. 'The Emergence of Ultra-Orthodoxy', in *The Uses of Tradition: Jewish Continuity in the Modern Era*, ed. J. Wertheimer. New York, NY, 1992, pp. 25–84.

Slutski, Y. 'The Growth of Jewish-Russian Intelligentsia', in *The East European Jewish Enlightenment* [Hebrew], ed. I. Etkes. Jerusalem, 1993, pp. 269–99.

Sorkin, D. *The Transformation of German Jewry 1780–1840*. Oxford, 1987.

Stanislawski, M. *For Whom Do I Toil? Judah Leib Gordon and the Crisis of Russian Jewry*. New York, NY, 1988.

Stein, S. 'Die Zeitschrift Sulamith', *Zeitschrift für die Geschichte der Juden in Deutschland* VII (1937), pp.193–226.

Stern, S. *Der preussische Staat und die Juden*, 7 vols. Tübingen, 1962–71.

Tipton, F. *Regional Variations in the Economic Development of Germany during the Nineteenth Century*. Middletown, CT, 1976.

Toury, J. *Soziale und politische Geschichte der Juden in Deutschland 1847–1871*. Düsseldorf, 1977.

—— 'Die Sprache als Problem der jüdischen Einordnung im deutschen Kulturraum', in *Gegenseitige Einflüsse Deutscher und Jüdischer Kultur*, ed. W. Grab (Beiheft 4, *Jahrbuch des Instituts für deutsche Geschichte*). Tel Aviv, 1982, pp. 75–96.

—— 'The Revolution that Did Not Happen. A Reapparaisal of Reform-Judaism', *Zeitschrift für Religions- und Geistesgeschichte* XXXVI (1984), pp. 193–203.

—— 'Das Phänomen des jüdischen Presse in Deutschland', *Qesher*, special issue [in German] (1989), pp. 4d–13d.

Volkov, S. *Jüdisches Leben und Antisemitismus im 19. und 20. Jahrhundert*. Munich, 1990.

—— 'Die Erfindung einer Tradition. Zur Entstehung des modernen Judentum in Deutschland', *Historische Zeitschrift*, 253 (1991), pp. 603–29.

—— 'Juden und Judentum im Zeitalter der Emanzipation. Einheit und Vielfalt', in *Die Juden in die europäischen Geschichte*, ed. W. Beck. Munich, 1992, pp. 86–108.

—— 'Introduction', in *Deutsche Juden und die Moderne*, ed. S. Volkov. Munich, 1994, pp. vi–xxiii.

—— 'Jews among the Nations: A Unique National Narrative or a Chapter in National Historiographies', [Hebrew], *Zion. A Quarterly for Research in Jewish History* LXI (1996), pp. 91–111.

—— (ed.) *Deutsche Juden und die Moderne*. Munich, 1994.

Wertheimer, J. *Unwelcome Strangers: East European Jews in Imperial Germany*. Oxford, 1987.

Yerushalmi, Y.H. *Zakhor: Jewish History and Jewish Memory*. Seattle, WA, 1982.

Zipperstein, S.J. *The Jews of Odessa: A Cultural History 1794–1881*. Stanford, CA, 1985.

Zmarion, Z. *Ha'Meassef*, [Hebrew]. Tel Aviv, 1988.

12

RELIGION BETWEEN STATE AND SOCIETY IN NINETEENTH-CENTURY EUROPE

Henk van Dijk

Introduction

European differences

Religion and the state in preindustrial societies were linked in a specific way. Kings legitimated their power with the help of a particular relationship with a supranatural order. At first glance we may think that this is no longer applicable to the situation in industrial societies. However, that is spurious, because religion can also play an important role in modern society. In some industrial societies, like Japan, for example, religion is still fundamental to the state. In some countries ideology took over the role of a state religion during the twentieth century. However, in pluralistic democratic societies, too, religion has still been able to influence public life. In some cases, consciously or unconsciously, states use religious symbols and metaphors. The American statement, 'In God we trust', is an example of this. The use of generally accepted or at least tolerated religious symbols has been called civil religion. It is particularly visible in societies with a population adhering to different confessions, but in which Protestantism dominated in the past.

Even if we leave aside these forms of public religion, we may notice that states have some relationship with religion. Although the legitimation of power in industrial societies is no longer grounded on supranatural powers, as in, for example, the absolutist states of the seventeenth and eighteenth centuries, the problem of legitimation still exists.

The concept of people's sovereignty, which has been applied since the French Revolution, seems convincing at first glance, but is a difficult one, because it is not clear how 'the people' has to be defined. The common practice of using the concept of the nation as a synonym of the people does not bring about any clarification.

The nation, as a group of people, who feel that they are belonging to a community, must provide the emotional bond, which the abstract state as such cannot give; it is, however, the state that defines the membership of the nation. The emotional bond also requires the symbolism and rituals, which have been so characteristic of religions. Myths and rituals are as important for nations as they are for the bonds of the community within religion. This applies to an even greater extent to those nations for which a common religion is the most important source of their nationhood.

Religion has customarily been identified with tradition and with a society mostly dominated by agriculture. For that reason one could expect a decline of the role of religion in nineteenth-century society at least in some areas, because industrialisation and urbanisation were important factors changing society during that period. However, it can be observed that during the first half of the nineteenth century a revival of religion took place. Although this revival diminished during the second half of the century, religion still influenced societies strongly in several ways.

In all West European states, with the exception of Britain, political battles between the state and religious institutions were fought over the control of the educational system. Also political parties with a religious affiliation developed. Although religion still dominated European society, the position of religion in society changed over the period in several respects, but these changes were influenced by various factors.

If we look to the countryside, the position of religious institutions was important, at least in many parts of Europe. It was there that clergymen and priests belonged to the local elite and played sometimes a role in the processes of societal change. Sometimes they stimulated innovations (one may think of farmers' leagues, cooperative movements etc., in particular at the end of the century), but sometimes they also slowed down developments.

In many cases clergymen were not born in the area, but came from outside. The Roman Catholic Church tried to avoid in its policy of appointments and displacements a strong emotional bond between the local priest and his parish. Sometimes the clergy identified with the established order. At least they belonged to a separate group. The Protestant clergy — at least the members of the established churches — saw themselves as intellectuals. Although their incomes were not very high, they had a status comparable with the professions (notaries, doctors etc.). The Anglican clergymen in the UK even saw themselves as gentlemen. In the eyes of their Methodist critics they were, with their gardens and spacious livings, a leisured class. This relatively affluent situation did not exist in urban society, yet, there too the clergy had some influence. However, the situation could differ according to local or regional circumstances. Important factors could be the existence of an established church, or specific political or economic situations.

It is even possible that differences in family structures could have played a role, as Emmanuel Todd tried to prove in a recently published book.[1] He linked the process of what he called 'de-christianisation' (by which he meant the loss of influence of religious institutions in society) to specific family structures in different European regions. Although his approach is very interesting, at the same it is time debatable. In this contribution I will not discuss the outcome of the process of the diminishing influence of religious institutions as such,[2] but will stress the differences in the relationship between state and religion, or crown and altar. Also a sociopolitical and institutional approach will be applied.

For several reasons my attention will focus on developments during the nineteenth century: firstly, contemporaries had the idea that religion was losing its position in society and they had lively and sometimes fierce debates about this topic. The question arises how far their impression was true. Secondly, during this period societies underwent not only important political but also massive social change (one may think of the influences of the revolutions, industrialisation, urbanisation and the impact of migration). And finally, different tendencies could be detected during this period. In general we may see a revival of the position of religion at the beginning of the century, in particular in the aristocracy and also parts of the working class, whereas some parts of the middle classes stayed critical. During the second half of the century we can detect a change of position. Large parts of the lower class, at least during the first half of the century, stayed only nominal members, whereas the middle classes became more attracted to these institutions. However, before we can say something about these changes, we have to define religion as such.

A definition of religion

Any attempt to define religion will depend on the starting point taken, whether it is a sociological, anthropological, historical or psychological viewpoint. It is clear, however, that although religion is related to individual ideas, social factors, such as community, are important. To quote the sociologist Talcott Parsons: 'Religion involves community.' Religion offers not only a system of significance and the possibility of understanding the world and one's place in it, but, with the help of rituals, these individual feelings and views are linked to those of the larger community. Rituals not only give a symbolic participation in this world, but also strengthen the feelings of community. Although there may be differences between various religious groups, in the majority of cases these communities have an institutional character.

Within nineteenth-century Christianity, four dominant institutional forms existed:

1. A hierarchical type without important influence of the laity, such as the Roman Catholic Church.

2. A hierarchical type with important influence of the laity and/or state such as the Russian Orthodox churches or the Episcopal Lutheran churches in Scandinavia and the German states.

3. A nonhierarchical type with important influence of the clergy, such as the Calvinist churches in the Netherlands, Switzerland and Scotland.

4. A nonhierarchical type with only minor distinction between clergy and laity, such as in the dissenting churches in the Netherlands, England, Wales, and in Switzerland.

Because these differences in organisational structure also influenced the relationship between religion and society we will return to this point later.

Religion not only has an important social impact, because it is formalised and institutionalised, but it also provides its adherents with norms of behaviour for the social setting. These norms and values can either be deduced from a supernatural origin or they can be rationalisations of what were originally mythical ideas. Ritual can also be important for the internalisation of values, and rituals can strengthen norms and normative structures. According to Parsons, particularly during periods of crisis, ritual serves as a safety net to bring structures back into balance.[3] But it may be clear that the existence of norms and values can have important social effects.

Secularisation

It is clear that religion plays an important role in many societies; but this role can change over time. In modern, pluralistic societies the influence of formal religion on the various aspects of society is limited. The development towards this situation is generally referred to as secularisation. One of the confusing aspects of the debate about secularisation is that the concept itself is understood in different ways. Sometimes it is used in relation to the individual, namely, the behaviour and attitudes of individuals, and at other times it is applied to religious institutions.

The most generally accepted definition is that secularisation is a process whereby religious thinking, practice and institutions lose their social significance.[4] That does not mean, however, that there needs to be a discrepancy between the individual and the institution. Individual forms of religiosity can exist, even if institutions lose their function in society. It is also possible that political or social movements can be inspired by religion, even though their adherents may no longer be members of a church in a formal sense.

For many people secularisation has been seen as a decline in the influence of religious institutions in society, including diminishing church attendance, a decrease in the income of the institutions and a decline in other aspects of religious institutions in the daily lives of their members. Although difficulties exist in the measurement of the institutional aspects of religion, it is questionable whether this decline in fact reflects a general decline of religion in society. Nevertheless, the institutional aspects are important, as we shall see.

If we attempt to define secularisation, several aspects come to mind. The word itself developed within the Christian world. This is not to say that this phenomenon did not manifest itself in other religions, but the concept seems to belong, at least in part, to the culture of Christian religions. Within Judaism, for example, similar developments can be seen, but these tended to occur later. It is clear, however, that within the major religions of Asia, such as Buddhism and Confucianism, the concept of secularisation does not exist. Also, to the third major religion of the Mediterranean world, Islam, the idea of secularisation is not a native concept. The only important exception to this general rule seems to be Turkey after Ataturk.

In Europe the idea of secularisation came into existence during the first half of the seventeenth century. By origin it was a legal term, involving the takeover of former ecclesiastical possessions by temporal powers. The concept itself was not new, because within canonical law during the Middle Ages, secularisation was used to describe the takeover of possessions of the regular clergy (i.e., monks living according to a rule) by the secular clergy (the ordinary priests). The devastating religious wars of the late sixteenth and early seventeenth centuries, as well as the development of the new absolutist monarchies in Europe, coined and used the term in this way.

With the emergence of new ideas during the seventeenth and eighteenth centuries, including expansion of the sciences, the idea of secularisation became embodied within other contexts. It became increasingly more desirable to separate the supernatural sphere (which was seen in stricter terms, as, for example, in deism) from the natural and verifiable sphere. Max Weber called this general process the disenchantment of the world (*Entzauberung der Welt*). It is debatable, however, as to how and to what extent this process was directly related to a diminishing influence of religion in general, and of religious institutions in particular. At least we may say that during the nineteenth century it was not a linear process.

The burden of the past

Although during the nineteenth and twentieth centuries religion had specific characteristics, which were partially moulded by society, these characteristics developed within a framework that had previously existed. This framework can be regarded as a result of national differences, or rather the result of state formation during the sixteenth and seventeenth centuries. These differences were a part of the former close relationships between religion and state policy, in particularly in the patrimonial states.

The French Revolution served to undermine this relationship, but if we try to detect more general structures, we see that within Europe four major zones existed at the beginning of the nineteenth century. There was a predominantly Roman Catholic zone (including France, Spain, the Italian States, Belgium and the Habsburg countries), a predominantly Protestant zone (including the Scandinavian countries), an Orthodox zone (Russia, Greece and Bulgaria) and finally a mixed one (Britain, the Netherlands, Switzerland and a major part of the German states). This situation was largely a result of the outcome of the Reformation and Counter-Reformation movements during the sixteenth century and the fierce religious wars that followed in their wake.

In those areas in which the Counter-Reformation was successful, a close link between the crown and altar was established, although during the late seventeenth and early eighteenth centuries the state was gaining power over the church. A well-known example which illustrates this situation is the expulsion of the Jesuit order from many European states and the development of the so-called national churches. In addition, general public education had become a state affair. The strict ties between the social and political establishments and the church, however, meant that in these areas political opposition was also opposition against the church.[5]

In the virtually homogeneous Roman Catholic areas, this led to the development of anti-clericalist movements, which were influenced by religion in both form and content. In France examples of this can be found within the Saint-Simonism and Comteianism movements. The state could be either religious or nonreligious. In contrast, the church was generally identified with political reaction in those areas, a situation different from that in the mixed areas.

A similar situation could be found in the largely homogeneous Protestant areas. In the Scandinavian countries some Free Churches existed, but their influence was not strong and they could not be seen as an alternative.[6] Their adherents were mainly lower class, whereas their members in the mixed areas were mainly middle class or so-called respectable working class. Nevertheless, the clashes between the church and its anti-clericalist opposition did not develop in the Protestant areas as in the homogeneous Roman Catholic areas. There are several reasons for this. During the first half of the nineteenth century Scandinavian Lutheranism was strongly influenced by Pietism. In Norway and Denmark particularly this led to specific movements of religious revival related to forms of nationalism and romanticism.[7] In Denmark Grundtvig, a parson as well as a poet and writer, had a strong influence on this movement, whereas Hauge, a merchant from Bergen, was the most influential person in Norway.[8] These movements not only stimulated popular attraction to Christianity, but also popular education (high schools for the people) and self-advancement for artisans and farmers. They also stimulated the democratisation of society.[9]

Secondly, during the nineteenth century it can be seen that when religion was related to some kind of national question there was no split in society between adherents and nonadherents of religion. This can be illustrated by the situation in Ireland and Poland, and it can also be seen in Finland, Denmark and Norway.[10] It is interesting to note that in Sweden, the only country in which religion and the national question did not play a role, these tensions developed to a greater extent.[11]

It was clear that within the Scandinavian countries the church was already totally subordinated to the state, therefore the establishment could not elevate the church as a sacred society above the state. This meant that the church adapted more easily to the state, even when the political structure of the state changed.

A third, mainly homogeneous area, was the Orthodox lands in Eastern Europe and the Balkans. Here, too, the church was mainly monopolistic and represented an instance of extreme collusion between the church and the state – particularly in Russia where, since Peter the Great, the Orthodox church was in fact a state department under the autocratic rule of the tsar. This model could also be found in the Balkans, where the Russian church played an influential role. The Turkish Empire had also been dominating the majority of these areas for a long time; therefore, the Byzantine heritage was very important.

Mixed areas could be found mainly in the border areas between Reformation and Counter-Reformation lands, such as Switzerland, the Netherlands and parts of Germany. Britain also belonged to this model, although it was not a border area in the strict sense. In these areas nothing of the strong antithesis between religion and nonreligion can be found, as was the case in the nonpluralistic areas. Not only was there an important Roman Catholic minority, which contributed to the processes of democratisation and parliamentary control, but also denominational dissent within Protestantism was strong. These dissenting movements played an important role within politics during the nineteenth century. In Britain, for example, they contributed much to liberalism and later to the Labour Party, whereas Anglicanism and conservatism tended to be more closely linked.[12]

In the mixed areas Roman Catholicism was not the conservative force that it was in the homogeneous Roman Catholic areas. During the nineteenth century there was a period of collaboration with liberalism (as in the Netherlands and in Belgium, although the latter belongs to the more homogeneous Catholic area). Also later in the nineteenth century and during the twentieth century, when Roman Catholic parties already existed they tended towards the centre-left of politics (in particular if they had many working-class voters). In the case of Britain a Catholic party was absent and with a great proportion of the working class being members of the Roman Catholic Church, votes went directly to the Labour party.

Dissenting religious groups contributed in general to the process of democratisation and growing parliamentary influence. This was also the case with neo-Calvinism, with its specific orthodox characteristics. The reason was its strong populist undertones, being in the tradition of the Covenanters. For example, in the Netherlands in the 1870s and 1880s neo-Calvinism was the first movement not only to break with the Reformed Church dominated by a liberal establishment, but also to create the first modern party, with structured organisation of its voters. This movement attracted many artisans, shopkeepers and traders.

Two aspects were particularly important in the mixed areas. In contrast to the situation in the predominantly homogeneous Catholic areas, the break with religion was not so strong in the mixed areas. Although the distance between state and religion increased in the aftermath of the revolutionary period, governments used vague but unmistakable religious symbols in their rhetoric. This symbolism and rhetoric was very pronounced in the USA, but can also be seen in the Netherlands, Denmark, Britain, Switzerland, etc. It has been called civil religion.[13] But the most important aspect was the necessity in those societies to find solutions for the increasing problem of pluriformity. The lack of a dominating religious group required solutions through compromises.

In some cases this pluriformity could be found in a situation of decentralisation of power. In such cases the state only served as an overall 'umbrella' organisation. This was the case in Switzerland, where the more urban areas became Protestant, whereas the more rural areas remained mainly Catholic. In spite of some troubled periods, with a short civil war in 1847, religion as well as education was organised on the canton level. This was particularly strong during the second half of the nineteenth century when liberalism tended to play down its secularising and centralising policies in favour of some cooperation with Catholics and conservative Protestants against the Labour movement. Swiss Catholicism therefore kept within some form of distinct pillar, as did its counterparts in the Netherlands, Austria and Belgium.[14]

A similar situation could be found in Germany. Here, the extreme decentralisation, and the effects of the Reformation as well as the religious wars, led to the establishment of different confessions according to regions. Although during the nineteenth century this geographical basis changed, due to industrialisation and urbanisation (as well as changes in state boundaries as a result of political movements during and after the Napoleonic period), some regional differences persisted. Catholicism could be found predominantly in the south and in the western Rhineland, whereas the Protestants dominated the north and the eastern areas. Although Roman Catholics had a strong foothold in some areas, after the unification of Germany under Prussian supremacy in 1871, their position within the whole empire was relatively weak. Whenever the Catholics did not vote for the (Catholic) Centre Party, they tended to vote for the left-wing parties.[15]

The political and social developments in Germany led to the emergence of a confessionally pluralistic society in which, due to the dominating position of Prussia, Protestantism had a prominent place. State and church were, however, strongly related to each other, as shown in the *Kulturkampf* (i.e. the conflict between Bismarck and the Catholic church, which was most violent in Prussia, but also played a role in other regions, such as Baden). As a result of the link between the state and the church(es), the nominal membership rates of the churches and synagogues were rather high.[16] However, by the end of the nineteenth century nonbelief was also rather high, at least in the larger cities.

Deviations from the model

We have seen that in the case of Scandinavia the effects of an almost monopolistic situation were different from the situation in the Latin countries. Also within predominantly Catholic areas, deviations could exist. The most well-known examples are those of Ireland and Poland and, to a lesser extent, Belgium. The Irish and Polish cases are examples of a situation in which external pressure or military and political occupation resulted in a close relationship between the nation and religion. The necessity for national unity tended to diminish criticism concerning the position and the role of the church. Consequently, religion seemed to play a unifying role and was generally accepted. Secularisation, defined as a diminishing influence of the religious institutions, was minimal in these cases.

Austria, too (at least the Austrian Republic after the First World War) seems to be an exception to the general rule within homogeneous Catholic areas. Although the development there – the autocratic rightwing government under Dollfuß – was similar to what occurred between 1934 and 1935 in other Catholic countries such as Spain and Portugal, the general tendency from the late nineteenth century was towards some form kind of pillarisation comparable to the Belgian, Swiss and Dutch situation.

Changes over time

Not only did the traditional cleavages within Christianity affect the position of religion within societies, but also general political and economic developments. Since the late eighteenth century, states developed from patrimonial monarchies towards more bureaucratic and centralised organisations, based on territory and legitimised by the concept of nationhood. This affected the role of religion within society in a different way. Whereas during the late eighteenth century religion was seen by 'Enlightened' monarchs as an obstacle to modernisation, these views changed in reaction to the political and social upheavals that culminated in the French Revolution.

The period between 1789 and 1848 showed a remarkable religious revival, compared with the eighteenth century. This revival was rooted in two developments. Political elites and the governments came to believe that the established churches could be an important force to hold back the tide of revolution. Romanticism as a cultural movement to some extent contributed to this development. New territorial divisions also created the need to define the concept of established churches in a new way. Examples of this situation could be found in the new kingdom of the Netherlands (where the future Belgian and Dutch territories were brought together), in Bavaria (where Protestant strongholds like the former *Reichsstädte* (city states) merged with a traditional Roman Catholic area) and in the enlarged Prussian state (with the Rhine provinces and the former Polish territory of Posen).

Another contribution to the revival of religion in society was the fact that religious sectarianism appealed to many groups of the middle and lower strata, who were in the process of establishing their own identity and cultural autonomy.[17] Although comparable movements in Roman Catholic areas did not exist, the Catholic Church at that time gained new influence because it was more tolerant than during the eighteenth century to various forms of popular belief and devotion.[18] The recruitment of priests from the lower strata also contributed to a stronger link between the population, the church and the religious revival.

During the same period, however, religion was challenged by the fact that political radicals popularised deistic and atheistic ideas on a broader scale.[19] The revolutionary French government also conducted one of the first state-directed anti-religious campaigns, which gained a mass following for the first time. Nevertheless, the impact of atheism on society was less influential than was the thought of, for example, Engels (*Die Lage der arbeitenden Klasse*),[20] at least during the first half of the nineteenth century. Royle investigated this topic for the English situation and concluded that atheism was not widespread among the working classes.[21] Although some relationship with Chartism existed (particularly among the artisans), atheism was, at least in England, a marginal phenomenon.

Whereas atheism did not increase during the second half of the nineteenth century, agnosticism increased remarkably. There were several reasons for the decline in active church membership. Urbanisation and industrialisation became more general phenomena in the majority of European societies. In particular, in the industrial areas, social conflict between the working classes and the middle classes, on the one hand, and the upper class, on the other, increased. More traditional forms of poor relief, mostly related to church organisation, came under pressure. The state, to an extent, took over education and charity, areas previously dominated by the church. This meant that the necessity to attend church services diminished for the lower classes.

Moreover, the development of more well-to-do neighbourhoods with their own churches led to greater financial problems for churches in working-class areas, particularly where the church organisation was a parish system. Also, working-class movements developed a more anti- or nonreligious standpoint. They were particularly opposed to the unionism related to churches, which emerged in Catholic areas with the new social policy of Pope Leo XIII, and in Protestant areas with the development of neo-Calvinism.[22] The increasing influence of Marxism on the working-class movement on the Continent, particularly in Germany, also contributed to this situation, mainly because it propagated a more scientific view of the world. Besides that, some working-class movements adopted socialism as a substitute for religion.

In addition, within the upper and middle classes agnosticism became stronger during the second half of the nineteenth century. Intellectual developments including Darwinism, liberal theology with its biblical criticism, and the increasing prestige of science contributed to these developments, both in urban and rural areas. Scientific methods of agriculture undermined the more traditional forms, which were often related to Christianity. It was not only these developments, but also Judaism that affected the Christian churches.[23] Assimilation not only implied the adoption of a different lifestyle but also, in some cases, a more critical stance towards religion.

At the end of the nineteenth century new forms of leisure gained popularity, which often detracted from traditional forms of church attendance. Some churches tried to cope with this problem by offering a combination of worship and leisure activities, even sport facilities on Saturdays. But in general the majority spent their Sunday on other activities other than attending church.

Although contemporary writers complained about these developments, in reality the situation was not so unambiguous. Political fights about the relationship between the state and the church, as, for example, in Germany during the so-called *Kulturkampf* and in France during the Third Republic, strengthened the ties between clergy and people. Movements to combine more traditional religious views with some aspects of modernisation, as in Dutch neo-Calvinism and in Catholic neo-Thomism in reaction to these developments, tended to strengthen the position of the churches. The development of the so-called People's Parties (*Volksparteien*) in Austria, Switzerland, Belgium and the Netherlands also contributed to this situation. The *pillarisation* of society with a political party, associations and an educational system related to a religious organisation led to counter-reactions from socialist working-class movements. Although pillarisation in this sense did not exist in Germany, similar reactions against the Centre Party existed.[24] It is undeniable that during the second half of the nineteenth century there was a massive decrease in working-class participation in church life in most countries, although this development was partially compensated by the bourgeoisie's return to the churches, most notably in France. Questions about the relationship between the church and the state, particularly the problem of education, led to a greater sense of cohesion among members of the churches.

During the second half of the nineteenth century there was not simply just a general tendency towards 'de-christianisation'. In some areas, not only political parties and social movements related to specific churches, but also the clergy itself participated in the modernisation processes. In specific areas, like Belgium, the Netherlands and parts of Germany, the Roman Catholic Church was involved in the establishment of banks, the forming of cooperatives and the organisation of the sale of fertilisers.

Changes in society as a factor influencing religion

It was not only regional divisions between Catholicism and Protestantism (related to historical events and cultural developments) that influenced the relationship between religion and society, but also specific changes within society itself. The process of modernisation of society in general,[25] and the Industrial Revolution in particular, contributed to a changing relationship between religion and society. Two aspects were of key importance: urbanisation and the changing relationship between towns and the countryside. Migration also played an important role during the nineteenth century. Several factors were important in this process.

The general increase in population, particularly in the countryside, led to a constant and sometimes dramatic mobility (examples can be found during and after the so-called 'hungry forties').[26] The constant factor was that people tried to combine the income from small properties in the countryside with temporary incomes elsewhere. Irish peasants went to England to earn a living, while their families stayed home to care for the animals and the property.[27] Similar situations could be found in Westphalia, where peasants worked in Dutch agriculture during harvest times, as well as in Denmark and parts of Germany. Besides the movement to other agricultural areas, people were also attracted by urban areas. Peasants from the mountainous areas in France went to Lyon or Paris to supplement their earnings in construction or other industries, as did the Flemish peasants from the North and from Belgium.

Although this pattern of migration was rather traditional (but in ever-increasing numbers), this was not true for other types of typically nineteenth-century migration. Political and economic changes led to a modified situation in the countryside and also to emigration. The most obvious example is the so-called enclosure movement of the British countryside, which also existed on the Continent in slightly different forms. The so-called Prussian reforms during the Napoleonic period had similar effects.[28] The result was a different division of property and, in particular, a rationalisation of agriculture. This led to an enormous increase in the mobility of the population.

Migration and urbanisation affected not only society in general, but also the role and position of religion within society.[29] Nineteenth-century authors, with their contemporary ideas about the strong influence of the environment on ideology and morality, took these trends and movements very seriously. Diminishing church attendance and widespread disbelief were anticipated. In reality, however, the developments were less clear cut. Religion, rather than ethnicity or geographical origin, tended to bind immigrants together, particularly in the United States.[30]

The expulsion of population led to a more definitive break with country life. Urban centres in general, and particularly the new industrial centres, experienced an enormous increase of inhabitants. Thus, the nineteenth century became a period of urbanisation. Cities such as London, Paris, Vienna, Berlin and Petersburg were striking examples of this process, as were the boom towns of the English Midlands, the Ruhr area, Northern France and Italy, as well as the traditional transport centres of Liverpool, Marseilles, Genoa, Rotterdam, Antwerp, Hamburg and Le Havre. The formation of nation states, with their policy of centralisation and their bureaucracies, also resulted in an increasing number of capital cities with rapidly growing populations.

Adaptation to urban environment and forms of identity

It is clear that these developments affected not only society as a whole, but also the position of religion within society. Contemporary authors, writing on this topic, feared a loss of belief and morality.[31] They considered that the environment influenced people and that the urban environment exerted a bad influence.[32] It is debatable, however, to what extent migration and urbanisation affected religion. Studies on specific groups of emigrants to the United States show that religion played a stronger role in group identification than factors such as language or ethnicity.[33] We have to remember, however, that in the USA the denominational model encompassed all groups, including Roman Catholics and Jews.

In Europe, where this was either absent, or related to specific Protestant groups, the situation was different – although here also religion could play a role in the adaptation of migrants to their new surroundings. In general, it seemed that the first generation stuck to their traditional belief. One of the greatest problems was a lack of money. The majority of the immigrants were of humble origin and the expanding urban areas were only provided with limited religious services. In many cases, the state was no longer inclined to contribute to the building of new churches.

In specific Protestant areas this problem was moderated by the activities of Free or dissenting churches, and the so-called 'internal mission' (a movement against de-christianisation of cities and towns, appearing in different forms in different European countries).[34] Churches with a parish system, like the Roman Catholic church and the Anglican church, were more vulnerable to the effects of the separation of the social classes into distinct urban and suburban neighbourhoods, than other types of church organisations which provided a system of solidarity between different local churches. Sometimes, however, the increase in the numbers of immigrants created new opportunities for specific churches. A good example was the influx of Irish migrants to English cities, which stimulated the Roman Catholic Church in England. Without such influx the position of this church would have been weaker, in spite of the upper-class interest during the last decades of the nineteenth century.[35] But even within the Irish Catholic community in England, church attendance decreased with the second generation. However, the popular anti-Catholicism in Victorian England was partially rooted in the strong Irish influence in English Catholicism.[36]

Similarly, for the Polish workers emigrating to the Ruhr area or Belgium and Northern France, religion was an important instrument for maintaining their identity. In the Western parts of Germany this led to clashes with the Prussian government, which not only had problems with Roman Catholics, but also tried to diminish Polish national feelings and the use of the Polish language.[37]

In general, however, the process of urbanisation and the migration to towns tended to decrease church attendance of the working classes. In Britain, where a strong relationship existed between Nonconformism and the working classes, even the dissenting churches were losing influence by the end of the century. Only the so-called respectable working class and labourers in the mining areas remained members of the church, rather than the traditional working class.[38]

Widespread migration also served to intensify tensions inside religious communities. Within the Jewish communities in Western Europe, complaints about the poorer and more pious Eastern immigrants increased towards the end of the century; this was also the case with some Christian communities. The arrival of masses of people from the countryside represented a threat to the established urban community.

As well as industrialisation and urbanisation, another important development was the emergence of the (nation) state, with its tendency towards homogeneity and centralisation. In different countries this led to a series of clashes, particularly on the subject of education. Although these developments influenced the role of religion in society, the effects were mainly political and do not need to be discussed here.

Conclusions

In spite of the general idea that religion is not important in industrial societies, we may conclude that – at least during the nineteenth century – there was no linear development towards a decline in religion. In the first half of the nineteenth century Christian churches were regaining ground in several ways. Agnosticism and nonbelief was not widespread, and also the working class – who later in the century had a widespread tendency towards lower church attendance – was involved in the church in many ways. Within the Roman Catholic Church, popular belief played an important role, and in Protestant areas dissenting churches and Free Churches were important, particularly for the artisans and lower middle classes.

This situation changed during the second half of the nineteenth century. Although many migrants moving to towns and industrial areas found that religion could play a role in the process of adaptation, giving them some feeling of identity, in the long run migration and urbanisation negatively affected the relationship between religion and society. Even in Britain, where the Roman Catholic Church benefited from the large number of Irish immigrants, there was gradual decline in church attendance over the years. Other factors contributed to this change, including the increasing influence of modern science and the development of a working-class movement with its rather anti-religious tendencies.

But even during the second half of the century, it is difficult to say that there was a tendency towards a diminishing influence of religion in society. Church membership remained attractive for the middle classes. New political and social movements related to church membership also played a role in this process, especially in Austria, Switzerland, Belgium, the Netherlands and in Germany (although a Roman Catholic political party only developed in the latter).

Europe in the nineteenth century showed many differences in the relationship between religion and society, and religion and politics. However, it was not so much the differences between the contemporary nation states that influenced these divisions. Structural divisions were a result of developments in the past, in particular during the sixteenth and seventeenth centuries. State formation in early modern Europe was also strongly influenced by these religious quarrels.

The areas with religious pluralism and the border areas were different from the more homogeneous areas. These differences influenced the outcome of the process of secularisation. This process was not a linear one, thus one cannot speak of a steady decline of religion in society. Finally, the role of religious institutions did become weaker, but the process was slow and was certainly not smooth. Even the results of the process of social and economic change, which affected Europe enormously, were partially influenced by this structural division.

Notes

1. E. Todd, *L'invention de l'Europe*, Paris, 1990.

2. The result was a decrease in the influence of the Roman Catholic Church in some areas during the eighteenth century and a stabilisation of this church during the nineteenth century up until the 1960s. In contrast to that there was a relatively lasting influence of Protestant churches until 1880 and a very rapid decline thereafter.

3. T. Parsons, 'Sociology of Religion', in *Action Theory and the Human Condition*, ed. T. Parsons, New York, 1978, pp. 167–324.

4. B.R. Wilson, *Religion in a Secular Society*, London, 1966.

5. D. Charlton, *Secular Religions in France*, Oxford, 1963; A. Dansette, *The Religious History of Modern France*, New York, 1962; F. Goguel, 'Religion et politique en France', *Révue française de science politique* 16 (1966), pp. 1174ff., A.C. Jemolo, *Church and State in Italy 1850–1950*, Oxford, 1969.

6. A. Hassing, 'Methodism in Norwegian Society', Ph.D. thesis, Northwestern University, 1973; J. Gusfield, *Svensk Kyrkogeographi*, Malmö, 1966; K. Kjær, 'Free Churches in Denmark', Ph.D. thesis, University of Copenhagen, 1968; M. Balle-Petersen, *Guds folk i Danmark: nogle synspunkter på studiet af religiøse grupper*, Lyngby, 1977; C. Bjørn, 'De folkelige bevægelser i Danmark', Fortid og Nutid 26 (1976), pp. 346–57.

7. G. Kaser, 'L'eveil du sentiment national. Rôle du piétisme dans la naissance du patriotisme', *Archives de sociologie des religions* 12 (1966), pp. 59–80.

8. D. Breistein, *Hans Nielsen Hauge, Merchant of Bergen: Christian Belief and Economic Activity*, Bergen, 1855; Bjørn, 'De folkelige bevægelser i Danmark'.

9. H.P. Clausen et al., *Kulturelle, politiske og religiøse bevægelser i det 19. Århundrede*, Århus, 1973; A.E. Christensen, *Danmarks Historie*, København, 1992; H.J.H. Glædemark, *Kirkeforfatningssporgsmaalet i Danmark, indtil 1874. En historiskkirkeretlig studie*, København, 1948; P.G. Lindhardt, *Vækkelse og kirkelige retninger*, Århus, 1977.

10. E. Allardt, 'Factors Explaining Variations and Changes in the Strength of Finnish Radicalism', in *Proceedings of the Fifth World Congress of Sociology*, Washington, 1962.

11. G. Gustafsson, *Religion och Politik*, Lund, 1967; S. Rydenfelt, *Kommunismen i Sverige*, Lund, 1954.

12. T. Brennan, E.W. Cooney and M. Pollins, *Social Change in South-West Wales*, London, 1954; C. Davies, *Religion in the Industrial Revolution in South Wales*, Cardiff, 1965; K.S. Inglis, *Churches and the Working Classes in Victorian England*, London, 1963; H. McLeod, *Religion and Class in the Victorian City*, London, 1974; B. Semmel, *The Methodist Revolution*, London, 1974; E.P. Thompson, *The Making of the English working class*, 2nd edn, Harmondsworth, 1968.

13. J.A. Coleman, 'Civil Religion', *Sociological Analysis* 31 (1970), pp. 67–77.

14. H. Righart, *De katholieke zuil in Europa: Het ontstaan van verzuiling onder katholieken in Oostenrijk, Zwitserland, België en Nederland*, Amsterdam, 1986; H.H. Kerr, *Switzerland: Social Cleavages and Partisan Conflict*, London, 1974.

15. E.L. Evans, *The German Center Party 1870–1933: A Study in Political Catholicism*, Carbondale, IL, 1981.

16. H. McLeod, 'Secular Cities? Berlin, London, and New York in the Later Nineteenth and Early Twentieth Centuries', in *Religion and Modernization*, ed. S. Bruce, Oxford, 1992, pp. 59–89, p. 66.

17. There exists a vast literature on this theme for the UK. Examples can be found in: Inglis, *Churches and the Working Classes in Victorian England*; McLeod, *Religion and Class in the Victorian City*; D.H. McLeod, 'Class, Community and Religion: The Religious Geography of Nineteenth Century England', *Sociological Yearbook of Religion*

in Britain 6 (1973), pp. 29–73; Brennan et al., *Social Change in South-West Wales*; Davies, *Religion in the Industrial Revolution in South Wales*; C. Field, 'Methodism in Metropolitan London 1820–1920', Ph.D. thesis, Oxford, 1975; Semmel, *The Methodist Revolution*; Thompson, *The Making of the English working class*; J. Baxter, 'The Great Yorkshire Revival 1792–6', *Sociological Yearbook of Religion in Britain*, London, 1974. See for other countries: L. Brunt, 'The "Kleine Luyden" as a Disturbing Factor in the Emancipation of the Orthodox Calvinists (Gereformeerden) in the Netherlands', *Sociologica Neerlandica* 8 (1972), pp. 89–102; Hassing, 'Methodism in Norwegian Society'; Kjær, 'Free Churches in Denmark'; G. Tiegland, 'Study of the Haugean Movement as a Case Study of Mobilisation', Ph.D. thesis, Bergen University, 1970; L.H. Mulder, *Revolte der fijnen: een studie omtrent de Afscheiding van 1834 als sociaal conflict en sociale beweging met een bronnenonderzoek in een achttal Friese dorpsgebieden*, Meppel, 1973; Balle-Petersen, *Guds folk i Danmark*; Bjørn, *De folkelige bevægelser i Danmark*; Glædemark, *Kirkeforfatningsspørgsmaalet i Danmark indtil 1874*; Lindhardt, *Vækkelse og kirkelige retninger*; A. Pontoppidan Thyssen, 'De religiøse bevægelsers samfundskritik og den demokratiske udvikling', in *Kulturelle, religiøse og politiske bevægelser i det 19. århundrede*, ed. A. Pontoppidan Thyssen, H.P. Clausen and P. Meyer (Det Lærde Selskabs publikationsserie, Ny serie I), Århus, 1973; R.J. Evans, 'Religion and Society in Modern Germany', *European Studies Review* 12 (1982), pp. 249–88.

18. E. Larkin, 'The Devotional Revolution in Ireland, 1850–1875', *American Historical Review* 77 (1972), pp. 625ff.; W. Schieder, 'Religion in der Sozialgeschichte', in *Sozialgeschichte in Deutschland*, ed. V. Sellin, Göttingen, 1987.

19. Charlton, *Secular Religions in France*.

20. S. Royle and E. Royle, *The Infidel Tradition: From Paine to Bradlaugh*, London, 1976.

21. E. Royle, *Radicals, Secularists and Republicans: Popular Freethought in Britain*, 1866–1915, Manchester, 1980.

22. For a more elaborate list of literature on this topic see: Righart, *De katholieke zuil in Europa*; F.A. Isambert, *Christianisme et classe ouvrière*, Paris, 1961; Inglis, *Churches and the Working Classes in Victorian England*.

23. D. Bensimon, 'Aspects of the Abandonment of Religious Practice in the French Jewish Milieu. Preliminary Results of an Inquiry', *Social Compass* 18 (1971), pp. 413–25.

24. Protestantism in Germany did not create political parties in Germany: R.M. Biglers, *The Politics of German Protestantism: The Rise of the Protestant Church Elite in Prussia 1815–1848*, Berkeley, 1972; G. Hübinger, 'Kulturprotestantismus und Politik. Zum Verhältnis von Liberalismus und Protestantismus, Bürgerliche und liberaler Revisionismus im wilhelmischen Deutschland', in *Religion und Gesellschaft im 19. Jahrhundert*, ed. W. Schieder, Stuttgart, 1993.

25. The concept of modernisation is rather unclear and controversial. A useful introduction for the historian is: H.U. Wehler, *Modernisierungstheorie und Geschichte*, Göttingen, 1975.

26. In particular the Irish migration to England and America was an example of the dramatic effects during a period of economic stagnation. See e.g., S.H. Cousens, 'Emigration and Demographic Change in Ireland', *Economic History Review* 2nd series, 14 (1961), pp. 275–88.

272 HENK VAN DIJK

27. S.H. Cousens, 'The Regional Variations in Emigration from Ireland between 1821 and 1841', *Transactions and Papers of the Institute of British Geographers* 37 (1965), pp. 15–30.

28. F. Tennstedt, *Sozialgeschichte der Sozialpolitik in Deutschland: Vom 18. Jahrhundert bis zum Ersten Weltkrieg*, Göttingen, 1981.

29. McLeod, 'Secular Cities?' in *Religion and Modernization*, ed. Bruce; F. Charpin, *Pratique religieuse et formation d'une grande ville: Marseilles 1806–1956*, Paris, 1964.

30. W.I. Thomas and F. Znaniecki, *The Polish Peasant in Europe and America*, 2 vols, New York, 1927.

31. E.g. Jacques-Victor-Albert, 4e duc de Broglie, Conservative French statesman and man of letters who served twice as head of the government during the early crucial years of the Third French Republic, but failed to prepare the way for the return of a king. He wrote the incompleted *L'Église et l'empire romain au IVe siècle*, 6 vols (1856–66).

32. L. Chevalier, *Classes laborieuses et Classes dangereuses à Paris dans la première moitié du XIXe siècle*, Paris, 1982.

33. P. Berger, *The Social Reality of Religion*, London, 1969; Thomas and Znaniecki, *The Polish Peasant in Europe and America*.

34. H.D. Loock, ed., *Seelsorge und Diakonie in Berlin*, Berlin, 1990; D.B. McIlhiney, 'A Gentleman in Every Slum: Church of England Missions in East London 1837–1914', Ph.D. thesis, Princeton University, 1977.

35. G.A. Beck, ed., *The English Catholics, 1850–1950*, London, 1950.

36. E.R. Norman, *Anti-Catholicism in Victorian England*, London, 1968.

37. C. Kleßmann, *Polnische Bergarbeiter im Ruhrgebiet 1870–1945: Soziale Integration und nationale Subkultur einer Minderheit in der deutschen Industriegesellschaft*, Göttingen, 1978.

38. C. Field, 'The Social Structure of English Methodism', *British Journal of Sociology* 28 (1977), pp. 199ff.

Bibliography

Allardt, E. 'Factors Explaining Variations and Changes in the Strength of Finnish Radicalism', in *Proceedings of the Fifth World Congress of Sociology*. Washington, DC, 1962.
Balle-Petersen, M. *Guds folk i Danmark: nogle synspunkter på studiet af religiøse grupper*. Lyngby, 1977.
Baxter, J. 'The Great Yorkshire Revival 1792–6', in *Sociological Yearbook of Religion in Britain* 7. London, 1974.
Beck, G.A. (ed.) *The English Catholics, 1850–1950*. London, 1950.
Bensimon, D. 'Aspects of the Abandonment of Religious Practice in the French Jewish Milieu. Preliminary Results of an Inquiry', *Social Compass* 18 (1971), pp. 413–25.
Berger, P. *The Social Reality of Religion*. London, 1969.
Biglers, R.M. *The Politics of German Protestantism: The Rise of the Protestant Church Elite in Prussia 1815–1848*. Berkeley, CA, 1972.

Bjørn, C. 'De folkelige bevægelser i Danmark', *Fortid og Nutid* 26 (1976), pp. 346–57.

Breistein, D. *Hans Nielsen Hauge, Merchant of Bergen: Christian Belief and Economic Activity.* Bergen, 1955.

Brennan, T., Cooney, E.W. and Pollins, M. *Social Change in South-West Wales.* London, 1954.

Brunt, L. 'The "Kleine Luyden" as a Disturbing Factor in the Emancipation of the Orthodox Calvinists (Gereformeerden) in the Netherlands', *Sociologica Neerlandica* 8 (1972), pp. 89–102.

Charlton, D. *Secular Religions in France.* Oxford, 1963.

Charpin, F. *Pratique religieuse et formation d'une grande ville: Marseilles 1806–1956.* Paris, 1964.

Chevalier, L. *Classes laborieuses et Classes dangereuses à Paris dans la première moitié du XIXe siècle.* Paris, 1982

Christensen, A.E. *Danmarks Historie.* København, 1992.

Clausen, H.P. et al., *Kulturelle, politiske og religiøse bevægelser i det 19. Århundrede.* Århus, 1973.

Coleman, J.A. 'Civil Religion', *Sociological Analysis* 31(1970), pp. 67–77.

Cousens, S.H. 'Emigration and Demographic Change in Ireland', *Economic History Review*, 2nd series, 14 (1961), pp. 275–88.

'The Regional Variations in Emigration from Ireland between 1821 and 1841', *Transactions and Papers of the Institute of British Geographers* 37 (1965), pp. 15–30.

Dansette, A. *The Religious History of Modern France.* New York, NY, 1962.

Davies, C. *Religion in the Industrial Revolution in South Wales.* Cardiff, 1965.

Evans, E.L. *The German Center Party 1870–1933: A Study in Political Catholicism.* Carbondale, IL, 1981.

Evans, R.J. 'Religion and Society in Modern Germany', *European Studies Review* 12 (1982), pp. 249–88.

Field, C. 'Methodism in Metropolitan London 1820–1920', Ph.D. thesis, Oxford, 1975.

'The Social Structure of English Methodism', *British Journal of Sociology* 28 (1977), pp. 199ff.

Glædemark, H.J.H. *Kirkeforfatningssporgsmaalet i Danmark, indtil 1874: En historiskkirkeretlig studie.* København, 1948.

Goguel, F. 'Religion et politique en France', *Révue française de science politique* 16 (1966), pp. 1174ff.

Gusfield, J. *Svensk Kyrkogeographi.* Malmö, 1966.

Gustafsson, G. *Religion och Politik.* Lund, 1967.

Hassing, A. 'Methodism in Norwegian Society', Ph.D. thesis, Northwestern University, 1973.

Hübinger, G. 'Kulturprotestantismus und Politik. Zum Verhältnis von Liberalismus und Protestantismus, Bürgerliche und liberaler Revisionismus im wilhelmischen Deutschland', in *Religion und Gesellschaft im 19. Jahrhundert*, ed. W. Schieder. Stuttgart, 1993.

Inglis, K.S. *Churches and the Working Classes in Victorian England.* London, 1963.

Isambert, F.A. *Christianisme et classe ouvrière.* Paris, 1961.

Jemolo, A.C. *Church and State in Italy 1850–1950.* Oxford, 1969.

Kaser, G. 'L'eveil du sentiment national. Rôle du piétisme dans la naissance du patriotisme', *Archives de sociologie des religions* 12 (1966), pp. 59–80.

Kerr, H.H. *Switzerland: Social Cleavages and Partisan Conflict.* London, 1974.

Kjær, K. 'Free Churches in Denmark', Ph.D. thesis, University of Copenhagen, 1968.

Kleßmann, C. *Polnische Bergarbeiter im Ruhrgebiet 1870–1945: Soziale Integration und nationale Subkultur einer Minderheit in der deutschen Industriegesellschaft.* Göttingen, 1978.

Larkin, E. 'The Devotional Revolution in Ireland, 1850–1875', *American Historical Review* 77 (1972), pp. 625ff.

—— *The Roman Catholic Church and the Home Rule Movement in Ireland, 1870–1874.* Chapel Hill, NC, 1990.

Lindhardt, P.G. *Vækkelse og kirkelige retninger.* Århus, 1977.

Loock, H.D. (ed.). *Seelsorge und Diakonie in Berlin.* Berlin, 1990.

McIlhiney, D.B. 'A Gentleman in Every Slum: Church of England Missions in East London 1837–1914', Ph.D. thesis, Princeton University, 1977.

McLeod, D.H. 'Class, Community and Religion: The Religious Geography of Nineteenth Century England', *Sociological Yearbook of Religion in Britain* 6 (1973), pp. 29–73.

—— *Religion and Class in the Victorian City.* London, 1974.

—— 'Secular Cities? Berlin, London, and New York in the Later Nineteenth and Early Twentieth Centuries', in *Religion and Modernization*, ed. S. Bruce. Oxford, 1992, pp, 59–89, p. 66.

Mulder, L.H. *Revolte der fijnen: een studie omtrent de Afscheiding van 1834 als sociaal conflict en sociale beweging met een bronnenonderzoek in een achttal Friese dorpsgebieden.* Meppel, 1973.

Norman, E.R. *Anti-Catholicism in Victorian England.* London, 1968.

Parsons, T. 'Sociology of Religion', in *Action Theory and the Human Condition*, ed. T. Parsons. New York, NY, 1978, pp. 167–324.

Pontoppidan Thyssen, A. 'De religiøse bevægelsers samfundskritik og den demokratiske udvikling', in *Kulturelle, religiøse og politiske bevægelser i det 19. århundrede*, ed. A. Pontoppidan Thyssen, H.P. Clausen and P. Meyer (Det Lærde Selskabs publikationsserie, Ny serie I). Århus, 1973.

Righart, H. *De katholieke zuil in Europa: Het ontstaan van verzuiling onder katholieken in Oostenrijk, Zwitserland, België en Nederland.* Amsterdam, 1986.

Royle, E. *Radicals, Secularists and Republicans: Popular Freethought in Britain, 1866–1915.* Manchester, 1980.

Royle, S. and Royle, E. *The Infidel Tradition: From Paine to Bradlaugh.* London, 1976.

Rydenfelt, S. *Kommunismen i Sverige.* Lund, 1954.

Schieder, W. 'Religion in der Sozialgeschichte', in *Sozialgeschichte in Deutschland*, ed. V. Sellin. Göttingen, 1987.

Semmel, B. *The Methodist Revolution.* London, 1974.

Tennstedt, F. *Sozialgeschichte der Sozialpolitik in Deutschland: Vom 18. Jahrhundert bis zum Ersten Weltkrieg.* Göttingen, 1981.

Thomas, W.I. and Znaniecki, I. *The Polish Peasant in Europe and America*, 2 vols. New York, NY, 1927.

Thompson, E.P. *The Making of the English Working Class*, 2nd edn. Harmondsworth, 1968.

Tiegland, G. 'Study of the Haugean Movement as a case study of mobilisation', Ph.D. thesis, Bergen University, 1970.

Todd, E. *L'invention de l'Europe.* Paris, 1990.

Wehler, H.U. *Modernisierungstheorie und Geschichte.* Göttingen, 1975.

Wilson, B.R. *Religion in a Secular Society.* London, 1966.

PART 3

A GENERAL VIEW

13

SOCIAL PARTICULARITIES OF NINETEENTH- AND TWENTIETH-CENTURY EUROPE

Hartmut Kaelble

More than the other essays in this volume, this paper will treat historical issues. It will raise the question of whether in the nineteenth and twentieth centuries, alongside the multiplicity of unchanged or new regional and national differences, one can locate long-term tendencies towards a European society, i.e., towards more commonalities, more convergence and a more intense interrelationship between the national European societies, and also to a growing consciousness of them. The essay will treat primarily those developments that reach into the present, that is, continuing historical processes.[1] Such a view of European society opens up two different perspectives. On the one hand, it draws our attention to the development of commonalities, convergence and interconnections that become apparent only when studied in retrospect. On the other hand, European society cannot be regarded simply as the discovery of social historians. It makes sense only if it was experienced, discussed and desired by European contemporaries. Thus the experiences of Europeans that transcended their own regions or nations and the debates they conducted about a European society are also part of its development.

These two basic perspectives have determined the structure of this essay. At the outset the first aspect mentioned above will be discussed. The first sections will treat the commonalities of European societies, then the decrease or persistence of social differences between European countries and, finally, the interconnections between them. Adopting the second perspective, I will sketch the widening of Europeans' geographical experiential framework and, in the last section, I will briefly address the debates among European contemporaries about European society[2]

This volume treats only the twelve members of the European Community before its recent enlargement. Was the emergence of European society limited to these twelve countries? Do these twelve countries, taken together, really differ substantially from other Western European societies – the northern (i.e.Scandinavian) countries and Austria and Switzerland? Has the European Community, in the more than forty years of its existence, really affected the societies of its members so deeply that one can speak of a society of the European Community now? This essay proceeds from the assumption that, from the very beginning, the emergence of a European society extended beyond the continually changing borders of the European Community and later Union, and included the Scandinavian countries, Austria and Switzerland, and to some extent the countries of Eastern and Central Europe even before 1989 – at any rate, that it was not restricted to the European Community within its various historical borders. Certainly, we should not underestimate the historical influence of the European Community. It represented a profound and radical change in European history, in stabilising peace within Europe, establishing parliamentary democracy and human rights, developing a large, dynamic European common market, replacing the principle of hegemony with that of partnership, both in the cooperation between small and large nations in Europe and in Europe's global role. The European Community's jurisdiction in family, education, social and housing policy and other areas of social policy did not, however, extend far enough to create a new society. Alongside European integration, other factors, which we will address in greater detail below, contributed to the emergence of a European society. For that reason I will not only trace the European Community within its ever-expanding borders since 1957, but also examine it within its West European framework, with frequent references to the societies of Eastern and Central Europe as well — a perspective that focuses not just on today's European Union, but that of the future as well.

Commonalities among European societies

In the course of the nineteenth and twentieth centuries a whole series of social commonalities arose within the European nations. Such common attributes may be observed in the realms of the family, employment and social milieux, as well as urbanisation, the welfare state and consumption. Commonalities in the first three areas were more readily visible in earlier years than they are today; those in the last three areas, in contrast, are rather new and have persisted up to the present day. Certainly there are also further commonalities, for example in the areas of religiosity and secularisation, in enterprises, bureaucratisation and the role played by intellectuals. I shall restrict my remarks not just to social commonalities, but more narrowly to those that have already been subjected to precise comparative studies by social historians.

To be sure, these commonalities have their obvious limits, which I shall discuss at the outset. The common attributes of European societies did not, of course, develop in complete isolation from each other, but neither can they be reduced to some simple formula. They represent a great diversity. They are hardly ever centuries-old, permanent structures, but nearly always have been subject to major historical change; often they are only a few decades old. They thus possess a quite different character from the basic constants of European intellectual history, about which there has been increasing discussion of late. In addition, the following social commonalities are not present in all European countries, but mainly in the heart of Europe, which was already industrialised by the end of the nineteenth century, and less in what was then the European periphery. These were, however, common attributes in the sense that the majority of Europeans lived in societies characterised by them. Certainly, such commonalities were limited to particular societal arenas and could not be found everywhere. Other areas, such as demographic developments, the development of social conflicts, or more generally the development of institutions in many sectors of society, were characterised by enormous differences.[3] A further limitation: these commonalities scarcely made a lasting impression on the consciousness of Europeans, but rather are to a great extent the discovery of social historians. They have not yet become the object of a European social identity. For reasons of space, these six areas of common ground among European societies can only be presented briefly and cursorily here rather than treated in empirical detail.

The European family, which has been studied above all by Austrian and British social historians,[4] represents an early European social commonality that is no longer so apparent in the present. The European family is characterised by particular structures, but also by particular ways of life. The core of this European peculiarity was the circumstance that, unlike in Japan or Eastern Europe, newly-weds did not marry into the families of their parents or grandparents, but rather founded their own households. Thus the coexistence of three generations under one roof was far less widespread in Europe than elsewhere. The financial means needed to establish one's own household generally required saving money for a number of years. Thus in Europe both men and women also married much later in life than elsewhere. This late age at marriage also meant that European families had lower birth rates than those in other parts of the world. Not all young adults could amass the financial resources to found their own households. For this reason the European family also included a large number of members who never married. Particular ways of life were associated with these familial structures. The European family separated itself more strictly than elsewhere from the outside world, from the extended family, neighbours, the community and also the state. Familial intimacy was more highly developed, creating stronger emotional bonds between parents and children. The relationship between spouses was also more strongly shaped by the ideal of the love match than elsewhere. Parent–child relationships were characterised not only by stronger emotional ties, but also by parents' more exclusive responsibility for child rearing and, in turn, by children's stronger orientation towards their parents. At the same time, European family life also prepared children to leave their family of origin when they reached young adulthood. This could take the form of moving from the family home to boarding school, an apprenticeship or domestic service, as was the case from the early modern period into the twentieth century, or of a protracted adolescent crisis, which is still the case today.

This European family, which I have sketched very briefly here, did not exist everywhere in Europe. Until the nineteenth century it was largely limited to the northern and western parts of Europe, to Britain, northern France, the Benelux countries, Scandinavia and the German-speaking lands, and had not yet become established in Southern or Eastern Europe. A discussion of the reasons for this would take us too far afield. In the late nineteenth and twentieth centuries the European family spread throughout Europe, while at the same time relinquishing some of its peculiarities. Even today, though, the three-generation family remains significantly less common in Western Europe than, for example, in Eastern Europe or Japan, the age at marriage significantly later than, for example, in the USA, and the birth rate substantially lower than in other parts of the world. The intimate family may also continue to be more widespread. We will, however, need to seek new explanations for these persistent differences.

A second peculiarity of European society is the dominance of industrial employment.[5] If we follow the development of employment during the nineteenth and twentieth centuries, we find that the proportion of workers in industry and the crafts was significantly higher in Europe and, at the same time, employment in the service sector significantly lower than elsewhere. For this reason, only Europe experienced a period in which more people were employed in industry than in the agricultural or service sectors. According to our textbooks, which often refer to this period as the era of 'industrial society', all industrialising societies go through such a phase. This phase, however, existed in Europe and nowhere else, neither in the early industrialising societies such as the USA and Canada nor in today's newly industrialised nations, and also not in Tsarist Russia or the Soviet Union. To be sure, not all European countries experienced this intensity of industrial labour. It was lacking in the Netherlands, Norway, Denmark, Greece and only weakly developed in France, yet clearly apparent in Europe as a whole. This peculiarity is no longer as marked today as it was even in the 1970s, since in today's Europe the service sector has also become the largest employer. To this day, however, the industrial sector is still stronger in Europe than elsewhere. The reasons for this predominance of industrial employment in nineteenth- and twentieth-century Europe are partly historical, and partly still in force today. The historical reasons include the phenomenon of emigration from Europe, especially to America, which is unique in the history of the world. As a result, the poorly paid service occupations that were held by migrants from the country to the city were less common in Europe than elsewhere. A further historical reason is that social, national and regional differences in consumption were particularly pronounced in Europe, creating an especially strong demand for individual, nonstandardised products, which in turn generated employment in industry and the crafts. As its productivity during industrialisation grew more slowly than, for example, in the USA, for many years European agriculture also bound more workers, which also led to a slower growth in the service sector. The reasons for this, which are still applicable today, are as follows: more than the American economy, and for many years more also than its Japanese counterpart, the European economy was orientated towards overseas markets, and exported a significantly higher proportion of its products, which created more demand for industrial workers – to produce goods for exports – than for service sector employees, since a large part of the distribution of these goods took place outside of Europe. The much higher population density in Europe as compared to the USA or the Soviet Union also contributed to a relatively smaller service sector. This high population density decreased the need for personnel in commerce and transport, but also in a number of other service occupations. Finally, the European family also played a role in the high rate of industrial employment. Because of late marriage, Europe always had a particularly large number of young, mobile adults not tied down by family who were prepared to move to where the industries were, which were generally strongly concentrated in certain regions. Thus it was particularly easy to build up industries in Europe.

There may be a connection between the great importance of industrial employment and the accompanying strict regulation of working hours and the distribution of work, on the one hand, and the development of an attitude towards work – particularly in pre-Second World War Europe – that differed from that prevailing in non-European countries, on the other. In several respects, the line between work and nonwork was more strictly drawn in Europe than elsewhere. Weekly and particularly yearly working hours were reduced more quickly in Europe than elsewhere. The annual long vacation, which arose particularly after the Second World War, is an economic but also cultural peculiarity of Europe. Europeans also came to have a shorter working life than workers in other parts of the world. They began their occupational lives later and, particularly because of developments in the welfare state, to which we will turn below, stopped working at an earlier age. Older European traditions of late entry into paid employment and early retirement were taken up here. One characteristic of the peculiarly European division between work and nonwork appears to have resulted at least in part from the strong emphasis on family intimacy and the ties between parents and children: Particularly after the Second World War, female labour market participation grew less quickly in Europe than elsewhere, which means that women who were primarily housewives for most of their lives are far more common in Europe than in the USA, Japan or – at least before 1989 – Eastern Europe (with clear North–South differences within Western Europe). Finally, Europeans also appear to have felt a greater distance towards work. Europeans speak far less often than, for instance, Americans or Canadians, of being proud of their work. They also tend to be more sceptical of instructions from their superiors. Their job satisfaction seems more limited. This does not change the fact that for Europeans work was and remains an important and central part of life, but it is one they assess differently than North Americans, for example.[6]

A further social peculiarity, which can only be sketched here and which has receded considerably in importance in recent decades, are the social milieux: the (upper) middle class, the proletarian milieu, the petty bourgeois milieu, the farming milieu and, until the beginning of the twentieth century, the milieu of the landed aristocracy. These milieux did not exist in isolation from each other, but were strongly interrelated and were based to a great extent on the drawing of mutual boundaries. I shall limit myself to those milieux that survived the Second World War, remains of which are thus still visible today, in spite of their diminished significance.

The European (upper) middle class, the oldest of these milieux, was composed of members of various occupations – entrepreneurs, the free professions, higher civil servants, and pastors – which also existed in other modern societies. In Europe, however, these occupations had a professional ethos of their own, an autonomous labour market, organisations and forms of social intercourse. At the same time they were closely intertwined without any one of these professions becoming dominant. They shared values of family, work, individual freedoms, the inviolability of property and its transmission through the family, education and culture; furthermore, strong social contacts, marriage circles, shared social origins, education and training in the same institutions, associations, clubs, social events such as visits to the theatre, opera, concerts, museums, restaurants and dinner parties. Finally, they also set themselves off from other milieux – in the nineteenth century particularly from the aristocracy and farmers, in the twentieth century rather from the proletarian milieu, the petty bourgeoisie and also farmers. This (upper) middle-class milieu arose in the late eighteenth and early nineteenth centuries in opposition to institutions that did not exist in the same form in other societies and thus shaped the European middle class in particular ways: opposition to strong state intervention in the market, to interference by highly bureaucratised churches in the private sphere, and to a culturally and politically dominant landed aristocracy. These commonalities coexisted with substantial social, national and regional differences. What is more, they also had clear limits in the political sphere, since middle-class liberalism developed along sharply divergent lines in the different European countries. The (upper) middle-class milieu also weakened substantially from the 1950s and 1960s on. In Eastern Europe, the middle classes were systematically undermined and eliminated by the communist regimes. Only certain segments of the middle class, such as pastors or medical doctors, survived communist rule. In Western Europe the unity of bourgeois values and lifestyles gradually disintegrated. The most important means of setting boundaries, particularly to the lower classes – property and higher education – were opened to wider segments of the population and became ever less appropriate as the means for a narrow stratum to set itself off from other social groups.[7]

A second peculiarly European social milieu was the proletarian milieu, which developed only in the late nineteenth and early twentieth centuries and which has been studied in detail above all in Britain, Germany, Austria, Belgium and France. This working-class milieu had three primary functions. Firstly, it represented a mutual-aid network among neighbours in urban districts for assistance in the vicissitudes of life such as serious illness, starting a family, unemployment, poverty in old age or the death of a parent. The working-class milieu thus supplemented assistance within the family. The pub or café, the local shopkeeper, the workplace, the trade union and sometimes also the church were important spaces for social contacts in the working-class milieu. In a society in which members of the working class were largely excluded from social life, had few opportunities for mobility and scant access to institutions of higher education, the proletarian milieu also provided a context for developing dignity and self-respect. Workers' educational associations, savings associations, pubs, support funds, clothing and eating styles, weekend outings, but also trade unions all fulfilled this function. Thirdly, the European proletarian milieu also had political significance. The working-class milieu provided the basis for the political labour movement, socialist parties and socialist trade unions. The ties between social milieu and the political labour movement were closer in some European countries than in others; they were stronger in Germany and Austria than in Britain or France. This proletarian milieu was also something that did not exist in non-European industrial societies. It began to decline, however, in the 1950s and 1960s. There were a number of reasons for this: the number of industrial workers, particularly of male skilled workers, the classic backbone of the proletarian milieu, was shrinking; the rise of the modern welfare state, to which we will turn later, reduced the importance of neighbourhood mutual aid; the rise of modern consumer society blurred the lines between the various class milieux; the expansion of education greatly improved access to higher education for working-class children; the classic working-class neighbourhoods disintegrated with the expansion of cities and the rise in mobility brought about particularly by the spread of automobiles; finally, in some countries like Germany and Austria, the classic working-class milieu had been deliberately destroyed by the Nazi regime and the Social Democratic Parties did not pick up the continuities of the labour movement's culture.[8]

A third peculiarly European social milieu was the lower middle class, which arose in its modern form in the second half of the nineteenth century and was composed mainly of independent artisans, shopkeepers, publicans and small transport enterprises. In modern industrial society this milieu was characterised above all by its precarious economic situation and continual pressure from large industrial or commercial enterprises. The European lower middle class became increasingly distinct from the bourgeoisie, from which it was increasingly excluded. The family played a particular role in this milieu. Since small businesses were normally family firms, familial solidarity and the duty of all family members to work to maintain the business were particularly important in the lower middle class. Familial self-exploitation was particularly frequent. At the same time, this milieu was characterised by an unusual degree of social mobility. Members of the petty bourgeoisie originated from many social strata, and their children entered many different social strata. The European lower middle class developed its own culture in rifle clubs, singing clubs, guilds and other trade corporations. In small European towns the lower middle class not infrequently set the tone, while it rarely played an important role in the big cities. These characteristics shared by the European petty bourgeoisie did not pertain to the political arena, however. As early as the second half of the nineteenth century, the political orientations of the European lower middle class began to diverge widely in the individual nations. While in France the lower middle class remained a pillar of republicanism and in Britain represented an important base of British liberalism, in Germany most members of this stratum shifted their loyalties from liberalism in the mid-nineteenth century to conservatism in the late imperial period and developed a strong inclination towards National Socialism at the end of the Weimar Republic.[9] This milieu, too, diminished in importance from the 1950s on, above all because of the sharp decline in the number of small craft and retail enterprises and thus of the size of the milieu, but also because familial solidarity and the mutual responsibility of all family members could no longer be maintained in the face of the development of welfare state institutions for all citizens, including those of the lower middle class, and an opening up of educational opportunities.

Finally, the farming milieu and its relationships to urban society were also a European peculiarity. In Europe as a whole, in which agriculture remained the largest employment sector until after the Second World War, this milieu possessed great significance. The fundamental orientation of the European farming milieu was towards the preservation of family farms and a high degree of self-sufficiency, even though twentieth-century European farmers were seldom fully independent of the market. A substantial proportion of European farmers not only produced their own food, clothing, and heating fuel, but also repaired their own machinery and houses. In this respect the occupation of farmers differed fundamentally from urban labour. The rhythm of work was different; the line between work and nonwork was less clearly drawn. Above all, farmers were generalists who performed a diversity of tasks without a clear-cut occupational profile or formal training. The economy of the farm was strongly dependent on the family and the participation of all its members, with a certain division of labour between men and women, parents and children, and older and younger adults. The standard of living in the broader sense of the word was substantially lower than in the cities. Households spent money on completely different things. Agricultural life was characterised by isolation in the village or even the individual farm household. The occupational mobility of farmers' sons and the marriage mobility of farmers' daughters was limited. Most sons of farmers became farmers themselves, and most daughters married farmers; at the same time the number of unmarried sons and daughters was high. Only in recent decades has this farming milieu experienced a massive decline. Farmers have been replaced by small agricultural entrepreneurs who specialise in a particular branch of agricultural production, have formal training, and are primarily motivated by profit. Since the 1950s, agricultural productivity has undergone a steady and historically unprecedented increase; at the same time, the number of family farms has declined rapidly. This radical transformation has led to fundamental changes in the farming milieu. The living standard of agricultural families quickly approached that of the comparable urban milieus, with certain differences such as more frequent ownership of automobiles or deep freezers among farmers. Farm households became completely dependent on the market. Particularly because of developments in the media, farm families have come to participate much more in general cultural developments. The choice of occupation and marriage partner have become broader. Only a minority of farmers' sons become farmers nowadays, and only a minority of their sisters marry farmers. In large parts of Europe the peasant village has disappeared, to be replaced by villages in which few of the inhabitants are farmers, and the majority of people pursue the same occupations as town-dwellers.[10]

A fourth European peculiarity, which has only developed fully since the 1950s and persists today, is the European welfare state. This European welfare state, too, does not exist in the same form in all European societies. In some late-industrialising nations, such as Portugal or Greece, it was less highly developed, and until 1989 it took quite another path in Eastern than in Western Europe. For a number of reasons, the welfare state developed differently in Western Europe than in non-European societies. Firstly, the European welfare state could look back on a longer tradition. In some European countries, the first state social insurance schemes, public housing programmes, and policies of equal educational opportunity were introduced in the nineteenth century and had been substantially intensified after the Second World War. In most industrial societies outside Europe, in contrast, the prehistory of the welfare state began only in the 1930s or even during or after the War. More importantly still, the European welfare state was always far ahead of its non-European counterparts in social spending and the proportion of the population covered by it. This Western European lead has scarcely diminished in more recent years. Not all, but most Western European nations had a head start in this field. Furthermore, in international debates on the welfare state it was always Europe that was the model. During the prehistory of the modern welfare state German social insurance and the English garden city served as models. In the postwar period it has been England and Sweden above all that have served as international models, for many years in a positive sense and in the 1980s also in a negative one. Thus despite the great differences in the development of the welfare state in the various European countries, West European societies have a good deal in common if compared with non-European welfare states and with the East European type of social security.[11]

A fifth European historical peculiarity, which still persists today, is related to the development of cities in the nineteenth and twentieth centuries. Despite the apparently rapid urbanisation in Europe since the late nineteenth century, urbanisation proceeded more slowly in Europe than in all non-European countries. Between 1910 and 1980 the urban population in Europe rose 0.6 percent annually, compared to 0.9 percent in the USA, 1.7 percent in Russia (and later in the Soviet Union), and 3.7 percent in Japan. To be sure, urban growth was much larger in some parts of Europe, such as Germany, Switzerland, Scandinavia before 1914, or Eastern Europe particularly after the Second World War. Taken as a whole, however, urban growth was markedly slower in Europe than the international average. Even in the 'hot' period of urban growth in the heart of Europe, the percentage of urban dwellers still grew more slowly than in the 'hot' period of international urban growth since the Second World War. In addition, European urbanisation, unlike urbanisation in other industrial societies, was characterised by the lesser importance of very large cities, and a predominance of middle-sized cities of between 100,000 and 1,000,000 inhabitants. This limit on the expansion of very large cities in Europe is nicely illustrated by a list of the world's twenty largest cities. At the beginning of the twentieth century about one-half of the twenty largest cities were still in Europe. At the beginning of the next century probably not a single European city will be on the list. Life in the middle-sized cities had many consequences for political culture, local elites, urban identity and the accessibility of services of all kinds. The stronger weight of middle-sized cities is doubtless related to the fact that population density is greater in Europe than in other large industrial societies and that middle-sized cities have a better chance in Europe because they are always closer to the great metropolises than in the USA, the Soviet Union, Canada or Australia. A further reason is that in the nineteenth century European urbanisation, unlike that in most other industrial societies, could already build on a tight network of cities, which frequently expanded during the urbanisation process and formed the core of middle-sized cities. Such cores were generally absent in non-European societies. Another European peculiarity may be that debates about the city were conducted differently there than elsewhere. At least in comparison to the USA, scepticism about large cities seems to have been stronger in Europe. Representatives of extremely diverse political tendencies regarded the big city as a symbol of the destruction of values, alienation and social decline. This fear of the big city was not infrequently unfounded, but it was still an important part of the contemporary reaction to urbanisation. It also had something to do with the existence, from the late nineteenth century until well into the postwar period, of a type of city that was much rarer outside of Europe: the purely industrial city, inhabited almost exclusively by industrial workers, which thus appeared politically threatening to the upper classes of the time. This type of European industrial city was closely linked with the above-mentioned clear dominance of industrial employment in Europe. The curb on urban growth and the predominance of middle-sized cities, but also European reservations about large cities, were important preconditions for a further European peculiarity: the massive and often highly efficient intervention, particularly since the end of the nineteenth century, of national and local government in urban development and planning, not only in the construction of railway stations, boulevards, opera houses, theatres, town halls, and public buildings in city centres, but also in planning the functions of individual neighbourhoods and urban expansion. This specially developed urban planning rested on a long European tradition of planning cities, reaching back to antiquity. This city planning contributed significantly to the quality of life in European city centres, which was much higher than in the towns of the USA, Japan or the developing world. To be sure, there were differences within Europe with regard to the development and planning of cities, and the debate about their size, but this should not cause us to overlook common European characteristics altogether.[12]

A final commonality, which is mentioned here because it has also been studied in some detail, are the European peculiarities in the area of the mass consumer society. The term mass consumer society is usually used to refer to the commercialisation of what were originally often personal relationships between consumers and producers, the establishment of standardised consumer goods, the removal of production from the household, the sharp decline in relative private household expenditures for food and clothing, and the strong increase in household investment expenditures; to the establishment of more uniform consumption and the weakening of differences in consumption between social milieux, but also between regions and nations, and finally, to the fundamental change in the debate about consumption, which shifted from cultural to environmental criticism. The development of modern mass consumer society has doubtless been a global process shaped above all by the United States, a process in which the societies of neither Western nor Eastern Europe have fundamentally stepped out of line. Nevertheless, there are clearly European, and until 1989 largely West European, particularities within the framework of this global development. These particularities, in turn, arose above all in the heart of Europe, already industrialised by the early twentieth century, gradually reaching the periphery after the Second World War, with different results for the East and West European peripheries. The first European peculiarity in this area is that, on the one hand, European societies clearly lagged behind the USA in the development of mass consumer societies. While in the USA mass consumer society had already developed in the 1930s and 1940s, in Western Europe it did not assert itself until the 1950s and in Eastern Europe not until the 1970s. On the other hand, Western Europe differed fundamentally from other latecomers in that all elements of mass consumer society had European as well as American roots. The standardisation of consumer products, department stores, the automobile, fast food restaurants, packaged foods and even the self-service shop had developed equally in Europe and North America. The USA only assumed the role of a motor of mass consumer society, because two world wars robbed Europe of several decades of developmental opportunities. Mass consumer society was thus not a foreign way of life thrust upon Europe, but rather – in many respects – a European development reimported from the United States. A second peculiarity is the particular debate that arose in Europe during the period when mass consumer society was becoming entrenched, which spurred decades of especially heated discussions about consumer society among Europeans. As part of the debates surrounding emerging mass consumer society, Europeans developed a particular historical self-image (above all in contrast to the USA), which was characterised by four elements: Europeans regarded themselves as less materialistic and more interested in education and culture, and thus more indifferent to material consumption than Americans. They were more sceptical of technological progress, more aware of the costs of such progress, and more attached to older ways of life; they had a stronger preference for individual, less standardised consumer goods designed for their own personal needs. On the whole, European society, it was claimed, allowed greater scope for the individual and less pressure to conform in everyday life, accompanied by a stronger preference for social differences between classes, ethnic groups, regions and nations – differences that were also strongly expressed in consumption. This European critique of mass consumer society has largely retreated today, but it strongly influenced the European debate for decades and often sought to convey the impression that modern mass consumer society was a purely American phenomenon that had nothing to do with European developments whatsoever. Finally, even today European mass consumption remains characterised by several obvious peculiarities: European households spend more money on food and clothing than US households with comparable incomes. Certain central indicators of modern mass consumer society, such as automobiles, televisions and telephones, remain permanently weaker in Europe, such that one cannot simply speak of later development, but rather of a long-term structural difference. Significantly fewer Europeans than North Americans have motorcars, television sets or telephones, in particular. There is an explanation for this. Greater population density in Europe makes cars and telephones less necessary; the different use of time by Europeans, particularly working hours and the length of working life, led to different consumer patterns, as did the somewhat lower tendency of European women to work outside the home. The stronger development of the welfare state in Europe, the greater dominance of state educational institutions and the intervention of local governments in public transport and housing also led to differences in consumption between Europe and the USA. There were, to be sure, also massive differences within Europe, particularly between Western and Eastern Europe, but we should not altogether overlook shared developments.[13]

The decrease of differences within Europe

These common attributes of European societies are, to be sure, only one side of the story. They coexisted with severe national and regional differences between European societies. Have these differences increased or decreased over the course of the twentieth century, and did this tend to make the above-mentioned commonalities more or less important?

There is no doubt that the differences between regions, countries and entire groups of countries within Europe have remained very significant throughout the twentieth century and up until the present. This applies not just to historical reality, but also to the way Europeans perceive themselves. Even today Europeans remain particularly interested in the social *differences* between European countries. Some intellectuals even go so far as to regard Europe's internal diversity as the element that most truly characterises European civilisation, and to overlook social commonalities altogether.[14]

In addition, growing differences may be observed in both the long-term perspective of the nineteenth and twentieth centuries and the short-term perspective of the period since the Second World War. Viewed in a long-term perspective, European societies took very diverse paths to industrialisation and modernisation. In this way, the differences between European societies rather tended to increase in the nineteenth and early twentieth centuries, and certainly did not simply disappear. Even in the shorter postwar perspective there were above all two strong reasons for new social differences between the European countries. On the one hand, the Second World War tended to intensify differences within Europe, not only because it affected the various countries involved very differently, but also because the European governments and populations drew very different conclusions for social policy after the war; in some countries massive social reforms were pushed through, while others rather attempted to restore prewar society.[15] On the other hand, the East–West division of Europe since the 1940s has also produced new, fundamental differences between Eastern and Western Europe, which are still intensely tangible today, and which will surely continue to play a major role in the immediate future. It is by no means clear that the end of the East–West divide in Europe after 1989 will lead to a new rapprochement between European societies. The war in former Yugoslavia drastically revealed the deep potentials for conflict lurking in Eastern Europe; in Western Europe, this only exists in certain isolated pockets.

Despite such persistent or even newly emerging social differences within Europe, there have also been obvious tendencies towards a decrease, if not a fundamental weakening, of such differences between European countries or groups of countries, particularly since the 1950s, but earlier as well. There are two reasons for this narrowing of intra-European differences: an economic impetus, which will be treated first here, and a political impetus.

The economic impetus for a reduction of social differences between European countries came above all from two closely related directions: on the one hand from the thorough industrialisation of Europe, that is, the industrialisation of the southern, northern and eastern peripheries. The process of industrialisation as a whole took particularly long in Europe, beginning in the late eighteenth century in England and not extending to all of Europe until after the Second World War. Only from the 1960s onwards we can speak of Europe as a whole as industrialised, even if certain regions or an entire country like Albania remained largely agricultural. This thorough industrialisation of Europe also brought about growing social similarities. On the one hand, the period following the Second World War, particularly the 1950s, 1960s and 1970s, saw an unprecedented increase in real wages and standards of living. Certainly, this development did not take place in all European countries at the same time or to the same extent, but the basic tendency is observable everywhere, in the heart of Europe and on the periphery, in the East as well as the West. In Western Europe these two processes were largely associated with the new world economic order that was established under the leadership of the United States, and with European integration since the 1960s, but also with extremely diverse national economic policies.

This economic impetus led to a shrinkage, if certainly not to a complete levelling, of social differences within Europe, particularly in three areas. Firstly, the massive differences in labour market structure among the various European countries and regions declined. The sharp contrast that had still existed in 1950 between countries with only minimal employment in the agricultural sector, such as Britain and the Netherlands, and those with a large agricultural labour force, such as Portugal, Spain, Italy and a number of Eastern European countries was substantially diminished. Today, with the exception of Albania, only a minority of the labour force in all European countries is employed in agriculture. The enormous differences in industrial employment that still existed in 1950 between countries with a high rate of industrial employment, such as Britain, Belgium, Germany, Austria, Switzerland and the Czech Republic, and those with a lower rate, such as Portugal, Italy and many

Eastern European countries, also diminished sharply. In the service sector, which today has become the strongest labour market sector in nearly all European countries, the differences in employment rates between the European countries are much smaller. To be sure, in the 1970s and 1980s new differences arose, particularly between countries such as the GDR and Czechoslovakia, with their consistent rate of industrial employment of about 50 percent of the working population, and the Western European countries, including Germany, in which industrial employment had been steadily declining since the 1970s. In a quick and brutal levelling process, though, this high rate of industrial employment in East Germany and the Czech Republic plummeted after 1989, which made their pattern of employment converge back to the European trend.[16]

Secondly, the enormous differences in urbanisation within Europe also declined as a result of the economic impetus. At the end of the Second World War there were still great differences between highly urbanised societies such as Britain or the Netherlands, on the one hand, and largely rural societies in Southern Europe, parts of Scandinavia such as Norway and Finland, and a number of Eastern European countries on the other. As a result of the further urbanisation of Europe in the decades since the War, today nearly all European societies are predominantly urban and most Europeans live in towns and have adopted urban values and ways of life.[17]

The third and probably most important decline in intra-European differences, at least in Western Europe, concerns the standard of living, which has become more similar since the Second World War,[18] even though one cannot speak of an equalisation. As late as the 1950s there was still an enormous difference between the industrialised heart of Europe and Southern Europe, for example. In 1960, per capita private consumer income in Portugal was only one-fifth and in Italy only two-thirds of the Western European average. By 1990 per capita private consumer income in Portugal had managed to reach a level of two-thirds of the European average. Taken as a whole, Italy by no means lags behind the European average any longer. A similar decrease of the enormous differences that were still present in the 1950s and 1960s can be registered for the central indicators of the standard of living: housing quality, the number of telephones, televisions, refrigerators and automobiles per capita of the population.[19] The differences in Europe and also within the European Community have doubtless not disappeared and will continue to require active Community policies to reduce inequality. In addition, the enormous differences between Western and Eastern Europe became evident after 1989. The closing gap between West European standards of living since the Second

World War, however, offers hope that the differences between East and West may also diminish in the future.

All of these reductions in the differences within Europe are not merely global trends that also diminished social differences between Europe or Western Europe as a whole and the societies of the rest of the world. Even after the triumph of the service economy, the structure of the European labour market remained industry-intensive.[20] The above-mentioned European peculiarities – the slower rate of urbanisation and the greater dominance of the big city – did not really hold back urbanisation in Europe. The de-urbanisation of the 1980s was also less marked in Western Europe than in the United States. As already mentioned, European peculiarities also remained in the standard of living. The decline of differences in available private consumer income is also observable only in Western Europe; however, not between Western Europe as a whole and the non-European member societies of the OECD.

A second impetus for the reduction of social differences in Europe came from politics, although not from any individual institution, group of politicians or political organisation. The decisive political background to shrinking social differences was, rather, the fact that on the one hand, for the first time in many years, all of Western Europe adopted the same basic political principles, namely those of democracy and human rights, and that at the same time European integration, the Pax Americana and the decline of the European colonial empires created a novel, lasting peace, for the first time excluding war as an instrument of conflict resolution in Europe. Both of these novel developments greatly facilitated the intra-European exchange of societal models and ideas, because it was now an exchange among fundamentally similar political systems, and also because no country saw itself compelled any longer to reassure itself of the superiority of its own nation through unique social reforms. From the national to the municipal level, the exchange of societal models and of the objectives of social policy was made a good deal easier. The European Community made a central contribution to establishing democracy in Europe and stabilising a lasting European peace, a contribution more important than the ultimately insoluble task of standardising social institutions and policies within the European Community. This background also helps explain why, although the institutions in many areas of society did not necessarily become more similar, the results of policies did. The welfare states became much more similar, if not in their institutions, at least in their monetary benefits and the proportion of the population they covered.[21] Educational institutions remained quite diverse, to be sure, but when it came to the proportion of children attending kindergarten, and of young people completing an academic secondary school or studying at university, the differences within Europe, or at least within Western Europe, lessened substantially, particularly after the Second World War.[22] Housing policy in Europe remained quite diverse with regard to aims, legislation and programmes, but housing standards, and in particular the quality of flats and houses, became much more similar in the postwar period.

These reductions of differences were not simply global processes that also lessened the differences between Western Europe and other industrialised nations. Clear differences between Western Europe and other industrialised countries, both those of the non-European West and Eastern Europe, persisted. We have already mentioned that the differences between Europe and the non-European Western welfare states, in terms of both benefits and coverage of the population, continue into the present. Conversely, despite the worldwide expansion of education, Western Europe, with its much smaller proportion of students, continues to lag behind the USA. When it comes to housing standards Europe, the USA and Japan have not simply become more similar. The same is true of Eastern Europe. Obvious differences from Western Europe in the period before 1989 clearly existed. The social structure remained fundamentally different. The proportion of pupils completing secondary school with a qualification to study and of university students in their respective age groups lagged significantly behind Western Europe. There was also no equalisation in housing standards. The growing similarities within Western Europe were thus not simply an international trend, but rather a Western European peculiarity.

Exchange and interconnections between European societies

The social commonalities among European countries and the decreasing differences between the individual nations were not in themselves enough to pave the way to a European society. An important third element was necessary: the interconnections and exchange between individual societies. Such exchange relationships and interconnections have correctly been emphasised by some social scientists and historians.[23] Such social interconnections include occupational and educational migration, marriage ties across national boundaries, consumer and cultural exchange, and, as a foundation of all of these, the development of foreign language skills.

This decisive third aspect was also characterised by contradictory developments. Interconnections and growing exchange in some cases were accompanied by break-ups and the interruption of exchange in others. Let us look at three very different examples of this phenomenon. Firstly, in the period before 1918, because of international familial ties among the European royalty and the high nobility, there were much stronger interconnections on the highest political level than today. These interconnections lost their significance above all with the abolition of the monarchy in a number of large European countries, along with the growing political power of governments and parliaments in those monarchies that continued to exist. Secondly, to name an example from the opposite end of the social spectrum, since the late nineteenth century the migration of workers from the European periphery to the industrial heartland of Europe led to increased interconnections between various European countries, however one may judge them. This migration reached a high point during the boom of the 1950s and 1960s. Since that period these interconnections have not increased much, since with the economic difficulties that began in the late 1970s demand for foreign labour has greatly diminished, and this migration from both European and non-European countries outside the EU has also been deliberately curbed by the European governments. A third example of imposed interruption of migration and relationships of exchange is the East-West division of Europe, which meant that interconnections between East Central and Western Europe fell drastically for almost fifty years.

Nevertheless, on the whole the average European has seen social interconnections and relationships of exchange intensify, particularly since the 1950s. This is, at least, the impression left by the (albeit quite inadequate) data collections that have been undertaken up until now, which address various aspects of exchange and interconnection. Lacking Europe-wide compilations, we will cite the German example, which is surely not unusual. Education expanded markedly in other European countries. Thus the number of German students studying at universities in other European countries rose from a few hundred in 1910 to 7,000 during the 1960s and 25,000 in 1989. The number of students from other European countries at German universities, in turn, rose from 6,000 in 1910 to 11,000 in the 1960s and 18,000 in 1989, although, for political and scholarly reasons, the quality and reputation of German universities had quite clearly fallen over the course of the twentieth century. Short- and long-term occupational migration between European countries also rose substantially, particularly in the 1970s and 1980s. Thus there were more British and French citizens living in Germany in 1980 than at any previous period. Immigration to Germany was in large part immigration from within Europe. Around 1980 as many immigrants came to Germany from the European Community states as from Turkey. It is very probable that this immigration is not solely composed of labour migrants, but also consists of people from a wide range of professions and social strata. Travel between European societies has also risen sharply, especially since the 1950s. Thus the number of hotel guests from other European countries in Germany rose from 800,000 in 1950 to almost 15 million in 1989. In other Western European countries the number of tourists and business travellers rose even more rapidly. This wave of travel not only took Northern Europeans to the South of Europe, but also to a growing extent brought Southern Europeans to the North. Among young Europeans in 1990 only a minority had never visited another country, which usually means a European country. Marriages between people from different countries certainly remained less frequent than one might expect, but they, too, increased. In Germany, the percentage of men who married women from other European countries rose from 0.5 percent in 1955 to 2 percent of all men marrying in 1980. The percentage of German women marrying men from other European countries rose from 1 percent to 2.5 percent in the same period.

Doubtless much more important were changes in the exchange of consumer goods and with them often changes of lifestyles. The proportion of consumer goods from other European countries rose massively beginning in the 1950s. The average European encountered consumer goods from other European countries in two fundamentally different ways: on the one hand as consumer goods that were sold as the national products of another country, and often associated with the aura and culture of another land (e.g., furniture, perfume, cheese, wine, cars or flowers), and, on the other, since the 1950s, as fully internationalised European consumer products, which were sold in multilingual packaging and whose national origins remained in the background (e.g., refrigerators, hotel rooms, toys and entire retail chains). This exchange of consumer goods between European countries internationalised, and mostly Europeanised, the lifestyle of most European countries from the 1950s on. Even today the mass of imported consumer goods originate from other European countries rather than the USA or Japan. Finally, another decisive precondition for interconnections between European societies, the knowledge of foreign languages, also increased massively. Among West Germans who went to school before the Second World War, only about 15 percent speak English, as compared to about 50 percent of those who began school after the War. At the end of the 1980s some 90 percent of young West Germans stated that they could carry on a conversation in English. West Germany is no exception here. The overwhelming majority of young citizens of the European Community learn a foreign language in school.[24]

All of these interconnections linked Europeans primarily with other European societies, even if the extent of the interconnections within Europe varied from country to country. Let us take the German case once again. Here ties with other European countries clearly dominated. Approximately 80 percent of West German students who studied abroad did so at a European university. Three-quarters of the foreign guests who booked hotel rooms in Germany in 1990 were Europeans. Some 80 percent of West Germans who went on holiday abroad in 1990 travelled to another European country. If Germans marry foreign citizens, men (largely) and women (increasingly) marry other Europeans. Foreign-made consumer goods in Germany were largely European. In terms of value, three-quarters of the imported consumer goods sold in Germany came from European OECD member countries. Growing international business interconnections meant above all European interconnections. One also gains the overall impression that intra-European relations have become increasingly dynamic particularly since the 1970s and 1980s.

There are international, but also specifically European, reasons for these growing interconnections between European countries. Six of these reasons were particularly important.

1. Above all, the internationalisation of the European economy since the Second World War, which was grounded in European integration, the new world economic order and the Pax Americana greatly promoted not only international economic but also social interconnections.

2. In addition, the already mentioned unique increase in real incomes, above all during the unprecedented economic boom between the late 1950s and the early 1970s, also facilitated the social interconnections in many respects, from travel abroad and the purchase of foreign-made consumer goods to school exchange programmes and language courses in foreign countries.

3. Since the Second World War a frequently ignored transformation in educational qualifications has also taken place. Most European countries underwent a change from societies in which the majority of the population attended only elementary school, and in which there were only small academically educated elites, to societies in which those without secondary education were in the minority and the mass of citizens possessed intermediate or higher educational qualifications. With these fundamental changes in the level of educational qualifications, the knowledge of foreign languages and the interest in foreign countries, consumer goods and lifestyles increased. Surveys substantiate this different attitude of academic secondary school leavers and university graduates towards all things foreign. Alongside these global reasons for stronger international interconnections there were also more specifically European reasons.

4. The revolution in transportation and communication has made exchange with other, particularly European, societies significantly easier. The motorcar, which only became a

means of mass transport for Europeans after the Second World War, has made travel to other European countries much cheaper and thus more accessible. The aeroplane has made it possible to spend a holiday at the beach in another European country for a relatively low price. Since the 1970s and 1980s, automatic telephones and the fax machine have also made it easier and cheaper for Europeans to keep in contact with each other.

5. The establishment – unthinkable as recently as the 1930s – of democracy and a liberal economy first in Germany and Italy immediately following 1945, then in Spain, Portugal and Greece in the 1970s, and finally in Eastern Europe after 1989, has facilitated and encouraged many relationships of exchange that had been inconceivable in a divided Europe. Political exchange programmes such as school exchanges or town twinning have created many close relationships between Europeans, frequently between opinion-leaders. Growing exchange between university teachers and intellectuals has been greatly facilitated by shared basic convictions about politics and civil rights.

6. Finally, the European Community also intensified these tendencies towards growing interconnection and exchange through the greater opening of national labour markets to Europeans from other member countries, the unprecedented mobility of high-level bureaucrats, politicians and experts between the European capitals and to Brussels, less complicated regulations for citizens moving from one country to another within the European Community, and, in recent years, through successful student exchange programmes.

European social commonalities, the reduction of social differences between the European countries and the growing interconnections within Europe have quite obviously been studied in varying depth. Some aspects can only be formulated in the form of hypotheses, or only for a few countries. It nevertheless appears that the tendencies towards a European society have intensified particularly since the 1950s, a phenomenon frequently, but by no means always, limited before 1989 to Western Europe, and which – since 1989 – has at least the potential to include East Central Europe.

These are, however, conclusions drawn in retrospect by social historians. The question remains of whether contemporary Europeans also thought within this framework of European society and were aware of such tendencies towards the development of a European society. Given what we have said up to this point, we can only speak of a European society discovered retrospectively. Did Europeans perceive themselves as living in a European society, or were they perhaps even consciously aware of it, so that it framed their way of thinking? Put differently, were they imagining Europe?

Europeanising Europeans' geographical experiential framework

As yet no one has devoted serious study to how the experiences of Europeans changed in the twentieth century. Much remains to be done. It is apparent, however, that the way in which Europeans experienced other countries in Europe also underwent a fundamental change, beginning in the 1950s, and that the basic character of their experiential framework changed and became Europeanised.

Until about the middle of the twentieth century, the geographical horizons of the mass of Europeans did not normally extend beyond their own country, and often not even beyond their own region. Only a small minority of Europeans, the upper classes, members of certain occupations, and people who lived in border regions, knew other European countries from frequent personal experience. Under everyday conditions, the mass of Europeans were familiar with other European countries only from newspapers, books and radio – that is, through the often highly selective reports of others. Their personal encounters with foreign countries were either overseas, or in European countries under traumatic circumstances. A segment of Europeans had lived overseas as colonial officials, missionaries, military officers, doctors, travellers, servants or soldiers, or as returning emigrants from America, of whom there were many in Europe. This personal experience of living abroad tended to turn the gaze away from Europe. In the first half of the twentieth century, a large number of Europeans experienced other European countries primarily through war, whether as soldiers, prisoners of war, deportees or refugees. Their personal experiences of other European countries were thus marked by the exceptional situation of war and fundamental enmity towards the citizens of another European country. Even if these wartime experiences in other European countries occasionally ended in positive personal relationships, this mass experience did not take people into the everyday life of other European societies and did not represent a normal everyday situation that could be repeated under other conditions. Another mass experience of other European countries was that of labour migrants, mainly unskilled workers, farm labourers and domestic servants. This experience, too, was very specific, since it frequently placed migrants in ghetto-like situations, and thus did not necessarily expose them to the normality of everyday life in other countries. Unlike experiences of other countries in wartime, this experience of mainly unskilled migrants was scarcely publicly acknowledged or discussed, since most migrants did not record their lives. Unlike wartime experience, this experience remained largely unspoken. A third type of personal experience of other European countries involved a narrow stratum of the upper middle class. Sons of entrepreneurs were not infrequently sent for a longer stay in the firms of friends, business partners or subsidiary companies abroad. Young upper middle-class women often spent time at finishing-school or as governesses in other European countries. These experiences certainly exposed them to normal everyday life in other European countries, but they were also strongly shaped by a specific phase of life – adolescence – and were certainly restricted to a tiny part of the population. Thus for the mass of Europeans who travelled abroad at all, their personal experience of other European countries was generally a traumatic or once-in-a-lifetime affair, which rarely took them into the everyday life of other lands. In a survey conducted during the 1950s, for example, 70 percent of German men stated that they were acquainted with other European countries from the War, but only 26 percent from travel or work. The experience of war and of other Europeans as enemies was thus wholly dominant.[25]

Beginning in the 1950s and 1960s, Europeans' experiential framework underwent a radical change in several respects: experiences of living or going abroad became Europeanised, more widespread, more intensive and more normal.

More than in the first half of the twentieth century, experiences of going abroad were concentrated within Europe. They often signalled a broadening of Europeans' spatial experience. At the same time, the process of decolonialisation after the Second World War transferred the experiences of many of the British, French, Belgians, Dutch, Spanish and Portuguese from overseas back to Europe. The slowing of European emigration to both Americas since the 1950s also shifted the gaze of many Europeans back to Europe. At the same time, experience of foreign lands became far more widespread in Europe. Well into the first half of the twentieth century, the experience of visiting foreign countries drew a class line between aristocrats and members of the upper middle class, on the one hand, and the lower middle class, workers and farmers, on the other. As late as 1950 an overwhelming majority of 75 percent of West German citizens had no experience of foreign countries aside from the War.[26] In recent decades, in contrast, the majority of Europeans have seen foreign countries with their own eyes. Most travel, education and training in other countries, business trips and working abroad, marriages with foreigners, foreign tourism, retirement abroad and town twinning have occurred within a European context. In 1990 only a minority of about 25 percent of young people in the European community had never visited another country. In Western Europe, at least, including those countries like Portugal or Spain that had long been cut off from the rest of the Continent, travelling or living abroad became common.[27] The countries of East Central Europe and East Germany will doubtless catch up quickly.

Furthermore, visits to foreign countries also became much more frequent and intensive, and no longer represented the once-in-a-life-time experience of a narrow stratum of students, au pairs, young people beginning their careers or those caught up in wars. Many Europeans have had regular and continuous experiences of being abroad. It is estimated that, apart from the nearly 5,000 senior civil servants from European Community member countries permanently based in Brussels, a further 36,000 senior civil servants from member countries constantly or frequently travel to Brussels. The same is true of countless European politicians. With the development of a European network of motorways and air travel the managers of large enterprises, not only from the international trade and transport sectors, but also from industry and banking, have found the geographical framework of short business trips expanding beyond their own borders to include all of Europe. During the past few decades the majority of Europe's large cities have become accessible for short or even day trips. A top manager of the prewar period like Walther Rathenau, in contrast, usually spent at least a week when he went abroad on business. Nowadays, the majority of Europeans are familiar with other European countries through holiday travel, consumer products and encounters with other Europeans in their own country. In 1990, about one-third of the young people in the European Community had not only travelled to other European countries but also had more intensive experiences there during stays of three months or more. Among students, more than half of them had experienced a longer stay abroad.[28]

The experience of other European countries became normal and was increasingly a part of everyday life in education and training, work or holidays. While in the first half of the twentieth century living abroad was often associated with an exceptional situation such as war, unemployment and leaving one's homeland, separation from one's family of origin, adolescence and the beginning of occupational life, in the second half of the century travelling to another European country has become more and more a part of normal everyday reality, repeatedly experienced during regular business trips, annual holidays or – even more frequently – during short vacations. The everyday range of consumer goods from other European countries lost the unusual, eccentric and individualistic character it had often had for average Europeans in the first half of the century. Travel literature changed accordingly. Travel accounts about other countries, both in Europe and overseas, which were published in large numbers in the nineteenth and early twentieth centuries, gradually disappeared, only to be replaced in the 1960s and 1970s by travel guides which described in detail how the reader him- or herself could turn travel into an experience. The experience of other countries, above all in Europe, became a component of the European standard of living and lifestyle; it became an interest in its own right.

This is only a crude outline of the interconnections between European societies and of the emergence of a new experiential framework for Europeans. The individual stages of this development, their intensity, their spatial extension within Western Europe and in East Central Europe as well need – to emphasise the point once again – further and more detailed study. Is all of this part of a society's identity?

The debate on Europe's social identity

The debate concerning Europe's social identity has intensified in recent years. In this debate, however, as in similar earlier discussions, questions of intellectual history and philosophical theses about the basic constants of European thought[29] and the origins of Europe in the Middle Ages and the early modern period play an important role.[30] This debate only partially addresses the theme of this book, social commonalities in Europe.

All of the above-mentioned signs of the emergence of a European society, the social commonalities, the – however not entirely unambiguous – decrease of social differences between the individual European countries, the general increase in interconnections and relationships of exchange, the expansion of Europeans' geographical experiential framework and ever more frequent personal experience of the everyday life of other European countries were all no mere inventions of social historians after the fact, but rather the subjects of continual debates among Europeans beginning as early as the nineteenth century. To be sure, such debates were conducted by small circles of people only. They cannot be compared to the broad discussions that have taken place in a number of European countries in recent years in the run-up to referenda concerning the Maastricht Treaty or joining the European Union. Nevertheless, in the nineteenth and twentieth centuries one can find clear traces not only of an experienced but also of an imagined European society. These debates have been little studied, and much less attention has been paid to them than to the rarer discussions of European political unity. Already, though, three peculiarities of this debate are fairly clearly recognisable.

Firstly, even in the period of the triumph of national consciousness in the nineteenth century and the first half of the twentieth century, notions of a common European society coexisted with the certainly dominant idea of national societies. This idea of a European society was not a purely historical one, and it did not refer only to Europe's historical social roots in antiquity, in the Judeo-Christian tradition, and the shared Middle Ages, Renaissance, and Enlightenment. Rather, the discussion also treated the peculiarities of European society in the present. The debate was filled with desires, ideology and speculations but also with inspiring and acute observations. Such well-known figures as Alexis de Tocqueville, James Bryce, Hugo von Hofmannsthal, Wilhelm Liebknecht, Max Weber, Werner Sombart, André Siegfried, Arnold Toynbee and Simone de Beauvoir, but also hundreds of unknown authors, contributed a large number of books and articles to this public debate.[31] This debate was, to be sure, conducted by an educated public and was thus restricted to a small minority of Europeans at any given time. It nonetheless shows that the idea of a European society is not a recent invention. The debate was also conducted in most European coun- tries: in France, Britain, Italy, Germany, Switzerland, Austria, the Netherlands, Belgium, Poland, the Czech lands and Hungary. A few countries, notably Spain, largely kept out of this debate. It is astonishing how similar the arguments in the various European countries were, and how minute the differences between them. How the substance of this idea of a European society changed, how it was assessed, how strongly it was based on an experience of the various European societies, under what conditions the debate waxed or waned, remains to be studied.

Secondly, one gains the impression that this discussion revolved to a great extent around the modernisation of Europe, and that it was used to come to terms with the social modernisation of European societies and with the changes, fears and enthusiasms it unleashed. Certainly, the European debate about social modernisation extended far beyond this European focus, but the subject of European society was a part of this lit- tle-studied debate about non-European models, the superiority or inferiority of European civilisation, and the advantages and disadvan- tages of a modernised Europe. American society and the comparison of Europe as a whole with America played a central role in this debate, because the realities of American society were regarded as a promising or menacing vision of Europe's own future. The differences between American and European society, the absence of hierarchies in American social life, the lesser degree of intimacy and seclusion of the American family, the more independent role of American women, more frequent upward mobility and changes of occupation, the different role played by education, and the rapid expansion of large cities in the USA were particularly important themes in this debate. This discussion about the modernisation of European society in the nineteenth and twentieth centuries appears to have intensified particularly in times of crisis, above all during the years following 1918 and 1945. Thus in 1949 Klaus Mann, writing from the perspective of the effects of the Second World War, noted that the intellectuals were 'Europeans now. Shared suffering has a unifying force'.[32] Such times of crisis also included periods in which Europe fell behind other societies, such as the decades preceding 1914 when the United States gained ascendancy. The debate on European modernisation stirred particularly strong emotions and seldom produced a consensus on how common European values, attitudes and structures should be assessed. To be sure, the observations made in this debate on the social peculiarities of European societies were surprisingly similar, and included the intimacy of and strong emotional ties to the family, the sharpness of social distinctions and limited social mobility, the great attachment to occupation, the aesthetic beauty of European cities and the strong intervention of municipal governments, the patriarchalism of entrepreneurs, the numerous but not necessarily violent strikes, the diminished contrast between rich and poor after the Second World War and the advanced development of the welfare state. This assessment of the peculiarities of European society remained highly contested, however. These controversies only died down after the boom of the 1950s and 1960s, and after the 1970s when Europe gradually caught up with the USA.

Thirdly, the political role of notions about a common European society underwent a fundamental change during the period following the Second World War. In the nineteenth and early twentieth centuries ideas on European civilisation, its historical roots and present state were frequently a substitute for the absent political unity of Europe, a sort of cultural consolation and conjuration in a period of national fragmentation and wars in Europe. With the beginning of European integration in the 1950s and the emergence of a European power centre in Brussels, the idea of a European society gradually relinquished this role. A new kind of position began to emerge in the debate about European society: On the one hand, in view of the increasing economic standardisation of European ways of life through the common market, and in the light of the growing concentration of power in Brussels there was, so to speak, a growing emphasis on the social and cultural diversity of the European nations and regions, and an attempt to view this variety as the European peculiarity. 'What counts in the life and future of European culture', wrote the French sociologist Edgar Morin in 1987, 'is the fruitful encounter of differences, oppositions, competitions, and complements. It is the logic of dialogue that represents the heart of European cultural identity, and not this or that peculiarity or driving force.'[33] On the other hand, some have argued that, with the advance of European integration and the emergence of a power centre in Brussels, European intellectuals now have responsibilities not just within the framework of their respective national publics but also for critically observing European politics. Social scientists and historians – so the argument goes – should thus devote more intense research and discussion to the strengths and weaknesses of social and cultural commonalities and interconnections within Europe. This thorough transformation from a discussion rather far removed from political decisions, which was often utopian and sought to compensate for the absence of European institutions, to a far more realistic debate revolving around existing political institutions and decisions, which would be incomprehensible without the background of a European power centre, has also strongly influenced the historical development of the idea of a European society.

Summary

This historical contribution has attempted to show that, alongside the European diversity of persistent and often newly developed national and regional social differences in structures, institutions, norms, mentalities, ways of life and social policies, there are also tendencies towards a European society, which may be demonstrated or at least assumed.

They include a number of *social commonalities*, which, to be sure, are not present in every European country, and yet have influenced, and are still influencing, the majority of Europeans: commonalities in the family, employment and labour, social milieux, urbanisation and urbanity, the welfare state and mass consumption. These social commonalities were not secular, permanent structures but rather underwent constant change. Some of them have tended to become less important, while others have gained in significance in recent years.

Another tendency within European society has been towards a decrease, if certainly not a disappearance, of social national differences, encouraged on the one hand by the thorough industrialisation of Europe, including the periphery, since the 1950s and 1960s, and the historically unusual increase in real incomes, and on the other by the democratisation of Europe and the accompanying increased opportunities for an exchange of social ideas, models and ways of life.

Tendencies towards a European society also existed in the increasing interconnections between European societies in the form of education, employment, business travel, tourism and marriages in other European countries, and through the growing exchange of consumer goods and ways of life, but also through a rise in knowledge of foreign languages. This massive increase in the interconnections between European countries is related in part to global internationalisation, and in part also with an additional specific Europeanisation.

The tendencies towards a European society do not only consist in the retrospective observations and discoveries of historians and social scientists. They are also expressed in changes in Europeans' geographical experiential framework. Since the 1950s Europeans have not only been travelling to other European countries far more frequently and concentrating more on Europe after the collapse of the colonial empires. The experiences of other European countries have also changed in character, no longer consisting mainly of traumatic wartime encounters or the ghettoisation of labour migrants. They became repeatable at will, belonged to everyday experience, and tended to allow encounters with the everyday lives of other European countries; they were no longer based on relationships between enemies, or between occupiers and the occupied, but rather on those of partners within the framework of a politically integrated Europe. At the same time, they also became part of European ways of life, and of the material interests of Europeans.

Finally, the progress towards a European society also includes the debate about Europe as a society. This debate about social commonalities has been conducted by Europeans since the nineteenth century, albeit for many years only in very small circles, and was largely concerned with the modernisation of European societies, and how to deal with and assess it. This debate has been given a new focus in recent decades, since Europeans have become aware of a European power centre in Brussels. It is no longer a discussion revolving around an ultimately purely cultural European civilisation removed from the political arena. Instead, it has become a debate about concrete political decisions on the European level, such as that to join the European Union or make alterations to the Union Treaty, and about basic decisions on expanding the jurisdiction or membership of the European Union.

Notes

1. For a good sociological overview of research on European society, see S. Immerfall, *Einführung in den europäischen Gesellschaftsvergleich*, Passau, 1994; *Lebensverhältnisse und sozialer Konflikt im neuen Europa*, ed. B. Schäfers, Frankfurt am Main, 1993 contains a number of contributions treating individual aspects of European society; for overviews of European social history in the nineteenth and twentieth centuries, most of which do not, however, address the question of Europe-wide or specifically European developments, see the introductions by W. Fischer, 'Wirtschaft und Gesellschaft Europas 1850–1914', in *Handbuch der europäischen Wirtschafts-und Sozialgeschichte*, ed. W. Fischer, vol. 5, Stuttgart, 1985, pp. 1–207, W. Fischer, 'Wirtschaft, Gesellschaft und Staat in Europa 1914–1980', in *Handbuch der europäischen Wirtschafts-und Sozialgeschichte*, ed. W. Fischer, vol. 6, Stuttgart, 1987, pp. 1–221 and G. Ambrosius and W.H. Hubbard, *Sozial- und Wirtschaftsgeschichte Europas*, Munich, 1986; and H. van Dijk, *De modernisering van Europa*, Utrecht, 1994.

2. The basic theses of this essay have already been addressed in H. Kaelble, 'L'Europe "vécue" and "pensée" au XXe Siècle: les spécificités sociales de L'Europe', in *Identité et conscience européennes au XXe siècle*, Paris, 1994, pp. 27–45 and H. Kaelble, 'Social History of European Integration', in *Western Europe and Germany: The Beginnings of European Integration 1945–1960*, ed. C. Wurm, Oxford, 1995, pp. 219–47; H. Kaelble, 'European Integration and Social History Since 1950', in *Europe after Maastricht*, ed. P.M. Lützeler, Providence, Oxford, 1994, pp. 89–111. The following theses on European social commonalities and the lessening of differences within Europe are based on my 1987 book *Auf dem Weg zu einer europäischen Gesellschaft*, Munich, 1987 (French translation 1988, English and Italian 1990, Japanese 1997); for a more detailed account of a number of aspects touched on below, see H. Kaelble, 'La grande modernisation', in *Les Européens*, ed. H. Ahrweiler and M. Aynard, Paris, 2000, pp. 509–41; on an aspect not treated here, see H. Kaelble, 'Eine europäische Geschichte des Streiks', in *Von der Arbeiterbewegung zum modernen Sozialstaat. Festschrift für G. Ritter zum 65. Geburtstag*, ed. J. Kocka, H.J. Puhle and K. Tenfelde, Munich, 1994, pp. 44–70.

3. Despite the enormous differences in social conflicts there were certain common tendencies. See Kaelble, 'Eine europäische Geschichte des Streiks'.

4. See J. Hajnal, 'European Marriage Patterns in Perspective', in *Population in History*, ed. D.V. Glass and D.E.C. Eversley, London, 1965, pp. 483–530; P. Laslett, *Family Life and Illicit Love in Earlier Generations*, Cambridge, 1977, chap. 1; P. Laslett, 'Household and Family as Work Group and Kin Group: Areas of Traditional Europe Compared', in *Family Forms in Historic Europe*, ed. R. Wall, J. Robin and P. Laslett, Cambridge, 1983, pp. 513–64; P. Laslett, 'The European Family and Early Industrialisation', in *Europe and the Rise of Capitalism*, ed. J. Baechler, Oxford, 1988, pp. 234–41; M. Mitterauer, *Sozialgeschichte der Jugend*, Frankfurt am Main, 1986, pp. 28–43; M. Mitterauer, 'Europäische Familienentwicklung, Individualisierung und Ich-Identität', in *Europa im Blick der Historiker*, ed. R. Hudemann, H. Kaelble and K. Schwabe, Munich, 1995, pp. 91–97; A. Burguière et al., *Histoire de la famille*, 2 vols, vol. 2, Paris, 1986.

5. See H. Kaelble, 'Was Prometheus Most Unbound in Europe? The labour Force in Europe During the Late 19th and 20th Centuries', *Journal of European Economic His-*

tory 18 (1989), pp. 65–104 (not pertaining to Eastern Europe); for Eastern Europe see the comparative data in B.R. Mitchell, *International Historical Statistics: Europe 1750–1988*, 3rd ed., Basingstoke, 1992, pp. 141ff. (up until 1988); OECD, *Short-term Statistics: Central and Eastern Europe*, Paris, 1992 (from 1988 on).

6. For working hours see G. Cross, *Time and Money: The Making of Consumer Culture*, London 1993; *ILO Yearbook*, Geneva, 1978, pp. 327ff., *ILO Yearbook*, Geneva, 1987, p. 675ff., *ILO Yearbook*, Geneva, 1992, pp. 728ff.; on women's work see: *Economically Active Population*, ed. International Labour Office, 5 vols, Geneva, 1986, vol. 5, pp. 87ff.; on values see S. Harding, D. Phillips and M. Fogarty, *Contrasting Values in Western Europe: Unity, Diversity and Change*, London, 1986; S. Ashford and M. Timms, *What Europe Thinks: A study of Western Europe Values*, Aldershot, 1992; S. Ashford and M. Timms, *The Meaning of Work*, London, 1987.

7. See: *Bürgertum im 19. Jahrhundert: Deutschland im europäischen Vergleich*, ed. J. Kocka, 3 vols, Munich, 1988; H. Kaelble, 'Die oberen Schichten in Frankreich und der Bundesrepublik seit 1945', *Frankreich Jahrbuch* 4 (1991), pp. 63–78; P. Bourdieu, *Die feinen Unterschiede*, 3rd edn, Frankfurt am Main, 1984; C. Kleßmann, 'Relikte des Bildungsbürgertums in der DDR', in *Sozialgeschichte der DDR*, ed. H. Kaelble, J. Kocka and H. Zwahr, Stuttgart, 1994, pp. 254–70; H. Siegrist, 'Ende der Bürgerlichkeit? Die Kategorien "Bürgertum" und "Bürgerlichkeit" in der westdeutschen Gesellschaft und Geschichtswissenschaft der Nachkriegsperiode', *Geschichte und Gesellschaft* 20 (1994), pp. 549–83.

8. H. Mendras, *La seconde révolution française 1965–1984*, Paris, 1988; K. Tenfelde, 'Vom Ende und Erbe der Arbeiterkultur', in *Gesellschaftlicher Wandel, soziale Demokratie*, ed. S. Miller and M. Ristau, Berlin, 1988, pp. 155–72; J. Moser, *Arbeiterleben in Deutschland 1900–1970*, Frankfurt am Main, 1984; W. Kaschuba, *Kultur der Unterschichten im 19. und 20. Jahrhundert*, Munich, 1990; R. McKibbin, *The Ideologies of Class: Social Relations in Britain 1880–1950*, Oxford, 1990; J.D. Young, *Socialism and the English Working Class: A History of English Labour 1883–1930*, New York, 1990.

9. G. Crossick and H.G. Haupt, 'Introduction. Shopkeepers, Master Artisans and the Historian. The Petite Bourgeoisie in Comparative Focus', in *Shopkeepers and Master Artisans in 19th century Europe*, ed. G. Crossick and H.G. Haupt, London, 1984, pp. 3–31; see also G. Crossick and H.G. Haupt, *The Petite Bourgeoisie in Europe 1780–1914: Enterprise, Family and Independence*, London, 1995; H.A. Winkler, 'From social protectionism to national socialism: The German small business movement in comparative perspective', *Journal of Modern History* 48 (1976), pp. 1–18.

10. R. Huebscher, 'Déstruction de la paysannerie?', in *Histoire des français XIXe et XXe siècles*, vol. 2: *La société*, ed. Y. Lequin, Paris, 1983, pp. 483–530; W. Roesener, *Die Bauern in der europäischen Geschichte*, Munich, 1993; M. Gervais, *La fin de la France paysanne: de 1914 à nos jours*, Paris, 1987; A. Ilien and O. Jeggle, *Leben auf dem Dorf: Zur Sozialgeschichte des Dorfes und Sozialpsychologie seiner Bewohner*, Opladen, 1978; H. Mendras, *La fin des paysans*, Paris, 1984.

11. See Kaelble, *Auf dem Weg zu einer europäischen Gesellschaft*, p. 73ff; P. Flora, ed., *Growth to limits*, 5 vols, Berlin, New York, 1986ff; OECD, ed., *OECD: Social Expenditure 1968–1990*, Paris, 1985; important comparative studies, however, tend to emphasise the differences among the West European welfare states; see, for example, G. Esping-Andersen, *The Three Worlds of Capitalism*, Princeton, 1990; S. Leibfried, 'Sozialstaat Europa. Integrationsperspektiven europäischer Armutsregimes', *Nachrichtendienst des*

Deutschen Vereins für öffentliche und private Fürsorge 7 (1990), pp. 295–305; G.A. Ritter, *Der Sozialstaat: Entstehung und Entwicklung im internationalen Vergleich*, Munich, 1989.

12. See P. Bairoch, *De Jéricho à Mexico: Ville et économie dans l'histoire*, Paris, 1985; J.L. Pinol, *Le monde des villes auf XIX siècle*, Paris, 1991; P. Hohenberg and L.H. Lees, *The Making of Urban Europe, 1000–1950*, Cambridge, 1985; A. Lees, *Cities Perceived: Urban Society in European and American Thought, 1820–1940*, Manchester, 1985; U.N., *Growth of the World's Urban and Rural Population 1920–2000. Population Studies*, New York, 1969; the growth rates of urban populations (cities over 20,000) have been calculated according to Mitchell, *International Historical Statistics: Europe 1750–1988* (Europe); P. Flora, *Indikatoren der Modernisierung*, Opladen, 1975 (USA up to 1970 and Japan up to 1950); *Japan Statistical Yearbook* 1986, p. 28 (Japan 1970, 1980); *Statistical Abstracts of the United States* 1982/83, p. 21 (USA 1980).

13. V. de Grazia, *Paths to Mass Consumption: Historical Perspectives on European-American Consumer Cultures*, unpublished manuscript, 1993; V. de Grazia, 'Mass Culture and Sovereignty: the American Challenge to European Cinemas, 1920–1960', *Journal of Modern History* 61 (1989), pp. 53–87; V. de Grazia, 'The Arts of Purchase. How American Publicity Subverted the European Poster 1920–1940', in *Remaking of History (Discussions in Contemporary Culture 4)*, ed. B. Kruger and Ph. Mariani, Seattle, 1989, pp. 221–57; S. Lebergott, *Pursuing Happiness: American Consumers in the 20th Century*, Princeton, 1993; Cross, *Time and Money*, London, 1993; A.S. Deaton, 'The Structure of Demand 1920–1970', in *The Fontana Economic History of Europe*, vol. 5, ed. C. M. Cipolla, Glasgow, 1976, pp. 11–112; OECD, ed., *Living Conditions in OECD Countries: A Compendium of Social Indicators*, Paris, 1986; H. Kaelble, 'Europäische Besonderheiten des Massenkonsums, 1950–1990', in *Europäische Konsumgeschichte: Zur Gesellschaftsgeschichte des Konsums vom 18. bis zum 20. Jahrhundert*, ed. H. Kaelble, J. Kocka and H. Siegrist, Frankfurt am Main, 1997, pp. 169–203; U. Becher, *Geschichte des modernen Lebensstils*, Munich, 1990; W. Schievelbusch, *Das Paradies, der Geschmack und die Vernunft: Eine Geschichte der Genußmittel*, Frankfurt am Main, 1990; M. Wild, *Am Beginn der 'Konsumgesellschaft': Mangelerfahrung, Lebenshaltung und Wohlstandshoffnung in Westdeutschland in den 1950er Jahren*, Hamburg, 1993; A. Sywottek, 'The Americanization of Everyday Life? Early Trends in Consumer and Leisure-time Behavior', in *America and the Shaping of the German Society 1945–1955*, ed. Michael Ermarth, Providence, Oxford, 1993, pp. 132–52; K. Wagenleitner, *Cocacolaization and the World War*, Chapel Hill, 1994.

14. See e.g., E. Morin, *Europa denken*, Frankfurt am Main, 1991.

15. The social historical study of the advent of a European society also has its costs: in a comparison involving many countries it is difficult to devote proper attention to and explain individual intra-European differences. For this reason, apart from a comparison of many countries, I have also analysed the development and decrease of long- and short-term differences using a comparison of France and Germany.

16. For Western Europe (the OECD nations without Turkey), the variation coefficient for national differences in industrial employment remained relatively stable at a low level. In 1980 it was 11 percent, in 1985 12 percent, in 1990 13 percent, but for service sector employment it fell even further from 16 percent in 1980 to 11 percent in 1990 (calculated according to *Historical Statistics 1960–1990*, OECD, Paris 1992, pp. 40–41). In 1990, the variation coefficient for intra-European differences was 13 percent for industrial employment and 12 percent for service sector employment, and had thus further weakened or remained the same in comparison to 1980 (figures calculated

according to *Historical Statistics 1960–1990*, OECD, Paris 1992, pp. 35ff.; for the period up until 1980 see Table 9 in Kaelble, *Auf dem Weg zu einer europäischen Gesellschaft*). For more recent developments and for Eastern Europe, which is not treated below, see OECD, *Short-term Economic Statistics: Central and Eastern Europe*, Tables 5.3 and 5.4; International Labour Office, ed., *Economically Active Population*, vol. 5, Geneva, 1986, pp. 87ff.

17. The variation coefficient for all of Europe (without the Soviet Union) was 58 percent in 1930, 41 percent in 1950, and 23 percent in 1980, and thus fell substantially on the whole (calculated according to Kaelble, *Auf dem Weg zu einer europäischen Gesellschaft*, Table 9; S.P. Shoup, *The East European Data Handbook: Political, Social and Developmental Indicators, 1945–1975*, New York, 1981); for Western Europe see Kaelble, *Auf dem Weg zu einer europäischen Gesellschaft*, Table 9. Unfortunately, no comparable data is available as yet on the rate of urbanisation in Europe in 1990.

18. See Kaelble, *Auf dem Weg zu einer europäischen Gesellschaft*, pp. 108ff, 162f.; see also H. Kaelble, *Soziale Mobilität und Chancengleichheit im 19. und 20. Jahrhundert. Deutschland im internationalen Vergleich*, Göttingen, 1983, pp. 210ff. This difference did not increase again in the 1980s: the variation coefficient for the proportion of university students among twenty- to twenty-four-year-olds in Western Europe fell from 37 percent (1980) to 35 percent (1988). In the light of the diverse and changing definitions of universities such variations do not, however, prove much (calculated according to Mitchell, *International Historical Statistics: Europe 1750–1988*, p. 863). It should be emphasised once again that this decrease of the differences in the achievements of the educational system occurred without any noticeable growth in similarities between the institutions themselves. On the maintenance of these differences see U. Teichler, *Europäische Hochschulsysteme: Die Beharrlichkeit vielfältiger Modelle*, Frankfurt am Main, 1990; G. Schink, 'Auf dem Weg in eine europäische Gesellschaft', in *Die europäische Option: Eine interdisziplinäre Analyse über Herkunft, Stand und Perspektiven der europäischen Integration*, ed. A.v. Bogdandy, Baden-Baden, 1993, pp. 269–83. The differences between Western Europe as a whole and Eastern Europe as a whole, however, increased after the Second World War, because in Eastern Europe the proportion of students expanded very rapidly immediately after the Second World War and was curbed in the 1960s, whereas in Western Europe the expansion began later and remained steady, so that in 1989 a much higher proportion of young people were students in Western than in Eastern Europe.

19. Calculated according to OECD, *Historical Statistics 1960–1980*, OECD, Paris, 1982, pp. 14ff; OECD, *Historical Statistics 1960–1990*, Paris, 1992, pp. 18ff. (available private consumer income); Mitchell, *International Historical Statistics: Europe 1750–1988*, pp. 714ff., 744ff. (for the decreasing international differences for automobiles, telephones, and television sets).

20. In the European OECD countries (without Turkey), the proportion of industrial workers in the working population was 39 percent in 1960, 37 percent in 1980, and 32 percent in 1990. In the non–European OECD industrial nations the figures were 35 percent in 1960, 32 percent in 1980, and 28 percent in 1990. In the USA the figures were 35 percent in 1960, 31 percent in 1980, and 26 percent in 1990 (calculated according to OECD, *Historical Statistics 1960–1990*, p. 40).

21. On the reduction of the differences in welfare state benefits see Kaelble, *Auf dem Weg in eine europäische Gesellschaft*, pp. 119ff, 162f. (up to 1980). This reduction contin-

ued after 1980 as well. The variation coefficients for social expenditures as a proportion of national product fell from 38 percent in 1980 to 32 percent in 1989 (calculated according to OECD, *Historical Statistics 1960–1990*, p. 67; without Spain and Luxemburg because the OECD figures for 1989 are missing).

22. The variation coefficient of the proportion of university students in the cohort of the twenty- to twenty-four-year old in Western Europe was 33 percent in 1970, and rose to 37 percent in 1980, before falling to 35 percent in 1988, as mentioned above in note 18.

23. See the classic studies by K.W. Deutsch et al., *Political Community and the North Atlantic Area: International Organisations in the Light of Historical Experience*, Princeton, 1957; K.W. Deutsch et al., 'Integration and Arms Control in the European Political Development: A Summary Report', *American Political Science Review* 60 (1966), pp. 354–65; more recently: M. Espagne, 'Sur les limites du comparatisme en histoire culturelle', *Genèses* 17 (1994), pp. 112–21.

24. For figures on studying abroad see *Schätzungen nach der Preußischen Statistik*, vol. 236, 1913, pp. 132ff.; UNESCO, *Statistical Yearbook*, Paris, 1966, p. 483; Bundesministerium für Bildung und Wissenschaft, *Grund- und Strukturdaten 1991–92*, Bonn, quoted in: Felix Grigat, '"Publish in English or Perish"? oder: Durch sprachliche Vielfalt die Gewandheit des Denkens mehren', *Mitteilungen des Hochschulverbandes* 40 (1992), pp. 18f., 19; for foreign citizens living in the Federal Republic of Germany, see *Statistisches Jahrbuch der Bundesrepublik Deutschland*, 1987, p. 106; for hotel stays, see *Statistisches Jahrbuch der Bundesrepublik Deutschland*, 1953, p. 394; *Statistisches Jahrbuch der Bundesrepublik Deutschland*, 1991, p. 266 (only registered guests from other European countries). On marriages with other Europeans, see *Statistik der Bundesrepublik Deutschland*, vol. 175: *Die natürliche Bevölkerungsbewegung im Jahre 1955*, Wiesbaden, 1956, p. 13; *Bevölkerung und Wirtschaft, Fachserie 1, Reihe 2: Bevölkerungsbewegung*, Statistisches Bundesamt, Wiesbaden, 1980, p. 39; for knowledge of foreign languages and experiences in other countries, see H. Kaelble, *Nachbarn am Rhein*, Munich, 1991, pp. 58ff.; *Eurobarometer* 41 (1994), tables 27–30.

25. *Jahrbuch der öffentlichen Meinung der Bundesrepublik 1947–1955*, ed. E. Noelle and E.P. Neumann, 3rd edn, Allensbach, 1956, p. 49.

26. Ibid: only 26 percent of men and 22 percent of women in Germany had travelled abroad.

27. Commission of the European Communities, *Young Europeans in 1990*, Brussels, 1991, p. 58 (surveys conducted in 1987 and 1990 among young Europeans between the ages of 15 and 24 in the European Community).

28. Ibid., p. 58: 44 percent of young Europeans with eighteen or more years of education and training had spent three months or more abroad. M. Bach, *Die Bürokratisierung Europas: Verwaltungsstrukturen, Experten und politische Legitimation in Europa*, Frankfurt am Main, 1999.

29. See, for example, C. Millon-Delsol, *L'irréverence: Essai sur l'esprit européen*, Paris, 1993; R. Brague, *Europa: Eine exzentrische Identität*, Frankfurt am Main, 1993; E. Morin, *Europa denken*, Frankfurt am Main, 1991; R. Swedberg, 'The idea of "Europe" and the Origin of the European Union – A Sociological Approach', in *Zeitschrift für Soziologie* 23 (1994); pp. 378–87; for a historical account on a segment of this debate, see P.M. Lützeler, *Die Schriftsteller und Europa: Von der Romantik bis zur Gegenwart*, Munich, 1992; H. Kaelble, 'Europabewußtsein, Gesellschaft und Geschichte', in *Europa im Blick der Historiker. Europäische Integration im 20. Jahrhundert: Bewußtsein und*

Institutionen, ed. R. Hudemann, H. Kaelble and K. Schwabe, Munich, 1995, pp. 1–29; R. Girault, ed., *Identité et conscience européennes au XXe siècle*, Paris, 1994; on other aspects of the debate see: H. Schulze, *Die Wiederkehr Europas*, Berlin, 1990; J. Rovan and G. Krebs, eds, *Identités européennes et conscience européenne*, Paris, 1992; G. Schwan, 'Europa als Dritte Kraft', in *Europäisierung Europas*, ed. P. Haungs, Baden-Baden, 1989, pp. 13–40; F. Braudel, 'Zivilisation und Kultur. Die Herrlichkeit Europas', in F. Braudel, *Europa: Bausteine seiner Geschichte*, Frankfurt am Main, 1991; W. Lepenies, *Fall und Aufstieg der Intellektuellen in Europa*, Frankfurt am Main, 1992; E. Weede, 'Der Sonderweg des Westens', *Zeitschrift für Soziologie* 17 (1988), pp. 172–86; E. Weede, 'Ideen, Ideologie und politische Kultur des Westens', *Zeitschrift für Politik* 36 (1989), pp. 27–43; A. Minc, *La grande illusion*, Paris, 1989; H. Lübbe, *Abschied vom Superstaat: Vereinigte Staaten von Europa wird es nicht geben*, Berlin, 1994; R. Münch, *Das Projekt Europa: Zwischen Nationalstaat, regionaler Autonomie und Weltgesellschaft*, Frankfurt am Main, 1993; N. Dewandere and J. Lenoble, eds, *Projekt Europa: Personale Identität, Grundlage für eine europäische Demokratie*, Berlin, 1994; F.W. Scharpf, 'Die Politikverflechtungsfalle. Europäische Integration und deutscher Föderalismus im Vergleich', in *PVS* 26 (1985), pp. 323–56; M.R. Lepsius, 'Europa auf Stelzen. Die EG muß den Irrweg des Zentralstaates vermeiden', in *Die Zeit* no. 25, 16.6.1969; M.R. Lepsius, 'Die Europäische Gemeinschaft: Rationalitätskriterien der Regimebildung. Papier auf dem 25. deutschen Soziologentag', Frankfurt am Main, 1990; M.R. Lepsius, 'Nationalstaat oder Nationalitätenstaat als Modell für die Weiterentwicklung der Europäischen Gemeinschaft', in *Staatswerdung Europas? Optionen für eine Europäische Union*, ed. R. Wildenmann, Baden-Baden, 1991, pp. 19–40; R. Picht, 'Die Kulturmauer durchbrechen', *EA* 42 (1987), pp. 279–86; R. Picht, 'Europa im Wandel: zur soziologischen Analyse der kulturellen Realitäten in europäischen Ländern', *Integration* 15 (1992), pp. 216–24; J. Schmierer, *Die neue alte Welt oder wo Europas Mitte liegt*, Klagenfurt, 1993; J. Derrida, 'Kurs auf das andere Kap – Europas Identität', *Liber* 3 (1990), pp. 110–21; D. Grimm, 'Effektivität und Effektivierung des Subsidiaritätsprinzips', *Kritische Vierteljahrschrift für Gesetzgebung und Rechtswissenschaft* 77 (1994), pp. 6–12; D. Grimm, 'Mit einer Aufwertung des Europa-Parlaments ist es nicht getan – Das Demokratiedefizit der EG hat strukturelle Ursachen', in *Jahrbuch zur Staats- und Verwaltungswissenschaft* 6 (1992/93), pp.13–18.

30. See M. Mann, 'European Development: Approaching a Historical Explanation', in *Europe and the Rise of Capitalism*, ed. J. Baechler, J.H. Hall and M. Mann, Oxford, 1988, pp. 6–19; M. Mann, *Geschichte der Macht*, 4 vols, Frankfurt am Main, 1990; E. Jones, *The European Miracle*, Cambridge, 1981.

31. I have analysed this debate in a project supported by the Deutsche Forschungsgemeinschaft, using the accounts written by Europeans on their travels in the USA from the second half of the nineteenth century to the 1960s as my main sources. These travel accounts are full of ideas and observations comparing American society with European society as a whole. Kaelble, H. *Europäer über Europa: Die Entstehung des modernen europäischen Selbstverständnisses im 19. und 20. Jahrhundert*, Frankfurt am Main, New York, 2001.

32. K. Mann, 'Die Heimsuchung des europäischen Geistes', in *Plädoyers für Europa: Stellungnahmen deutschsprachiger Schriftsteller 1915–1949*, ed. P.M. Lützeler, Frankfurt am Main, 1987, pp. 298–318, 304f.

33. E. Morin, *Penser l'Europe*, Paris, 1987, p. 129.

Bibliography

Ambrosius, G. and Hubbard, W.H. *Sozial- und Wirtschaftsgeschichte Europas*. Munich, 1986.

Ashford, S. and Timms, M. *The Meaning of Work*. London, 1987.

—— *What Europe Thinks: A Study of Western Europe Values*. Aldershot, 1992.

Bach, M. *Die Bürokratisierung Europas: Verwaltungseliten, Experten und politische Legitimation in Europa*. Frankfurt am Main, 1999.

Bairoch, P. *De Jéricho à Mexico: Ville et économie dans l'histoire*. Paris, 1985.

Becher, U. *Geschichte des modernen Lebensstils*. Munich, 1990.

Bourdieu, P. *Die feinen Unterschiede*, 3rd edn. Frankfurt am Main, 1984.

Brague, R. *Europa: Eine exzentrische Identität*. Frankfurt am Main, 1993.

Braudel, F. 'Zivilisation und Kultur. Die Herrlichkeit Europas', in F. Braudel, *Europa: Bausteine seiner Geschichte*. Frankfurt am Main, 1991, pp. 149–73.

Bundesministerium für Bildung und Wissenschaft, *Grund- und Strukturdaten 1991–92*, Bonn.

Burguière, A. et al. *Histoire de la famille*, (2 vols) vol. 2. Paris, 1986.

Commission of the European Communities, ed. *Young Europeans in 1990*. Brussels, 1991.

Cross, G. *Time and Money: The Making of Consumer Culture*. London 1993.

Crossick, G. and Haupt, H.G. 'Introduction. Shopkeepers, Master Artisans and the Historian. The Petite Bourgeoisie in Comparative Focus', in *Shopkeepers and Master Artisans in 19th Century Europe*, ed. G. Crossick and H.G. Haupt. London, 1984, pp. 3–31.

—— *The Petite Bourgeoisie in Europe 1780–1914: Enterprise, Family and Independence*. London, 1995.

—— *Die Kleinbürger. Eine europäische Sozialgeschichte des 19. Jahrhunderts*. Munich, 1998.

Deaton, A.S. 'The Structure of Demand 1920–1970', in *The Fontana Economic History of Europe*, vol. 5, ed. C.M. Cipolla. Glasgow, 1976, pp. 11–112.

Derrida, J. 'Kurs auf das andere Kap – Europas Identität', *Liber* 3 (1990), pp. 110–21.

Deutsch, K.W. et al. *Political Community and the North Atlantic Area: International Organisations in the Light of Historical Experience*. Princeton, NJ, 1957.

—— 'Integration and Arms Control in the European Political Development. A Summary Report', *American Political Science Review* 60 (1966), pp. 354–65.

Dewandere, N. and Lenoble, J. (eds) *Projekt Europa: Personale Identität, Grundlage für eine europäische Demokratie*. Berlin, 1994.

Dijk, H. van. *De modernisering van Europa*. Utrecht, 1994.

Espagne, M. 'Sur les limites du comparatisme en histoire culturelle', *Genèses* 17 (1994), pp. 112–21.

Esping-Andersen, G. *The Three Worlds of Capitalism*. Princeton, NJ, 1990.

Eurobarometer 41 (1994).

Fischer, W. 'Wirtschaft und Gesellschaft Europas 1850–1914', in *Handbuch der europäischen Wirtschafts-und Sozialgeschichte*, ed. W. Fischer, vol. 5. Stuttgart, 1985, pp. 1–207.

—— 'Wirtschaft, Gesellschaft und Staat in Europa 1914–1980', in *Handbuch der europäischen Wirtschafts-und Sozialgeschichte*, ed. W. Fischer, vol. 6. Stuttgart, 1987, pp. 1–221.

Flora, P. *Indikatoren der Modernisierung*. Opladen, 1975.

—— (ed.). *Growth to Limits* (5 vols). Berlin, New York, NY, 1986.

Gervais, M. *La fin de la France paysanne: de 1914 à nos jours.* Paris, 1987.

Girault, R. *Identité et conscience européennes au XXe siècle,* ed. R. Girault. Paris, 1994.

Grazia, V. de. 'Mass Culture and Sovereignty: the American Challenge to European Cinemas, 1920–1960', *Journal of Modern History* 61 (1989), pp. 53–87.

—— 'The Arts of Purchase. How American Publicity Subverted the European Poster 1920–1940', in *Remaking of History (Discussions in Contemporary Culture 4),* ed. B. Kruger and Ph. Mariani. Seattle, WA, 1989, pp. 221–57.

—— *Paths to Mass Consumption: Historical Perspectives on European-American Consumer Cultures.* Unpublished manuscript, 1993.

Grigat, Felix, '"Publish in English or Perish"? oder: Durch sprachliche Vielfalt die Gewandheit des Denkens mehren', *Mitteilungen des Hochschulverbandes* 40 (1992), pp. 18f.

Grimm, D. 'Mit einer Aufwertung des Europa-Parlaments ist es nicht getan – Das Demokratiedefizit der EG hat strukturelle Ursachen', in *Jahrbuch zur Staats- und Verwaltungswissenschaft* 6 (1992/93), pp. 13–18.

—— 'Effektivität und Effektivierung des Subsidiaritätsprinzips', *Kritische Vierteljahrschrift für Gesetzgebung und Rechtswissenschaft* 77 (1994), pp. 6–12.

Hajnal, J. 'European Marriage Patterns in Perspective', in *Population in History,* ed. D.V. Glass and D.E.C. Eversley. London, 1965, pp. 483–530.

Harding, S., Phillips, D. and Fogarty, M. *Contrasting Values in Western Europe: Unity, Diversity and Change.* London, 1986.

Hohenberg, P. and Lees, L.H. *The Making of Urban Europe, 1000–1950.* Cambridge, MA, 1985.

Huebscher, R. 'Déstruction de la paysannerie?', in *Histoire des français XIXe et XXe siècles,* vol. 2: *La société,* ed. Y. Lequin. Paris, 1983, pp. 483–530.

Ilien, A. and Jeggle, O. *Leben auf dem Dorf: Zur Sozialgeschichte des Dorfes und Sozialpsychologie seiner Bewohner.* Opladen, 1978.

ILO Yearbook. Geneva, 1978.

ILO Yearbook. Geneva, 1987.

ILO Yearbook. Geneva, 1992.

Immerfall, S. *Einführung in den europäischen Gesellschaftsvergleich.* Passau, 1994.

International Labour Office (ed.). *Economically Active Population* (5 vols). Geneva, 1986

International Labour Office (ed.). *Economically Active Population,* vol. 5, Geneva, 1986.

Jones, E. *The European Miracle.* Cambridge: Cambridge University Press, 1981.

Kaelble, H. *Soziale Mobilität und Chancengleichheit im 19. und 20. Jahrhundert: Deutschland im internationalen Vergleich.* Göttingen, 1983.

—— *Auf dem Weg zu einer europäischen Gesellschaft.* Munich, 1987 (French translation 1988, English and Italian 1990, Japanese 1997).

—— 'Was Prometheus Most Unbound in Europe? The Labour Force in Europe during the late 19th and 20th Centuries', *Journal of European Economic History* 18 (1989), pp. 65–104.

—— 'Die oberen Schichten in Frankreich und der Bundesrepublik seit 1945', *Frankreich Jahrbuch* 4 (1991), pp. 63–78.

—— *Nachbarn am Rhein.* Munich, 1991.

—— 'Eine europäische Geschichte des Streiks', in *Von der Arbeiterbewegung zum modernen Sozialstaat: Festschrift für G. Ritter zum 65. Geburtstag,* ed. J. Kocka, H.J. Puhle and K. Tenfelde. Munich, 1994, pp. 44–70.

—— 'European Integration and Social History since 1950', in *Europe after Maastricht,* ed. P.M. Lützeler. Providence, Oxford, 1994, pp. 89–111.

—— 'L'Europe "vécue" and "pensée" au XXe Siècle: les spécificités sociales de L'Europe', in *Identité et conscience européennes au Xxe siècle,* ed. R. Girault. Paris, 1994, pp. 27–45.

—— 'Europabewußtsein, Gesellschaft und Geschichte', in *Europa im Blick der Historiker: Europäische Integration im 20. Jahrhundert. Bewußtsein und Institutionen*, ed. R. Hudemann, H. Kaelble and K. Schwabe. Munich, 1995, pp. 1–29.

—— 'Social History of European Integration', in *Western Europe and Germany: The Beginnings of European Integration 1945–1960*, ed. C. Wurm. Oxford, 1995, pp. 219–47.

—— 'Europäische Besonderheiten des Massenkonsums, 1950–1990', in *Europäische Konsumgeschichte: Zur Gesellschaftsgeschichte des Konsums vom 18. bis zum 20. Jahrhundert*, ed. H. Kaelble, J. Kocka and H. Siegrist. Frankfurt am Main, 1997, pp. 169–203.

—— 'La grande modernisation', in *Les Européens*, ed. H. Ahrweiler and M. Aynard. Paris, 2000, pp. 509–41.

—— *Europäer über Europa: Die Entstehung des modernen europäischen Selbstverständnisses im 19. und 20. Jahrhundert*. Frankfurt am Main, New York, NY, 2001.

Kaschuba, W. *Kultur der Unterschichten im 19. und 20. Jahrhundert*. Munich, 1990.

Kleßmann, C. 'Relikte des Bildungsbürgertums in der DDR', in *Sozialgeschichte der DDR*, ed. H. Kaelble, J. Kocka and H. Zwahr. Stuttgart, 1994, pp. 254–70.

Kocka, J. (ed.). *Bürgertum im 19. Jahrhundert: Deutschland im europäischen Vergleich* (3 vols). Munich, 1988.

Laslett, P. *Family Life and Illicit Love in Earlier Generations*. Cambridge, 1977.

—— 'Household and Family as Work Group and Kin Group: Areas of Traditional Europe Compared', in *Family forms in historic Europe*, ed. R. Wall, J. Robin and P. Laslett. Cambridge: Cambridge University Press, 1983, pp. 513–64.

—— 'The European family and early industrialisation', in *Europe and the Rise of Capitalism*, ed. J. Baechler. Oxford, 1988, pp. 234–41.

Lebergott, S. *Pursuing Happiness: American Consumers in the 20th Century*. Princeton, NJ, 1993.

Lees, A. *Cities Perceived: Urban Society in European and American Thought, 1820–1940*. Manchester, 1985.

Leibfried, S. 'Sozialstaat Europa. Integrationsperspektiven europäischer Armutsregimes', *Nachrichtendienst des Deutschen Vereins für öffentliche und private Fürsorge* 7 (1990), pp. 295–305.

Lepenies, W. *Fall und Aufstieg der Intellektuellen in Europa*. Frankfurt am Main, 1992.

Lepsius, M.R. 'Europa auf Stelzen. Die EG muß den Irrweg des Zentralstaates vermeiden', in *Die Zeit* no. 25, 16.6.1969.

—— 'Die Europäische Gemeinschaft: Rationalitätskriterien der Regimebildung. Papier auf dem 25. deutschen Soziologentag'. Frankfurt am Main, 1990.

—— 'Nationalstaat oder Nationalitätenstaat als Modell für die Weiterentwicklung der Europäischen Gemeinschaft', in *Staatswerdung Europas? Optionen für eine Europäische Union*, ed. R.Wildenmann. Baden-Baden, 1991, pp. 19–40.

Lübbe, H. *Abschied vom Superstaat: Vereinigte Staaten von Europa wird es nicht geben*. Berlin, 1994.

Lützeler, P.M. *Die Schriftsteller und Europa: Von der Romantik bis zur Gegenwart*. Munich, 1992.

Mann, K. 'Die Heimsuchung des europäischen Geistes', in *Plädoyers für Europa: Stellungnahmen deutschsprachiger Schriftsteller 1915–1949*, ed. P.M. Lützeler. Frankfurt am Main, 1987, pp. 298–318.

Mann, M. 'European Development: Approaching a Historical Explanation', in *Europe and the Rise of Capitalism*, ed. J. Baechler, J.H. Hall and M. Mann. Oxford, 1988, pp. 6–19.

—— *Geschichte der Macht* (4 vols). Frankfurt am Main, 1990.

McKibbin, R. *The Ideologies of Class: Social Relations in Britain 1880–1950*. Oxford, 1990.

Mendras, H. *La fin des paysans*. Paris, 1984.
—— *La seconde révolution française 1965–1984*. Paris, 1988.
Millon-Delsol, C. *L'irréverence: Essai sur l'esprit européen*. Paris, 1993.
Minc, A. *La grande illusion*. Paris, 1989.
Mitchell, B.R. *International Historical Statistics: Europe 1750–1988*, 3rd edn. Basingstoke, 1992.
Mitterauer, M. *Sozialgeschichte der Jugend*. Frankfurt am Main, 1986, pp. 28–43.
—— 'Europäische Familienentwicklung, Individualisierung und Ich-Identität', in *Europa im Blick der Historiker*, ed. R. Hudemann, H. Kaelble and K. Schwabe. Munich, 1995, pp. 91–97.
—— *Europa denken*. Frankfurt am Main, 1991.
Morin, E. *Penser l'Europe*. Paris, 1987.
Moser, J. *Arbeiterleben in Deutschland 1900–1970*. Frankfurt am Main, 1984.
Münch, R. *Das Projekt Europa: Zwischen Nationalstaat, regionaler Autonomie und Weltgesellschaft*. Frankfurt am Main, 1993.
Noelle, E. and Neumann, E.P. (eds) *Jahrbuch der öffentlichen Meinung der Bundesrepublik 1947–1955*, 3rd edn. Allensbach, 1956.
OECD (ed.). *OECD: Social Expenditure 1968–1990*. Paris, 1985.
—— *Living Conditions in OECD Countries: A Compendium of Social Indicators*. Paris, 1986.
—— *Historical Statistics 1960–1980*. Paris, 1982.
—— *Historical Statistics 1960–1990*. Paris, 1992.
—— *Short-term Economic Statistics: Central and Eastern Europe*. Paris, 1992.
Picht, R. 'Die "Kulturmauer durchbrechen"', in *Europa Archiv* 42 (1987), pp. 279–86.
—— 'Europa im Wandel: zur soziologischen Analyse der kulturellen Realitäten in europäischen Ländern', in *Integration* 15 (1992), pp. 216–24.
Pinol, J.L. *Le monde des villes au XIX siècle*. Paris, 1991.
Ritter, G.A. *Der Sozialstaat: Entstehung und Entwicklung im internationalen Vergleich*. Munich, 1989.
Roesener, W. *Die Bauern in der europäischen Geschichte*. Munich, 1993.
Rovan, J. and Krebs, G. (eds). *Identités européennes et conscience européenne*. Paris, 1992.
Schäfers, B. (ed.). *Lebensverhältnisse und sozialer Konflikt im neuen Europa*. Frankfurt am Main, 1993.
Scharpf, F.W. 'Die Politikverflechtungsfalle. Europäische Integration und deutscher Föderalismus im Vergleich', in *PVS* 26 (1985), pp. 323–56.
Schätzungen nach der Preußischen Statistik, vol. 236. 1913.
Schievelbusch, W. *Das Paradies, der Geschmack und die Vernunft. Eine Geschichte der Genußmittel*. Frankfurt am Main, 1990.
Schink, G. 'Auf dem Weg in eine europäische Gesellschaft', in *Die europäische Option: Eine interdisziplinäre Analyse über Herkunft, Stand und Perspektiven der europäischen Integration*, ed. A.v. Bogdandy. Baden-Baden, 1993, pp. 269–83.
Schmierer, J. *Die neue alte Welt oder wo Europas Mitte liegt*. Klagenfurt, 1993.
Schulze, H. *Die Wiederkehr Europas*. Berlin, 1990.
Schwan, R. 'Europa als Dritte Kraft', *Europäisierung Europas,* ed. P. Haungs. Baden-Baden, 1989, pp. 13–40.
Shoup, S.P. *The East European Data Handbook: Political, Social and Developmental Indicators, 1945–1975*. New York, NY, 1981.
Siegrist, H. 'Ende der Bürgerlichkeit? Die Kategorien "Bürgertum" und "Bürgerlichkeit" in der westdeutschen Gesellschaft und Geschichtswissenschaft der Nachkriegsperiode', *Geschichte und Gesellschaft* 20 (1994), pp. 549–83.
Statistical Abstract of the United States, 103rd edn, 1982/83.

Statistik der Bundesrepublik Deutschland, vol. 175: *Die natürliche Bevölkerungsbewegung im Jahre 1955*. Wiesbaden, 1956.

Statistisches Bundesamt. *Bevölkerung und Wirtschaft, Fachserie 1, Reihe 2: Bevölkerungsbewegung*. Wiesbaden, 1980.

Statistisches Jahrbuch der Bundesrepublik Deutschland, 1953.

Statistisches Jahrbuch der Bundesrepublik Deutschland, 1987.

Statistisches Jahrbuch der Bundesrepublik Deutschland, 1991.

Swedberg, R. 'The Idea of "Europe" and the origin of the European Union – A Sociological Approach', *Zeitschrift für Soziologie* 23 (1994), pp. 378–87.

Sywottek, A. 'The Americanization of Everyday Life? Early Trends in Consumer and Leisure-time Behavior', in *America and the Shaping of the German Society 1945–1955*, ed. Michael Ermarth. Providence, Oxford, 1993, pp. 132–52.

Teichler, U. *Europäische Hochschulsysteme: Die Beharrlichkeit vielfältiger Modelle*. Frankfurt am Main, 1990.

Tenfelde, K. 'Vom Ende und Erbe der Arbeiterkultur', in *Gesellschaftlicher Wandel, soziale Demokratie*, ed. S. Miller and M. Ristau. Berlin, 1988, pp. 155–72.

UN. *Growth of the World's Urban and Rural Population 1920–2000. Population Studies*. New York, NY, 1969.

UNESCO. *Statistical Yearbook*. Paris, 1966.

Wagenleitner, K. *Cocacolaization and the World War*. Chapel Hill, NC, 1994.

Weede, E. 'Der Sonderweg des Westens', *Zeitschrift für Soziologie* 17 (1988), pp. 172–86.

—— 'Ideen, Ideologie und politische Kultur des Westens', *Zeitschrift für Politik* 36 (1989), pp. 27–43.

Wild, M. *Am Beginn der 'Konsumgesellschaft'. Mangelerfahrung, Lebenshaltung und Wohlstandshoffnung in Westdeutschland in den 1950er Jahren*. Hamburg, 1993.

Winkler, H.A. 'From Social Protectionism to National Socialism: The German Small Business Movement in Comparative Perspective', *Journal of Modern History* 48 (1976), pp. 1–18.

Young, J.D. *Socialism and the English Working Class: A History of English Labour 1883–1930*. New York, NY, 1990.

NOTES ON THE CONTRIBUTORS

Ida Blom is a professor at the University of Bergen. Her main recent books are: *Gender as an Analytical Tool in Global History*, in Sølvi Sogner, ed., *Making Sense of Global History*, Oslo, 2001; editor and coauthor of *Gendered Nations: Nationalisms and Gender Order in the Long Nineteenth Century*, New York, 2000; coeditor with S. Sogner of *Med kjønnsperspektiv på norsk historie, fra vikingtid til 2000-årsskiftet*, Oslo, 1999.

Christophe Charle is a professor at the Sorbonne (Paris I), and director of the Institute of Early Modern and Contemporary History. His main recent books are: *La crise des sociétés impériales*, Paris, 2001; *Paris fin de siècle: Culture et politique*, Paris, 1998; *Les intellectuels en Europe au XIXe siècle, Essai d'histoire comparée*, Paris, 1996; *Histoire des universités*, Paris 1994; *La république des universitaires*, 1870–1940, Paris, 1994; editor of *Histoire sociale, histoire globale?* Paris, 1993; *Histoire sociale de la France au XIXe siècle*, Paris, 1991; *Naissance des 'intellectuels' 1880–1900*, Paris, 1990.

Geoffrey Crossick is a professor and Pro-Vice Chancellor at the University of Essex. His main recent books are: coeditor with S. Jaumain, *Cathedrals of Consumption. The European Department Store 1850–1939*, Aldershot, 1999; *The Artisan and the European Town 1500–1900*, Aldershot, 1997; with H.-G. Haupt, *The Petite Bourgeoisie in Europe 1780–1914: Enterprise, Family and Independence*, London, 1995.

Henk van Dijk is a professor at the Erasmus University, Rotterdam. His main recent book is: *De modernisering van Europa. Twee eeuwen maatschappelijke geschiedenis*, Utrecht, 1994.

Heinz-Gerhard Haupt is a professor at the University of Bielefeld. His main recent books are: coeditor with D. Dowe and D. Langewiesche, *Europa 1848. Revolution und Reform,* Bonn, 1998; together with M.G. Müller, S. Woolf (eds), *Regional and National Identities in 19th and 20th century Europe*, Leiden, 1997; coeditor with J. Kocka, *Geschichte und Vergleich. Ansätze und Chancen einer international vergleichenden Geschichtsschreibung*, Frankfurt, New York, 1996; together with G. Crossick, *The Petite Bourgeoisie in Europe 1780–1914*, London, New York, 1995; editor, *Orte des*

Alltags. Miniaturen einer europäischen Kulturgeschichte, Munich, 1994; coeditor with P. Marschalck, *Städtische Bevölkerungsentwicklung in Deutschland im 19. Jahrhundert. Soziale und demographische Aspekte der Urbanisierung*, St. Katharinen, 1994; *Histoire sociale de la France depuis 1789*, Paris. 1993.

Dick Geary is a professor at the University of Nottingham. His main recent books are: *Hitler and Nazism*, 2nd edn, London, 2000; *Aspects of German Labour*, Leicester, 1997; *European Labour Politics from 1900 to the Depression*, Basingstoke, 1991; *Labour and Socialist Movemnents in Europe before 1914*, Oxford, 1989.

Hartmut Kaelble is a professor at the Humboldt University, Berlin. His main recent books are: coeditor with J. Schriewer, *Vergleich und Transfer*, Frankfurt, 2002; *Europäer über Europa. Die Entstehung des modernen europäischen Selbstverständnisses im 19. und 20. Jahrhundert*, Frankfurt, 2001; *Wege der Demokratie. Von der Französischen Revolution zur Europäischen Union*, Munich, 2001; *Der historische Vergleich. Eine Einführung zum 19. und 20. Jahrhundert*, Frankfurt, 1999; coeditor with Y.S. Brenner and Mark Thomas, *Income Distribution in Historical Perspective*, Cambridge, 1991; *Nachbarn am Rhein. Entfremdung und Annäherung der französischen und deutschen Gesellschaft seit 1880*, Munich, 1991; *Auf dem Weg zu einer europäischen Gesellschaft: Eine Sozialgeschichte Westeuropas, 1880–1980*, Munich, 1987 (English version: *A Social History of Western Europe, 1880–1980*, Dublin, Savage (USA), 1990).

Jürgen Kocka is a professor of modern history at the Free University of Berlin, and president of the Wissenschaftszentrum Berlin. His main recent books are: coeditor with C. Conrad, *Staatsbürgerschaft in Europa*, Hamburg, 2001; coeditor with C. Offe, *Geschichte und Zukunft der Arbeit*, Frankfurt, New York, 2000; coeditor with M. Hildermeier, *Europäische Zivilgesellschaft in Ost und West. Begriff, Geschichte, Chancen*, Frankfurt, 2000; *Industrial Culture and Bourgeois Society: Business Labour, and Bureaucracy in Modern Germany*, New York, Oxford, 1999; *Vereinigungskrise: Zur Geschichte der Gegenwart*, Göttingen, 1995; coeditor with Allan Mitchell, *Bourgeois Society in Nineteenth-Century France*, Oxford, Washington, 1993; editor, *Historische DDR-Forschung*, Berlin, 1993; coeditor with H. Kaelble and H. Zwahr, *Sozialgeschichte der DDR*, Stuttgart, 1994; editor, *Sozialgeschichte im internationalen Überblick*, Darmstadt, 1989.

Maria Malatesta is a professor at the University of Bologna, Italy. Her recent books are: *Il Resto del carlino: Potere politico ed economico a Bologna dal 1885 al 1922*, Milan, 2000; with S. Bellassai, *Genere e mascolinità nella storiografia moderna e contemporanea*, Bulzoni, Rome, 2000; *Le aristocrazie terriere nell'Europa contemporanea*, Rome-Bari, 1999; editor, *I professionisti*, Torino, 1996; editor, *Society and the Professions in Italy, 1860–1914*, Cambridge, 1995; *I signori della terra. L'organizzazione degli interessi agrari padani 1860–1914*, Milan, 1989.

Michael Mitterauer is a professor at the University of Vienna. His main recent books are: *Dimensionen des Heiligen: Annäherungen eines Historikers*, Vienna, 2000; *Die Entwicklung Europas – ein Sonderweg? Legitimationsideologien und die Diskussion der Wissenschaft*, Vienna, 1999; *Millennien und andere Jubeljahre. Warum feiern wir Geschichte?* Vienna, 1998; editor, *Familie im 20. Jahrhundert: Traditionen, Probleme, Perspektiven*, Frankfurt, 1997; *Familie und Arbeitsteilung. Historisch-vergleichende Studien*, Cologne, 1992; *Sozialgeschichte der Jugend*, 3rd edn, Frankfurt, 1992; *Vom Patriarchat zur Partnerschaft. Zum Strukturwandel der Familie*, 4th edn, Munich, 1991; *Historisch-anthropologische Familienforschung: Fragestellungen und Zugangsweisen*, Vienna, 1990.

Hannes Siegrist is a professor at the University of Leipzig. His main recent books are: *Advokat, Bürger und Staat. Sozialgeschichte der Rechtsanwälte in Deutschland, Italien und der Schweiz (18.–20. Jh.)*, 2 vols, Frankfurt, 1996; editor, *Bürgerliche Berufe*, Göttingen, 1988; coeditor with Charles. E. McClelland and Stephan Merls, *Professionen im modernen Osteuropa/Professions in Modern Eastern Europe*, Berlin, 1995; together with Etienne François and Jakob Vogel, eds, *Nation und Emotion. Deutschland und Frankreich im Vergleich. 19. und 20. Jahrhundert*, Göttingen, 1995; coeditor with David Sugarman, *Eigentum im internationalen Vergleich (18.–20. Jahrhundert)*, Göttingen, 1999.

Shulamit Volkov is a professor of modern history and incumbant of the Konrad-Adenauer-Chair for Comparative European History at Tel Aviv University, Israel. His main recent books are: *Das Jüdische Projekt der Moderne*, Munich, 2001; *Antisemitismus als kultureller Code*, 2nd edn, Munich, 2000; *Die Juden in Deutschland 1780–1918*, 2nd edn, Munich, 2000, editor, *Deutsche Juden und die Moderne*, Munich, 1994.

INDEX

Aachen 126
absolutism 17, 207
academic proletariat 193
acculturation 237
Africa 144, 207
agnosticism 10, 263f, 268f
agriculture 19, 28, 44, 46f, 49, 53, 55,
     58–61, 173, 254, 264, 266, 280, 291
agrarian association 58–61
agrarian crisis 46, 49–51, 55, 57
agrarian sociability 58
agricultural labour force 121, 291
agricultural parties 61
agricultural sector 122, 280, 284, 291
Albania 144, 291
Aleichem, Shoylem 243
Alpine regions 52, 143
America (US) 2f, 44f, 53, 70–72, 123,
     165–69, 169, 187, 194, 208, 238, 240,
     253, 261, 266f, 279–81, 286–88, 293f,
     299f, 303f
Americanisation 167
Amsterdam 239
ancien régime 17, 20f, 79
anthropology 144, 164
anti-Semitism 77, 232, 241
Antwerp 266
apprentices 97, 142, 147, 171
aristocracy 6, 17f, 20–22, 25, 27, 29f, 32f,
     44–61, 71, 81, 91, 103, 177, 194, 210,
     255, 281f, 295
aristocratic culture 32
aristocratic identity 6f, 45, 55, 58–61
Aristotle 109
Armenia 146
Arons, Leo 198
Asia 9, 205–7, 214–20, 257
assimilation 228, 264
association 18, 26, 29, 32, 54, 60, 58, 77,
     92f, 98, 100, 102, 116, 120, 124, 198,
     241, 265, 283
Australia 128, 287

Austria 46, 104, 21, 23, 120, 77, 167, 175,
     187–89, 192, 236, 261f, 265, 291, 303
Austria-Hungary 116, 121 124, 126, 188
Ataturk, Mustafa Kemal 257
Auerbach, Berthold 242
autonomy 74, 229
avant-garde 188, 192, 195–97

Baden 262
Baden-Württemberg 175
Balkans 144, 146, 260
Baltic Countries 25
banks 54f, 265
Barcelona 7, 116
Barrès, Maurice 194
Basque Provinces 121
Bavaria 21, 23, 77, 217, 263
Beauvoir, Simone de 303
Belgium 20, 23, 47, 52, 54f, 59, 90f, 101f,
     104–6, 108, 126, 170f, 174, 187, 258,
     260–63, 265f, 268f, 291, 300, 303
Benelux countries 279
Benson, John 173
Bergen 259
Berlin 31, 92, 116, 121, 170, 191, 193,
     198, 234–36, 239, 241, 266
Bielefeld 123
bien nationaux 50, 52
Bildungsbürgertum 6, 16, 22, 24f, 30
Birmingham 107, 191
Bismarck, Otto von 128, 193, 262
Blackbourn, David 100
blue-collar sector 33, 123
Boer War 197
Bohemia 21, 54, 121
Bolshevik/Russian Revolution 25, 116
Booth, Charles 102
Bordeaux 173, 228, 236
borghesia 15, 24
Boucicaut, Aristide 170
Bourdieu, Pierre 163
bourgeois class 91

bourgeoisie 15, 20, 34, 45, 48, 50f, 53, 56–58, 124, 168, 177, 227, 230, 236, 265, 284
bourgeoisie culture *see* middle-class culture
bourgeois elite 25, 29
Brants, Victor 109
Bratislava 230
Braudel, Fernand 162, 165
Bremen 103
Breuilly, John 117
Bromme, William 128
Bryce, James 303
Buber, Martin 243
Buddhism 257
Bürgertum 15f, 19, 31
Bulgaria 49, 258
bureaucratisation 34, 70, 72, 278
businessmen 16, 22, 24, 30, 51, 54, 75, 107

Calvinism 256, 260, 264
Canada 194, 280f, 287
capital 24, 49, 101, 105, 108, 117, 162
  symbolic 44, 60
capitalism 19, 27f, 33, 212
Cardiff 191
Catalonia 119, 121
Catholicism 108f, 260f, 266f
Catholic area 10, 199, 258–60, 263f
Catholic Church (Roman) 59, 254, 256, 260, 262, 262f, 265–69
Catholic minority 260
Catholics (Roman) 109, 126, 261, 267f
Caucasus 145
census 90, 92, 95, 122, 171, 188f
Charle, Christophe 162
Chartism 107, 116f, 120, 263
Chassidism 229f
Chemnitz 121
China 144f
Christianity 146f, 256f, 259, 262, 264, 268
Cisleithania 190, 192
city 7, 10, 15f, 18f, 20f, 23, 26–28, 30, 48, 54f, 56, 71, 75, 92f, 95, 98, 100f, 105, 108, 142, 168–173, 192, 262, 265, 269, 280, 283–87, 293, 301, 304. *See also* urban area
civil service 24, 71, 76, 188
civil society 17
class identity 116, 120, 125, 127f, 218
Cologne 126

communism 34
comparative analysis/studies/research 90–93, 106, 110, 70f, 73, 161, 166f, 176, 213, 219, 278
comparative gender history 205, 220
comparison 4, 6, 19, 21, 50, 70, 73, 90f, 99–102, 110, 141, 166, 187, 194, 206, 214–16, 303
Confino, Michael 45
Confucianism 257
consumption 8, 10, 161–76, 277, 280, 288, 305
corporation 19, 26, 68, 91, 101, 104f, 172, 284. *See also* guilds
Counter–Reformation 258, 260
countryside 19–21, 28, 47, 50, 53, 56, 59, 75, 142, 173, 254, 265f, 268, 280
Coventry 117
Crimean War 27
Crouch, Colin 3
culture 5, 10, 21, 31, 48, 56, 68, 73, 81, 218–20, 239, 288, 304
cultural capital 59, 18
cultural products 187, 189, 243
Czech Republic 24, 175, 291f, 303

Darwinism 264
democracy 5, 33, 194f, 196f, 207, 210, 212, 293, 297
democratisation 31, 33, 72, 259f, 305
Denmark 46, 116, 205, 210, 259, 261, 266
Dessau 235
Diaspora 226, 233
difference strategy 211, 215, 217
discourse 15, 70, 73, 75, 77, 97, 109, 194, 212, 229, 236
divorce 145, 150
Dollfuß, Engelbert 262
Dresden 116, 121, 168, 193
Dreyfus affair 186, 195f, 198
Dubnov 232
Durkheim, Emile 163

economic crisis 94
economic cycle 56, 59
economic logic 45, 54
economic policy 59f
education 18, 23f, 27, 29–31, 34, 60, 70, 72f, 79, 95, 97, 101, 211, 187, 196, 238f, 254, 259, 264, 268, 283, 288, 293f, 297, 301
Edwardian England 32

Eichel, Isaac 235
Elbe 21
elites 6, 9, 20, 24f, 27, 30f, 48, 68, 81, 102,
    194–96, 198f, 263, 297
  alternative elite 195
  composite elite 32f
  elite formation 44
  landed elite 28, 44f, 47–49, 52f, 55f, 58,
    60
  local elites 69, 82, 92, 254, 287
  national elites 69, 82
  professional elite 73
  rural elites 20
  scientific elite 69
  urban elites 20, 28, 47
Emilia Romagna 172
Engel, Ernst 167
Engels, Friedrich 162, 263
England (Great Britain) 2, 4, 16, 20–23,
    27f, 31, 33, 47–50, 52, 54–57, 59, 70f,
    76, 81, 90f, 99, 101–8, 116–20, 124–26,
    143, 164, 166, 170, 173–75, 188–94,
    196f, 214, 217, 127, 240, 244, 255, 258,
    260f, 263, 266, 268f, 254, 278f, 283,
    286, 291f, 295, 299f, 303
Enlightenment 27, 35, 229, 234, 239, 303
enterprise 89f, 92, 94–98, 100, 103, 105–9,
    278, 301
entrepreneual strategy 52f, 171
equal rights strategy 212, 216
Essen 125
estates 22, 46, 49–55, 57, 73, 108f, 145,
    163
Ethiopia 146
ethnicity 19, 81, 127f, 208, 267
ethnic distinctiveness 48
Ettinger, Jakob 240
Europe
Central Europe 6f, 10, 15, 19, 21, 23–25,
    27, 29f, 33, 50, 70–72, 77, 143, 188,
    190, 192, 197, 227, 236, 277
Eastern Europe 6f, 9, 16, 19, 21, 24f, 27,
    33, 45–49, 53f, 61, 77, 121, 144f, 167,
    187, 192, 227–30, 232, 237f, 240, 242f,
    260, 277f, 281f, 285, 288f, 291f, 298
East Central Europe 25, 29, 147, 174, 295,
    298, 300, 302
Northern Europe 27, 52, 57, 143, 148f,
    174, 187, 219, 296
Southern Europe 46, 51, 53, 72, 148f,
    165f, 173f, 187, 219, 279, 292, 296
West Central Europe 234, 227, 236

Western Europe 2, 6f, 9, 16, 19, 21, 23–25,
    33, 45, 49, 52f, 61, 70, 161, 164f, 174,
    187, 190, 192, 227, 229, 236, 254, 268,
    277, 279, 281f, 285f, 288f, 293–96, 298,
    302
Europeanisation 306
European commonalities 144, 277f, 282,
    290, 298, 305
  exchange 294–98, 302, 305
  society 277, 303, 306
  Union 3, 82, 277, 293, 296–98, 301f,
    306

Fabians 197
family 7, 10, 18, 21–23, 26, 29f, 35, 57f,
    95–97, 99f, 108f, 140–52, 161, 163f,
    167f, 211, 219, 221, 255, 266, 277–81,
    283–85, 301, 304
farming milieux 281, 284
fascism 33
feminism 205–21, 207
  feminist strategy 216
feudalism 26
  defeudalisation 27, 44, 48–50
  feudal rights 52, 55
  feudalisation 31f
fideicommissum 57
financial crisis 51
financial sector 55f
fin de siècle 32
Finland 25, 46, 116, 208, 218, 292
Foucault, Michel 78
Fourth Republic 167
France 2, 4, 20–23, 28, 31, 46f, 49, 50–53,
    55f, 59, 70–72, 77, 80f, 90f, 99, 101–9,
    115–21, 123, 125–27, 143, 162, 165,
    170, 173–176, 187–92, 194f, 197–99,
    228, 237, 240f, 258f, 263–66, 268–70,
    295, 300, 303
Frankel, Jonathan 233
Frankfurt (Main) 231, 242
Frankfurt School 128
Fransoz, Karl Emil 242
Frederick II. 80
Frontier (USA) 45
Franché-Comté 53

Galicia 21, 227, 229f, 237, 239f
GDR (Eastern Germany) 292, 300
gender 9, 19, 35, 127f, 140, 147, 152, 167,
    172, 205f, 211f, 214, 216f, 220f
  identity 217f

generation 23, 49, 57, 151f, 146, 165, 196, 231, 267, 278f
Genoa 121, 266
German speaking countries 79, 191, 279
Germany 2, 4, 7, 9f, 16, 23f, 28–31, 46f, 51f, 55, 57, 59f, 70–72, 81, 91, 96, 100–5, 108, 115–26, 161, 170, 174–76, 188–91, 193f, 197–99, 228f, 231f, 234–37, 240f, 243, 256, 258, 260f, 265f, 269, 283f, 286, 291f, 295, 298, 303
Ghandi, Mahatma 215
Ginzburg, Marek 243
globalisation 82
Goethe, Johann Wolfgang von 198
Gordon, Yudah-Leib (Yalag) 236
Great Depression 48, 55, 59, 96
Greece 24, 167, 258, 280, 285, 298
Grundtvig, Nikolaj Frederik Severin 259
guilds 19, 26–28, 76, 99, 101f, 104, 147, 284. See also corporations
Guipozcoa 119
Ha'Am, Ahad 232
Habermas, Jürgen 229
Habsburg Empire/Monarchy 24, 71, 80f, 258
Halbwachs, Maurice 163, 168
Halifax 117
Hamburg 21, 80, 103, 192, 230, 239, 266
Hanagan, Michael 117
Hauge, Hans Nielsen 259
Haupt, Heinz-Gerhard 90, 94
Heilbronn 175
Heine, Heinrich 242f
Hermann, Georg 242
Hessen-Kassel 21
Hideko, Fukuda 215f
Hinduism 214, 219
historcism 242
Hitler, Adolf 4
Hobsbawm, Eric 161, 208
Hofmannsthal, Hugo von 303
Holocaust 244
Hubscher, Ronald 171
Huddersfield 117
Hugo, Victor 186
Hungary 48, 120, 188, 192, 230, 303

identity
 legal 29
 middle-class 32, 34
 multiple 128
 national 92, 73, 205f, 208, 212, 216–18

political 119f
 social 17, 96, 278, 302
 working-class 118f, 121, 128
independence 7, 18, 28, 34, 48, 74, 93–96, 98, 100, 108, 146
India 9, 145, 206f, 209, 214–17, 219f
industrialisation 5, 24, 28f, 46f, 51, 53–56, 59, 89, 116, 120f, 140, 142, 148f, 152, 162, 173, 219, 228, 254f, 261, 263, 268, 280, 290f, 305
industrialists 30f, 50f, 58, 117
industry 10, 59, 61, 96, 28, 75f, 115, 122–24, 162, 280, 301
 automobile 117, 122
 engineering 117, 122f
 industrial sector 54f
 leisure 124
 textile/clothing/woollen 6f, 45, 55, 58–61, 117
inheritance 7, 20, 56f, 147, 206
intellectual professions 187–99
intelligentsia 25, 193, 195f, 242
interconnections 294f, 297f, 302, 305f
investments 50f, 54–57, 59, 100
Ireland 46, 48, 125f, 167, 259, 262, 266f, 269
Islam 219, 257
Israel 226, 237
Italy 20f, 24, 29, 46–57, 59f, 71, 77, 80f, 116f, 125, 167, 172, 176, 188f, 194, 199, 258, 266, 291f, 298, 303

Jackson Turner, Fredereck 45
James, Henry 44
Japan 9, 49, 53, 55, 206f, 209, 214–17, 219f, 253, 278–80, 281, 286f, 294
Jerusalem 226
Jevons, William St. 163
Jewry 9, 226–244, 267
 culture 243
 identity 226f, 233
 religion 146, 230
Jews 48, 24, 77, 198, 226, 244, 267f
Joyce, Patrick 117
Judaism 230–32, 234–36, 238, 241–43, 257, 264

Kaelble, Hartmut 161, 166
Karlsruhe 23
Kautsky, Karl 124
Kleinbürgertum 16
Kocka, Jürgen 17, 91, 108f

Konigsberg 235
Koselleck, Reinhard 141
Krog, Gina 217f
Kuisel, Robert 167
Kulturkampf 262, 264
Kulturkritik 32

labour movement 34, 116, 124, 283
Labrousse, Ernest 162
Laichlingen 169
Lancashire 117, 125
land management 53
landownership 21, 45f, 49, 59
Lang, Ferdinand 175
language 15, 58, 91, 93, 109, 116, 140,
    207, 214, 235, 238, 242, 296f, 306
Languedoc 121
Lassalle, Ferdinand 128
Latin countries 49f, 79
Leeds 191
Le Havre 266
Leipzig 116, 121, 193
Lenin, Vladimir Ilych 124
Leo XIII 264
Léon, Pierre 161
Le Play, Frédéric 163, 168
Lequin, Yves 162
Levy-Leboyer, Maurice 173
liberalism 24, 29, 31, 102f, 107, 109, 125,
    197, 233, 260f, 282, 284
Liebknecht, Wilhelm 128, 303
life-cycle 94, 141
lineage 56, 56
Lithuania 235
Liverpool 191, 266
Lombardy 54, 172
London 28, 31, 92, 97f, 102, 107, 128,
    170, 193, 236, 238, 240, 266
lower class 16, 27, 194, 255, 264, 282
Lublin 239
Lutheran religion 219
Lyon 30, 90, 96, 266

MacKay, Thomas 109
Madrid 56, 168
Maimon, Salomon 235
Manchester 191
Mann, Klaus 304
Mannheim 23
manufacturing sector 54
Marseille 126, 266
Marxism 17, 22, 89, 118, 232, 264

Marx, Karl 22, 116, 128, 162f
mass society 56, 165, 288f
Masurian 126
Mazamet 125
McKibbin, Ross 124
Medick, Hans 169
Meiji Revolution 207
men 16, 122f, 147, 167, 169, 171, 205–21,
    242
Mendelssohn, Moses 234f
Mendras, Henri 3
Metz 228, 239
Meyer, Carl 163
middle-class 6, 15–35, 49, 61, 74, 79, 94,
    169, 175, 217, 227, 237, 255, 259, 263f,
    281f
middle-class culture 7, 18f, 21–29, 31–35,
    75, 80
migration 92, 266, 268, 294f
Milano 51, 55, 117, 121
Mill, John Stuart 22
mines 27, 54, 120, 148, 268
Mirabeau, Honoré Gabriel 80
Mittelstand 91, 108f
modernisation 34, 53, 68, 73, 121f,
    140–42, 148f, 152, 162, 228, 230, 232f,
    262, 264f, 290, 303, 306
modern state 5, 68, 73
Moltke, Helmuth General von 128
Mombert, Paul 164
Mommsen, Theodor 198
Montebello, Fabrizio 169
Montenegro 141
Morin, Edgar 304
Moscow 25
Moss, Bernhard 117
Munich 193

Naples 71, 80
Napoleon 20, 30, 57f, 71, 209, 261, 266
nation 6, 9, 19, 61, 70f, 73, 81, 128, 140,
    151, 211, 254
nationalism 19, 59, 24f, 32, 68, 70, 82,
    105, 126, 205–21, 207, 231f, 234, 243
national minority 171
nation state 4, 29, 80, 90–92, 110, 121,
    128, 174, 208, 212, 221, 266, 268f
nation/state building 28, 128, 205, 209f,
    213, 216, 221
neighbourhood sociability 95, 98
Netherlands 10, 20, 47, 126, 164, 174, 256,
    258, 260–66, 269, 280, 291f, 300, 303

New York 231, 239
Newcastle 191
Nicaud, Gérard 167
Niort 107
nobility *see* aristocracy
Nordic countries 46. *See also* Europe,
    Nothern
Normandy 54
Norway 9, 25, 46, 116, 174, 205–7,
    209–213, 215–17, 259, 280, 292
notables 20, 22, 28, 31

Odessa 231, 237, 239
OECD 293, 297
Offermann, Toni 117
Oppenheimer, Moritz 243
Orient 144–146

Palermo 192
Paris 30, 52, 90, 92, 105, 107, 116, 122,
    170, 176, 192, 228, 238, 240, 266
Parsons, Talcott 256
Pas-de-Calais 118, 171
patriotism 127
peasants 6, 16, 20f, 46, 48f, 52f, 60, 95,
    143, 147, 266
Peretz, Y.L. 243
Perkin, Harold 22
Perrot, Marguerite 169
Perrot, Michelle 118
Peter the Great 260
petite bourgeoisie 7, 16, 25, 31, 89–110,
    282, 284
    culture 7, 99f, 284
Philippson, Ludwig 240
Pirmasens 122
Poland 24, 48, 126f, 229, 231, 259, 262,
    268, 303
political culture 287
political impetus 293
political party 61, 105f, 115, 124, 213,
    265, 269
popular culture 119, 124
Portugal 47, 51, 167, 262, 285, 291f, 297,
    300
Prague 121, 175, 236, 289
pressure groups 60f
profession 6–8, 28, 59, 68–82, 194, 233
    professional class 196
    professionalisation 7, 30, 59, 72f, 78,
    190, 255

professional/occupational culture 68–70,
    74, 76–79
professional/occupational identity 73
professionals 7, 16, 23, 29f, 32, 50f, 68,
    75f, 95
proletarian milieu 282f
property 21, 33, 34, 44, 49f, 55f, 73, 59,
    90, 99f, 105, 107, 109, 266
protectionism 77
Protestantism 253, 260, 263, 265
    areas10, 147, 199, 258–60, 264, 267f
Protestants 71, 73, 126
Proudhon, Pierre Joseph 100
Prussia 21, 23, 46f, 49–52, 60, 71, 77, 80,
    235, 239, 241, 261f, 266, 268
Pulkkhinen, Tuija 218

radicalism 30, 98, 104f, 118, 237
railways 54, 228
Rathenau, Walther 301
real estate 22, 54, 56
Reformation 258, 260f
religion 9, 17, 19, 26, 29, 34, 126f,
    145–47, 199, 229, 235–69
rent 51, 54–56
rentiers 16, 18, 22, 26, 28, 34, 54
Renzsch, Wolfgang 117
republicanism 104, 108, 284
Restoration 51
Revel, Jaques 164
rhetoric 79f, 261
Rhine 20f
Rhineland 21, 28, 71, 261
Roche, Daniel 176
Romania 49, 187, 241
Romanticism 263
Rome 170
Rotterdam 266
Rousseau, Jean Jacques 211
Royle, Edward 263
Ruhr 118, 120–23, 126f, 266, 268
rural class 50
ruralisation 55–57
Russia (*also* Soviet Union) 21f, 25, 27, 49,
    53, 71, 80, 116, 121, 124, 187–89,
    192–95, 227, 232f, 235–37, 239–41,
    243f, 256, 258, 280, 286f

Sandgruber, Roman 167
Sardinia 168
Satha, Salvadore 168
Saxony 21, 54, 120, 122

Scandinavia 209, 214f, 218f, 256, 258f, 262, 277, 279, 286, 292. *See also* Europe, Nothern
Schaffhausen 123
Scholem, Gershom 238
Scotland 127, 192, 256
secularisation 236, 256f, 262, 269, 278
Segalen, Martin 168
Serbia 144
serfs 53
service sector 165, 280
Sheffield 191
Sicily 49
Siegfried, André 303
Silesia 30, 54
Slovakia 24
Smiles, No Samuel 117
social differences 290, 293, 298
social distinction 44f
social history 1–11, 70, 91, 110, 164
social milieux 95, 97, 281, 288, 305
social mobility 45, 48f, 50, 94f, 229, 284, 304
social policy 59, 264, 290, 293, 305
socialisation 120, 148–50, 206
socialism 30, 98, 101, 105, 118f, 231f, 234, 264
Sombart, Werner 303
Spahn, Martin 198
Spain 46, 47, 49–56, 58 119, 121, 125, 167, 187, 192, 194, 219, 239, 242, 258, 262, 291, 298, 300, 303
Stand 91, 108f, 17
state 59, 70f, 75–77, 81, 91, 93, 100f, 103–105, 108, 110, 119, 186, 194, 196, 198f, 253
Stearns, Peter N. 2
St Etienne 104, 119, 170
St Petersburg 7, 25, 32, 146, 236, 266
Strasbourg 192, 228, 239
strike 30, 60, 95, 115f, 118, 127f, 304
Stuttgart 123
suffrage 105, 209f, 213
Sweden 9, 20, 46, 116, 174, 206f, 209–15, 217, 259, 286
Switzerland 10, 20, 27, 71f, 256, 258, 260–62, 265, 269, 277, 286, 291, 303
syndicalism 119

Taine, Hippolyte Adolphe 194
Tarnopol 237
taxation 93, 105, 110

Tenfelde, Klaus 174
Therborn, Göran 3
Thomson, F.M.L. 162
Tilly, Charles 172
Tocqueville, Alexis de 303
Todd, Emmanuel 255
Torlonia of Rome 52
Toynbee, Arnold 303
trade union 115f, 120f, 124, 283
transfers 4, 8, 49, 56, 70, 151, 166
Treitschke, Heinrich von 198
Trieste 146
Tsarist Russia 81, 118, 124, 231, 280
Turin 121, 170
Turkey 174, 257, 260, 296
Tuscany 172

university 23, 29, 69, 71f, 81, 188, 195f, 198, 297
upper class 10, 45, 51, 142, 164, 210, 264, 299
urbanisation 7, 29, 48, 54, 56, 116, 148, 170, 173, 227f, 254f, 261, 263, 265f, 268f, 277, 286, 286f, 292f, 305. *See also* city
urban class 56
urban neighbourhood 97
USA *see* America

Valencia 51f
Venetia 51
Vesuvius 80
Vetterli, Rudolf 123
Vienna 116, 121, 128, 170, 175, 191f, 236f, 266
Vilnius 236f, 239
violence 60, 116
Vogtland 122
Voltaire, Francois Marie Arouet 186
Vormärz 30

wage-labour 94, 96, 116f, 129, 148
Wales 128
Walras, Léon 163
Warsaw 71
Wassermann, Jacob 242
wealth 20, 24, 27f, 30, 32, 44, 55, 100
Webb, Sidney 197
Weber, Max 17, 162f, 258, 303
Wehler, Hans-Ulrich 161
welfare state 10, 30, 33, 219, 277, 281, 283, 285f, 288, 304f

West Germany 296f
Westphalia 266
white-collar workers 16, 33, 123
    employment 95, 101
Wilhelm II. 128
Wilhelmine Germany 32, 124
Wirtschaftsbürgertum 6, 16, 22, 24, 28, 30
women 16, 26, 58, 72, 97, 124f, 147, 150f,
    167, 169, 171f, 175, 205–21, 281, 299,
    303
women's emancipation 35
    enfranchisement 212
working class 6f, 18, 23, 33f, 61, 94,
    97–99, 101, 107–9, 115–29, 143, 163f,
    168f, 171, 174, 212, 255, 259, 265,
    168f, 183
working-class solidarity 127, 143

youth 35, 145

Zionism 232f, 241
Zola, Emile 176, 187

Related Titles of Interest from *Berghahn Books*